AF531620

Punjab's Economic Development in the Era of Globalisation

Essays in Honour of R.S. Ghuman

Punjab's Economic Development in the Era of Globalisation

Essays in Honour of R.S. Ghuman

Edited by

Inderjeet Singh
Sukhwinder Singh
Lakhwinder Singh

LG PUBLISHERS DISTRIBUTORS

First Published, 2014

ISBN 978-93-83723-03-4

Published by
LG PUBLISHERS DISTRIBUTORS
49, Gali No. 14, Pratap Nagar
Mayur Vihar Phase I, Delhi 110 091
Tel : 011 2279 5641 email: lgpdist@gmail.com

Printed at
Saurabh Printers Pvt. Ltd., A 16, Sector IV, Noida

Contents

PART IV: Consequences of Agrarian Distress in Punjab

PART V: Gender Employment and Social Security Perspectives in Punjab

PART VI: Critical Issues in Punjab's Education Sector

PART VII: Emerging Health Scenario in Punjab

Preface

Ranjit Singh Ghuman is a man of many facets; an economist, an academician, an administrator, and a social activist. This book, in fact, is a collection of essays written by his colleagues and friends to honour his commitment towards the teaching profession, research output and best practices established as an economist and social activist. Though these essays are marked by a perceptible diversity, yet their focus is on the vital aspects of Punjab's economy; the issues that have agitated his mind and remained a primary concern throughout his academic career. Born on April 6, 1951 in Pandori village of Gurdaspur district—a bordered and most backward district of Punjab, he studied in the nearby village government school up to the matriculation. With sheer hard work and luck, he built up a brilliant academic record by getting the second position in order of merit in the M.A. (Economics) examination of Punjabi University, Patiala in 1973. He taught for more than 37 years—first in the Government Colleges of Punjab and then in the University—where he groomed many research students in Economics. For him, this time was indeed a period of learning which sharpened his academic acumen and social inclinations.

At the university level, he developed a long tradition of team work and his team work has still been flourishing in terms of generating innovative ideas which are now known as the Patiala School of Thought. The uniqueness of this school of thought has been reflected in the generation of many new ideas/ approaches to achieve inclusive economic growth. One of his studies along with his team members helped the Government of Punjab to formulate a pro-rural education and employment policy by creating additional seats in general and professional education courses in the universities and by reserving seats in government jobs for rural students. Along with this, he remained very active in the teachers' politics and was elected as the Secretary, Punjabi University Teachers Association (PUTA) for two terms. He further graduated to the university administration and remained the Dean, College Development Council of the University for two years. He subsequently chaired the Department of Economics from 2009-11. During his stewardship, the SAP status of the department was upgraded to Centre for Advanced Study (CAS) by the University Grants Commission (UGC), New Delhi.

He authored, co-authored, edited and co-edited 12 books, 20 project reports and 86 research papers on many significant themes such as Indo-Pak trade relations, regional economy, block planning, university finances, higher education, agricultural labour, farmers/labour suicides, corporate social responsibility, local-self governance, globalisation and change; the issues that are crucial for the marginalised masses in India and for the economic development in general. His research work is a guiding post for the new students and scholars working on the Punjab economy. His doctoral thesis titled 'Indo-Pakistan Trade Since 1947' is highly acclaimed in the academic, political and economic policy circles. In fact, the book has become an important policy input document highlighing mutual gains of trade relations between India and Pakistan, especially through the Wagha land route. Armed with strong arguments, he went to various forums such as FICCI's Trade Delegation to Pakistan (1997), Folklore Research Academy, Amritsar, Hind-Pak Dosti Munch and Candle Light March (an annual feature) for promoting people-to-people contacts and for establishing permanent peace, friendship and brotherhood across two hostile bordered nations.

As the policy formulation in Punjab is now largely distant from the poor people's perspective like non-performance of public education, public health and other welfare schemes that affect and also get affected by the process of economic transformation prevalent in the state, Professor Ghuman devoted considerable attention to such neglected aspects of economic transformation in the state. He went an extra mile to collaborate with non-economists to bring out a few studies in the relatively unexplored area of human rights. He has maintained a very long association with the Association for Democratic Rights (AFDR), Punjab as an active member and office bearer of AFDR's Patiala unit. Throughout his life, as an economist he has been continuously highlighting that the Green Revolution strategy in Punjab has provided a much needed food security to the Indian economy, but the small/marginal farmers and poor rural labourers are pushed into a much deeper and multi-dimensional crisis which is more serious in its cultural, social, political, and ecological connotations. And, as a social activist, he continuously highlighted human rights violation in the state.

This book has been conceived and planned at his superannuation from the Punjabi University in June 2011. For this purpose, when we approached many known experts and his friends to write research papers, their responses were nothing short of overwhelming as his hard work on the Punjab economy has created a niche for Prof. Ghuman and impacted state public policy in a big way. Possibly for this reason, we got an overwhelming response and spontaneous cooperation of the contributors. If we had accepted all contributors' essays, this book could have been much larger. Inevitably, we had to be selective in choosing a few contributions. We are very grateful to all these contributors for their timely help and unstinted support for preparing this volume. The editors also want to put on record our profound gratitude to the departmental colleagues—Professor Jaswinder Singh Brar, Professor Kesar Singh Bhangoo and Dr. Parmod Kumar—for their comments and suggestions on the first draft of the manuscript of this book. The editors are also grateful to Mr. Baltej Bhathal for preparing several drafts of the book and Mr. Rahul Saxena of LG Publishers Distributors for bringing this book out meticulously and in a short span of time. The errors and omissions, if they still remain, are the sole responsibility of the editors.

February 2014 **Editors**

1

Economic Development in Punjab: An Introduction

Inderjeet Singh, Sukhwinder Singh and Lakhwinder Singh

Punjab before 1947 was known as the land of the five rivers. Two rivers and the most productive and agriculturally developed areas of Punjab were allocated, during the partition, to Pakistan. The partition of the country erected artificial borders, not only blocking the natural flow of economic transactions but also played havoc with the institutional infrastructure. During this time, in the recorded history of the displacement of population, Punjab suffered heavily on this count with unprecedented transfer of population (10 million) and the communal riots killed between 0.5 to 0.8 million of human beings (Ahmed, 2011). The biggest challenge, in the post-partition period with the government and the people of Punjab, was the rehabilitation of the uprooted population. The difficult task of rehabilitation of the uprooted population, which came from West Punjab, was carried forward rather quickly to allocate productive assets like the land for cultivation and also loans for constructing houses both in the villages and towns of East Punjab (Randhawa, 1954). Along with this, several measures related to agrarian reforms such as abolishing intermediaries between the state and the actual cultivators, conferring property rights to occupancy tenants, consolidation of land holdings, imposition of ceilings on land holdings, fixing and regulating rent on tenanted land were carried out to provide security to the tenants. The agrarian policy followed by the government of Punjab, rather emphasised building capability for production base while making heavy investments in developing the irrigation system via canal network and rural electrification, agricultural credit, regulated grain market system, agricultural research and extension system, and rural road networks (Gill, 2001). The public policy succeeded in enacting and developing a network of institutional arrangements during the decade of the 1950s and early 60s that played a pivotal role in initiating modern agricultural development in the state.

Punjab state was further divided in 1966, to carve out two new states, Himachal Pradesh and Haryana. The present-day Punjab came into existence on November 1, 1966, which coincided with the revolutionary rise in the productivity of wheat and paddy popularly called the 'Green Revolution'. Punjab economy prospered during the faster pace of agricultural development, in the late 1960s and the decade of the 1970s. This early Green Revolution period was supported by unique institutional arrangements, such as minimum support price system, procurement of the produce for central pool, public distribution system, and subsidies to farmers and to the companies producing the fertilisers. Rural development in Punjab got a big push and necessary dynamism for economic transformation of the state economy, as predicted by the theory of economic development (Chenery, 1960). Many studies of the early Green Revolution period testified to the fact that its gains were shared by every section of society in the country. However, the gains at the most were unevenly shared by the Punjab farmers in relation to the proportion of ownership/operational size of the land holdings (Bhalla and Chadha, 1983). The income gains and surpluses generated have prepared the ground for other sectors of the Punjab economy to prosper. It has certainly made the Punjab economy achieve a distinctive status of the number one state of India, in terms of per capita income and surpassed the so-called 'Hindu rate of economic growth' of the Indian economy (Singh and Singh, 2002). It is pertinent to note here that the big promotion of agricultural development in

Punjab has changed the structure of the Punjab economy from a diversified to less diversified (wheat-paddy rotation), so far as the proportion of income generated and workforce employed in the agriculture sector of the economy is concerned. This can be ascertained from the remark that 'Punjab continues to be an agricultural state' (Bhalla and Chadha, 1983).

The impact of the Green Revolution has been visible in terms of rising living standards and dramatic reduction of population below the poverty line. Punjab has emerged as the lowest poverty incidence state, as compared with other Indian states. This can be described as the single most important achievement of modern agriculture. Another important impact of the Green Revolution that can be ascertained from the investment, out of the surpluses generated by the rapid pace of agricultural development, has been made in the transportation sector, by the farmers of Punjab. The industrial sector of Punjab also got some dynamism in terms of establishing small sized firms especially to meet the growing agriculture machinery/implements demand. It is significant to note here that the establishment of large sized units, both by the private corporate sector and the public sector, required licences from the union government. The licensing regime had a limited scope of large sized units that were expected to be launched in Punjab. The growing prosperity, during the early years of the Green Revolution period, generated a huge demand for consumer goods and also of inputs required for the agriculture sector. The growing demand for consumer goods and agricultural inputs was fulfilled by the manufacturing sector of the other states of India. This kind of leakage, not only adversely affected the industrial development of the state, but also reduced the impact of multiplier in the Punjab economy. Growing demand for labour for various operations in the agriculture sector generated the employment opportunities for manual labour that has increased inflows of migratory labour from other states of India, such as Uttar Pradesh, Bihar and other neighbouring states. The migratory labour has been sending remittances back home to their families which were the other source of leakage and a source of reduction of the value of multiplier in the Punjab economy.

A well-known characteristic of human capital of Punjab is their entrepreneurial abilities and their capability to adapt new innovations. When the biological and mechanical innovations emerged on the scene in the second-half of the 1970s and the early 1980s, the Punjab peasantry made full use of them. These innovations entirely changed the organisational structure of Punjab agriculture. It dramatically increased the dependence of Punjab peasantry on market transactions. They have started organising operations while hiring all inputs from the market including labour. The agriculture production system became a capital-intensive enterprise and almost eliminated the use of family labour in various farm operations that made even the small peasants managers of capitalist farming. Financial needs for conducting farm operations increased tremendously. The intensive agriculture based on capitalist rules of operation, raised cost of production and reduced profit margins of farmers due to higher increase in input prices and slow increase in output prices. Technological innovations towards the early 1980s showed signs of exhaustion and as a result of it, deceleration in the productivity growth of wheat and rice crops have started occurring. The modern agriculture based on high doses of chemical fertilisers, pesticides, insecticides and water has severely damaged the environment (Singh and Kumar, 2010). This process has set in the crisis of Punjab's agrarian economy and the political leadership gauging the gravity of the situation started diverting the attention of the people while initiating 'protest movements' related to the long pending/ unsettled issues with the union government. The base of these protests was the religion and, therefore, the religious fundamentalist elements hijacked the protest movements and established their supremacy over the political leadership. Political turmoil, which started in the late 1970s and ended in the early 1990s, disrupted the normal course of economic development in the state, discouraged new investments and turned the economic governance institutions to be dysfunctional. The fiscal policy was jeopardised and the state underwent transformation from a developmental to non-developmental mode that resulted in a high fiscal deficit. The government resorted to borrowing, to meet expenditure needs, especially of the security forces that resulted in a high degree of indebtedness in Punjab (Gill, Singh and Brar, 2010; Singh, 2013).

The response to the growing crisis of capitalist economic development of the Punjab economy from the professionals trained in economics was based on two fundamental approaches. One, several scholars of the Punjab economy questioned the long-run sustainability of economic development of the state on the basis of agriculture growth only. Agriculture growth provided essential preconditions for economic transformation from low productivity-low wage to high productivity-high wage industrial development. The structural stagnation of the Punjab economy and trapping of workforce in the agriculture sector of the Punjab economy is the root cause of the brewing economic crisis in the state. Therefore, it has been suggested that the state must shoulder its responsibility to develop the industrial sector of the economy in a manner to generate synergy between the agriculture and industrial sector of the Punjab economy (for a detailed discussion, see Chadha, 1986; Gill, 1988). Two, many scholars who are closely researching the agriculture sector of Punjab's economy emphasise that since the crisis is being faced by the agriculture sector and, therefore, the solution should be seen within the agriculture sector. Therefore, they have mooted an idea that the agricultural stagnation can be solved through diversifying the agriculture, from low value added to high value added products. They believed that this will strengthen the income base of the farmers and the local labour. This idea was more suitable to the political leadership of the state which had farming as their main source of income and more specifically a consolidated vote bank. Thinking on these lines, the state government appointed a committee under the chairmanship of Dr. S.S. Johl—a reputed agricultural economist—and a report was submitted and accepted in 1986. The diversification of agriculture idea was fundamentally based on providing a central role to the market (Johl, 1986). This market-led model of diversification of agriculture development in Punjab was also adopted by many farmers but failed to succeed due to volatility of the market; and farmers reverted back to wheat-paddy rotation. The state government, in fact, developed a neutrality to solve the brewing economic crisis that has deepened and intensified which resulted in the farmers' suicides in the green revolution and the highest per capita income state of India (Gill and Singh, 2006). Still, diversification of agriculture, as an idealistic solution, has remained on the scene of economic policy making in Punjab for the three long decades, without solving the basic problems of crisis-ridden capitalistic economic development of Punjab's economy.

Punjab's development experience, therefore, has become quite instructive during the last five decades, particularly for those who want to examine the close relationship between state efforts and high economic growth on one hand, and between the economic slowdown and governance problems on the other. It is true that the Punjab economy achieved an impressive growth rate compared to the Indian economy as a whole, during the three decades spanning the period: 1960s to the 1980s. This impressive growth was largely due to the right kind of economic policies and institutional framework developed in Punjab, with the state efforts. However, the annual growth rate of Punjab's economy began to slow down during the 1980s and decelerated further during the 1990s (Singh and Singh, 2002). Consequently, Punjab slipped down in terms of per capita income ranking across major Indian states from the first rank (till 1991-92) to the second rank (1992-93) and the sixth rank (2009-10). The CSO data also pointed out that Punjab's economy has experienced a much lower growth rate than that of the fast growing Indian states such as Haryana, Maharashtra, Kerala, Gujarat and Tamil Nadu, during the 1990s, as well as during the first decade of the 21st century. In fact, on the basis of per capita income, Punjab was overtaken by Haryana, for the first time in 1992-93. Later, the state has not only lost its glorious position to other states, but it has also lagged behind in relation to all-India average figures of per capita income.

Mainstream growth experts from time to time also cited many reasons responsible for slowdown of Punjab's economy.

Some of them are of the opinion that an over-emphasis on agriculture alone, in the absence of the right kind of supporting and dynamic industrialisation, has been found to be one of the main causes of slow down of the Punjab economy. In the agriculture sector also, stagnated per hectare yield and production, rising input costs compared to output prices, non-viability of marginal/small farmers, fast depletion of underground water, degradation of soil fertility, unsustainable mono-cropping pattern, etc. are the factors behind slow down and the low growth syndrome. Many others are of the opinion that Punjab state, having an active international border with Pakistan, is unable to attract heavy private investment/capital, particularly in the medium/large scale industries, even in the post-liberalised policy regimes. Non-availability of any worthwhile basic metals needed for the modern industries put limits on the industrialisation of the state. Even, locational disadvantages of the state, far away from sea-ports/routes, also discourages establishment of large-scale industrial units in the state. Further, at policy level, tax concessions given to new industrial ventures in the neighbouring hilly states (Himachal Pradesh, and Jammu & Kashmir) have led to the shifting of already established industrial units from Punjab to these hill states; what to speak of attracting new industrial units in the state. Thus, both the commodity producing sectors (agriculture and manufacturing), within given policy framework, are unable to stimulate adequate growth in the state.

Even the services sector, both organised and unorganised, is also facing many obstacles that consistently limit the state's future growth potentials; the former known as the provider of quality jobs is known for shrinkage of jobs with fewer government jobs and more low paid jobs (ad hoc/part-time, contract, basic pay only, low social security benefits, etc.); and, the latter is notorious for in-decent work, temporary, casual and low paid work where labour laws and other regulations are either not adhered to or poorly implemented. The poor farmers, SC workers and other marginalised sections of society, who want to leave odd occupations, cannot do so because of inadequate growth of non-farm employment, as well as, lack of adequate skills or expertise among them to join new occupations. They, therefore, have no option but to become casual labourers or face unemployment. Mechanisation of all agricultural operations, except the paddy transplanting and cotton picking, has not only reduced labour absorption capacity of the agriculture sector in the state (Gill, 2002; Sidhu and Singh, 2004; and Singh, 2010), but also swelled the ranks of unemployed and under-employed persons. Consequently the rate of unemployment among the youth (15-29 years) in the state is quite high (11.1 per cent), during 2009-10, as compared to the national average of 9.5 per cent and neighbouring states of Haryana (8.6 per cent), Jammu & Kashmir (5.1 per cent) and Himachal Pradesh (6.4 per cent). Even, the social security measures for the working poor, like the pensions to the aged, widows/destitute women, dependent children and disabled persons, are not only meagre/low, but are also delayed for most of the time in the state (Gill, Singh and Brar, 2013).

The development process of any region within a country is complex and multifaceted phenomenon. It is, in fact, the product of interplay of natural resources, historical factors, policy formulations, politico-economic agenda and vested interests of the state's ruling elites. Besides, it also depends on how economic activities are being organised, and for whom these are beneficial. The pace of development can be accelerated by the policy measures, which supplement the activities of economic agents, both directly by organising productive activities and indirectly by creating infrastructure facilities. Effective/ineffective implementation of policy measures, technological innovations and responses of economic agents (labour, capital, entrepreneurs, etc.) also determines the pace of economic development. The educated and skilled workforce is an additional advantage to the region. On this count, the people of Punjab are known for their dynamism and pragmatic approach towards life. They are very quick to adapt new technology and innovations in the productive processes. They always respond positively to the policy measures. Keeping in view the above-mentioned issues, we approached many experts/scholars, to whom we consider an authority on the given subject, to write papers on specific theme/s related to the Punjab economy. These papers are organised under seven major sub-themes:

I. Genesis of Slow Down of the Punjab Economy
II. Core Issues Before Agricultural Development in Punjab
III. Emerging Alternatives for Sustainable Agriculture in Punjab
IV. Consequences of Agrarian Distress in Punjab
V. Gender Employment and Social Security Perspectives in Punjab
VI. Critical Issues in Punjab's Education Sector
VII. Emerging Health Scenario in Punjab

'Genesis of Slow Down of the Punjab Economy', Part I of the book, includes two articles on issues related to causes of slow down of the economy, weak economic policies and lack of governance in the state. The first paper has been written by Sucha Singh Gill, an authority on the development economics in this region. In his paper 'Slow Down of Punjab Economy and Governance Crisis', Gill has discussed the inherent causes behind the slow down of Punjab's economy. Even the success of the Green Revolution in Punjab agriculture has also brought out some of the worst consequences to the farmers and ecology of the state. For instance, bio-diversity has been destroyed and it has been replaced by the mono-cropping pattern which led to massive soil degradation, depletion of macro and micro nutrients, over-exploitation of ground water, poisoning of soil and water resources by unrestricted use of pesticides/ insecticides. Though a number of policy suggestions have been made by various committees and individual scholars from time to time, yet the state is unable to achieve any major success, because the organisations/institutions responsible for policy implementation are either paralysed or become non-functional for want of funds and good governance. Tracing the role of institutions and rule-based governance in promoting economic activities, the author highlighted poor governance in the state, which is manifested in the poor management of the economy, persistent fiscal imbalance, income disparities across regions/

districts, denial of basic needs (food, shelter, water, etc.), threat to life and personal security, and many more. And, the study suggests a multi-pronged strategy to revive its sagging economy, where the state government has to play a leading role by making the state administration more efficient, transparent and inclusive in nature. For this, improving rule based governance in the state is urgently needed.

Another paper on this theme is by Lakhwinder Singh. In his paper 'Economic Governance and Punjab's Economic Growth', he clearly identified the factors that have contributed to the slow growth of Punjab's economy. Over-emphasis on the agriculture sector, lack of dynamic action in the industrial sector, and non-exploitation of new opportunities in emerging services sectors has pushed the growing economy into a sluggish mode. This is largely due to the chronic shortage of fresh investments in the state as well as the poor institutional response to the emerging sectors of Punjab's economy. To sustain the economic growth momentum, the state should bring much needed structural transformation in the agriculture sector (crop diversification and agro-processing industries) for promoting agriculture-industry linkages in the state. Further, the high value-added products like horticulture and knowledge-based industries such as bio-technology, micro-electronics, pharmaceutical, information technology, and skill-oriented education must be encouraged in the state. The study also suggested introducing drastic changes in the organisational skills and institutions of the state. New generation cooperatives based strictly on democratic principles like Amul which adhere to market rules with accountability and transparency, suggested by the author should be established in Punjab. Furthermore, the state government should enact a suitable industrial policy that attracts new industries by providing incentives and is helpful in creating exclusive industrial parks, particularly for the agro-processing zones, IT industry, farmers' cooperatives, etc. on a similar pattern, as has been provided and offered to the foreign and domestic private industry.

'Core Issues Before Agricultural Development in Punjab', Part II of the book, includes two articles. Surjit Singh, in a much wider spectrum and scope, has analysed rice-based systems in India with special reference to Punjab, where the rice is neither a traditional natural crop like wheat nor falls in the consumption basket of its populace. The study revolves around to answer many pertinent questions: how has rice become the state's main crop?; who is cultivating/growing rice in the state?; which factors favour rice cultivation in the state?; how have advances in technology affected rice cultivation and yields in the state?; how has rising yield impacted the rice growers in the state?; why is the cost of rice production rising in the state?; how are rising costs affecting the economy of rice growers?; how are field impressions useful for driving policy conclusions?; and what is the future of rice cultivation in the state? These are some of the questions, to which the author tried his best to give cogent and meaningful answers. For instance, the rice in the shortest span has become the most important commercial crop of Punjab's Kharif season. Even, the small farmers are likely to grow rice, despite declining water and rising costs syndrome. Application of HYVs, chemical fertilisers and plenty of water has ensured a stable yield and made the growers earn more money because of MSP for their entire surplus produce. Punjab farmers, therefore, are likely to grow rice in future so long as the government supports them. Furthermore, the author emphasised that the situation still demands the state subsidies as well as more market support. Otherwise, the free market will destroy small rice producers because the free market regime always favours the traders and the consumers, not the real producers.

In their joint paper 'Agriculture Sector in Punjab: Retrospect and Prospect', M.S. Sidhu and Varinder Pal Singh stated that the state's agriculture sector has witnessed a major breakthrough in the crop production, particularly of wheat and rice crops, since the late 1960s. This rising farm production has improved the economic status of the peasantry, by bringing out all-round societal changes in Punjab. A number of factors, like application of HYVs of wheat-paddy, assured market clearance at MSP and supporting infrastructure for supplying of inputs and dissemination of technical knowledge, have made it possible.

The prime-movers of this growth, however, were the hardy farmers themselves who were quick enough to adapt and exploit new production possibilities. With a limited geographical area (1.53 per cent) of India, the state contributed about 60-65 per cent of wheat and 30-35 per cent of rice procured for the central pool of foodgrains during the last four decades or so. They argued that the Punjab agriculture which grew at a faster rate earlier has now reached a sort of plateau, both in terms of productivity and production. Farm profitability has also declined in the recent years due to rising input costs and MSP squeeze. Farming alone is not sufficient to generate enough income for the small and marginal farmers. Comparatively also, the annual growth rate in Punjab agriculture sector's GSDP for the period 2000-01 to 2007-08 was also low (2.40 per cent), compared to 3.20 per cent for India as a whole. And, rural debt incidence rose to Rs. 35000 crore during 2008-09, out of which Rs 13000 crore (37 per cent) was from non-institutional sources. Nearly 64 per cent farmers (up to 10 acres), in Punjab, reported difficulties in repaying the debt/loan. And, they are likely to fall into a debt trap in the next 10 to 15 years. One can also see the rising number of suicides across otherwise hardy farmers of the state. In the wake of a declining land-man ratio, agriculture alone cannot generate gainful employment for the growing population. All these facts highlight that Punjab farmers, in general, and marginal and small farmers, in particular, are in a deep economic crisis. They propagated an urgent need to promote sustainable agriculture in the state. For this, non-farm employment opportunities for rural youth must be generated. Re-structuring rural education is stressed. A delay of a few years will not be in the interests of state authority and the country-side, they warned.

Part III of the book, 'Emerging Alternatives for Sustainable Agriculture in Punjab', examines two alternative approaches, one dairy and another organic farming, for sustainable agriculture in the state. Along with the food grains, livestock population has emerged as another pillar of Punjab's agrarian economy. Over the time period, Punjab state produced a significant proportion of India's total milk production. The significance of milk and milk products (dairy products) has been on the rise, even when the share of the primary sector in the NSDP of Punjab has declined. For instance, the share of livestock and dairy products in the NSDP produced by the agricultural sector has increased from 33.52 per cent in 1980-81 to 40.41 per cent in 2005-06. In fact, livestock, in general, and dairy, in particular, are regarded as the growth engine of Punjab's agricultural sector in the recent years. The dairy sector is now regarded as a 'treasure house' of the state's rural economy, as the dairy provides nutritious products, organic manure, supplementary employment, continuous income flows, and acts as a cushion against the income-shocks arising due to crop failure. Further, dairying enterprises provide a support base to the milk producers without disturbing their agro-economic and cultural chains. In the recent decade, dairying has become a backbone of the diversification plan of the state's agriculture sector. Alternately, dairying and livestock have become important topics for research and policy making in the state.

Kaur et al., in their joint paper 'Growth and Performance of the Dairy Sector in Punjab', examined the trends in the livestock growth, milk production/yield and constraints inhibiting the growth of the dairy sector in the state. Regarding the growth of the dairy sector, they found three main trends: one, declining proportion of 'work animals' and of less productive bovines (indigenous cattle) is largely synchronised with the mechanisation of agriculture adopted in the state. Second, the rising number of productive milk bovines (crossbred cows and buffaloes) in the state have increased milk production in leaps and bounds during the last three decades; at the growth rate of 3.96 per cent per annum. Per capita availability of milk in the state rose from 541 grams per day in 1980-81 to 915 grams per day in 2009-10 — much higher than the all-India average of 128 grams and 258 grams in respective times. Third, rising milk production is mainly due to the yield effect than that of population effect across the crossbred cows; whereas in the case of buffalo milk, though the yield effect is slightly stronger than that of the population effect, but not as strong as in the case of cow milk. These facts indicate the adoption of new technology in breeding and feeding animals – a welcome step. The dairy sector of the state, however, faced some constraints such as shortage of fodder, redundant and less productive animals, and lack of veterinary services in the state. The study argued in favour of improving animal health and feeding practices, both quantitatively and qualitatively, in the state.

No doubt, chemical intensive agriculture is successful in raising food production in the state. This success has made the country self-sufficient in the food grains production. In his paper, 'Organic Farming for Sustainable Agriculture in Punjab', G.S. Romana presented a critique of chemical intensive agriculture adopted in the state. To him, this increased food production has happened at huge costs in the form of degradation and depletion of the state's natural resources such as the soil, water and environment. Intensive agriculture led to an ever-increasing application of farm inputs, particularly the chemical fertilisers, which in turn consistently raised the cost of cultivation. Stagnant yields in the absence of the corresponding rise in farm-output prices have reduced profit margins of the farmers. As a result, beleaguered farmers began to commit suicides in the state. And, a severe agrarian crisis is clearly manifested in the contamination/deterioration of groundwater quality, depletion of soil fertility, growing incidence of pests, presence of pesticides' residue in the soil/ crop residues, milk and milk products, mothers' milk, etc. The health experts even attributed the rising incidence of chronic diseases in the state to the ever-rising use of agro-chemicals (including pesticides/insecticides, etc.). Visualising the bleak future of chemical the intensive agriculture in the long run, the author suggested an alternative system of 'organic farming' for sustainable agriculture in Punjab—which is relying mainly upon application of crop rotations, crop residues, animal manure, green manures, off-farm wastes, biological pest control, etc. to maintain the soil fertility, supply of plant nutrients and control of pests. On the question of economic viability, the debate is still inconclusive and demands more research inputs. However, one thing is indeed true that organic farming is the right answer to the depleting natural resource base, pesticide pollution and environmental degradation caused by the present cropping system. A few regional studies, though based on the small-sized sample/s, pointed out that a large chunk of educated population favours organic food, provided it is easily available. Till date, there is no state support so far as easy testing of organic food, certification of produce, proper checks, any promotion campaign and any reserve national/international market for the organic produce is concerned. The author also suggested that the state must promote organic farming by eliminating these impediments.

Part IV of the book, 'Consequences of Agrarian Distress in Punjab', tries to find causes and consequences of agrarian distress and their impact on the farmers and agricultural labour. Kesar Singh Bhangoo, in his paper 'Political Economy of Agrarian Distress in Punjab', visualises that the roots of agrarian distress lies in the state's political economy perspectives. He states that under the neo-liberal policy era, agriculturally advanced regions like Punjab have witnessed a scourge of rural suicides among the farmers and agricultural labourers. This frightening and shocking phenomenon continues, without any sign of abatement. The study also reveals the plight of deceased farmers and agricultural labourers, and their living dependents' conditions are worse than the victims. Agrarian distress in the state, in fact, is the result of neo-liberal policies pursued by the state government along with the stagnated yield in agriculture, successive crop failure/damage and non-implementation of crop diversification programme. Further, agrarian distress has been aggravated by the increasing production costs, low farm returns, non-viability of small/marginal holdings, and over-capitalisation/mechanisation with under-utilisation of farm machinery. Marginalisation of the agriculture sector and weakened political-clout of the farmers, during the new policy regime, has doomed the farmers' economy especially of small/marginal farmers to a nadir, and that has compelled the farmers to borrow heavily with a hope of revival of agriculture which landed them into the debt trap. He makes it clear that this agrarian distress, indebtedness and farmers' suicides in the state are interlinked, deep-rooted, complex and multi-dimensional;

which can be tackled and resolved through the multi-pronged short-term and long-term policy initiatives. In the wake of the changing agrarian political economy and disjunction between the interests of farmers and political elite, it is desired that the farmer/*kisan* unions must be consolidated and the state should come forward to protect them from the onslaughts of the new capitalist regime, by reorienting and reorganising its policies. The farmers must form a united force to press upon the state to initiate policy changes, so that the agrarian distress is phased out.

When the agriculture sector of a progressive region like Punjab is facing an unprecedented and multifaceted agrarian crisis that was manifested in (i) deceleration of growth in output, (ii) reduced profitability, and (iii) less employment elasticity in agriculture, in such a scenario, one can imagine the plight of agricultural labourers in the state. In fact, they are the worst sufferers. Being poor, unskilled and less mobile, on the one hand, they are unable to find adequate employment in the agricultural sector itself and, on the other, could not get better jobs in other sectors of the economy like the industrial services. Sukhpal Singh and Ms. Sangeet, in their paper 'Economic Conditions of Agricultural Labourers and Public Policies in Punjab' examined the impact of this agrarian crisis on the economic conditions of agriculture labour and how many benefits they derived from the government schemes. The study makes it clear that mechanisation of almost all major agricultural operations (man vs. machine) has reduced the demand for hired agriculture labour in the state to the lowest ebb. Consequently, an overwhelming majority of them are either employed as casual workers or on a seasonal basis (under-employed) or engaged in low paid manual/unskilled jobs or remained unemployment. They also become victims of low income, under-nutrition and indebtedness. More than two-thirds of their average consumption expenditure is incurred only on food items. Further, the quantity and quality of civil amenities enjoyed by them is far from satisfactory. Only 20 to 30 per cent of the agricultural labour families got benefits of old age pension, free education and *shagun* schemes, though the ration cards and free electricity were enjoyed by many households. In the absence of liberal social security measures (old age pensions, sickness benefits, etc.), they live under constant stress and strain, and are consistently facing vulnerable situations. They should be made partners of economic development through inclusive state policies. For this, a progressive increase in their wage rates is recommended. Non-farm sectors should be developed, so that they can get additional and remunerative employment. Moreover, functional efficiency of government institutions needs to be improved. Similarly, flow of institutional credit to them at cheaper rates with easy repayment facilities must be increased. Rural education and health services should be revamped in the state so that they can acquire proper skills to get better jobs. However, in the given socio-economic and political structure in the state, all these measures may not be helpful for solving their problems. The authors favoured radical changes in pro-poor policies/schemes to improve the living conditions of agricultural labour.

Part V of the book, 'Gender Employment and Social Security Perspectives in Punjab', deals with the issues related to gender discrimination in labour markets and social security mechanisms, prevailing in an affluent state. It is true that, according to the Constitution, all men and women enjoy equal status, irrespective of caste, creed, sex, religion, location, etc. Both should have an equal access to adequate means of livelihood and get wage/payment as per 'equal work – equal pay' principle. Unfortunately, these pious principles/rights are not fully translated into practice. The women lagged behind in sharing the gains of economic development initiated in India and across other states. In the present era, which is influenced by liberalisation, privatisation and globalisation policy based on sophisticated technology, many questions arise about the gender employment: What has happened to the gender employment under the new policy regime? How are women workers marginalised in the new era? How does this policy influence women's wages and working hours? What are the main determinants of rising/falling women's work participation rates? Which sector/s is/are more attractive to the women workers? Which occupational shift will be more beneficial to the women-folk? In her paper, 'Gender Dimensions of Employment in Punjab', Kanwaljit Kaur Gill tried to find answers to these questions by using the NSSO data of different rounds since 1983, both at rural and urban levels, in Punjab. She noticed a gender gap to the tune of 33 percentage points between 1983 and 2004-05. Further, women's employment scenario in the state has also changed during this time period. Still, most of the working women are employed either in the primary sector or in other informal sectors of the economy. The occupational shift across the rural women is not as sharp as in the case of urban women; indicating that rural women are at a disadvantage and are at the receiving end. More women over the time period have shifted to the self-employment category, leading us to believe that regular job opportunities in the state are shrinking, and the latest technology is pushing the women out of regular/formal jobs to casual/informal ones. The much propagated 'inclusive growth' strategy has not benefited poor women workers in the state. Though, a shift from traditional occupation/s (agriculture sector) to the services sector is visible to some extent, but that has happened mostly in the unorganised (informal) private sector – low paid jobs. The situation demands that the state should come forward to protect the interests of women's labour force by creating more and more jobs in the formal/organised sector and by enforcing their right to have 'equal pay for equal work'. There is great need to break the traditional 'glass ceiling' at the entry level of certain types of jobs and professions to reach the women up to the higher level of the cadre. It is suggested by the author that more and more women-centric investments should be made in the state.

Although overall growth of Punjab's economy has decelerated during the post-reforms period, the state is still enjoying a status of affluence. For instance, Punjab on the basis of per capita income maintained its first rank till 2001-02, second rank for the next three years (2002-03 to 2004-05), and slipped to the sixth/seventh place in recent years (GOI, 2013). In terms of monthly per capita consumption expenditure, however, the state still ranked first or second for most of the years, as per the data generated by the NSSO, since 1972-73. Further, instead of equally shared, gains of economic growth are iniquitous and exclusionary in nature (Bhalla and Chadha, 1982; Rangi, et al. 2004; Ghuman, Singh and Brar, 2006; 2009). Still, the state has 20.9 per cent (22.1 per cent rural and 18.7 per cent urban) of its population living below the poverty line in 2004-05 (GOI, 2013). And, Varinder Jain, in his paper 'Affluence, Vulnerability and Social Security Evidence from Punjab', produced a terse commentary on the economic affluence vis-à-vis a weak social security mechanism in the state. To him, Punjab being an affluent state, both in terms of income/expenditure, could not do much to protect the interests of the poor and vulnerable masses. The legislative measures taken to protect the working poor, in spite of their existence, have largely remained ineffective. For instance, institutions like the Labour Welfare Board, and State Planning Board, despite their existence, could not promote the interest of the working poor. The implementation of various social security schemes like the pensions (for old-aged, widows/destitute women, dependent children and disabled persons) are not only meagre/low, but the payments are delayed for most of the time. In fact, social security/welfare efforts made by the state are still negligible both in absolute and relative terms, because the Punjab economy enjoyed a relative affluence vis-à-vis other states. Such findings disappoint even the casual readers of the Punjab economy who want cogent answer to such a basic question like: how an affluent state having better factor endowments and political struggles could not become the 'model state' for the welfare of the poor populace? The answer, in fact, lies in its weak socio-economic and cultural movements in the past that did not force the state to take care of the poor despite dominance of Sikh religious philosophy in the politico-religious discourse of the state. The emerging 'inclusive growth' strategy demands from the state government to start pro-poor policy measures like the social security benefits to protect the poor and vulnerable masses.

Part VI of the book, 'Critical Issues in Punjab's Education Sector', includes two articles showing significance of education, state efforts and issues related to delivery of higher education sector in the state. In the modern era, educational expenditure, whether public or private, is considered to be the most important investment for human beings as such. Investment in this context is helpful in the formation and accumulation of human capital by producing new knowledge and creating better skills, positive values and attitudes across the people (Mittar, Singh and Brar, 2002). Such qualities of the workforce have now become essential inputs for a country/region's high economic growth and ever-rising personal incomes. In addition, education expansion helps the state to strengthen civil institutions, to build national competencies and to promote good governance; all these are recognised as most critical elements in effective implementation of economic and social policies. However, on the educational front, Punjab does not fall into the category of a forward looking state because almost all education-related indicators do not show desirable improvements compared to the southern states like Kerala and Tamil Nadu (Brar, 2002), though Punjab has enjoyed a higher level of income over a considerable long period of time.

A.S. Sethi and Baljit Kaur in their joint paper, 'Public Expenditure on the Education Sector in Punjab: A Comparison with Some Adjoining States', examines some dynamic aspects of public expenditure on the education sector in Punjab as well as in adjoining states. The study found a dismal and disturbing picture as far as the public expenditure allocated to the education sector of these states is concerned. As per the findings, the relative share of public expenditure on the education sector across all four neighbouring states (Punjab, Haryana, Himachal Pradesh and Jammu & Kashmir) has declined, whereas the share of non-developmental expenditure (NDE) increased perceptibly during the last 21 years (1985-86 to 2005-06). In comparative terms, Punjab has experienced a severe dip in the public expenditure on education, the biggest jump in the proportionate share of NDE and the least value of public expenditure on the education-GSDP ratio. The study also highlights that the Punjab state is already facing a severe decline in its fiscal health as more than one-half of its aggregated expenditure went towards non-developmental activities. However, such a retrogressive phase should not be continued in the future. This is, in fact, a poor reflector of governance adopted in the state, thereby calling for a mature political will to raise more public resources, provide good governance, change development priorities and do something serious to promote educational activities in the state.

The paper by Jaswinder Singh Brar, 'Market Dispensation, State Contraction and Emerging Practices in Delivery of Higher Education in Punjab', falls in the ambit of delivery of higher education in Punjab which is fully functional and operating under the market-oriented business mode. The state's role as a promoter of higher education has diminished, when it is viewed as a proportion of the total budgetary expenditure, state income and on per student basis. Naturally, a scarcity of public funds has seriously eroded the quality and affordability aspects of public-funded higher education institutions of the state. In fact, these institutions are either allowed to deteriorate or forced to levy high users' charges. The public sector institutions though few in numbers have considerably lost the sheen and glory both for the existing and emerging disciplines. For instance, in the professional courses, the best ranking students in all-India competitive tests/examinations or the students having paying capacity do not prefer to study in the state institutions located in Punjab. On the other side, the private educational colleges/ institutes charge extremely high fees and funds with a larger variety of fines and forced sale of uniforms, mess/canteen food, etc. These charges are, in fact, de-linked from the socio-economic reality and requirements of the state. Already, exclusion of students from the benefits of higher education has been reported in the state. Probably, this exclusion will increase further when someone views the prevalence of income inequalities, poverty and vulnerability of masses in the state. Punjab's higher education system as such has drifted away from the pious principles of equity and easy accessibility, inherent in the constitutional mandate. Instead, it caters to the vested interests consisting of the pressure groups and business lobbies of neo-educational entrepreneurs. Moreover, the credibility of the higher education sector has reached its nadir. The faculty is grossly under-paid, working without any service/social security and faculty improvement programmes. The institutions frequently change the courses not in a planned manner but in an undue haste and whimsical ways to earn high profits. These profits induce over-experimentation in the academic spheres/courses, which, in turn, disturbing the academic equilibrium. The study favoured a complete overhauling of higher education in the state which ensures inclusion, transparency, and quality aspects in order to generate high rated human resources.

Part VII of the book, 'Emerging Health Scenario in Punjab', deals with the health-related issues of women and the plight of cancer-afflicted families in the state. Though the women in Punjab added a few more years to their lives than that of men, yet they (women) did not enjoy a better health status. In fact, women's health issues in Punjab remained a neglected area of research in the past (Singh, 1991), but gained importance since the 1990s (Singh and Brar, 1997). In their paper 'Exploring Women's Health Issues in Punjab: Current Status, Problems and Emerging Policy Issues', Sukhwinder Singh and Rupinder Kaur clearly show that women's health is a function of demographic, socio-economic and cultural factors prevalent in the society. The study revealed that, in Punjab, illiteracy, low income status, rural residence, low work participation, spousal violence and other cultural factors are affecting the women's health and their living conditions adversely. Till the gender equality and women's empowerment are achieved, better health for women will remain a dream in the state or elsewhere. Further, when the girls/women are married at an early age, such girls/women are exposed to the early/repeated pregnancies and unsafe abortions. And, when a high proportion of pregnant women face malnutrition or anaemic conditions or are unable to get adequate maternal care, then the probability of attracting illness and mortality will be very high. The NFHS-3 data revealed three disturbing trends about the women's health in Punjab: First, nearly one-tenth of women aged 20-49 years were married before the age of 18 years—a minimum and legal age for a girl's marriage. Second, a little less than one-half of surveyed women (48.8 per cent) were termed as unhealthy by weight-for-height norms because 18.9 per cent women in the state were categorised as too thin (BMI < 18.5) and 29.9 per cent as overweight/obesity (BMI > 25.0); Third, nearly two-fifths of women (38 per cent) were anaemic, including 26 per cent as mildly anaemic, 10 per cent moderately anaemic, and 1 per cent severely anaemic. Further, neonatal, infant and child mortality rates are still very high in the state. Nearly one-half of childbirths (48.7 per cent) were not delivered in any health institution. Surprisingly, cent per cent surveyed women (15-49 years age) knew at least about one contraceptive method. But, 36.7 per cent of married women were currently not using any contraceptive method; and those who were using any contraceptive, 30.8 per cent favoured women-centric terminal method, 24.1 per cent spacing methods and 7.2 per cent a traditional method. It means that if Punjab continuously ignores the women's health issues, health of newborns and of the whole family will be in great peril. For better health status of women as well as equal participation in all spheres of development, the study suggested reorganising the state's developmental and health policies, raise women's education level, popularise late marriages and benefits of the small family in the state.

As reported earlier, success of the Green Revolution in Punjab has brought much needed food security to the nation, but at the same time, it has an adverse impact on the state's resource base (soil, water, etc.) and ecological balance. In their joint paper entitled 'Cancer Suffering Households in Punjab: Economic and Financial Consequences', Inderjeet Singh, Lakhwinder Singh and Parmod Kumar captured the gravity of the man-made cancer situation in Punjab and its adverse consequences on the lives of people. Because of adoption of intensive agricultural practices in the post-green revolution era, not only did the underground water level decline, but the state has also become the biggest consumer of agro-chemicals (fertilisers, insecticides/pesticides, etc.), on per hectare basis. This alarming increase in health diseases/ailments is identified with the indiscriminate and uncontrolled use of these agro-chemicals in the state. In fact, many news reports and a few research studies also highlighted the unusual rise of cancer deaths/patients in the last few years across the cotton-belt (Malwa region) of the state. Based on the census survey of four villages of Muktsar district (Punjab), conducted during the December 2012-February 2013, the study identified 136 cancer cases—103 dead and 33 alive cancer patients—in these villages. Most of them were either engaged directly in the agriculture (45.59 per cent) or doing household work (39.71 per cent). Further, 56 per cent of them had a direct exposure to the pesticides. On the whole, only 2.21 per cent of cancer cases have a life insurance cover, but no health insurance. The average length of the cancer patient's life remained very short; it is 1.9 years. Per patient treatment cost borne by cancer households was Rs. 2.75 lakhs, against per household income of Rs. 2.30 lakhs. In the absence of a health insurance system and meagre savings, cancer victim families have to borrow funds on highly unfavourable terms and conditions. State government support to cancer patients in the state is insufficient, untimely and cumbersome. And, this high cancer treatment costs certainly affects other expenditures made by the households. Findings of the study can help the state to quantify the insurance support that can bring the family out of perpetual distress. The study advised the state to design a better financial support system for the cancer victim families that must cover not only the cancer treatment costs, but also their basic needs, capabilities and functionalities of living family members.

At the end, we want to reiterate our commitment to explore all fundamental aspects/factors of economic development of Punjab's economy which will make Punjab again a prosperous and a leading state. The study highlights all major obstacles and policy lacunas which have not only decelerated its economic growth, but also held up its leading position to the laggard one; despite the fact that Punjab is a major recipient of diaspora remittances. In future, these obstructions will also put a question mark on the state's future growth potentials and economic sustainability. Interestingly, when the Indian economy, as a whole, is witnessing a resurgent growth in the post-1991 era, the Punjab economy is facing a relative decline and is apparently besetted with societal and environmental problems. More ironically, the fact is that the invisible surpluses generated in the rural economy have been used to the advantages of agriculture and allied activities only; not for building a modern industrial culture out of rural enterprises (Chadha, 1986). A familiar joke that is circulating in academic circles that Punjab has no 'culture' but only agriculture signifies the popular perceptions of the agrarian model of development pursued in the Punjab by the British colonial state and the independent Indian nationalist state (Singh, 2012). It means that the agrarian-oriented development path is unsustainable for the long run growth of the state. That is why Punjab's economy slides down to the sixth/seventh place in terms of per capita income criterion (GOI, 2013).

There are many cogent explanations behind this phenomenon. First, a slowdown in the Punjab economy is attributed largely to the poor governance of economy, persistent fiscal imbalance, lack of dynamic industrial sector, chronic shortage of fresh investments and social sector institutional framework. Secondly, excessive emphasis on agriculture alone, particularly in the long run, is also questioned by many experts because the future potentials of Punjab agriculture to sustain the state's further economic development is almost exhausted. Thirdly, there is a mismatch between the proportionate share of NSDP originated in the agriculture sector and the proportionate share of population engaged in this sector; indicating a low income to those dependent on agriculture alone. Fourthly, over-exploitation of ground water is not only creating a very dangerous ecological crisis that can lead to exhaustion of this renewable water source, but also raise the cost of cultivation in the state. Fifthly, profit margins of the farming community, across major crops grown in the state, have been shrinking primarily because of the Centre's decisive role in determining agricultural inputs and output prices. Sixthly, the diversification plan of agriculture, as a strategy to rid this sector of the saturation crisis, has not been gaining a worthwhile ground because of insufficient incentives to the farmers to move away from the wheat-paddy cropping pattern.

Even if the crop diversification is successful in the state, but this strategy will still reinforce the state economy in an agrarian-dependent model (Singh, 2012). This again raises a number of questions about the possible transition of the agrarian economy towards non-agrarian economic structures. In such a scenario, Punjab can keep up and improve its economic growth by moving and emphasising non-agrarian economic segments. For this, Punjab state must move towards building modern and dynamic industrial and tertiary sectors and reinvigorate the state-owned education and health sectors. Here comes the role of the state government to promote appropriate steps to improve the functioning of these sectors. Moreover, if the state wants to shed the 'dependent path' of development, it needs to explore new industrial zones that can cherish and revolve around a new independent and decentralised path of development. While charting its independent path, the state must respond to its internal strengths, needs of other states and vital changes in global economy in accordance with their own needs, requirements and compulsions. Further, the state must protect the poor and marginalised sections of society by providing a worthwhile and pro-poor social security mechanism.

The paper contributors have put in a considerable amount of research in their respective fields. These articles provide many fresh perspectives on the issues exploring various linkages between Punjab's economic developments on the one hand and visible governance crisis, unchanging agrarian structure, environmental concerns, lack of modern industrial sector, gender bias, weak social security, non-performing social sectors, and alarming rise of cancer, on the other. These articles contribute immensely towards understanding the macro, sectoral and other dimensions of Punjab's economy. Innovative suggestions related to creation of new efficient institutions and public policies for reducing the constraints on future economic development of Punjab are based on the grass root realities. This volume, comprehensive in nature and intensive in its analysis, gives new dimensions to the ongoing debate on 'how to rebuild the laggard Punjab economy' and will initiate new explorations for the benefits of policy makers, academia and the general public.

REFERENCES

Ahmed, Ishtiaq (2011), *The Punjab Bloodied: Partitioned and Cleansed*, Rupa & Co., New Delhi.

Bhalla, G.S. and G.K. Chadha (1982), 'Green Revolution and the Small Peasant: A Study of Income Distribution in Punjab Agriculture: I & II', *Economic and Political Weekly*, Vol. 17 (20 and 21): pp. 826-33 and 870-77.

Bhalla, G.S. and G.K. Chadha (1983), *Green Revolution and the Small Peasant: A Study of Income Distribution among Punjab Cultivators*, Concept Publishing Company, New Delhi.

Brar, J.S. (2002), 'Basic Education, Health Care and Economic Growth in Punjab: Achievements, Gaps and Imbalances', *Man and Development*, Vol. 24 (1), pp. 51-63.

Chadha, G.K. (1986), *The State and Rural Economic Transformation: The Case of Punjab 1950-85*, Sage Publications, New Delhi.

Chenery, H.B. (1960), 'Patterns of Industrial Development', *American Economic Review*, Vol. 50 (4), pp. 624-54

Ghuman, R.S., Sukhwinder Singh and J.S. Brar (2006), *Rural Students in Universities of Punjab*, Publication Bureau, Punjabi University, Patiala.

Ghuman, R.S., Sukhwinder Singh and J.S. Brar (2009), *Professional Education in Punjab: Exclusion of Rural Students*, Publication Bureau, Punjabi University, Patiala.

Gill, Anita and Lakhwinder Singh (2006), 'Farmers' Suicides and Response of Public Policy: Evidence, Diagnosis and Alternatives from Panjab', *Economic and Political Weekly*, Vol. 41 (26), June 30 (*Review of Agriculture*), pp. 2762-68.

Gill, S.S. (1988), 'Contradictions of Punjab Model of Growth and Search for Alternatives', *Economic and Political Weekly*, Vol. 23 (42), October 15, pp. 2167-73.

Gill, S.S. (2001), *Land Reforms in India: Intervention for Agrarian Capitalist Transformation in Punjab and Haryana*, Sage Publications, New Delhi.

Gill, S.S. (2002), 'Agriculture, Crop Technology and Employment Generation in Punjab', in S.S. Johl and S.K. Ray (eds.) *Future of Agriculture in Punjab*, Centre for Research in Rural and Industrial Development, Chandigarh, pp. 56-68.

Gill, S.S., Sukhwinder Singh and J.S. Brar (2010), *Globalisation and Indian State: Education, Health and Agricultural Extension Services in Punjab*, Aakar Books, New Delhi.

Gill, S.S., Sukhwinder Singh and J.S. Brar (2013), 'Social Security in

Punjab: A Blend of State and Central Schemes', in K.P. Kannan and Jan Breman (eds.) *The Long Road to Social Security: Assessing the Implementation of National Social Security Initiatives for the Working Poor in India*, Oxford University Press, New Delhi, pp. 504-38.

GOI (2013), *Economic Survey 2012-13*, Oxford University Press, New Delhi.

Johl, S.S. (1986), *Diversification of Agriculture in Punjab*, Report of Expert Committee, Government of Punjab, Chandigarh.

Mittar, V., Sukhwinder Singh and J.S. Brar (2002), *Changing Structure of Education in Punjab: Some Issues and Policy Recommendations*, Publication Bureau, Punjabi University, Patiala.

Randhawa, M.S. (1954), *Out of the Ashes: An Account of the Rehabilitation of Refugees from West Pakistan to the Rural Areas of East Punjab*, Public Relations Department, Chandigarh.

Rangi, P.S., M.S. Sidhu and Harjit Singh (2001), Casualisation of Agricultural Labour in Punjab, *The Indian Journal of Labour Economics*, Vol. 44 (4), pp. 957-70.

Sidhu, R.S. and Sukhpal Singh (2004), 'Agricultural Wages and Employment in Punjab', *Economic and Political Weekly*, Vol. 39 (37), pp. 4132-35.

Singh, Inderjeet and Parmod Kumar (2010), 'Ecological Implications of Agricultural Development in Punjab', in Sucha Singh Gill, Lakhwinder Singh and Reena Marwah (eds.) *Economic and Environmental Sustainability of the Asian Region*, Routledge-Taylor and Francis Group, New Delhi, pp. 183-200.

Singh, Pritam (2012), 'The Role of Externally-Governed Economic Policies in Shaping Punjab's Agrarian-Oriented Development Pattern', *Journal of Agricultural Development & Policy*, Vol. 22 (2), pp. 1-19.

Singh, Lakhwinder and Sukhpal Singh (2002) 'Deceleration of Economic Growth in Punjab: Evidence, Explanation and a Way-Out, *Economic and Political Weekly*, Vol. 37 (6), February 9, pp. 579-86.

Singh, Lakhwinder (2013) 'Vision of Economic Development in Punjab', Paper Presented at the International Conference on *'Rebuilding Punjab: Political Economy, Society and Values'*, Organised by the Institute for Humanities Research and The Sikh and Punjabi Studies, University of California, Santa Cruz, USA, March 29-30.

Singh, Sukhpal (2010), 'The Status of Agricultural Resources in Punjab: Need for Alternatives', in R.S. Ghuman, Surjit Singh and

Jaswinder Singh Brar (eds.) *Globalisation and Change: Perspectives from Punjab*, Rawat Publications, Jaipur, pp. 257-74.

Singh, Sukhwinder (1991), Development and Use of Health Care Services in Rural Areas: A Case Study of Punjab, *Unpublished Ph.D. Thesis*, Department of Economics, Punjabi University, Patiala.

Singh, Sukhwinder and J.S. Brar (1997),'A Caste-wise Study of Utilisation of Health Care Services during Child Birth in Punjab: Based on Sample Survey of Households in Patiala District', in V.S. Mahajan and B.S. Mann (eds.), *Economic Development of Scheduled Castes in Punjab*, Anmol Publications, New Delhi, pp. 171-90.

PART I

Genesis of Slow Down of the Punjab Economy

2

Slow Down of Punjab Economy and Governance Crisis

Sucha Singh Gill

The pace of economic development of the economy of a country or a region depends on the activities of economic agents such as the labour and entrepreneurs when they act upon natural resources and organise economic activities. This pace can be accelerated by the policy measures, which supplement the activities of individual economic agents both directly by initiating productive activities and indirectly by creating infrastructure facilities. Truly, the pace of economic development is the product of effective/ineffective implementation of policy measures and responses of economic agents to these policy measures. The people of Punjab whether they are the entrepreneurs or labourers/employees are known for their dynamism and pragmatic attitude towards life. They are very quick to adopt new technology and innovations in productive activities. They recovered very quickly from the shock of partition and they were, in fact, the first in the country to enact the Green Revolution. They responded positively to the policy measures and the state achieved first position in the per capita income among the major states in the country in the mid-1950s and retained that position till 1991-92.

But the slow down of the Punjab economy vis-à-vis other states and the all-India average has changed the position of the state. In fact, the governance process in the state was derailed in the 1980s—the period known for political turmoil. In the subsequent period, however, the process of governance could not be put on the rails in spite of the restoration of political normalcy in the early 1990s. This chapter makes an attempt to relate the slow down in the Punjab economy to the crisis of governance. It is divided into three sections. Section I tries to explain the slow down and its roots in the state. Section II examines the issues related to governance. And, Section III makes concluding observations and policy suggestions.

I

The Punjab economy experienced an impressive growth rate during the 1960s and 1970s of the 20th century. But the growth rate began to slow down during the 1980s and decelerated during the 1990s. The growth rates of gross state domestic product (GSDP) and also of per capita income in the state became significantly lower than that of the national average. Consequently, the state has slipped down in its ranking among major states from the first rank in 1991-92 to the second rank in 1992-93 and to the sixth rank in 2009-10. This happened because the economy of the state has been experiencing a growth rate much lower than the fast growing states like Haryana, Maharashtra, Kerala, Gujarat and Tamil Nadu, which have overtaken the Punjab state in the per capita income since 1992-93. The state has also lost its position in relation to the all-India average. In 1999-2000, Punjab's per capita income was 61.4 per cent higher than that of the all-India average, which has come down to be more than the all-India average by 30.3 per cent in 2007-08. This is because of the growth rate of the Punjab economy has been one of the lowest in the country. Ever since India introduced the new economic policy and entered the era of fast and accelerating rates of growth, Punjab has entered the phase of slow and stagnating growth rate. During the Eighth Five Year Plan (1992-97), the state achieved 4.7 per cent annual growth rate in the GSDP against the national average of 6.5 per cent. During the Ninth Five Year Plan (1997-2002), the state achieved 4.4 per cent growth rate of GSDP against the national average of 5.5 per cent. In the Tenth Five Year Plan (2002-07), the state experienced a growth rate of 4.5 per cent against the all-India average of 7.7 per cent (Planning Commission, 2002). Furthermore, amongst the major states, Punjab's growth rate was the lowest in the country during the Tenth Five Year Plan, and during the earlier two Five Year Plans (8th and 9th), it was among the five lowest growing states in the country. The state has targeted to grow at 5.9 per cent per annum against the national average of 9.9 per cent during the Eleventh Five Year Plan (2007-12). Again, the growth rate in Punjab's economy is the lowest amongst the major Indian states (Planning Commission, 2007).

The slow growth rate in the state is also found in its three sub-sectors such as primary, secondary and tertiary sectors compared to all-India averages. The agriculture and allied activities, which forms the backbone of the economy of the state, is suffering from a serious crisis. The crisis is manifested in the form of stagnating production and per hectare yields. In fact, the state has exhausted the potentials of Green Revolution technology among the major crops by achieving more than 83 per cent of the potential yield level in the case of rice and BT Cotton and above 90 per cent in the case of wheat (Sidhu and Singh, 2011). Besides, this technology has brought out disastrous economic, environment and social consequences in the state. The commercial agriculture with intensive farming techniques have added to the costs of cultivation at a rate higher than that of output prices reducing the diminishing per hectare income for the farmers/peasants (Ghuman, 2002; Sidhu and Johl, 2002). This has made a large proportion of small and marginal farmers unviable. It has pushed a large number of them into the debt trap (Shergill, 2010). In addition, commercial agriculture has weakened the traditional social ties as well as community support to the peasants. The pauperised peasants, agricultural labourers and those who fell into the debt trap have resorted to suicides (AFDR, 2000; Gill, 2005; Gill and Singh, 2006; Gill, 2010; Iyer and Manick, 2000). The commercialised capitalist agriculture has intensified the process of de-peasantisation of pauperised peasantry and their land is being transferred to more prosperous, middle and big (rich) farmers through the mechanism of reverse tenancy, mortgage and sale deeds. An exhaustive study (Singh et al., 2009) on differentiation of peasantry and process of throwing peasantry out of agriculture covering 40 villages from the state indicates that 10.9 per cent of farmers have left agriculture between 1990 and 2008. Those who left cultivation mostly belonged to the small and marginal category of farmers and 21.7 per cent of them have become wage labourers. Those who became entrepreneur/commission agents largely belonged to the upper/rich category farmers. The land leased-out or mortgaged/sold by the farmers leaving agriculture has gone to the middle and bigger (rich) farmers. The differentiation process and commercial nature of contracts have weakened community sense in the rural/agricultural economy. The poor farmers who have left cultivation lack the skills and expertise to join new occupations. They, therefore, have no option but to become casual labourers and face unemployment. The mechanisation of agricultural operations has reduced the labour absorption capacity of agriculture (Gill, 2002).

The Green Revolution has also disastrous consequences both for farmers and environment in the state. The bio-diversity has been destroyed and replaced by mono-cropping culture. There has been massive soil depletion in the state leading to deficiency in micro nutrients, over exploitation of ground water resources, poisoning of soil and water resources due to high/intensive use of insecticides and pesticides. This has also created several health problems like cancer, diabetes, blood pressure and heart ailments along with continuation of traditional water-borne diseases (Shiva, 1991; Khurana, 2011). This is accompanied by collapse of rural health and education. In terms of literacy rate, infant mortality rate, maternal death rate, etc., the state ranks at fourth or fifth place among the major states of the country. Although its position in per capita income, health and education indicators is higher than the all-India average, the gap is being reduced over a period of time. There is a high rate of unemployment among the population in the age group of 15-19 years. The unemployment rate in the state was 11.1 per cent in 2009-10 compared to the national average of 9.5 per cent. This is very high when it is compared with the neighbouring states of Haryana (8.6 per cent), Jammu & Kashmir (5.1 per cent) and Himachal Pradesh (6.4 per cent). This is also very high when compared to the high income states of Haryana (8.6 per cent), Maharashtra (5.8 per cent); Gujarat (9.6 per cent), Tamil Nadu (5.9 per cent) and Kerala (11.0 per cent) (Labour Bureau, 2010). The quality of wage and salary employment has deteriorated over time. The government jobs have lost their sheen with passing of legislation in 2011 to make all government appointments on contract at lower salary (only basic pay) for the initial period of 3-5 years for all posts except for those filled through the PCS, IPS and IAS examinations. The qualified youth of the state is leaving the country by hook or by crook to earn their livelihood in foreign lands. Two Expert Committees (1986; 2002) know as The Johl Committee-1 (1986) and Johl Committee-2 (2002) have highlighted diversification issues and the Punjab Government launched diversification of agriculture programme in 2003. But this programme failed to take off in the absence of adequate provision of assured market clearance at assured/pre-determined prices. There have been suggestions to diversify the rural economy through generation of extensive non-farm employment and setting up of agro-processing industries. At present, the produce of major agricultural crops is being sold in the raw form. Surprisingly, the Punjab government is unable to develop a balanced link between agricultural and industrial development in the state (Khurana, 2011; Singh, 2011).

There are a number of policy suggestions made by a large number of committees set up during the last two and a half decades and also individual scholars in the region to recover the lost glory of Punjab in its socio-economic development. But, the state is unable to implement successfully some of the viable policies and programmes. This is because the organisations and institutions in the state are paralysed and the delivery mechanism of services has become non-performing. This, in fact, is connected to the poor governance in the state.

II

Governance is one of the key factors in the socio-economic transformation of any society. Governance, in economic literature, is treated as a part of institutions of the societies. These institutions have a much more fundamental role in determining long run performance of economies. Institutions can provide incentives for economic performance or create disincentives to efficiency. However, these institutions are treated as a non-economic factor for economic development and a critical element for determining economic performance. These make markets to function or not to function. They affect markets in a variety of ways but commonly through reducing or adding to the transaction costs. The incentives to cheat, free ride or so on contribute to high transaction costs, add to inefficiencies and lead to failure of many policies or making them ineffective. The incapacity of formal financial markets to eliminate the informal rural credit market dominated by moneylenders and commission agents is a classic example of institutional factors leading to failure of public policy due to high transaction costs and poor functioning of formal rural credit, labour and commodities markets.

Institutions are defined as the 'rules of the society or organisations that facilitate coordination among the people by helping them form expectations, which each person can reasonably hold in dealing with others' (Ruttan and Hayami, 1984). They are also viewed as complex norms and behaviour that persist over time by serving socially valued objective (Uphoff, 1991). Some scholars make a distinction between institutions and organisations. Institutions are defined as rules of the game in a society or more formally and humanly devised constraints that shape human interaction and organisations as groups of individuals bound by some common purpose to achieve objectives (North, 1990). The institutions are a cluster of rules, norms and societal concepts while the organisations are instrumental concentrations of institutional patterns (Kotter, 1988). The formal institutions are devised and socially recognised rules and sanctioned expectations in a society with regard to legal relations which define a choice set of individuals with respect to a choice set of others. The governance is practically an operation and enforcement of formal rules and norms of the government to achieve societal objectives. In fact, the working of institutions is mirrored through the governance and reflected in the progress of the society.

Recognising the crucial role of the governance, the World Bank in its *World Development Report 1997* focused on this issue and subtitled it *The State in a Changing World*. The report was devoted to the role and effectiveness of the state, especially what the state should do, how it should be done and how it could do better in a rapidly changing world (World Bank, 1997). The report came to the conclusion that the state's central institutions work better for meeting a broad range of collective needs more effectively, therefore, its capability must be increased. The state capabilities can be raised by reinvigorating public institutions. This means redesigning effective rules and restraints to check arbitrary state actions and combat corruption. This means to increase efficiency, the state has to be more responsive to people's needs and it has to be closer to the people through broader participation and decentralisation. Thus, reinvigorating state institutions demand the following three aspect: (i) effective rules and constraints, (ii) greater competitive pressure and (iii) increased citizens' voices and partnership. These three factors lead to the issue of a well-functioning, effective and accountable governance system. Since the justice system is a major part of the governance, a functioning and effective legal system is critical to good governance.

When the World Bank raised the issue of governance, this immediately became part of public concern in India. The document of the Ninth Five Year Plan (1997-2002) added a chapter on 'Implementation, Delivery Mechanism and Institutional Development'. This chapter reviewed the implementation of different Five Year Plans in India with a view to identify weak spots in the formulation and implementation of plan programmes and to find solutions to these weaknesses. The issues of decentralisation in development planning, accountability of implementing agencies and monitoring/ evaluation of programmes were raised. This was followed by a more specific chapter titled 'Governance and Implementation' in the Tenth Five Year Plan (2002-07) and an exclusive chapter on 'Governance' in the Eleventh Five Year Plan (2007-12). These documents highlight the features of the good governance as well as the poor governance. The good governance consists of:

(i) Exercise of legitimate political power;
(ii) Formulation and implementation of policies and programmes that are equitable, transparent, non-discriminatory and socially sensitive;
(iii) Accountability to the people at large; and
(iv) Decentralised and participatory governance.

And, the poor governance is manifested in:

(i) Poor management of economy, persisting fiscal imbalances, disparities in pace and level of development across regions/districts;
(ii) Denial of basic needs of food, water and shelter to substantial population;
(iii) Threat to life and personal security in the face of inadequate state control on law and order;
(iv) Marginalisation, exclusion, persecution of people on account of social, religious, caste or gender affiliations;
(v) Lack of sensitivity, transparency and accountability of state machinery in interface with people;
(vi) Inadequate incentives/disincentives for people, subversion of rules, evasion of taxes and failure in getting justice;
(vii) Lack of decentralised participatory governance and development in spite of the provisions of the 73rd and 74th amendments of the constitution; and
(viii) Deterioration of the physical environment.

These issues of poor governance need to be addressed to improve the capability of the state to increase the rate and level of socio-economic development in a country, a region or a state. From the point of view of standards of governance, Punjab state has seen a change over the time period. For instance, immediately after India's independence when the state was partitioned, Punjab state was able to establish the standards and norms of governance which were a model for other states. This was manifested from the settling of resettlement claims after the partition of Punjab, consolidation of landholdings and updating of land records. In spite of some weaknesses (poor implementation of land reforms), the state was able to change the orientation of the administration from the colonial attitude of maintenance of law and order to promotion of economic development. Consequently, the people of the state were able to quickly recover from the shock of partition and the state became a leader in enacting the Green Revolution in the mid-1960s and turned out to be the number one state in socio-economic development by 1956. But this could not be sustained beyond the mid-1970s when the governance began to deteriorate and ultimately collapsed during 1982-92 (militancy dominated period) when the protection of life and property came under a question mark in the state.

The governance of the state in relation to the economy and its economic development can be measured in several ways. One, it has been measured in terms of proportion of the government expenditure incurred for development and non-development purposes. An examination of government expenditure from 1978-79 to 2009-10 on the basis of the three-year triennium period bring out very clearly the shift in pattern of expenditure of the Punjab Government. In the triennium ended year 1980-81 (before the terrorism began in the state), 72.98 per cent of the state budget was spent for development purposes. The share of non-development expenditure in the total state expenditure stood at 27.02 per cent. This increased slowly but remained in the range of 30.24 per cent to 35.15 per cent up to the early 1990s. However, these proportions changed very rapidly after the state attained political normalcy and the new economic policy was implemented in the state. The proportion of development expenditure fell to 42.88 per cent during the triennium ended year 1995-96 from 72.98 per cent during the triennium ended year 1980-81. The share of non-development expenditure rose from 27.02 per cent to 57.12 per cent. Thus, the proportion of non-development expenditure doubled while that of development fell to slightly more than one-half during this period. In the recent years (triennium ended year 2009-10), proportion of non-development expenditure has slightly declined to 56.95 per cent from 58.95 per cent during the triennium ended year 2004-05. Consequently, the share of development expenditure has increased from 41.05 per cent during the triennium ended year 2004-05 to 43.04 per cent during the triennium ended year 2009-10 (Table 2.1). The data bring out that the priorities of government have shifted from the development activities to non-development activities involving general administration, maintenance of law and order and servicing of public debt. This also fits into priorities of the government under the new economic policy where more space in the development activities have been granted to the private companies, especially those belonging to the corporate sector.

Table 2.1: Distribution of Public Expenditure by Major Heads in Punjab

(Rs. in Crores at 1993-94 Prices)

Triennium Period	*Total Public Expenditure (All Heads)*	*Non-Development Expenditure*	*Development Expenditure*
1978-78 to 1980-81	1520.24 (100.00)	410.71 (27.02)	1109.53 (72.98)
1981-82 to 1983-84	1889.60 (100.00)	571.45 (30.24)	1318.14 (72.98)
1984-85 to 1986-87	2383.50 (100.00)	837.89 (35.15)	1545.62 (64.85)
1987-88 to 1989-90	2994.60 (100.00)	955.39 (31.90)	2039.17 (68.09)
1990-91 to 1992-93	4025.37 (100.00)	1365.99 (33.93)	2689.78 (66.70)
1993-94 to 1995-96	4686.01 (100.00)	2676.80 (57.12)	2009.18 (42.88)
1996-97 to 1998-99	5537.74 (100.00)	2697.89 (48.72)	2839.84 (51.28)
1999-00 to 2001-02	7044.19 (100.00)	4108.59 (58.33)	2935.60 (41.67)
2002-03 to 2004-05	9152.56 (100.00)	5395.67 (58.95)	3756.89 (41.05)
2007-08 to 2009-10*	25744.53 (100.00)	14658.28 (56.96)	11086.25 (43.04)

Figures in parentheses are percentages.
* Figures for 2007-08 to 2009-10 are at current prices
Source: Gill, Singh and Brar, 2010.

The second way one can look at the relationship between governance and economic development is the commitment of the state government to convert promised outlays on the development into actual expenditure on development. For this

Table 2.2: Head-wise Approved Outlay and Expenditure in Punjab during the Ninth Five Year Plan (1997-2002)

S. No.	*Major Heads of Development*	*Approved Outlay (Rs. Lakh)*	*Total Expenditure (Rs. Lakh)*	*Absolute Gap (Rs. Lakh)**	*Relative Gap (%)***
1.	Agriculture & Allied Activities	80173.90	45157.52	35016.38	43.68
2.	Rural Development	99773.40	43391.01	56382.39	56.51
3.	Special Area Programme	1675.29	8961.74	-7286.45	-434.94
4.	Irrigation & Flood Control	159816.05	106267.51	53548.54	33.51
5.	Energy	368025.00	420235.77	-52210.77	-14.19
6.	Industry & Minerals	34979.00	7309.97	27669.03	79.10
7.	Transport	73948.00	62519.10	11428.90	15.46
8.	Science, Technology & Environment	5382.00	299.73	5082.27	94.43
9.	General Economic Services	113361.79	17531.09	95830.70	84.54
10.	Social Services	472026.65	278024.86	194001.99	41.10
11.	General Services	20838.72	11439.41	9399.31	54.11
	Grand Total	**1430000.00**	**1003283.79**	**426716.21**	**29.84**

* Between allocated and spent resources.
** Percentage between allocated and spent resources.

Source: Punjab State Planning Board, Chandigarh.

purpose, an exercise has been done for the period from 1997-2007 covering the Eight, Ninth and Tenth Five Year Plans. The data show that except for the Eighth Five Year Plan (1992-97), the state government did not release the necessary funds to match plan expenditure to plan outlay for the remaining two plans (Ninth and Tenth). Table 2.2 and Table 2.3 show that during the Ninth Five Year Plan (1997-2002), plan expenditure fell short of plan outlay by 20.55 per cent. The deficiency in plan expenditure over the plan outlay during the Tenth Five

Year Plan (2002-2007) in Punjab was to the extent of 29.84 per cent. The implementation of the Eleventh Five Year Plan (2007-12) for the first three years brings out that deficient expenditure of the plan outlay turned out to be 10.51 per cent. The sector-wise details of deficient expenditure makes it clear that vital sectors like agriculture, rural development, industry and minerals, science and technology and general economic services had born the brunt of deficient expenditure during the Ninth Five Year Plan. And, sectors like agriculture, irrigation and flood control, science and technology, transport, social and economic services suffered more during the Tenth Five Year Plan. This trend has continued during the Eleventh Five Year Plan. The gap/deficient expenditure has been much larger for Scheduled Caste Special Plan. This stood at 49.97 per cent for the Ninth Five Year Plan and 60.92 per cent for the Tenth Five Year Plan.

The governance crisis in Punjab is also reflected more clearly in the fiscal management of the state. The state is unable to collect revenue both through taxes and non-tax sources to meet its rising expenditure. This is reflected in the fiscal deficit of the state. The data on fiscal deficit is shown in Table 2.4. The data bring out that the fiscal deficit of Punjab and Haryana respectively stood at 3.37 per cent and 3.78 per cent of GSDP during 1980-81 to 1982-83 (three year average). In the case of Punjab, this increased to 8.03 per cent during 1989-90 to 1991-92, but declined to 3.23 per cent in the case of Haryana during these years. The divergence can be explained in terms of disturbed conditions in Punjab while Haryana continued to be in a normal situation. The fiscal deficit of Punjab decreased to 5.98 per cent during 1999-2000 to 2001-02 which it increased to 4.4 per cent in the case of Haryana. After enactment of the Fiscal Responsibility Act in 2003, the fiscal deficit of Punjab state decreased to 3.32 per cent during 2006-07 to 2008-09 against the maximum limit of 3.0 per cent of GSDP. In the case of Haryana, the fiscal deficit declined to 0.70 per cent of GSDP. Thus, even after achieving normalcy, the state has not been able to contain the fiscal deficit compared to the neighbouring state of Haryana, a top performing state in the country in per capita terms (Table 2.4). This has led to accumulation of public debt of the Punjab government. Starting with a public debt of a few hundred crore rupees in the early 1980s, this increased to Rs. 67,721 crores on March 31, 2010 in Punjab compared to Rs. 40,324 crores in Haryana. The annual interest payment reached Rs. 5,349 crores (3.07 per cent of GSDP) in Punjab compared to Rs. 3,001 crores (1.55 per cent of GSDP) in the case of Haryana. If interest

Table 2.3: Head-wise Approved Outlay and Expenditure in Punjab during the Tenth Five Year Plan (2002-07)

S. No.	*Major Head of Development*	*Approved Outlay (Rs. Lakh)*	*Total Expenditure (Rs. Lakh)*	*Absolute Gap (Rs. Lakh)**	*Relative Gap (%)***
1.	Agriculture & Allied Activities	63540.79	40648.74	22892.05	36.03
2.	Rural Development	12650.00	165221.54	-39171.54	-31.08
3.	Special Area Programme	13437.36	11003.79	2433.57	18.11
4.	Irrigation & Flood Control	261151.28	96726.50	164424.78	62.96
5.	Energy	59973.00	509997.10	89875.90	14.98
6.	Industry & Minerals	5588.00	16125.08	-10537.08	-188.57
7.	Transport	271150.00	182827.00	88323.00	32.57
8.	Science, Technology & Environment	3875.00	1294.18	2580.82	66.60
9.	General Economic Services	15015.00	113161.90	-98146.90	-653.33
10.	Social Services	485836.57	331214.09	154622.48	31.83
11.	General Services	20183.00	14100.82	6082.18	30.14
	Grand Total	1865700.00	1482320.74	383379.26	20.55

* Between allocated and spent resources.

** Percentage between allocated and spent resources.

Source: Punjab State Planning Board, Chandigarh.

payments are combined with instalment of debt payment, it eats away nearly one-third of the state budget and one-half of the state's own revenue. The poor fiscal health of the state has undermined the capacity of the state government to undertake new initiatives to solve the pressing problems of unemployment, slow down of growth rate and poor urban infrastructure. There are reports that the work of revenue and taxation officers is interfered by the powerful/influential persons in the ruling parties. The poor tax collection is accompanied by unsustainable populist measures to benefit a section of population which has negatively impacted on economic performance in the state.

Table 2.4: Gross Fiscal Deficit and its Percentage in GSDP in Punjab and Haryana

Year	*Gross Fiscal Deficit (GFD) (Rs. Crores)*		*GFD Ratio to GSDP (%)*	
	Punjab	*Haryana*	*Punjab*	*Haryana*
1980-81	160	112	3.6	3.69
1981-82	178	102	3.37	2.92
1982-83	183	189	3.13	4.72
1989-90	909	393	6.04	3.96
1990-91	1242	386	7.42	3.15
1991-92	2151	375	10.62	2.58
1999-2000	3195	2133	5.23	4.51
2000-01	3904	2285	5.76	4.27
2001-02	4958	2740	6.96	4.55
2002-03	4401	1471	5.99	2.21
2006-07	4384	-1179	4.07	-0.99
2007-08	1604	1284	1.25	0.98
2008-09 (RE)	6856	3708	4.63	2.2
2009-10 (BE)	9660	8557	5.55	4.42

Source: 1. RBI (2010), *Handbook of Statistics on State Government Finances*, RBI Occasional Publication
2. RBI (2012), *Handbook of Statistics on Indian Economy*, RBI Publication.

As the performance of the Punjab economy has slowed down, the problems of unemployment, poor quality of employment, non-payment of arrears to the employees, de-peasantisation induced by pauperisation of peasantry, suicides by agricultural labourers and farmers, etc. are rising. The suffering sections of population can express their voice of resentment to impress upon the government to solve their problems through the protest movements. In democracy, the sections of population not represented in the government can represent themselves through these protest movements. But the government has become intolerant towards such movements and has passed two acts (The Punjab Prevention of Damage to Public and Private Property Act, 2010 and The Punjab Special Security Group Act, 2010) in the state to contain these movements and reduce public representation of population not represented in the government policies and programmes. They are intended to contain protest movements. The implementation of these acts will reduce representation of issues of unrepresented sections. It is an attempt to rule through force rather than consent of the people. It is a sign of poor governance and indication of psyche to conceal people's problems instead of solving them. This will further alienate people from the government of the day and negatively affect economic performance of the state.

III

Slow down of economic development in Punjab is the manifestation of the deep-rooted governance crisis in the state. The rural economy led by the agriculture sector has already been heading for stagnation. The pauperisation of the peasantry is leading to their proletarianisation. The downward mobility accompanied by high incidence of debt and involvement of poor peasants in the debt trap is leading to farmers' suicides. The growth of high level of unemployment and underemployment due to shrinking labour absorbability of agriculture has pushed a section of agricultural labour in neck deep debt and also to their suicides. In fact, the initial agricultural development could not be transformed into industrial development in the state. Most of the agricultural produce is sold in raw form and disjunction prevails between agriculture and manufacturing sectors in the state.

The collapse of rural education and rural health has created a disability among the rural youth to adopt non-farm activities both in the villages and towns. A process of integrated development ensuring upward mobility has come to a stand still with the widening of rural-urban differences in living standards. This requires multipronged efforts with a leading role of the state government. The capacity of the state government has crippled on one side due to poor fiscal health of the state and apathy of the government machinery on the other. It is becoming very difficult for the state government to implement some of the centrally sponsored programmes. The prevalence of massive corruption makes most of the policies and programmes ineffective. The whole process of governance has been inefficient and alienating in nature. This needs to be rectified to make it more efficient, people-friendly and responsive in nature. This would require the political class in the state to contain bureaucracy and make administration efficient, transparent and non-partisan in functioning. Without improving governance, the fiscal health of the state can not be restored. With per capita income of the state nearing US $ 1500, the tax GSDP ratio can be raised from 8.0 per cent to 12.0 per cent and above without raising the rate of taxes. It means that a better tax compliance is urgently required in the state.

With better delivery of services such as the education and health especially in the rural areas can pay rich dividends in revival of the high growth trajectory in the state. The improvement of infrastructure, agricultural research and extension services along with institutional reforms towards farmers' cooperatives/collectives can help solve the agrarian crisis and establish a healthy/balanced relationship between agriculture and manufacturing. Increased public investment in power, irrigation and ground water management, and improvement in urban infrastructure can create conditions for raising private investment. The increase in the minimum wage rate and improvement in working and service conditions can make employment decent and economic growth inclusive in nature. All these measures can improve the working of the economy. To achieve a high growth trajectory and make it people-friendly and more inclusive, an improvement in governance is a necessary condition. These are some of the lessons, which can be learnt from better performing states in the neighbourhood as well as in other regions of the country and abroad. The bills/acts, which block democratic participation of the people, need to be withdrawn. The Panchayati Raj Institutions and Urban Local Bodies need to be empowered for the participative and decentralised governance in the true sense.

REFERENCES

AFDR (2000), *Suicides in Rural Punjab: A Report* (in Punjabi), Association for Democratic Rights, Ludhiana.

Expert Committee (1986), also known as Johl Committee-1, *Diversification of Agriculture in Punjab*, Government of Punjab, Chandigarh.

Expert Committee (2002), also known as Johl Committee-2, *Agricultural Production Pattern Adjustment Programme in Punjab for Productivity Growth*, Government of Punjab, Chandigarh.

Ghuman, R.S. (2002), 'World Trade Organisation and Indian Agriculture with Special Reference to Punjab: Crisis and Challenges', in S.S. Johl and S.K. Ray (eds.), *Future of Punjab Agriculture*, CRRID, Chandigarh, pp. 125-159.

Gill, Anita (2010), 'Punjab Peasantry: A Question of Life and Death', in R.S. Deshpande and Saroj Arora (eds.) *Agrarian Crisis and Farmer Suicides*, Sage Publications, New Delhi, pp. 293-311.

Gill, Anita and Lakhwinder Singh (2006), 'Farmers' Suicides and Response of Public Policy: Evidence, Diagnosis and Alternative from Punjab', *Economic and Political Weekly*, Vol. 41 (26), June 30, pp. 2762-68.

Gill, Sucha Singh, Sukhwinder Singh and Jaswinder Singh Brar (2010), *Globalization and Indian State: Education, Health and Agricultural Extension Services in Punjab*, Aakar Books, New Delhi.

Gill, Sucha Singh (2005), 'Economic Distress and Farmer Suicides in Rural Punjab', *Journal of Punjab Studies*, Vol. 12 (2), pp. 219-37.

Gill, Sucha Singh (2002) 'Agricultural Crop Technology and Employment Generation in Punjab', in S.S. Johl and S.K. Ray (eds.) *Future of Punjab Agriculture*, CRRID, Chandigarh, pp. 56-68.

Iyer, K. Gopal and M.S. Manick (2000), *Indebtedness Impoverishment and Suicides in Rural Punjab*, India Publishers and Distributors, New Delhi.

Khurana, M.R. (2011), 'Agrarian Crisis in Punjab and the Way Out', in H.S. Shergill, Sucha Singh Gill and Gurmail Singh (eds.),

Understanding North-West Indian Economy, Serials Publications, New Delhi, pp. 36-108.

Kotter, Herbert (1988), 'Institutions and Organisations in Rural Development', *Quarterly Journal of International Agriculture*, Vol. 27 (1), pp. 7-19.

Labour Bureau (2010), *Report on Employment and Unemployment Survey (2009-10)*, Government of India, Shimla.

North, D.C. (1990), *Institutions, Institutional Change and Economic Performance*, Cambridge University Press, Cambridge.

Planning Commission (2002), *Tenth Five Year Plan 2002-07*, Government of India, New Delhi.

Planning Commission (2007), *Eleventh Five Year Plan 2007-12*, Government of India, New Delhi.

Rattan, V.W. and Yujiro Hayami (1984), 'Towards a Theory of Induced Institutional Innovation', *Journal of Development Studies*, Vol. 20 (4), pp. 203-23.

Shergill, H.S. (2010), *Growth of Farm Debt in Punjab*, Institute for Development and Cummunication (IDC), Chandigarh.

Shiva, Vandana (1991), *The Violence of Green Revolution: Third World Agriculture, Ecology and Politics*, Zed Books, London.

Sidhu M.S. and Varinder Pal Singh (2011), 'Problems and Prospects of Agriculture in Punjab', in H.S. Shergill, Sucha Singh Gill and Gurmail Singh (eds.), *Understanding North-West Indian Economy*, Serials Publications, New Delhi, pp. 11-35.

Sidhu, R.S. and S.S. Johl (2002), 'Three Decades of Intensive Agriculture in Punjab: Socio-Economic and Environment Consequences', in S.S. Johl and S.K. Ray (eds.) *Future of Punjab Agriculture*, CRRID, Chandigarh, pp. 16-39.

Singh, Karam, Sukhpal Singh and H.S. Kingra (2009), 'Agrarian Crisis and Depesantisation in Punjab: Status of marginal Farmers who Left Agriculture', *Indian Journal of Agricultural Economics*, Vol. 64 (4), pp. 585-603.

Singh, Lakhwinder (2011), 'Post Reform Economic Development in Punjab: A Comparative Perspective and Alternative Strategies', in H.S. Shergill, Sucha Singh Gill and Gurmail Singh (eds.), *Understanding North-West Indian Economy*, Serials Publications, New Delhi, pp. 329-55.

World Bank (1997), *The World Development Report: The State in a Changing World*, Washington D.C.

Uphoff, N. (1991), *Managing Irrigation: Analysis and Improving Performance of Bureaucracies*, Sage Publications, New Delhi.

3

Economic Governance and Punjab's Economic Growth

Lakhwinder Singh

Introduction

Punjab's experience of economic development remained quite instructive for examining the relationship between economic governance and economic growth. The modern economic growth that started with the advent of the Green Revolution has made Punjab's economy a symbol of economic prosperity which lasted more than three decades. The rank of Punjab state, in terms of per capita income, among major Indian states remained number one for the three decades since the Green Revolution. Before the Green Revolution, the government of Punjab has taken a series of measures to develop institutional infrastructure that was conducive for preparing the ground to initiate new economic activities. Punjab state, apart from providing the right kind of institutional arrangements, has initiated the process of public investment that enabled private sector economic activities to flourish. It is a widely known fact that Punjab state was not only known as a 'model state of capitalist economic development', but was also able to govern well the markets to achieve a higher rate of economic growth when the Indian economy as a whole was trapped in the Hindu rate of growth.

It is somewhat surprising that in the post-reform period

when the Indian economy has started achieving a faster rate of economic growth, the Punjab economy, however, has turned towards the syndrome of the Hindu growth rate. These divergent growth trends, i.e. from a leading state to a laggard state of the Indian economy, prod the scholars to provide satisfactory explanations why this has happened in the Punjab state. There are two kinds of explanations one can turn to. One, the standard economic growth theory (Solow-Swan) states that the rapidly growing state/countries will slow down due to decreasing returns to scale to the scarce factor of production, i.e. capital. This explanation has been challenged by the endogenous growth theory on the ground that many ways and means exist through which decreasing returns to scale can be converted into increasing returns to scale through investing in the research and development/innovations as well as in the human capital. Two, the structural-evolutionary theory of economic growth states that the economic development is path dependent but fundamentally determined by the governance pattern, in terms of regulation of markets via the investments in enacting institutional arrangements and generating innovations suitable for the structure and stage of economic development. Both theoretical constructs allow us to think of growing without bounds.

This chapter has made an attempt to examine the status of the Punjab economy with a view to identify the factors that have contributed to the slow/slower growth of Punjab's economy. Identification of the factors that have contributed to the slow growth of the Punjab economy can help us to devise alternative policy measures for regulation and governance of markets for achieving a higher growth path along with distributive justice.

Economic Growth of Punjab in Comparative Perspective

According to available comparable per capita income estimates of major states of India, Punjab's per capita income in 2008-09 at constant prices was Rs 33,198 and, on this basis, Punjab state ranked fourth. First, second and third ranks went to Haryana, Maharashtra and Kerala respectively. It is also expected that the other two fast growing states, i.e. Gujarat and Himachal Pradesh will soon cross the level of per capita income of Punjab state. This evidence clearly establishes the fact that the status of Punjab's economy in the national reckoning has been eroded and declining further at a fast pace. The falling behind of Punjab state compared with other states has happened largely due to the slow rate of economic growth of Punjab's economy, especially in the post-reform period. It is pertinent to mention here that during the Eight Five Year Plan (1992-97), the Punjab economy attained the growth rate of state domestic product of the order of 4.7 per cent per annum against the national average growth rate of 6.5 per cent per annum (Table 3.1). The growth performance of Punjab's economy further declined marginally during the Ninth Five Year Plan (1997-2002) when the rate of economic growth was recorded at 4.4 per cent compared to the Indian economy's growth rate of 5.5 per cent per annum during the same period. Further more, when the Punjab economy grew at a rate of 4.5 per cent per annum during the Tenth Five Year Plan (2002-07) against the targeted growth rate of 6.4 per cent per annum and, during the same period, the Indian economy entered into the high growth trajectory of 7.7 per cent per annum. Even the target rate of growth for Punjab during the Eleventh Five Year Plan (2007-12) has been fixed at 5.9 per cent per annum, whereas the Indian economy sets a target to grow at the rate of 9 per cent per annum (Planning Commission, 2008). It means that Punjab state has recorded an economic growth rate much below the national average for a considerable period of time, i.e. for the last two decades.

Sources of Economic Growth of Punjab Economy

To identify sources of slow growth experience of Punjab's economy, an analysis of structural change and decomposition of aggregate growth rate of the economy into sub-sectors can be useful. It is true that the agriculture sector in Punjab's economy as well as in the Indian economy as a whole occupied a prime place both in terms of generating income and providing employment to the workforce. For instance, the

Table 3.1: Growth Rates in State Domestic Product in Different States

S. No.	*State/UT*	*Eighth Plan (1992-97)*	*Ninth Plan (1997-02)*	*Tenth Plan (2002-07)*	*Eleventh Plan (2007-12)*
1.	Andhra Pradesh	5.4	4.6	6.7	9.5
2.	Bihar	2.2	4.0	4.7	7.6
3.	Goa	8.9	5.5	7.8	8.6
4.	Gujarat	12.4	4.0	10.6	12.1
5.	Haryana	5.2	4.1	7.6	11.2
6.	Karnataka	6.2	7.2	7.0	11.0
7.	Kerala	6.5	5.7	7.2	9.8
8.	Madhya Pradesh	6.3	4.0	4.3	11.2
9.	Maharashtra	8.9	4.7	7.9	9.5
10.	Orissa	2.1	5.1	9.1	6.7
11.	Punjab	4.7	4.4	4.5	9.1
12.	Rajasthan	7.5	3.5	5.0	8.8
13.	Tamil Nadu	7.0	6.3	6.6	5.9
14.	Uttar Pradesh	4.9	4.0	4.6	7.4
15.	West Bengal	6.3	6.9	6.1	8.5
16.	Chhattisgarh	NA	NA	9.2	6.1
17.	Jharkhand	NA	NA	11.1	9.7
18.	Arunachal Pradesh	5.1	4.4	5.8	6.4
19.	Assam	2.8	2.1	6.1	6.5
20.	Himachal Pradesh	6.5	5.9	7.3	9.5
21.	Jammu & Kashmir	5.0	5.2	5.2	6.4
22.	Manipur	4.6	6.4	11.6	5.9
23.	Meghalaya	3.8	6.2	5.6	7.3
24.	Mizoram	NA	NA	5.9	7.1
25.	Nagaland	8.9	2.6	8.3	9.3
26.	Sikkim	5.3	8.3	7.7	6.7
27.	Tripura	6.6	7.4	8.7	6.9
28.	Uttaranchal (now Uttarakhand)	NA	NA	8.8	9.9
	All India	**6.5**	**5.5**	**7.7**	**9.0**

Source: Twelfth Five Year Plan (2012-17), Government of India, 2012.

agriculture sector in 1970-71 generated 58 per cent of the state domestic product in Punjab, whereas 48 per cent income was generated by the agriculture sector of the Indian economy

(Table 3.2). There is enough evidence to state that Punjab state in the post-green revolution period became a highly agricultural-oriented economy. Its economic dynamics revolved more around this sector of the economy. The industrial sector, during the same period, was quite small, both in Punjab and India so far as its contribution to state/national income was concerned. However, the contribution of the industrial sector to the state income in Punjab was just 15 per cent, which was much lower compared with the national percentage, i.e. 20 per cent. The share of the service sector was also much higher in the Indian economy than that of the Punjab state.

Table 3.2: Structure of Punjab Economy vs. Indian Economy

Sector/Year	*1970-71*		*2008-09*	
	Percent Share in GDP		*Percent Share in GDP*	
	India	*Punjab*	*India*	*Punjab*
Agriculture	48	58	18	32
Industry	20	15	26	23
Service	32	27	56	45

Source: Government of India, *Economic Survey, 2010* and Government of Punjab, *Statistical Abstract of Punjab, 2010.*

The dramatic changes in the structure of Punjab/Indian economy have occurred since 1970-71. The relative income shares in 2008-09 showed a dramatic change in the structure of the state/Indian economy. The relative share of agriculture has declined by 30 percentage points in the case of the Indian economy and 26-percentage points in the case of Punjab's economy. The service sector emerged as the most dominant sector both of the Indian economy and of the Punjab economy. The relative contribution of the service sector to India's GDP in 2008-09 was 56 per cent, whereas the service sector contributed 45 per cent to Punjab's GSDP. This analysis of structural change brings out the fact that the industrial sector never occupied a prime place in the growth story of the Punjab/Indian economy. This is contrary to the development experience witnessed by the industrially advanced countries of the Western world and also of the newly industrialising countries of East Asia. It needs to be mentioned here that Punjab state has recorded a much lower level of industrial development when one compares it with the Indian economy.

The sectoral rate of growth based on net state domestic product (NSDP) presented in Table 3.3 reveals that the performance of Punjab state is deteriorating when one compares with its own performance and achievements in the past. There is a strong evidence of deceleration in economic growth rates of the Punjab economy in terms of NSDP recorded during the period of 2000-01 to 2007-08 compared with the period of 1990-91 to 1999-2000. It also revealed that the agriculture sector remained the core sector of the Punjab economy. Although the relative share of the agriculture sector declined from 44 per cent in 1990-91 to 39 per cent in 1999-2000 and further to 32 per cent in 2007-08 (GOP, 2009), yet the agriculture sector contributed a major share in the NSDP of the Punjab economy. The growth rate of the agriculture sector as indicated from the post-reform period not only remained quite low (3.33 per cent), but also decelerated (2.21 per cent) in the second sub-period, i.e. 2000-01 to 2007-08. During the decade of the 1990s, the agriculture sector of the state has grown at a rate 4.45 per cent per annum compared to 2.21 per cent during the period 2000-01 to 2007-08. Surprisingly, the agriculture sector has grown at a rate of 5.15 per cent per annum during the 1980s (Singh and Singh, 2002). The foregoing discussion brings out the fact that the deceleration of growth rate of the agriculture sector has contributed substantially to the slow down in the growth rate of per capita income of the Punjab economy.

The industrial sector has been regarded as the most dynamic sector of an economy and provides the desired economic transformation from low wage-low productivity economic activities to high wage-high productivity economic activities. However, in the case of Punjab, the industrial sector's contribution to the NSDP, in a relative sense, has remained quite small. For instance, the manufacturing sector in Punjab contributed 15.1 per cent of NSDP in 1990-91 and declined to 13.6 per cent in 2007-08. The relative share of the registered manufacturing sector in the NSDP has also declined from 8.8

Table 3.3: Sectoral Net State Domestic Product Average Annual Growth Rates, 1999-2000 to 2007-08 (at 1999-2000 prices)

Sector/Year	*1990-91 to 2007-08*	*1990-91 to 1999-2000*	*2000-01 to 2007-08*
Agriculture	3.33	4.45	2.21
Manufacturing	4.73	4.43	5.03
Registered Manufacturing	4.59	5.35	3.84
Unregistered Manufacturing	5.68	4.71	6.66
Electricity	11.84	12.46	11.23
Construction	7.61	4.42	10.80
Trade	4.60	4.24	4.96
Transport	11.92	11.14	12.7
Banking	10.33	9.99	10.68
Real Estate	2.42	4.66	1.79
Public Administration	6.74	9.16	4.32
Other Services	7.80	13.06	2.54
NSDP	5.26	5.73	4.79
PCI	3.32	3.7	2.9

Note: Estimates are based on the data compiled from Government of Punjab, *Statistical Abstract of Punjab* (various issues).

per cent in 1990-91 to 7.4 per cent in 2007-08. The rate of growth in the registered manufacturing sector has also grown during the period of 2000-01 to 2007-08 compared with the period of 1990-91 to 1999-2000. The registered manufacturing sector has grown at the rate of 5.35 per cent per annum during the 1990s, which was much below the level achieved during the 1980s. However, the growth rate for the period 2000-01 to 2007-08 was just 3.84 per cent per annum. Contrary to this, the unorganised manufacturing sector has recorded a higher growth rate during the 2000-01 to 2007-08 compared with the growth experience of the 1990s (Table 3.3). That was precisely the reason that the manufacturing sector as a whole has shown marginal acceleration of the rate of growth in the later period compared with the period of the 1990s.

The other sectors, which have recorded deceleration of economic growth during the 2000s compared with the 1990s, are the electricity, real estate, public administration and other services. It is worth mentioning here that the combined share of all those sectors of the Punjab economy, which observed deceleration in the growth rate during the 2000s, was 68.52 per cent in 1990-91 compared to this share declined to 57.74 per cent in 2007-08. Obviously, the slow growing sectors have contributed to the slow growth of per capita income and NSDP of Punjab's economy. Although, the fast growing sectors failed to arrest the deceleration of economic growth in Punjab because of their relative share in the NSDP was less than 32 per cent in 1990-91. But these have triggered the process of structural transformation in terms of changing the relative contribution of the sectors to the state's economy. From the foregoing analysis, it can be safely said that the engine of growth of Punjab's economy still continued to be the 'agriculture sector'.

On the other side, Punjab's agriculture sector has shown signs of fatigue in terms of slow down in its productivity growth, shrinking employment opportunities, rising input costs and environmental degradation. The long-term trends (1960 to 2006) in total cropped area, production and yield of various crops bring out the fact that the highly diversified cropping pattern of Punjab during the 1960s has been transformed into wheat-paddy rotation during the 2000s. Even, during the 1970s and the 1980s, the diversified rural economy of Punjab turned towards predominantly the wheat-paddy crop rotation. For instance, 21 different crops were sown in Punjab during 1960-61 and the number of crops declined to 9 in 1990-91 and remained so thereafter.

The area sown under crops other than wheat declined from 62.74 in 1960-61 to 17.12 per cent in 2004-05. The area under rice increased from merely 6.05 per cent in 1960-61 to 63.02 per cent in 2004-05. The crop diversification index for the winter season declined from 0.79 in 1960-61 to 0.30 in 2004-05 and this index for the summer crop season declined from 0.98 in 1960-61 to 0.58 in 2004-05 (Toor, Bhullar and Kaur, 2007). This indicates that there has occurred a clear 'reversal' of diversification of the rural economy of Punjab. Actually, the assured market and prices of two crops (wheat and paddy) provided by the state agencies facilitated this transformation.

It is also true that production and procurement of wheat

and paddy have been rising but the rate of increase has been slowing down since the 1980s (Table 3.4). The rate of growth of production of wheat increased at a rate of growth of 5.42 per cent over the period 1967-68 to 1979-80. This seems to be the peak period. Thereafter, the production growth rate of wheat crop increased at a slightly slower rate, i.e., 4.29 per cent during the decade of the 1980s. In the post-liberalisation period (1990-91 to 2006-07), the growth rate of production of the wheat crop was just 1.31 per cent per annum. This showed a dramatic deceleration of wheat production in Punjab. This was mainly due to three factors. One, the area expansion under the wheat crop slowed down from 1.25 per cent per annum during 1980-81 to 1989-90 to 0.45 per cent per during 1990-91 to 2006-07. Two, the rate of growth of yield also slowed down from 3 per cent per annum during the 1980s to 0.29 during the post-liberalisation period. Three, the depletion of micro-nutrients in the topsoil has also contributed to the decline in the rate of growth of the wheat production in Punjab. Somewhat similar trends were recorded for the paddy crop. The rate of growth of yield declined in all crops in Punjab except the maize and cotton. This is mainly because of degradation of soil fertility, declining innovations in agriculture and also decline of public investment to support to agriculture during the post-liberalisation period.

Further, slow down of the agriculture sector in general and non-exploitation of opportunities in other sectors has pushed the dynamic Punjab economy as a laggard economy across Indian states. This can precisely be noticed from the emergence of chronic shortage of fresh investments in Punjab. The data revealed that the investment-GSDP ratio of Punjab state has declined from 24.06 per cent in 1995-96 to 20.00 per cent in 2008-09, which is contrary to the rising trends of this ratio for the Indian economy as a whole, i.e. from 26.6 per cent to 34.9 per cent during the same period. The graphic presentation of the comparative series of India and Punjab clearly brings out the fact that the gap between investment-GDP ratios has increased substantially between 1998-99 and 2000-01. Thereafter, it started reducing marginally during the period 2001-02 to 2004-05 and declined slightly in 2005-06 but remained almost stagnant since 2006-07. If one measures the deficiency of investment and

Table 3.4: Average Annual Compound Growth Rates of Area (A), Production (P) and Yield (Y) of Major Crops in Punjab

(Per cent Per Annum)

Year	*1960-61 to 1966-67*			*1967-68 to 1979-80*			*1980-81 to 1989-90*			*1990-91 to 2006-07*		
	A	*P*	*Y*	*A*	*P*	*Y*	*A*	*P*	*Y*	*A*	*P*	*Y*
Rice	4.86**	7.18**	2.2	11.17**	18.90**	6.95**	5.34**	6.70**	1.30	1.86**	2.95**	1.07**
	(0.75)	(1.76)	(1.40)	(0.78)	(0.79)	(0.70)	(0.62)	(1.23)	(0.78)	(1.86)	(023)	(0.22)
Bajra	6.83	10.57	3.97	-8.54**	-9.04**	-0.55	-18.63**	-21.34**	-3.07*	-3.45*	-4.61**	-0.98
	(3.93)	(6.66)	(4.67)	(1.80)	(1.94)	(*0.80)	(2.31)	(2.21)	(1.24)	(1.26)	(1.48)	(0.6)
Maize	23.6	10.14*	5.11	-1.47	-1.38	-0.08	-5.64**	-6.83**	-1.27	-1.42**	1.68*	3.13**
	(20.51)	(3.65)	(3.82)	(0.82)	(0.85)	(0.83)	(0.55)	(1.49)	(1.74)	(0.19)	(0.65)	(0.57)
Wheat	2.20**	5.44*	3.17	2.95**	5.42**	2.40**	1.25**	4.29	3.0**	0.45**	1.31**	0.29
	(0.35)	(1.89)	(1.74)	(0.40)	(0.70)	(0.37)	(0.25)	(0.67)	(0.65)	(0.07)	(0.29)	(2.72)
Barley	4.54	8.59*	3.76	-4.98	-1.26	3.87**	-7.92**	-2.99	5.55**	-5.32**	-4.0**	1.38**
	(4.27)	(3.68)	(3.43)	(3.35)	(3.32)	(0.87)	(1.71)	(2.50)	(1.38)	(0.52)	(0.68)	(0.28)
Others	-32.60*	0.0	-	-1.89	-7.69*	-	1.42	-3.67	-	0.68	5.63	-
Cereals	(11.695)	(9.90)		(1.89)	(1.29)		(6.82)	(6.27)		(2.18)	(-5.41)	
Total Cereals	4.23**	6.64**	-	3.05	6.36**	-	1.81**	4.55**	-	0.92**	1.90**	-
	(1.23)	(1.53)		(0.2)	(0.53)		(0.26)	(0.57)		(0.10)	(0.23)	
Gram	-5.64**	-6.95**	-1.39	-2.86**	-3.27	0.12	14.15**	-10.20*	4.52	-13.61**	-12.30**	1.46**
	(1.07)	(3.58)	(3.22)	(1.09)	(1.83)	(0.95)	(2.15)	(3.83)	(2.84)	(0.90)	(0.94)	(0.48)
Other Pulses	-4.96*	-5.29*	-	0.71	0.01	-	0.88	1.89	-	-7.28**	-7.94**	-
	(2.43)	(2.30)		(1.18)	(1.46)		(1.64)	(3.32)		(0.72)	(0.72)	
Total Pulses	-5.58**	-6.87*	-	-2.51*	-2.63	-	-8.21*	-5.04*	-	-8.71**	-9.01**	-
	(1.14)	(3.43)		(1.10)	(1.68)		(1.54)	(2.50)		(0.57)	(0.62)	
Total Food	0.89	4.24*	-	2.46**	5.96**	-	1.58**	4.46**	-	0.81**	1.88**	-

Year	*1960-61 to 1966-67*			*1967-68 to 1979-80*			*1980-81 to 1989-90*			*1990-91 to 2006-07*		
	A	*P*	*Y*	*A*	*P*	*Y*	*A*	*P*	*Y*	*A*	*P*	*Y*
Grains	(0.52)	(1.77)		(0.17)	(0.48)		(0.32)	(0.57)		(0.10)	(0.23)	
Arhar	-	-	-	14.59**	18.05**	3.02*	2.40	0.55	-1.81	3.16**	-3.79**	-0.66
				(3.23)	(3.64)	(1.03)	(4.93)	(5.83)	(1.71)	-(0.49)	(0.76)	(0.69)
Moong	-11.34**	-6.38	5.62**	0.8	2.53	1.71	10.46**	8.78*	-1.52	-9.64**	-10.10**	-0.51
	(3.68)	(4.62)	(1.85)	(2.82)	(2.89)	(1.01)	(2.66)	(3.9)	(1.51)	(1.10)	(1.15)	(0.88)
Rapeseed &	-0.52	0.34	0.87	0.90	2.06	3.19*	-0.04	5.51	5.49**	-3.78**	-3.37**	0.41
Mustard	(2.70)	(1.27)	(3.02)	(2.58)	(3.08)	(1.25)	(2.57)	(3.59)	(1.66)	(0.83)	(0.93)	(0.55)
Sunflower	-	-	-	-	-	-	-	-	-	-1.39	-1.16	0.07
										(4.75)	(4.84)	(0.56)
Sesamum	7.85	9.61*	1.64	0.73	0.70	-0.03	-1.85	-1.2	0.67	-4.01**	-4.23**	-0.22
	(5.94)	(4.79)	(3.65)	(2.27)	(2.16)	(0.74)	(2.12)	(1.73)	(1.59)	(0.88)	(1.01)	(0.57)
Total	8.42**	15.40**	-	-3.30**	-3.33*	-	-4.53*	-2.56	-	-5.76**	-6.22**	-
Oilseeds	(1.85)	(2.11)		(1.10)	(1.18)		(1.72)	(2.38)		(1.24)	(1.63)	
Sugarcane	3.91	2.50	-1.32	-3.41**	0.77	4.31**	2.07	2.71	0.64	0.15	-0.13	0.29
	(2.87)	(3.47)	(1.99)	(0.92)	(1.30)	(0.65)	((1.59)	(1.56)	(0.70)	(1.18)	(1.21)	(0.25)
Dry Chillies	-	-	-	-0.98	-1.18	-0.2	-14.48**	-9.47**	2.28	-3.73*	-3.12*	0.64**
				(2.72)	(2.59)	(0.79)	(2.02)	(2.22)	(0.93)	(1.39)	(1.44)	(0.20)
Potato	9.46**	10.57*	0.95	10.31**	15.00**	4.32**	-2.37**	-2.47	0.29	8.07**	8.02**	-0.19
	(2.51)	(3.87)		(1.29)	(1.90)	(0.84)	(1.62)	(1.65)	(2.59)	(1.24)	(1.33)	(0.46)
Cotton A	-1.23	1.8	3.04**	7.67**	8.17**	-0.12	2.44	11.28**	8.61*	-2.32*	-0.85	1.51
	(2.01)	(2.51)	(0.90)	(0.77)	(0.76)	(0.42)	(1.70)	(2.81)	(1.85)	(0.86)	(2.39)	(2.03)
Cotton D	0.38	0.01	-0.36	-0.94	-2.35	-1.96*	-10.83**	-5.72	5.71	-2.10	1.18	3.32*
	(1.96)	(2.33)	(0.51)	(1.15)	(1.53)	(0.46)	(1.85)	(3.16)	(2.91)	(1.840)	(1.72)	(1.25)

** significant of 1 per cent level * significant of 5 per cent level.

Note: Figures in parentheses indicate standard error.

Source: Kumar and Singh, 2011.

compares it with the all-India average, it comes out to be nearly Rs.9,133 crores per annum (Table 3.5). It needs to be noted here that in the developing economies, apart from other factors, fresh investment drives the economic growth rate of an economy. And, the role of the state government is to correct this kind of deficiency of investment, which has a capacity to arrest the deceleration trends.

Figure 3.1:Comparison of Investment-GDP Ratio-India and Punjab

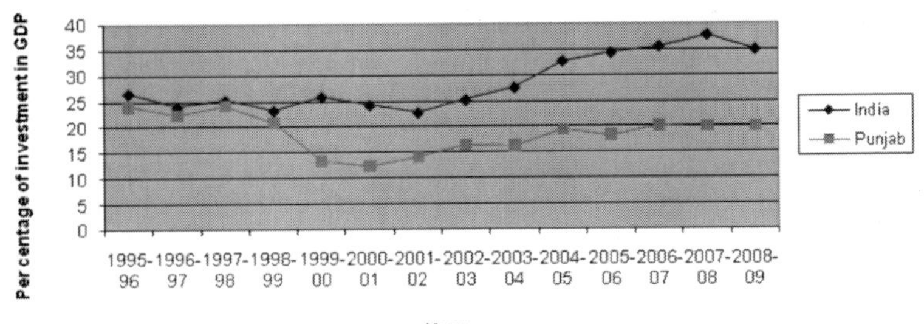

Table 3.5: Investment Deficiency in Punjab Compared to All India

Year	*GSDP of Punjab (Rs. Crores)*	*Investment-GDP Ratio (%)*		*Gap (%) (India-Punjab)*	*Investment Deficiency Gap Based on Gap in Investment-GDP Ratio* (Rs. Crores)
		India	*Punjab*		
1995-96	34218	26.6	24.06	2.54	869.14
1996-97	39112	24.0	22.50	1.50	586.68
1997-98	43099	25.3	24.17	1.13	487.02
1998-99	49612	23.3	20.98	2.32	1151.00
1999-00	61139	25.9	13.40	12.50	7642.38
2000-01	67779	24.3	12.41	11.89	8058.92
2001-02	71260	22.8	14.05	8.75	6235.25
2002-03	73494	25.2	16.44	8.76	6438.07
2003-04	79840	27.6	16.24	11.36	9069.82
2004-05	85761	32.7	19.48	13.22	11341.03
2005-06	96108	34.3	18.27	16.03	15406.11
2006-07	107591	35.5	20.05	15.45	16622.81
2007-08	128303	37.7	20.0	17.07	21901.32
2008-09	148008	34.9	20.0	14.90	22053.19
		Annual Average			**9133.05**

Source: (i) Government of India, *Economic Survey* (various issues).
(ii) Government of Punjab, *Statistical Abstract of Punjab* (various issues).

Alternative Strategy of Economic Growth in Punjab

The perusal of the existing structure of Punjab's economy allows us to conclude that the emerging future growth scenario in the state on current lines is unsustainable. This has also been noticed and argued by the leading thinkers of the Punjab economy as early as in the mid-1980s. It was then suggested that Punjab's economy needs structural transformation in general and the agriculture sector in particular requires diversification of crops to sustain future economic growth momentum. The sustainability of economic growth momentum of the Punjab economy was also questioned on the grounds that the production structure is oriented towards producing food grains only and selling these items in raw form. The processing of food grains is being largely done either in the urban locations or in the households. It means that value addition is being done at a distance from the farm gates. Till this gap is bridged, the primary producers cannot be sustained over the long run. The sustainability of the current cropping system has also been questioned on the grounds that it is based on mining of natural resources, such as water and soil nutrients, and generates environmental hazards, in terms of air, water and soil pollutions. The irrational cropping system is dependent on irrational use of factor inputs, which has started severely affecting human health.

The history of economic development of advanced capitalist countries and the newly industrialised countries of East Asia brings out the fact that agricultural development paves the way to high productivity based manufacturing industries. And, when the transformation of economy from the agriculture to industrial sector matures, i.e. income and employment opportunities stagnate in the agriculture sector, the industrial and service sectors largely emerge to bear the burden of dynamic gains in the income and employment to the population. The Punjab economy witnessed the Green Revolution more than four decades ago; however, it could not transform its economic and employment structure as has been observed in the developed and newly industrialised countries of the world. The remedy lies in the restructuring of the economic policy in a manner to initiate new economic activities, which ensures the desired structural transformation and diversification of the economy of Punjab. Some specific new initiatives desired to be undertaken are suggested here as follows:

1. Agriculture-based agro-processing industries need to be initiated in the countryside on a massive scale. These industries will link the agriculture production with manufacturing industries and can produce numerous products such as ready to serve food based on the wheat, rice, maize, soyabean, vegetables and spices, pulses, poultry, dairy, fishery and honey.
2. The agriculture sector of Punjab produces a huge amount of bio-mass, which is being burnt as waste especially of wheat and rice straw and cotton sticks. There are several possibilities to use this bio-mass to develop products such as paper and organic manure and can also be used for producing electricity.
3. Horticulture and floriculture are the other two high value-added options. This option can be used to produce high value-added products based on citrus fruit, mangoes, guavas, grapes, lichis, peaches, pears and ber.
4. The future path of industrialisation in any region including Punjab lies in developing highly skilled, labour-intensive and knowledge-based industries such as biotechnology, microelectronics, pharmaceutical sciences, information technology, education and health.

All these suggested four broad groups of industries need to be established for promoting an agriculture-industry linkage, which will facilitate the long awaited structural transformation of the Punjab economy from the agrarian to the industrialised one. The fundamental requirement for the success of this kind of strategy is to bring organisational changes. Two provisions, that is, amendments in company law and establishment of agro-processing zones can help us to develop modern industrial units for inclusive growth of the rural economy of Punjab state. The new organisation change from the individual/corporate initiatives to new generation cooperatives based on democratic practices has a capacity to integrate the agriculture and industry with each other. This new suggested organisation has a capacity to simultaneously conduct production, processing and marketing activities. It eliminates the intermediary agency which usually usurps surpluses generated through the processing and marketing activities. These saved surpluses can be ploughed back to generate the necessary rural infrastructure and institutional arrangements.

The new cooperatives suggested here are not the bureaucratic-state controlled cooperatives, but the modern cooperatives strictly based on membership and which adhere to market rules with accountability as an endogenous tool of organisational behaviour. There are many such examples of the cooperatives, which have succeeded in our own country. Amul is a remarkable success story of a small rural milk producers' cooperative in Gujarat, which has now highly diversified into consumer products. The creative organisation of Amul contributed to the generation of surpluses after the elimination of intermediary agencies and these surpluses have been used for developing local infrastructure and investment in the technology to raise the productivity of the farmers' output. It is, thus, suggested that the government of Punjab should enact a suitable policy and provide exclusive industrial parks as agro-processing zones for farmers' cooperatives on a similar pattern as have been provided and offered to the foreign and domestic private industry.

In a nutshell, the suggested strategy for the revival and rejuvenation of the Punjab economy have an additional advantage over the existing operative strategy that requires to provide adequate land to the private players both domestic and foreign, which is in the possession of the farmers, and it is very difficult to acquire the desired amount of land due to stiff resistance from the owners.

REFERENCES

Government of Punjab (2009), *Statistical Abstract of Pubjab 2008*, Economic and Statistical Organisation, Punjab, Chandigarh.

Kumar, S. and Parminder Singh (2011) 'Agriculture Development and Productivity Stagnation in Punjab', in H.S. Shergill, Sucha Singh Gill and Gurmail Singh (eds.) *Understanding North-West Indian Economy*, Serials Publications, New Delhi, pp. 109-39.

Planning Commission (2008), *Eleventh Five Year Plan 2007-12*, Government of India, New Delhi.

Singh, Lakhwinder and Sukhpal Singh (2002) 'Deceleration of Economic Growth in Punjab: Evidence, Explanation and a Way Out', *Economic and Political Weekly*, Vol. 37 (6), February 9, pp. 579-86.

Toor, M.S., A.S. Bhullar and Inderpreet Kaur (2007) 'Agriculture-Led Diversification and Labour Use in Punjab: Potentials and Constraints', *Indian Journal of Labour Economics*, Vol. 50 (4), pp. 737-46.

PART II

Core Issues Before Agricultural Development in Punjab

4

Rice-Based System in India: Some Perspectives for Rice Growers in Punjab

Surjit Singh

> Rice is a symbol of cultural identity and global unity. Rice is life. To millions of Indians, rice is a way of life. It is their culture and ethos. That is why, rice occupies a prominent place in marriage rituals as a sign of prosperity and fertility (anonymous).

1. Introduction

Rice is central to the food security in the world[1]. It is the main source of calorie intake for about half of the world's population and the predominant staple food in 34 countries in Asia, Latin America and Africa. In several Asian countries, people depend on rice for more than two-thirds of calories and 60 per cent of protein in their diets. Growing and processing rice has become the main source of employment and income for an estimated 2 billion people in the world. About 90 per cent of the world's rice is produced by small-scale farmers in the developing nations. In many poorest countries of Asia, 60 per cent of the cropped land is devoted to grow rice and the poorest segments of population spend between 20 and 40 per cent of their income on rice. Rice is the only major cereal that can withstand water submergence. And, rice-based systems can make productive use of all the available water and land resources. Rice is even cultivated in the hilly areas. In fact, terracing allows rice cultivation on steep slopes that, in turn, helps to prevent soil erosion and landslides, controls floods, minimises weed growth and promotes water percolation and groundwater recharge while submergence enables organic matter to accumulate in soils.

2. Rice-Based Systems in India

In India, rice is grown in high rainfall areas or in the areas where irrigation facilities are available. It is the staple food for the majority of population and mainly grown on small family farms. There were more than 200,000 varieties of rice at the time of independence in 1947, but now only 500 remain in the contention (Singh, 2005). A typical Indian farmer plants rice primarily to meet family needs, and hence, his/her marketable surplus is small. There are more than 30 rice-based cropping systems in India, where rice is grown along with other crops such as vegetables, cotton, jute, pulses, wheat, maize, sorghum, oilseeds, sugarcane, groundnuts, millets, coconuts and fruits such as bananas depending on the local agro-climatic conditions[2]. Rice-based eco-systems host a wealth of biodiversity, with much of the planting material derived from the seeds that farmers produce and that represent generations of local genetic resources. Rice-based farming systems also connect wells with other agricultural production such as raising fish or ducks on waterlogged rice fields, and rice straw can be fed to livestock, which help with transportation and land preparation, as well as provide organic fertiliser (particularly in small farms). Rice fields also host a wide variety of natural enemies that control harmful insects and pests[3]. In these ways, rice-based systems provide great opportunities for improved nutrition, diversified agriculture, increased income and the protection of genetic and agricultural resources.

Rice is the most important crop of India's kharif season. And, kharif[4] paddy in India is cultivated in Assam, West Bengal, eastern Uttar Pradesh, Bihar, Orissa, coastal Andhra Pradesh, and parts of Tamil Nadu, Karnataka, coastal Maharashtra and Kerala. During the last few decades, however, paddy has become a major crop in Punjab, Haryana, and to some extent in western Uttar Pradesh. Paddy is also one of the major crops in humid areas of eastern India comprising Manipur, Mizoram and Tripura too. In Meghalaya, paddy is alternated with cotton, vegetables and food crops. In parts of Assam, West Bengal, Bihar, Orissa and northern coastal districts of Andhra Pradesh, jute forms an important commercial crop as an alternative to paddy. In Bihar, pulses, wheat, jute, maize, oil seeds and sugarcane are alternative crops. Paddy is concentrated in the eastern part of Uttar Pradesh where pulses, groundnuts, sugarcanes and sorghum are alternative crops. Pulses, ragi, oilseeds, maize and small millets are the alternative crops in Orissa where paddy is grown on more than 50 per cent of the area. In Central India, paddy is grown mainly in Chhattisgarh state. The important alternative crops in this area are small millets, pulses and groundnuts. In southern states, namely, Andhra Pradesh, Tamil Nadu and Kerala, paddy is grown in more than one season. In Andhra Pradesh, pulses, groundnuts, jowar, maize and sugarcane are major alternative crops whereas, in Karnataka, alternative crops to paddy are ragi, plantation crops, cotton, groundnuts, sorghum and maize. In Kerala, plantation crops and tapioca are the main alternatives for paddy.

Further, South India is rice-deficit while the northern states are rice-surplus in India; the Green Revolution has brought significant changes in rice productivity in the northern Indian states. India today is among the top five rice-exporting countries. Rice accounted for 35.4 per cent of the total area under food grains and 41.9 of the total food grains production in 2007-08, which stood at 34 per cent and 42 per cent respectively in 2003-04. Though rice-based cropping systems in India are predominantly subsistence-oriented, still surplus rice is being generated for trade, both internal and external. This has become feasible following the Special Rice Development Programme started in 1994-95. The programme was meant to increase rice production through new varieties of seed, field demonstrations, and on-site training of farmers for technology transfer. The focus initially was on the Eastern Indian region, which was not touched by the Green Revolution of the 1960s. The programme helped in raising production in the eastern region, and made the region rice-surplus. This cropping system, predominated by small-scale and marginal farmers, has also an extensive capacity to support farm labour as the agriculture in the region is relatively less mechanised. Thus, a large proportion of the poor are dependent on rice-based cropping systems.

3. Rice Consumption Trends in India

Over the past 40 odd years, advances in technology and policy changes have fuelled rapid gains in rice production and a steep decline in prices. High-yielding varieties introduced during the Green Revolution gave a strong boost to rice production. Between 1961 and 1990, global production more than doubled, from 216 million to 518 million tonnes. Yields increased from less than 1900 kilograms to more than 3500 kilograms on per hectare basis. Real prices fell by more than 50 per cent. The increased availability and affordability of rice contributed to a rapid decline in the number of people suffering from hunger and malnutrition in the countries where rice is the main staple food, though diarrhoea is significant and is present because of cultural habits of cooking rice and polishing that reduces micro-nutrients, especially zinc. In Asia, the annual per capita rice consumption increased by more than 20 kilograms and the proportion of undernourished declined from almost 40 per cent to 16 per cent. Over the past four decades, rice consumption patterns in different regions have evolved and converged. In Asia, where rice has been the mainstay of diets for centuries, per capita consumption of rice increased rapidly during the 1960s and 1970s. Since then, consumption of other foods has increased and the relative contribution of rice has fallen. In parts of Africa, the Near East and Latin America and the Caribbean, on the other hand, rice consumption has increased significantly, both in volume and as a proportion of total calorie intake. Rice is now the most rapidly growing source of food in Africa as well.

Growth in demand for a staple grain depends on the level of per capita income, the population growth rate, and the changes in prices relative to those of substitute crops. Changing food habits, due to external influences, may also affect demand for rice. At low levels of income, when meeting energy needs is a serious concern, rice is considered a luxury commodity in most parts of India. At high-income level, rice becomes an inferior good. So the move is necessity to luxury to inferior grain. In eastern India, rice goes with fish; in southern India, it goes with curd (yoghurt); and in north India, it goes with pulses. This completes the nutrition components of diet of an average Indian. However, changes in rice consumption have occurred in India. The per capita consumption (kg/person/year) went up from 76 in 1969-71 to 86 in 1990-92 and then fell to 83 in 2000-02; the period of Agreement on Agriculture[5]. These changes can be ascribed to opening up of Indian markets and growing urbanisation that have dampened the demand for rice to some extent. Also, the share of rice in total dietary protein consumption has stagnated around 25 per cent while in total dietary fat consumption at around 4 per cent. Further, rice consumption over the period has either stagnated or declined across the Indian states. Major rice-consuming Indian states are Andhra Pradesh, West Bengal, Orissa, Kerala and Tamil Nadu (all consuming above 8 kgs per person per month. Non-rice eating states are Punjab, Rajasthan, Gujarat and Haryana. Over and above this, there is malnutrition prevalent in many states like Chhatisgarh, Madhya Pradesh and Rajasthan (Singh, 2007). Severe stunting is also found among children in rural India. Most of them belong to the poor households who are vulnerable to food security shocks. This group includes landless labourers, marginal farmers and small farmers. A sizeable proportion of women in India is anaemic too.

Thus, one needs to differentiate between national food security and household food security. The rural poor households are more vulnerable to the food security. About 30 per cent of per capita rural food expenditure is on wheat and rice. And, 60-70 per cent of rice produced by Indian farmers is kept for consumption needs, animal feed or for seed; diversity in rice-based system contributes greatly to the rural income and nutrition in a more balanced diet. Already most cereals are getting beyond the reach of the poor due to high food inflation.

4. Rice Cultivation in Punjab: A Background

Located in northwest India, Punjab is the most prosperous state in India with the highest per capita income and has the lowest proportion of population living below the poverty line. Basically an agrarian economy, the state is endowed with abundant resources and has an enthusiastic farming community. It lies between two great river systems, the Indus and the Ganga. Most of the land is an alluvial plain, irrigated by the canals developed by the state authorities from time to time. Punjab occupies only 1.6 per cent of the total land area and 2.6 per cent of the cropped area of the country. Punjab has more than 4 million hectares of well-irrigated land, with cropping intensity of 186 per cent[6]. Over 95 per cent of food grains that are moved inter-state to feed deficit areas through the public distribution system are from Punjab. It now (2009-10) produces 12.6 per cent of rice and 18.8 per cent of wheat production in India (GOI, 2012).

At the time of India's independence in 1947, Indian Punjab (after partition of the state between India and Pakistan), which then had a much larger area comprising also the present states of Haryana, parts of Himachal Pradesh and the Chandigarh Union Territory, was a foodgrain-deficit area. In 1951, Punjab produced only about 1.99 million tonnes of food grains, which included 1.1 million tonnes of wheat, 0.11 million tonnes of rice and other food grains. Its agricultural sector contributed 54.4 per cent of real gross state domestic product in 1950-51 (at 1970-71 prices). At that time (1951), food grain crops, occupying 68 per cent of the cropped area, dominated the cropping pattern and the remaining 32 per cent cropped area was under the pulses and coarse grains, mainly on unirrigated lands. With a net sown area of 3544 thousand hectares and gross cropped area of 4170 thousand hectares, intensity of cropping was 118 per cent only. Only 52.3 per cent of the cropped area was irrigated and land-holdings were quite fragmented. The farmers did not use fertilisers and pesticides, tube wells were conspicuous by their absence and tractors were hardly known in the state.

Since independence, Punjab started moving on a path of growth dominated by agriculture. Irrigation facilities began to increase through the Bhakra-Nangal dam (built in the early 1960s) based canal system. Simultaneously, availability of electric power from the Bhakra hydel project encouraged the installation of tube wells by the farmers that provided assured irrigation supplementing the canal water supply. Even, in 1960-61, the share of the agricultural sector in the state GDP was 54 per cent. Production of food grains stood at 3.83 million tonnes - 1.74 million tonnes of wheat, 0.25 million tonnes of rice, and 1.84 million tonnes of coarse grains and pulses[7]. The irrigated area increased to 54 per cent of the net sown area and intensity of cropping improved to 121 per cent. The cropping pattern was still dominated by wheat with 29.6 per cent of the cropped area, pulses 19.08 per cent, coarse grains 10.52 per cent and cotton 9.4 per cent of the cropped area. Productivity of main crops had started improving but only marginally. Rice productivity was only 1 tonne per hectare. This situation continued till the mid-1960s only with marginal improvements. Punjab since the early days has been caught in the wheat-rice cycle. And, after the success of the Green Revolution in Punjab (1966 onwards), the state has been literally feeding India, with its annual contribution of more than half of the wheat and around 40 per cent of rice to the food stocks of the country[8].

Regarding rice growers in Punjab, the data on number of land-holdings showed many interesting results. First, at the beginning of the 1990s, Punjab had 1.117 million land holdings and the number went down to 0.997 million (a reduction of 10.74%, Table 4.1) in 2000-01. During the same period, land-holdings at the national level improved by 13.9 per cent. In 1990-91, Punjab had 1.06 per cent of all holdings of the country, which declined to 0.83 per cent in 2000-01. Punjab also had 0.48 per cent of all marginal holdings in 1990-91 and this share fell to 0.16 per cent by 2000-01. India's 1.02 per cent small holdings were in Punjab in 1990-91 and 0.76 per cent in 2000-01. It means that in Punjab, land-holdings are concentrated in the upper categories, while at the national level marginalisation of holdings is taking place. Second, marginal and small farmers in Punjab are going down and during this decade things must have worsened significantly if the past trend is any indication. This is primarily due to land being sold by small holders producing rice and wheat to medium and large holders because of indebtedness. This is an indication of small farmers' livelihood being at stake in Punjab and opening up of markets would further erode his economic viability, as land would shift increasingly into non-agricultural purposes (Shergill, 2010).

Table 4.1: Number of Operational Holdings (000s) in Punjab vs India

Category of Farmers	*Punjab 1990-91*	*2000-01*	*(%) Change*	*% Share in India 1990-91*	*2000-01*	*India 1990-91*	*2000-01*	*(%) Change*
Marginal	296	123	-58.45	0.48	0.16	62110	75409	21.41
Small	204	173	-15.20	1.02	0.76	19970	22696	13.65
Semi-Medium	289	328	13.49	2.08	2.34	13910	14020	0.79
Medium	261	301	15.33	3.42	4.58	7630	6577	-13.80
Large	67	72	7.46	4.01	5.86	1670	1228	-26.47
Total	1117	997	-10.74	1.06	0.83	105290	119930	13.90

Note: Marginal - below 1 hectare, Small 1-2 hectares, Semi-medium 2-4 hectares, Medium 4-10 hectares, and Large 10 hectares and above

Source: Centre for Monitoring Indian Economy (CMIE), Agriculture 2010.

If numbers of marginal and small land-holdings are reducing in Punjab at a faster pace, then what is the status of area operated by them? Table 4.2 shows that during 1990-91 and 2000-01, the area operated by marginal holdings also declined by 52.44 per cent, while that of small farmers fell by 26.22 per cent in Punjab. In absolute terms, there were 0.164 million hectares of area under marginal holdings in 1990-91 compared to 78000 hectares in 2000-01. In the case of small holdings, the decline is from 0.328 million hectares to 0.24 million hectares. In other words, marginal and small farmers possessed 0.492 million hectares of land in 1990-91 and this area declined to 0.220 million hectares in 2000-01. At national level, however, marginal and small holdings gained in the area operated; 53.33 million hectares to 61.96 million hectares.

Table 4.2: Total Land Area Operated (000 Hectares) in Punjab vs. India

Category of Farmers	*Punjab*			*Share in India %*		*India*		
	1990-91	*2000-01*	*(%) Change*	*1990-91*	*2000-01*	*1990-91*	*2000-01*	*(%) Change*
Marginal	164	78	-52.44	0.67	0.26	24620	29815	21.10
Small	328	242	-26.22	1.14	0.75	28710	32144	11.96
Semi-medium	842	876	-4.04	2.20	2.29	38350	38192	-0.41
Medium	1622	1731	6.72	3.60	4.53	45050	38125	-15.17
Large	1077	1096	1.76	3.73	5.20	28890	21070	-27.07
Total	4033	4022	-0.27	2.44	2.52	165600	159436	-3.72

Source: CMIE, Agriculture 2010.

Further, the average size of land-holdings has improved from 3.61 hectares in 1990-91 to 4.03 hectares in 2000-01 in Punjab, whereas it has declined to 1.33 hectares in 2000-01 from 1.57 hectares in 1990-91 in India. However, marginal farmers in Punjab had the average size of land of only 0.63 hectares in 2000-01 compared to 1.40 hectares in the case of small farmers. These two categories of farmers saw a reduction in average holding size in the ten-years period. The significance of this fact is that decline in size of holdings is sharper in the case of small farmers compared to all other categories.

Table 4.3: Average Size of Holdings (Hectares)

Category of Farmers	*Punjab*			*India*		
	1990-91	*2000-01*	*(%) Change*	*1990-91*	*2000-01*	*(%) Change*
Marginal	0.55	0.63	14.46	0.40	0.40	-0.26
Small	1.61	1.40	-13.00	1.44	1.42	-1.49
Semi-medium	2.91	2.67	-8.33	2.76	2.72	-4.19
Medium	6.21	5.75	-7.46	5.90	5.81	-1.59
Large	16.07	15.14	-5.30	17.30	17.16	-0.82
Total	3.61	4.03	11.73	1.57	1.33	-15.47

Table 4.4: Distribution of Number of Operational Holdings (000s) in Punjab vs. India

Category of Farmers	*Punjab*				*India*			
	Number of Holdings		*(%) Share*		*Number of Holdings*		*(%) Share*	
	1990-91	*2000-01*	*1990-91*	*2000-01*	*1990-91*	*2000-01*	*1990-91*	*2000-01*
Marginal	296	123	26.50	12.37	62110	75409	58.99	62.28
Small	204	173	18.26	17.35	19970	22696	18.97	18.92
Semi-Medium	289	328	25.87	32.90	13910	14020	13.21	11.69
Medium	261	301	23.37	30.19	7630	6577	7.25	5.48
Large	67	72	6.00	7.22	1670	1228	1.59	1.02
Total	1117	997	100	100	105290	119930	100	100

Source: CMIE, Agriculture 2010.

Moreover, 44.8 per cent of the land-holdings in Punjab in 1990-91 were marginal and small and this proportion fell to 29.7 per cent in 2000-01, whereas at the national level, the proportion rose from 78 per cent to 81.2 per cent. As regards the area operated by marginal and small farmers, the share in land operated fell from 12.2 per cent to 8.73 per cent in Punjab and it improved from 32.21 per cent to 36.02 per cent at the national level. The data reveal that the marginal and small farmers are losers in Punjab and the changes are very significant and this group is losing land at a very fast pace. The situation in Punjab is worse than at the national level. This has implications for cultivation of rice by marginal and small farmers. If the area operated by them goes down, then naturally rice put under cultivation would also go down. It may be added that rice is not a staple food in Punjab and so marginal and small farmers may opt out of rice cultivation, if MSP is withdrawn or if the state wants to pursue the crop diversification plan vigorously.

4.1 Rice Production in Punjab

Rice is not a traditional crop in Punjab. The area under rice has increased from 0.39 million hectares in 1970-71 to 2.188 million hectares in 1995-96 when India joined the WTO and then went up to 2.614 million hectares in 2003-04 and 2.610 million tonnes in 2006-07 (Table 4.5). It has fluctuated over the years, may be because of weather conditions. In 1970-71, the share of Punjab in the national rice area was 1.04 per cent and it stood at 5.11 per cent in 1995-96 and then at 6.32 per cent in 2004-05 to fall to 5.94 per cent in 2007-08. This means that the contribution of Punjab in the Indian rice area is quite important and it has gone up over the period.

Similarly, production of rice in Punjab was only 0.688 million tonnes in 1970-71 (at the advent of the Green Revolution) and it increased to 6.845 million tonnes in 1995-96 and further to 10.489 million tonnes in 2007-08. The importance of Punjab as a rice-feeding bowl of India, after the wheat, becomes apparent when one observes that in 1970-71, it produced just 1.63 per cent of India's total rice output, its contribution went up to 8.89 per cent in 1995-96 and then to an all time high of 12.26 per cent in 2005-06; though declined in the next two years. In doing so, Punjab has to pay a very heavy price; in terms of depletion of ground water and environmental degradation.

Rice yield has also shown an increasing trend. For instance, the average yield of rice in Punjab was 1760 kgs/per hectare in 1970-71, and it rose to 3128 kgs/hectare in 1995-96 and an all time high of 4019 kgs/hectare in 2007-08. The corresponding yield rates at the national levels were low, i.e. 1120 kgs/hectare in 1970-71, 1797 kgs/hectare in 1995-96 and 2202 kgs/hectare in 2007-08. This means that during the last three decades and a half, the average yield rate of rice in Punjab has been much higher than that of India in each year.

Table 4.5: Rice Area, Production and Yield (Area 000' Hectares, Production 000' Tonnes, Yield Kg/Hectare)

Years	*Punjab*			*Punjab's Share in India %*		*India*		
	Area	*Production*	*Yield*	*Area*	*Production*	*Area*	*Production*	*Yield*
1970-71	390	688	1760	1.04	1.63	37592.0	42225.0	1120
1971-72	450	920	2040	1.19	2.14	37758.0	43068.0	1140
1972-73	476	955	2010	1.30	2.43	36688.0	39245.0	1070
1973-74	520	1189	2286	1.36	2.70	38285.4	44051.0	1150
1974-75	569	1179	2072	1.50	2.98	37888.4	39578.9	1040
1975-76	567	1447	2552	1.44	2.97	39475.4	48739.8	1230
1976-77	674	1741	2583	1.75	4.15	38511.1	41916.8	1090
1977-78	831	2494	3001	2.06	4.74	40282.6	52674.4	1310
1978-79	1052	3091	2938	2.60	5.75	40482.2	53773.4	1330
1979-80	1167	3041	2606	2.96	7.18	39414.3	42330.3	1070
1980-81	1182	3234	2736	2.97	6.03	39773.3	53621.0	1350
1981-82	1270	3743	2947	3.12	7.03	40708.0	53248.0	1310
1982-83	1320	4156	3144	3.46	8.82	38262.0	47116.0	1230
1983-84	1482	4539	3063	3.59	7.55	41244.0	60097.0	1460
1984-85	1644	5054	3074	3.99	8.66	41159.0	58336.0	1420
1985-86	1714	5485	3200	4.17	8.59	41137.0	63825.0	1550
1986-87	1786	5949	3331	4.34	9.82	41167.0	60557.0	1470
1987-88	1720	5442	3164	4.43	9.57	38806.0	56862.0	1470
1988-89	1778	4923	2769	4.26	6.98	41735.8	70488.7	1690
1989-90	1908	6697	3510	4.52	9.10	42166.9	73572.6	1740
1990-91	2024	6535	3229	4.74	8.80	42686.9	74291.4	1740
1991-92	2074	6755	3257	4.86	9.05	42648.7	74677.6	1750
1992-93	2073	7031	3392	4.96	9.65	41775.0	72867.7	1740
1993-94	2179	7645	3508	5.12	9.52	42539.3	80300.0	1890
1994-95	2276	7702	3384	5.32	9.41	42813.8	81814.0	1911
1995-96	2188	6845	3128	5.11	8.89	42836.7	76.975.3	1797
1996-97	2159	7334	3397	4.99	9.02	43283.0	81736.7	1882
1997-98	2281	7904	3465	5.25	9.58	43446.0	82534.5	1900
1998-99	2518	7940	3153	5.62	9.22	44802.3	86076.7	1921
1999-00	2604	8715	3347	5.79	9.72	45161.7	89682.9	1986
2000-01	2611	9154	3506	5.89	10.77	44712.0	84976.6	1901

2001-02	2487	8816	3545	5.57	9.45	44904.0	93340.0	2079
2002-03	2530	8880	3510	6.28	12.22	41176.1	71820.2	1744
2003-04	2614	9656	3694	6.15	10.94	42592.5	88526.0	2078
2004-05	2647	10437	3943	6.32	11.79	41906.7	83131.7	1984
2005-06	2642	10193	3858	6.05	12.26	43659.8	91793.4	2103
2006-07	2621	10138	3868	5.98	10.86	43813.6	93355.3	2131
2007-08	2610	10489	4019	5.94	10.85	43914.4	96692.9	2202

Source: CMIE, Agriculture 2010.

On the question of how much cultivable land in Punjab has been allocated to the rice cultivation, the data in Table 4.6 showed that in 1990-91, the rice area as a per cent of gross cropped area went up from 26.98 per cent to 33.16 per cent in 2007-08, whereas at the national level, it stagnated around 23 per cent only. In many South East Asian countries, the area under rice was affected by the world trade agreement on agriculture. These policy changes like India's entry into WTO and domestic subsidies reduction did not have an adverse effect on the area under rice in Punjab. The reason for this is that there is minimum support price for rice and it increases every year and then rice gives relatively higher returns to the farmers compared to other competitive crops. The Punjab farmers are in a cycle of surplus rice production and are increasingly suffering from over-production. This over-production in the changing policy regime at times leads to the distress sale of rice. Distress sale of rice is largely due to high indebtedness of farmers to the commission agents (traders in agriculture markets). Farmers borrow from the traders/ commission agents before the crop is ready for non-productive consumption along with purchase of inputs used for cultivation. These farmers do not sell the produce in the agriculture market, but to the traders at the farm gate. The average debt on a farmer household in Punjab is about Rs. 42000 (NSSO, 2005; Deshpande and Arora, 2010).

Further, since the Punjabis do not consume rice in large quantities, an overwhelming proportion of rice produced in the state goes to the national pool with slight processing. The only processing activity done here is the conversion of paddy to rice through shelling. Punjab's agricultural strategy is largely based upon bringing in larger cultivated areas under the rice and wheat; emphasising increase in productivity per unit of land area through intensive use of inputs; focusing on increasing the cropped area through intensive cropping; and envisaging increases in input use efficiency to reduce cost of production and raising profit margins for cultivators. Though rice is grown in all the districts of Punjab, it is concentrated in some parts. In 1990-91, when the liberalisation process was initiated[9], only five districts out of 17 districts—Sangrur, Patiala, Amritsar, Firozpur and Ludhiana—together accounted for 65 per cent of the area under rice in the state, and more or less maintained the same share in the area in the subsequent years.

For yield account, Punjab has performed fairly well. At the district level, most of the main rice-growing areas have higher

Table 4.6: Rice Area as Percent of Gross Cropped Area (GCA) (000 Hectares)

Years	*Punjab*			*India*		
	GCA	*Rice*	*% Share*	*GCA*	*Rice*	*% Share*
1990-91	7502	2024	26.98	185742	42686.6	22.98
1991-92	7518	2074	27.59	182242	42648.7	23.40
1992-93	7552	2073	27.45	185487	41775.0	22.52
1993-94	7623	2179	28.58	186420	42539.3	22.82
1994-95	7693	2276	29.59	188053	42813.8	22.77
1995-96	7752	2188	28.22	186561	42836.7	22.96
1996-97	7842	2159	27.53	189543	43283.0	22.84
1997-98	7833	2281	29.12	190570	43446.0	22.80
1998-99	7739	2518	32.54	192620	44802.3	23.26
1999-00	8240	2604	31.60	189740	45161.3	23.70
2000-01	7947	2611	32.90	185340	44712.0	23.72
2001-02	7941	2487	31.32	188286	44904.0	23.85
2002-03	7773	2530	32.55	175580	41176.1	23.45
2003-04	7907	2614	33.06	190777	42592.5	22.33
2004-05	7931	2647	33.38	191545	41906.7	21.88
2005-06	7868	2642	33.58	193649	43659.8	22.55
2006-07	7861	2621	33.34	193228	43813.6	22.67
2007-08	7870	2610	33.16	195835	43914.4	22.42

Source: CMIE, Agriculture, Various Years.

yield rates compared to the other areas. The majority of districts surpass the state average in rice yield. This means most districts are doing well in the case of yield rates of rice. During the 1990s, the rice yield rates in most districts have gone up. In some, the increase is significant and in others, it is only marginal. There are a few districts that have observed no change or yield rates fell. However, a few districts stand out. One does observe tapering of yield rates of rice in Punjab. Liberalisation, privatisation and globalisation (LPG), are thus presenting a huge challenge to the rice economy of Punjab.[10]

4.2 Rice Research and Adaptation by Punjab

Modern varieties of rice were first introduced to India in the 1960s, when two IRRI varieties (IR8 and IRS) were released. These varieties were not adapted to the Indian conditions, so their adoption was very slow. By 1972-73, less than 20 per cent of the rice area was under these varieties. Indian researchers were, however, able to develop more varieties suitable to the Indian conditions. These varieties performed better in a range of agro-climatic conditions and were widely adopted, leading to a large increase in productivity and production. With the development of hybrids, rice production technology has received another boost, particularly in Punjab. These hybrids are reported to give about 20 per cent higher yield than open pollinated semi-dwarf varieties.

More efforts to develop hybrid rice suitable for local conditions began when ICAR launched a National Hybrid Rice Project in the late 1980s in collaboration with IRRI under UNDP financial support. The project has led to the setting up of a National Research Network with 12 centres, working on hybrid rice development. Today, both the public and private sectors are engaged in the development of rice hybrids. While the public sector accounts for the development of a large number of lines used in the development of hybrids, however, the marketing of hybrids is largely done by the private sector. Nearly 15 private firms are engaged in the development and marketing of rice hybrid seeds in India. Hybrid Rice International, a Proagro group company, dominates the market. The other important companies include Mahyco, Pioneer and EID Parry. Over the years, some of these firms have built their own germ plasm collection and have breeding programmes to develop hybrids. However, as mentioned above, these firms have received considerable support from the public sector. For example, most of the germ plasm and breeding material used by these firms were originally obtained from public sector institutions. Some private companies without their own breeding programmes do market hybrids developed by the public sector.

Among the major challenges that rice research in India faces today, the two most important are the low productivity and large regional differences in performance (Alam, 2004). The increase in productivity has been slowing down since the early 1990s. This is due to several reasons. The most important of these is that no significant genetic yield breakthrough has been achieved since the introduction of early high yield varieties such as Jaya and IR-8. The other important reason is the low rate of adoption of improved varieties. This is shown by the fact that yield gap (percentage difference between potential and achieved yields) in most areas is between 35 per cent and 75 per cent. Only in Tamil Nadu and Punjab, it is lower to 15 per cent and 22 per cent, respectively. The adoption of hybrids has also been limited. This is because of poor grain quality[11]; high cost of seeds[12] and; difficulties in germ plasm exchange[13]. The other reasons for low productivity of rice include the problem of pests and diseases, which has become more complex and difficult to solve than in the past. As the genetic base used in the development of new varieties has shrunk, their vulnerability to disease and pests has increased. Bacterial leaf blight and blast diseases have emerged as particularly serious causes of damage in the rice-wheat combination prevalent in North India. Furthermore, high salinity (largely due to excessive and faulty use of irrigation water), imbalanced use of fertiliser nutrients and delayed planting has also affected rice yields adversely.

Further, there are also large regional differences in average yields. Average yields are particularly low in the rain-fed areas in states such as Assam, Bihar, Madhya Pradesh and Orissa. The average productivity in these areas, which account for 40 per cent of the total area under rice, is only 1,200 kgs/hectare. The productivity in these areas is limited by a lack of suitable modern varieties. The problem is compounded by the fact that the growing conditions in these areas are diverse and the development of suitable varieties for a large variety of agro-climatic regions is difficult and costly. Although the situation has improved since the 1990s (as a number of varieties for rain-fed, shallow lowland areas have been released), there is still a need to develop varieties for semi-deep water, deep water and drought-prone low land areas. As many farmers are affected by low productivity in these areas, this work should be given high priority. The slow down in the increase in rice productivity is a serious cause of concern. In order to meet its growing need for food, it is necessary that India continues to increase rice productivity and production. According to some estimates, in order to meet its food requirements in 2020, India needs to increase its rice production by three per cent every year (Bhalla and Hazell, 1997); so here lies the significance of rice research.

4.3 Cost of Rice Production in Punjab

Paddy is sown in Punjab in the months of June to August and harvested during September to November. As Punjab took up rice cultivation in a big way in the early 1970s, it started with the new high-yielding varieties, which required relatively high modern inputs like fertilisers, pesticides, etc and involved high cost. Since then fast changes in new high-yielding rice varieties have also taken place[14]. And, up to the 1980s as per the deliberate policy of the Indian government, liberal subsidies were being given on power, fertilisers and other purchased inputs to raise food grains production. Since 1990-91, under liberalisation policies, subsidies are being slowly withdrawn. Then there is pressure to reduce subsidies provided to agriculture. So, what happens to the cost of cultivation of rice gains is significant and demands attention.

The cost of cultivating rice in Punjab rose from Rs. 2894 per hectare in 1974-75 to Rs. 5474 in 1980-81 in just 6 years (almost doubled). The next decade also saw doubling of cost per hectare to Rs. 10,082 and then to Rs. 21,119 per hectare in 1999-2000. In

2001-02, the cost stood at Rs. 22,306. Further, over the years with increased mechanisation, use of human and bullock labour has reduced and that of machine labour has gone up. Human labour constitutes presently only 17.3 per cent of total cost and machine cost is 10.92 per cent. Surprisingly, seed cost in percentage terms has reduced to 2.3 per cent from 3.81 per cent in 1974-75 (Table 4.7). So is the case with fertiliser cost, it stands at 8.77 per cent. This could be due to reduced usage with rising prices of fertilisers. Irrigation cost has also gone down in percentage terms. However, the share of other costs include insecticides, interest on working capital, miscellaneous costs, rental value of owned land, rent paid for leased-in land, land revenue, cesses and taxes, depreciation on farm implements and buildings and interest on fixed capital has gone up significantly from 32.1 per cent in 1974-75 to 56.6 per cent in 2006.07. It means that rice cultivation has become a very costly proposition in Punjab over the years. The declining use of traditional inputs (human and bullock labour) has an important message that rice cultivation is no more a labour-intensive activity except the planting of paddy. This increasing cost will have a varying impact over different holdings sizes. Small and marginal farmers will increasingly find it difficult to cultivate rice. Those who are still cultivating rice must be incurring high debts. Increase in paid out cost always raises the question of profitability. In 2005-06, fertiliser cost per hectare stood at Rs. 191.70, while human labour cost was Rs. 437.50 per hectare[15]. The data of Commission for Agriculture Cost and Prices show that there is over-capitalisation of rice farms in Punjab. These trends would have adverse impacts on the profitability of rice cultivation in Punjab.

In the corporate world, every business enterprise must earn profits to keep itself in business, but farm business is such an activity where the farmer has to continue operating his unit as a way of life even when he is running into losses. Rice cultivation is no different. Net returns at current prices increased from Rs. 124 per hectare in 1970-71 to Rs. 2272 in 1995-96. Net returns at constant prices did not go up in 1990-91. It peaked at Rs. 684 in 1993-94, but declined thereafter (Sidhu and Johl, 2001). In 1995-

96, the net returns at constant prices were Rs. 298 per hectare. There is no growth in rice profitability over the period. Rising cost is eating into profits from rice. With liberalisation and withdrawal of subsidies, the post-1995-96 period has witnessed a rapid decline in returns from rice cultivation. In this situation, the small farmers in Punjab would be the worst sufferers. The small farmer's indebtedness would increase and he would be forced to sell his land or mortgage it. It is already happening in Punjab as we have seen earlier. In this scenario, the Indian government has to keep in tact the support system of subsidies at least targeting marginal and small farmers.

Table 4.7: The Structure of Cost of Cultivation of Rice (Per Hectare) %

Item	*1974 -75*	*1980 -81*	*1990 -91*	*1998 -99*	*1999 -2000*	*2000 -01*	*2002 -03*	*2003 -04*	*2004 -05*	*2005 -06*	*2006 -07*
Human Labour	30.46	21.85	18.36	19.43	17.21	17.29	15.65	15.09	16.60	16.99	15.65
Bullock Labour	7.32	2.74	0.70	0.12	0.05	0.08	0.12	0.28	0.09	0.30	0.12
Machine Labour	1.54	5.67	9.83	11.32	11.52	10.92	7.15	11.50	9.89	9.97	7.15
Seed	3.81	2.46	1.73	2.44	2.51	2.30	1.97	1.87	2.19	2.14	1.97
Fertil-iser	11.10	10.80	12.31	9.83	10.44	8.77	8.67	7.98	8.15	8.12	8.67
Irriga-tion	13.68	12.92	9.72	6.98	6.47	6.92	9.89	10.50	8.57	6.63	9.89
Other Costs	32.09	43.56	47.35	49.88	51.80	53.72	56.56	52.78	54.51	55.85	56.56
Total Cost	100	100	100	100	100	100	100	100	100	100	100
Total Cost Rs.	2894	5474	10082	19126	21119	22306	28926	31770	30007	30384	28926

Note: Other costs include insecticides, interest on working capital, miscellaneous costs, rental value of owned land, rent paid for leased-in land, land revenue, cesses and taxes, depreciation on implements and farm buildings and interest on fixed capital.

Source: Commission for Agriculture Cost and Prices, vearious years.

4.4 Rice Procurement in Punjab vs. India

The Government of India under its policy of food self-sufficiency, is not only giving price support in terms of minimum prices, but is also purchasing surplus wheat and rice in Punjab. And, Punjab over the time period has developed a significant number of regulated grain markets, and during the season, many temporary markets to procure grains from farmers are also set up. The Food Corporation of India, Punjab Food Civil Supplies Department and MARKFED (Marketing Federation of Punjab) are the three main agencies assigned the task of procurement of rice. Rice millers are also part of this scheme of things. Regulated markets have commission agents (licensed traders) who purchase rice and wheat on behalf of the state. Table 4.8 shows that since the liberalisation process was set in motion in India, rice procurement has seen improvement because production increased. In 1990-91, 4.814 million tonnes of rice was procured in Punjab, which constituted about 41 per cent of all rice procured in India. During the 1990s, the lowest procurement was done in 1995-96 (34.62 per cent share) in Punjab. And, the year 2004-05 saw a record procurement of 9.106 million tonnes in Punjab, but the relative share went down to 37.89 per cent. In 2008-09, Punjab's share stood at 35.67 per cent. Thus, Punjab has been increasingly contributing to India's food grains buffer stocks. There are diverse views on how this should be handled with cost of handling grains increasing over the years. It is however, viewed that even the small/marginal farmers gain from this system as they market their entire production. There is only an insignificant part of rice production kept for domestic production in Punjab.

4.5 Crop Diversification Plan and Contract Farming in Punjab

Rice fields, on an average, use 85 per cent of fresh water supplies. The crisis of overuse of water led the state to come out with a report 'Agricultural Production Pattern Adjustment Programme for Punjab' in the early 2000s. The Punjab government plans to divert one million hectares of land from under wheat and paddy to other crops like sunflowers, vegetables, flowers, etc. This would save about 14.7 billion cubic metres of water every year.

The state government is contemplating a compensation of Rs. 12500 per hectare to farmers who agree to shift away from wheat and paddy. It also plans to put the farmers under the bond not to grow wheat and paddy in the marked area. Any violation would attract penalty as stated by the Johl Committee on Diversification of Punjab Agriculture[16]. On the other side, the PAU has developed an irrigation schedule for rice for increasing water use efficiency and for conserving the natural water resource. Reducing the initial ponding period from 3 to 2 weeks and subsequent irrigation 2 days after soaking the ponded water has helped in saving at least 25 per cent of irrigation water in rice[17].

The Punjab Agro Foodgrains Corporation (PAFC) is the nodal agency for contract farming in Punjab. It provides/ arranges for the farmers high-yielding varieties of seeds (mainly

Table 4.8: Rice Procurement in Punjab and India (000 Tonnes)

Year	*Punjab*	*India*	*Share of Punjab %*
1990-91	4814	11745	40.99
1991-92	4248	9240	45.97
1992-93	4905	11793	41.59
1993-94	5486	13651	40.19
1994-95	5826	13403	43.47
1995-96	3462	9950	34.79
1996-97	4231	12222	34.62
1997-98	6035	14308	42.18
1998-99	4384	11788	37.19
1999-00	6787	17273	39.29
2000-01	6964	19587	35.55
2001-02	7282	21277	34.22
2002-03	7883	16316	48.31
2003-04	8662	22621	38.29
2004-05	9106	24031	37.89
2005-06	8855	26727	33.13
2006-07	7829	24029	32.58
2007-08	7908	27506	28.75
2008-09	8544	23951	35.67

Source: Commission for Agriculture Cost and Prices.

basmati rice)[18] from reputed companies, technical supervision and follow-up on agronomic practices and buy-back entire produce with returns comparable to/better than paddy and wheat. It lays down quality specifications of crops, in consultation with buyers/processors and specifies a contract price for the farmers to buy-back the quality crop (ground level reality is totally different as discussed below (also see the box). PAFC has identified basmati for contract cultivation. PAFC has helped to develop new equipment for paddy, viz. paddy disc puddler, paddy seedling marker, paddy pre-cleaner, paddy-transplanter, combine harvester. During the kharif (summer) 2003, the total area under basmati crop increased from 0.425 million acres to 0.550 million acres with a major contribution of 90500 acres under the contract farming programme. The extension agencies contracted are: Escorts India Limited, Rallies India Limited, Pepsi Foods Limited, Mahindras, and DCM. Exporters/buyers involved were : Pepsi Foods Limited, United Rice Land, Amira Foods, Satnam Overseas and LT Overseas[19]. Special machines were installed for cleaning basmati so that long delicate grains of basmati are not broken and the farmers get high value of their crop. The international agency SGS International was involved in evaluation/certification and assessing the quality of the produce brought by the contracted farmers so that there was no dispute between the buyers and the farmers. The contracted agencies/buyers purchased 25000 tonnes of basmati valued at Rs. 330 million. The end story is that despite all this PAFC had to intervene in the market to purchase 2800 metric tonnes of basmati in 2003 because contracting firms failed to lift the total production[20]. In the case of the Basmati contract, the farmers were made to pay Rs. 150 per acre as consultancy/extension service fee. Punjab Agro Foodgrains Corporation Ltd. (PAFC) has set up cleaning units at Dudhan Sadhan, Shatrana and Rajpura in Punjab. During 2004, they were not working leading to harassment of farmers. They paid a price in the range of Rs.1100-1250 per quintal. As soon as the companies closed their procurement, the price of basmati increased by Rs. 100-150 per quintal causing loss of income to farmers (Gill, 2004).

4.6 Field Impressions of Rice Cultivation in Two Punjab Villages

Field impressions are based on personal visits to two villages viz. Rampur Sahiwal and Dakaunda in Patiala district, which is very representative of rice producers in Punjab. Focus group discussions were held and structured schedules were also administered to small rice farmers. Dakaunda has 225 households and half of them are landless workers' families who are dependent on wage labour in agriculture within and in the neighbouring villages. Some landless workers, mainly adults, frequent Patiala city for wage labour. Ten households are rich farm households who own land of over 5 acres. There are 3 families holding 50 acres or more land. There are 104 families with land up to 5 acres of land. All households grow paddy/ rice in summer and wheat in winter. Social composition of the village reveals that half the households are Jat Sikhs (land owning clan in Punjab), 42 per cent are Scheduled Castes (landless workers' families). The rest are supporting caste groups mainly of artisan families like potters, barbers, etc. The total population of the village is 2200. Rampur Sahiwal village has 200 households of which 120 are Jat Sikhs and 80 households are Scheduled Castes (agricultural workers). It is more homogeneous socially compared to the other village. About 100 households are landless with another 80 being small and marginal farmers' households. The remaining are medium and large farmers' households. The total population of the village is 1500. Presently the average holding size in Dakaunda village is around 8 acres, while in the other village it is 4 acres. In the late 1980s, the average size of land was 12 acres in Dakaunda village and 8 acres in Rampur Sahiwal village. Some small farmers do lease in land. The going rate of land lease is Rs.17000 per acre. Wheat has remained as a major staple food. Rice is eaten occasionally.

Rice as a commercial crop in both villages was introduced around the Green Revolution time in the late 1960s. Earlier, basmati (local varieties) were grown for domestic consumption. In the early phase of the Green Revolution along with local varieties of basmati, two high-yield varieties of rice—PR-106 and IR-8—were grown. At present, many more varieties are being grown like PR 111, PR 114, PR 116, PR 118, Pusa 44 and basmati. These HYV rice varieties gave higher yield. Today the yield rates are around 2700 kgs/acre, which earlier was around 1000 kgs/acre. These new varieties are not affected by the wind like earlier local varieties, which fall down and get grain damaged. Rice covers around 90 per cent of the cropped area in both the villages during the season. The other crops grown are fodder crops and sugarcane. Maize, cotton, pulses and chillie crops have disappeared from the scene. Radio and Punjab Agriculture University played a major role in broadcasting new varieties of rice in both the villages. Initially, the large farmers adopted the HYVs and the other farmers followed them. Farmers do attend Kisan Melas (farmers' fairs) organised by Punjab Agricultural University. There is no contact farmer in both the villages. Rice was and still is sold through the regulated market, which is 5-8 kms away from each village. Farmers take the threshed rice in their own tractor-trolley or hired one to the market. He goes to the pre-determined traders' shop (invariably the trader has provided a loan for purchase of seeds, fertilisers and pesticides). The produce is de-loaded, cleaned and put out in the open in a heap for auction. The state procurement agencies visit the traders' shop in the market twice a day. Observing the rice grains quality and moisture content (10% moisture is allowed), fixes the price, which is not below the minimum support prices fixed by the government. The trader weighs the produce. The farmer is given a slip that gives the rate and total amount due to him. It takes 10-15 days for the farmer to receive the money for his paddy sale.

Most of the small farmers in both the villages had small families and women did not actively participate in rice cultivation. Only 2 per cent of farmers hired any permanent worker to cultivate rice. Wage labour is hired for transplantation of rice. All small farmers themselves prepared the bed for sowing seeds. They only prepared the field for rice transplantation. Only 15 per cent farmers hired workers to harvest the rice crop. Both local labour and migrant labour (from Uttar Pradesh and Bihar) are used. The family size in both villages varied between 4 and 8 members. All households are male-headed ones. This is because women in rural Punjab like rural India still do not have land rights. For ploughing either they use bullocks or hire a tractor from within the village. A small proportion of small farmers now own tractors. Tractors have also largely replaced bullock carts for transporting the produce to the market. Seeds used were local (*desi*), but now all seeds are procured from the market. Bullock carts were the traditional mode of transportation, but now tractors have largely replaced them. Earlier no pesticides/insecticides/weedicides were used, but now all farmers use these. Most of the small farmers do the weeding themselves. The upper crust of small farmers also use harvesting combines to harvest rice now, while none did so earlier. All farmers use farm manure.

Experiences of both villages confirm that the cost of rice cultivation has gone up in recent times. It is largely because of rising diesel prices, rising fertiliser prices and rising power tariff. The wages are also rising. An acre of rice transplantation now costs more than Rs. 600 which was just Rs. 200 ten years ago. As the underground water level is going down in both the villages, cost of irrigation has gone up with added use of diesel engines. Electricity is scarcely available, four/six hours daily. All small farmers have observed increases in rice output with new technologies. A tractor could be hired for Rs. 550 per acre earlier, but now cost Rs. 1700 per acre. All small farmers were of the view that cost recovery has become difficult now. Farmers at the lower end are selling off land to meet family and farming expenses. Most reported that they are in farming because of compulsion as there is no way out. So the debt burden is on an increase. About half the farmers contacted had leased-in land. The farmers felt that MSP should be continued and prices of rice should be raised. All feared the market forces as they felt no one would buy their produce because private traders do not have the capacity to buy huge quantities of rice. Prices paid would also be lower than what they get today. Traders already exploit the small farmers and in an open environment small farmers will be at their mercy. Most feared losing their land, which is their only means of livelihood. Government support is necessary and subsidies for small farmers should continue. They were concerned about subsidies. All small farmers favoured reduction in input cost. With the exception of a few small farmers, all were indebted. The range of debt is Rs. 37,000 to Rs. 125,000. Most of this accrues from the commission agents (agricultural commodity traders). For crop production credit, small farmers do borrow from the cooperative society within the village. The water table has gone down and now everyone uses submersible pumps instead of the centrifugal pumps. This increases the cost of irrigation. Agricultural extension services have reduced now. Finally, small rice producers are hard pressed even with the state support in terms of minimum support price, assured procurement and free electricity. Small farmers feel that they are passing through hard times. Debts are mounting and land which is their only source of income may not be with them for long. Small farmers require support of the state to be in farming till the time alternatives are available.

Small Rice Farmer's Woes

Darshan Singh from village Dakaunda is a typical small rice producer from Punjab. He inherited 3.5 acres of land from his father. Darshan's father could not send him to school, as the means were limited. Illiterate Darshan was married at an early age of 17 years. Today he has three children, two girls and a boy. His wife is illiterate too. The small farm does not have an irrigation source of its own. There is canal water, but is available only for three months in a year or 12 days for 3 hours a day only. Land is of good quality. Darshan grows wheat during winter and rice during summer on 3 acres. Half an acre is used for growing fodder for the milch animals. Dairy is what supports him on a day-to-day basis. He sells milk to the village milk vendor, who pays Rs.14 per litre of milk. Traditionally, he grew basmati rice for self-consumption on one acre. The yield was very poor. He used only farm manure and green manure. The Green Revolution brought new seeds to the village. The rich farmers were the first ones to plant HYVs rice. Darshan was a follower. In 1969, he planted his first HYV rice on half an acre. At that time he had a well and a good pair of bullocks. The first crop of rice gave him 10 times the yield he had earlier. But he had to purchase fertilisers as advised by extension workers. He got a good price for the produce.

Since 1969, Darshan has been growing rice and selling it in a nearby market. Initially, he borrowed from the village co-operative society for seeds, fertilisers, and pesticides. As the rice crop was sold, he would return the loan taken. Today he grows rice on 3 acres and produces 30 quintals of rice per acre. His input cost has gone up tremendously. He has to buy water from the neighbour, buy fertilisers and pesticides from the market. For this, he borrows from the commission agent. There is an unwritten contract between him and the commission agent that all the rice produced will be sold to the commission agent. In this sense, the crop is sold before it is ready for harvest. His debt has multiplied. He cannot afford to have an electric motor to draw water from the bore well. For Darshan, agriculture has become an activity as a last resort. On the marriage of his daughter, he borrowed money from the commission agent and the rich landlord of his village. To the land landlord, he mortgaged half an acre of land for Rs.50,000. Darshan has not heard of WTO, but knows that during the last 10-12 years, fertiliser and pesticide prices have gone up. So has the price of diesel. Wages have gone up. He cannot hire any worker, so his wife and son contribute their labour to produce rice. On the question, whether he will continue to grow rice, he is affirmative. The entire rice produced is sold in a regulated market. He, however, fears that if the government does not procure his produce, then he is doomed because he may not get the price he is getting today that keeps him going. He needs protection (field notes).

5. Conclusions

In all conditions, the small farmers in Punjab will continue to grow rice. The fear only is of declining water-table and rising cost. These poor farmers are not aware of WTO and its impact. Their concerns are more day-to-day livelihood strategies. They have lost the traditional varieties because of HYVs have replaced them[21]. This has made them earn more money, but put them in the high cost syndrome too. The cycle of agricultural production is such that virtually the entire farm yield comes to the market simultaneously. In a completely free and open market under WTO and AoA, the indebted small farmer would obviously find it hard to bargain with the economically more powerful trader. These farmers have so far survived because the government offered them minimum support price for rice.

India is a centre of genetic diversity of rice[22]. Out of this diversity, Indian peasants and tribals have selected and improved many indigenous high-yielding varieties. Comparative studies of 22 rice-growing systems in South Asia have shown that indigenous systems are most efficient when inputs of labour and energy are taken into account (Bayliss-Smith, 1984). Mechanisation of agricultural operations increases cost. Modern inputs like seeds, fertilisers, pesticides, insecticides, etc. link the farmers with the market and have to purchase these inputs. In the indigenous agriculture, manure is local and very few inputs are purchased from the market. Seeds are preserved over the years.

The Green Revolution package has reduced genetic diversity at two levels. First, it replaced mixing and rotations of crops like wheat, maize, millets, pulses and oilseeds with monocultures of wheat and rice in Punjab. Second, the introduced wheat and rice varieties came from a very narrow genetic base. Of the thousands of dwarf varieties bred by Norman Borlaug, only three were eventually used in the Green Revolution. On this narrow and alien genetic base, the food supplies of millions are precariously perched (Shiva, 1991). In Punjab, the rice variety PR-106 (developed by the Punjab Agricultural University), which currently accounts for 80 per cent of the area under rice cultivation, was considered resistant to white-backed plant hopper and stem rot when it was introduced in 1976. It has also become susceptible to rice leaf-folder, hispa, stem-borer and several other insect pests. Patenting of basmati by the multinationals means that indigenous knowledge and production inherited by farmers from ages no longer belongs to them. This is a gross injustice.

Small farmers have to give up chemical fertilisers and pesticides, opt for organic farming. When rice is grown as a mono-crop, it fails to control the increase of the pests, minimises bio-diversity. It is, therefore, suggested to opt for mixed cropping (along with rice, grow legumes, cereals/grams, chillies, etc). Growing paddy becomes a water intensive agricultural practice. For example, 2500 litres of water are required to produce 1 kg of paddy. Hybrid seeds consume more water and farmers should avoid growing them. The

Government of Punjab has been repeatedly asking farmers not to produce more rice, as it has no place to stock it. As American farmers are receiving an average subsidy of US$ 30000 per farm per year, to ask Punjab farmers to further increase productivity, means pushing them into a death trap. They are already suffering from producing more. There are already cases of distress sale in Punjab. Small rice producers in Punjab will continue to grow rice as long as the government supports them. This means there is need for subsidies, government setting up of procurement prices and purchase of produce. Power tariffs needs to be graded in favour of small farmers who cannot afford the market rates. Irrigation charges have to be progressive. The free market regime does not help the small producer; it helps the trader and the consumer.

NOTES

1. Rice is the focal point through which the interdependent relationships among agriculture, food security, nutrition, agro-biodiversity, environment, culture, economics, science, gender and employment can be clearly seen (www.rice2004.org).
2. Varying natural conditions cause shortages or surpluses in rice and consequently price instabilities. Rice is a strategic commodity in certain parts of India as it is the single most important element in the diet of the poor and an important source of income and employment for farmers and labour. The rice areas of Punjab and Haryana create employment for millions of migrant workers from Bihar and Uttar Pradesh. It therefore becomes a national objective to achieve self-sufficiency in rice and to maintain stable prices through government intervention. Government interventions have taken the forms of subsidies for and taxes on inputs and output, control on international trade, setting farm gate price or minimum support price (MSP) for rice, and procurement and distribution of rice to poor households through the public distribution system.
3. Brown, BPH, Green leafhopper (GLH), Blue leafhopper, Whitebacked, Leaf folder Stem borer, Aphid, Whitefly, Bandwing whitefly, and Spider mite are the pest paddy face.
4. Kharif crop is grown during May to October. In the southern states, it is also grown in the subsequent season, during November to April.

5. The growth rate of rice consumption during 1990-2001 declined to 1.4% compared to 2.8% during 1970-90.
6. It is defined as gross cropped area divided by net area sown.
7. Rice roughly contributes more than 15% of the gross domestic product (GDP) from the agricultural sector, and it will remain for years an important crop in the small-scale farmers' portfolio because of their household food security, for small-scale farmers still remain net food buyers.
8. Punjab was at the time of India's independence in 1947 a food grain deficit area with only 52% of its area under irrigation. The 1960s Green Revolution (GR) changed all this. This period saw the introduction of dwarf wheat and paddy germ plasm that resulted in a quantum jump in production. The high tide of the GR led to intensive production, which then resulted in the emergence of crop monoculture.
9. Since 1991, the Government of India has taken steps to reduce the subsidy on fertilisers, pesticides, electricity, diesel and other inputs. Agriculture market reforms were also initiated.
10. As input cost is increasing, farmers at lower end of holding are using less purchased inputs. This has had an impact on yield rates. If farmers shift from rice to other crops they confront the market situation that gives them fluctuating prices.
11. Most of the hybrids developed in India are based on one IRRI CMS line (IR58025A). The grain quality of this line is not very desirable. The large-scale diffusion of rice hybrids depends on the availability of hybrids with acceptable grain quality; susceptibility to pests and diseases. Another problem is that the hybrids released in India have very little resistance to diseases and pests. See for instance, Attavar, Manmohan (2000), 'Hybrid Rice: Bright Prospects Ahead', *The Hindu Survey of Indian Agriculture.* As the rice is grown in humid conditions, it is particularly prone to attack by diseases and pests. The damage caused by stem borer, perhaps the most important pest of rice, is estimated to be upto 30 per cent of production. Rice accounts for about 25 per cent of pesticide application in India. Bacterial leaf blight, blast, stem borer, leaf folder and hoppers are the major diseases and pests of rice.
12. The seed production costs of rice hybrids are also high and need to be brought down. Hybrid production on a large scale also faces difficulty in maintaining the purity of CMS lines and seeds.
13. The development of improved hybrids is constrained by a lack of free exchange of germ plasm between public sector research institutes and private sector seed firms.

14. Farmers traditionally grew basmati for domestic consumption. However, presently the varieties of basmati grown in Punjab are: basmati average, basmati (P. 2-33-14), basmati (P.40-40-17), basmati 217, basmati superior, basmati 3, sela basmati 370, basmati T.34 and basmati T.23. PUSA RH-10 (2001) was released (hybrid rice variety) released in 2001 having 120-125 days duration having a yield rate of 3.11 tonnes per hectare. The varieties changed over time to enhance yield rates.
15. Cost of production in terms of per unit of output of rice has declined over the years. The total cost at 1971-72 prices in 1971-74 was Rs. 55.10 per quintal (=100 kgs) and it declined to Rs. 35.35 per quintal in 1993-96. During the same period, fertiliser use cost increased from Rs.74 (kgs/hectare) to 176 (kgs/hectare), while labour cost declined from 720 (hours/hectare) to 519 (hours/hectares). The machinery cost increased remarkably from just Rs. 19.00 (at 1970-71 prices- Rs. per hectare) to Rs.128.70 (Source: CACP).
16. This report is being implemented partially through the agriculture department of the state.
17. *http://www.wis.cgiar.org/rwc/shared/asp/generealinforserver/intermediate.asp?InstitutionalID=51150*. Daler Singh of the JDM Foundation in Lodhowal, Ludhiana has been working on the concept of a low water-use variety of paddy. Since 2000, Singh has demonstrated to farmers in several locations in Punjab that paddy can survive and thrive on much less water. The innovation is simple: Rice seedlings are transplanted onto the ridges spaced 24 inches apart by furrows that are filled with water. While the crop is irrigated daily for the first week after transplantation, subsequent irrigation is at weekly intervals, with special attention during the tillering and grain setting stages. Since less water is used in ridge-furrow system of paddy cultivation than in flooded rice fields, the crop requires about 30 per cent less fertiliser application (Sudhirendar Sharma, HIMAL South Asian, October 2003).
18. The first contract was of tomatoes (Nigger Foods, Amritsar). It was followed by potato crop (Pepsi Foods). There is no clear information on increase or decrease in contract farming as every year new farmers get into the contract and most leave.
19. The Tatas and the Punjab government teamed up to undertake contract farming of basmati rice in Punjab. Under the plan, the Punjab government was to provide 35,000 acres of land to cultivate basmati rice in the state. Tata group company Rallis India, Punjab Agro Industrial Corporation (PAIC) and the New Delhi- based

company LT Overseas formed a partnership in April 2003 to execute the project. ICICI provided credit to farmers for participating in the initiative. LT Overseas markets the Dawat basmati rice brand. While Rallis provided farm end support services, LT overseas was to buy the rice that is produced. PAIC had signed an agreement with ICICI Bank for covering a broad gamut of services. In addition to providing credit for financing the distribution of seeds and fertilisers, the agreement provides for assistance to farmers for introducing new crops, varieties and in diversification of cropping systems. The initiative is part of the Punjab government's effort to promote contract farming in the state during the next 5 to 10 years. As part of the plan, PAIC is planning to forge marketing alliances with huge basmati rice exporters. Rallis had reportedly established farm management services to offer customised packages to farmers. The partnership was expected to give Rallis a chance to work closely with farmers in Punjab and help develop the best crop. LT Overseas, which has 40 years of experience in basmati rice processing and trading, was expected to buy the entire produce from the cultivators. Rallis had earlier formed an alliance with Hindustan Lever (HLL) for a contract-farming project for wheat in Madhya Pradesh, which was mainly intended to help farmers grow and sell wheat for making atta and basmati rice for export in Madhya Pradesh and Haryana. Rallis and ICICI had also tied up with big retail chains like Food World and Nilgiris, and juice Maker Sunsip (*Economic Times* April 3, 2003).

20. http/www.punjabagro.com/cf.htm
21. Traditional varieties were grown with farm manure, no pesticides and no chemical fertilisers and so the cost was very low.
22. In order to empower the small farmers, technological advances can boost yields and government policies can help to create a favourable environment for producing and marketing rice. But long-term success in improving food security depends on the ability of millions of small farmers to benefit from these gains and increase rice production as part of sustainable, diversified agricultural systems. One approach that has proven successful at engaging and empowering small farmers has been the use of Farmer Field Schools (FFS). Between 1990 and 2000, more than 2 million Asian rice farmers participated in FFS. They learned how to reduce their use of pesticides and how to make better and more sustainable use of fertilisers and water. Their lessons translated into reduced costs, increased yields and higher incomes, In Sri Lanka, for example, farmers who participated in FFS reduced pesticide use by more than 80% while increasing yields by over

20%. With substantial savings on pesticides and higher yields, incomes from rice production more than doubled (FAO, 2004).

REFERENCES

Alam, Ghayur (2004), *Technology Generation and IPRs Issues*, Academic Foundation, New Delhi.

Attavar, Manmohan (2000), 'Hybrid Rice: Bright Prospects Ahead', *The Hindu Survey of Indian Agriculture.*

Bayliss-Smith, T.B. (1984), 'Energy Flows and Agrarian Change in Karnataka:The Green Revolution at Micro Scale' in T.B. Bayliss-Smith and S. Wanmali (eds.) *Understanding Green Revolutions: Agrarian Change and Development Planning in South Asia*, Cambridge University Press, New York, pp. 153-72.

Bhalla, G.S. and Peter Hazell (1997), 'Food Grains Demand in India: to 2020: A Preliminary Exercise', *Economic and Political Weekly*, Vol. 32 (52), pp. A150-A154.

Deshpande, R.S. and Saroj Arora (2010), *Agrarian Crisis and Farmer Suicides*, Sage (India), New Delhi.

FAO, (2004), *The State of Food Insecurity in the World* 2004, Food and Agriculture Organisation of the United States, Rome (Italy).

Gill, S.S. (2004), 'Contract Farming Hurts Farmers', *Tribune*, September 27 (Monday).

GOI (2012), *Economic Survey 2011-12*, Oxford University Press, New Delhi.

NSSO (2005), *Situation Assessment Survey of Farmers: Indebtedness of Farmer Households*, 59th Round (January-December 2003) May.

Shergill, H.S. (2010), 'Rationalising the Diversion of Cultivated Land to No-agricultural Use: Theoretical and Empirical Analysis', in R.S. Ghuman, Surjit Singh and Jaswinder Singh Brar (*eds.)* *Globalization and Change: Perspectives from Punjab*, Rawat Publications, Jaipur, pp. 303-321.

Shiva, V. (1991), 'The Green Revolution in the Punjab', *The Ecologist*, Vol. 21, (2), March-April, pp. 57-60.

Sidhu, R.S. and S.S. Johl (2001), 'Three Decades of Intensive Agriculture in Punjab: Socio-Economic and Environmental Consequences', *Man & Development*, Vol. 23 (2), June, pp. 45-66.

Singh, Surjit (2005), 'Food, Trade and Nutrition in Select Asian Countries: Experience and Contours of Campaign', A Paper Published in the *Proceedings of FTN Coalition Asia, Bangkok*, June 28-30.

Singh, Surjit (2007), 'Millennium Development Goals in Chhatisgarh, Madhya Pradesh and Rajasthan: The Half Way', A Report Prepared for UNMC, Bangkok.

5

Agriculture Sector in Punjab: Retrospect and Prospect

M.S. Sidhu and Varinder Pal Singh

1. Introduction

Punjab witnessed a major breakthrough in the farm production starting in the late 1960s. The increase in wheat and paddy production improved the economic status of the peasantry bringing about an all-round development. A number of factors have made this possible. These include the application of high-yielding varieties (HYVs) particularly of wheat and paddy, assured price policy, supporting infrastructure for supply of different inputs and dissemination of the technical know-how. However, the prime movers in this growth process were the farmers themselves who were quick enough to exploit the new production possibilities. The result is that the state with 1.53 per cent of the geographical area of the country accounted for about 60-65 per cent of wheat and about 30-35 per cent of rice procured for the central pool of foodgrains during the last four decades or so.

The Punjab agriculture which was growing fast earlier has now reached a sort of plateau in terms of productivity and production. In the wake of a declining land-man ratio, it is not able to generate gainful employment and sufficient income for the growing population. Farm profitability has witnessed a decline in the recent years due to cost price squeeze (Sidhu,

Joshi and Kaur, 2006). There is almost stagnation in farm income. Farming alone is not able to generate sufficient income for the small and marginal farmers. It may be stated that the agricultural gross state domestic product (GSDP) growth rate had been 2.40 per cent per annum in Punjab for the period 2000-01 to 2007-08 as against 3.20 per cent per annum for the country as a whole.

Owing to economic distress, 2116 farmers had committed suicides during the last 15 years in Punjab (Nibber, 2004). However, some other organisations claim that the actual figure is staggering, somewhere between 10,000 and 13,000 farmers' suicides (*HT* Correspondent, 2006). A very recent study has revealed that 1757 farmers and 1133 agricultural labourers had committed suicides in two districts of Punjab—Sangrur and Bathinda—during 2000-2008 (PAU, 2009). The study further highlighted that of them, 73.31 per cent farmers and 59.22 per cent agricultural labourers committed suicides due to the indebtedness. The average outstanding debt of such farmers (who committed suicide due to debt) ranged from Rs 2.95 lakhs (Bathinda district) to Rs 3.36 lakhs (Sangrur district). The rural debt incidence had been estimated at Rs 35,000 crores during 2008-09, out of which the non-institutional component was Rs 13,000 crores (GOP, 2009). In the absence of some suitable policy measures, nearly 64 per cent farmers in Punjab (up to 10 acres) may not be able to repay the debt/loan and are likely to fall into a debt trap during the next 10 to 15 years (Ghuman, 2008). All these highlight that the Punjab farmers in general and marginal and small farmers in particular are in a deep economic crisis. Keeping all this in view, the present study has been undertaken to examine various problems faced by the farm sector in the state and its prospects in future.

2. Database

The study used the secondary data that were mainly taken from the published sources. Notable among these are the Statistical *Abstract of Punjab, Agricultural Statistics at a Glance*, etc. The data published in reputed English newspapers have also been used. The information has also been taken from the Department of Economics & Sociology, Punjab Agricultural University, Ludhiana.

3. Results and Discussion

3.1 Number of Operational Holdings

The data showed that there were 10.27 lakh operational holdings during 1980-81 in Punjab (Table 5.1). Their number increased to 11.17 lakhs in 1990-91, but declined marginally to 10.93 lakhs in 1995-96, then sharply to 9.97 lakhs in 2000-01 and this number increased marginally to 10.03 lakhs in 2005-06. The maximum decline was observed in the case of marginal and small farmers. Their number was 3.86 lakhs in 1995-96 which plummeted to 3.17 lakhs in 2005-06. These figures reveal that agriculture is becoming unremunerative, particularly for the marginal and small farmers, therefore, they were forced to lease out their tiny holdings. In many cases, they also sold their land to clear their debts and to meet other social obligations.

Another interesting aspect of operational holdings in the state is regarding the numbers of large farmers. Although their proportion was just six to seven per cent during the last two decades but they operated about 27 to 29 per cent of the area during this period. One can, therefore, say that modern farming is more favourable to the large farmers compared to their fellow marginal and small farmers. The average size of operational holdings was 3.79, 3.61, 3.79, 4.03 and 3.95 hectares during 1980-81, 1990-91, 1995-96, 2000-01 and 2005-06 respectively. At the national level, it is just 1.32 hectares. Therefore, the Punjab scenario is better than other states in terms of the average size of operational holdings.

3.2 Increasing Number of Agricultural Workers

The information on the number of agricultural workers—cultivators and agricultural labourers—are given in Table 5.2. It shows that the number of cultivators has increased from about 16 lakhs in 1961 to about 21 lakhs in 2001, whereas the number of agricultural workers jumped from 3.35 lakhs to 14.90 lakhs in the corresponding period. The trend of sub-division of land holdings is reflected more evidently in the land operated per cultivator and agricultural worker (taken together) which has declined gradually form 1.94 hectares of the net area sown in

Table 5.1: Number of Operational Holdings (OP), Area Operated and Average Size of Operational Holdings in Punjab

Farm category	1980-81			1990-91			1995-96		
	No. of OP (Thousand)	*Area Operated (Thousand ha.)*	*Av. Size of OP (ha)*	*No. of OP (Thousand)*	*Area Operated (Thousand ha.)*	*Av. Size of OP (ha)*	*No. of OP (Thousand)*	*Area Operated (Thousand ha.)*	*Av. Size of OP (ha)*
Marginal	197.32	118.33	0.60	295.67	164.13	0.56	203.88	122.00	0.60
(Below 1 hect.)	(19.21)	(3.04)		(26.47)	(4.07)		(18.55)	(2.94)	
Small	199.37	281.04	1.41	203.84	328.26	1.61	183.45	240.00	1.31
(1-2 hect.)	(19.41)	(7.22)		(18.25)	(8.14)		(16.78)	(5.79)	
Semi-medium	287.42	790.95	2.75	288.78	841.62	2.91	320.34	833.00	2.60
(2-4 hect.)	(27.99)	(20.32)		(25.86)	(20.87)		(29.31)	(20.09)	
Medium	269.07	1565.55	5.82	261.48	1621.95	6.20	305.79	1754.00	5.74
(4-10 hect.)	(26.20)	(40.22)		(23.41)	(40.22)		(27.98)	(42.30)	
Large (10	73.94	1136.60	15.37	67.17	1076.73	16.03	79.61	1198.00	15.05
hect. & above)	(7.19)	(29.20)		(6.01)	(26.70)		(7.28)	(28.88)	
All	1027.13	3892.46	3.79	1116.95	4032.69	3.61	1093.07	4147.00	3.79
Holdings	(100.00)	(100.00)		(100.00)	(100.00)		(100.00)	(100.00)	

Farm category	*2000-01*			*2005-06*		
	No. of OP (Thousand)	*Area Operated (Thousand ha.)*	*Av. Size of OP (ha)*	*No. of OP (Thousand)*	*Area Operated (Thousand ha.)*	*Av. Size of OP (ha)*
Marginal	123.00	77.00	0.63	134.00	83.00	0.62
(Below 1 hect.)	(12.34)	(1.91)		(13.36)	(2.09)	
Small	173.00	242.00	1.40	183.00	258.00	1.41
(1-2 hect.)	(17.35)	(6.02)		(18.25)	(6.51)	
Semi-medium	328.00	876.00	2.67	319.00	855.00	2.68
(2-4 hect.)	(32.90)	(21.78)		(31.80)	(21.57)	
Medium	301.00	1731.00	5.75	296.00	1701.00	5.81
(4-10 hect.)	(30.19)	(43.04)		(29.51)	(42.91)	
Large (10	72.00	1096.00	15.22	71.00	1067.00	14.93
hect. & above)	(7.22)	(27.25)		(7.08)	(26.92)	
All	997.00	4022.00		1003.00	3964.00	
Holdings	(100.00)	(100.00)	4.03	(100)	(100)	3.95

Note: Figures in parentheses indicate percentages to the total
Source: *Statistical Abstract of Punjab*, various issues.

1961 to 1.20 hectares in 2001. In terms of gross cropped area, this figure has also declined from 2.44 hectares to 2.23 hectares during the same period. The facts given above are not mere statistical figures, but rather have wider social, economic and political implications for the state as well as the country.

A further perusal revealed that the net area sown per cultivator has declined from 2.34 hectares in 1961 to 2.06 hectares in 2001. This figure per agricultural worker was 11.23 hectares and 2.85 hectares in the corresponding period. Owing to the increase in cropping intensity, the gross cropped area per cultivator has increased from 2.95 hectares in 1961 to 3.91 hectares in 1991 but declined to 3.85 hectares in 2001. As already discussed, there has been a rapid increase in the number of agricultural workers during the last four decades, i.e. from 1961 to 2001. Their number was 3.35 lakhs in 1961 which increased to 14.90 lakhs in 2001. It had an adverse impact on the gross cropped area available to each agricultural worker. The gross cropped area per agricultural worker declined from 14.14 hectares in 1961 to 5.33 hectares in 2001. The fast mechanism of agriculture in this state has also narrowed down the employment opportunities for the agricultural labourers. A recent study has shown that the use of each harvest combine eroded an estimated 24,000 person days of work in a year (Mander, 2004). Moreover, increased use of weedicides for controlling weeds across major crops, i.e. wheat, paddy and cotton, has obviated the need for human labour for inter-culture operations. The excessive use of weedicides has not only replaced human labour but has adversely affected the soil health too.

3.3 Land Use Pattern

The information on land use pattern shows that the total net area sown in the state was 4158 thousand hectares during the year 2009-10 out of a total geographical area of 5033 thousand hectares. It means that about 83 per cent of the reporting area is already under cultivation—the highest in the country. In Punjab, a negligible area is under the current fallows and other un-cultivated land. Actually, the net sown area increased from 3870 thousand hectares in 1966-67 to 4158 thousand hectares in 2009-10 which means an average increase of about seven thousand hectares per annum. It may be mentioned here that the net area sown reached nearly 4200 thousand hectares in 1980-81. After that, there has been no significant increase in the net area sown in the state. It happened mainly because of the fact that the size of the land is fixed and an increase in area under crops came mainly from increase in the area sown more than once.

Due to increase in the cropping intensity (from 134 per cent in 1966-67 to 189 per cent in 2009-10), the gross cropped area peaked to 7945 thousand hectares in 1998-99 (GOP, 2011) from 5171 thousand hectares in 1966-67. After that, it has almost become constant, in fact declined to 7876 thousand hectares in 2009-10 because there is a limit to increase the cropping intensity in the state. Therefore, there is little scope to increase cropping intensity in the near future and the gross cropped area will

Table 5.2: Net and Gross Cropped Area Available to Cultivators and Agricultural Labourers in Punjab, 1961 to 2001

Variable	*Year*				
	1961	*1971*	*1981*	*1991*	*2001*
Total Number of					
Cultivators	1602,666	1665,153	1767,286	1917,210	2065,067
Agri. Labourers	334,610	786,705	1092,225	1452,828	1489,861
Net Sown Area (hect.) Per					
Cultivator	2.34	2.43	2.37	2.2	2.06
Agri. Labourer	11.23	5.15	3.84	2.9	2.85
Both	1.94	1.65	1.47	1.25	1.2
Gross Cropped Area (hect.) Per					
Cultivator (hect.)	2.95	3.41	3.82	3.91	3.85
Agri. Labourer	14.14	7.22	6.19	5.16	5.33
Both	2.44	2.32	2.36	2.23	2.23

Source: Statistical Abstract of Punjab, various issues.

remain constant around 7900 thousand hectares. On the other hand, there is a possibility of decline in the net area sown in the state due to the high demand of land for non-agricultural purposes. This will have an adverse effect on the gross cropped area as well. Above all, the forest wealth of the state is very poor.

3.4 Major Shifts in Cropping Pattern

The cropping pattern in the state is shown in Table 5.4. The figures show that, during 2009-10, nearly 82 per cent of the gross cropped area was under the foodgrains, slightly more than nine per cent under the cash crops, i.e. cotton, sugarcane, oilseeds and potatoes. Further, about two per cent of the grossed area was reported under the fruits and vegetables and the remaining area was under fodder crops of rabi and kharif seasons. In fact, wheat is the principal crop of Punjab which alone had about a 46 per cent of gross cropped area, followed by rice (nearly 35 per cent area) and cotton (6-7 per cent area). Thus, two crops—wheat and rice—taken together occupied nearly 81 per cent of the area.

Rice is not a traditional crop of Punjab. The area under rice was just 227 thousand hectares in 1960-61 which increased to 390 thousand hectares in 1970-71, 567 thousand hectares in 1980-81, 1183 thousand hectares in 1985-86 and 2015 thousand hectares in 1990-91. It reached the level of 2612 thousand hectares in 2000-01 which further increased to 2802 thousand hectares in 2009-10. The major factors responsible for this increase are the high and stable yield compared to other kharif crops, assured minimum support price and public procurement. Since the net returns to the farmers from the paddy crop are high vis-à-vis other competing kharif crops, so paddy has replaced kharif pulses and oilseeds on a large scale in the last three decades. The area under wheat was 1400 thousand hectares in 1960-61 which increased to about 2300 thousand hectares in 1970-71, 2812 thousand hectares in 1980-81, 3273 thousand hectares in 1990-91, 3408 thousand hectares in 2000-01 which further increased to 3522 thousand hectares in 2009-10. Increasing area under wheat has also replaced rabi pulses particularly gram and oilseed crops. This crop has also a high and stable yield, assured price and public procurement as compared to other rabi crops. It is also a staple food of the Punjabis. Wheat bhusa, the by-product of wheat, is used on a very large scale by the farmers to feed dairy animals. Therefore, one can say that wheat is a natural crop of Punjab. Moreover, its irrigation requirements are not as high as in the case of paddy.

Table 5.3: Total Geographical Area, Cropped Area and Cropping Intensity in Punjab, 1966-67 to 2009-10

Year	*Figures in Thousand Hectares*					
	Net Sown Area	*Area Sown More Than Once*	*Gross Sown Area*	*Total Geographical Area*	*NSA to Total Area (%)*	*Cropping Intensity (%)*
1966-67	3870	1301	5171	5033	77	134
1970-71	4053	1625	5678	5033	81	140
1980-81	4191	2572	6763	5033	83	161
1990-91	4218	3284	7502	5033	84	178
2000-01	4250	3691	7941	5033	84	187
2009-10	4158	3718	7876	5033	83	189

Source: Statistical Abstract of Punjab, various issues.

Maize was also an important crop of the state in the pre-Green Revolution period. The maize area was 327 thousand hectares in 1960-61 which declined to 188 thousand hectares in 1990-91, 164 thousand hectares in 2000-01. Further, it plummeted to 139 thousand hectares in 2009-10. In percentage terms, the maize area declined from about seven per cent of the cropped area in 1960-61 to 1.76 per cent in 2009-10. Maize, in fact, is replaced by the paddy crop. Although the MSP is announced for the maize crop every year, but there is no effective public procurement. Therefore, to avoid price risk, the Punjab farmers, particularly in the central zone, shifted from maize to paddy on a large scale during every kharif season.

Further, the potato crop has gained importance as the area under this crop has increased during the last three decades from 17 thousand hectares in 1970-71 to 90 thousand hectares in 2006-07, but declined to 83 thousand hectares in 2009-10 largely due

Table [illegible] Shifts in Cropping Pattern in Punjab, 1960-61 to 2009-10 (Area 000 Hectares)

Years/ Crop	Wheat	Rice	Maize	Total Cereals	Total Pulses	Rapeseed & Mustard	Total Oilseeds	Cotton	Sugarcane	Potato
1960-61	1400	227	327	2160	903	107	185	447	133	9
	(29.58)	(4.80)	(6.91)	(45.65)	(19.08)	(2.26)	(3.91)	(9.45)	(2.81)	(0.19)
1970-71	2299	390	555	3514	414	103	295	397	128	17
	(40.48)	(6.87)	(9.77)	(61.89)	(7.29)	(1.81)	(5.19)	(6.99))	(2.25)	(0.29)
1975-76	2439	567	577	3891	441	122	315	580	114	27
	(38.99)	(9.06)	(9.22)	(62.21)	(7.05)	(1.95)	(5.03)	(9.27)	(1.82)	(0.43)
1980-81	2812	1183	382	4513	341	136	238	649	71	40
	(41.58)	(17.49)	(5.65)	(66.73)	(5.04)	(2.01)	(3.52)	(9.59)	(1.05)	(0.59)
1985-86	3112	1714	260	5169	225	151	211	559	78	43
	(43.47)	(23.95)	(3.63)	(72.21)	(3.14)	(2.11)	(2.95)	(7.81)	(1.09)	(0.60)
1990-91	3273	2015	188	5525	143	69	104	701	101	23
	(43.63)	(26.86)	(2.51)	(73.65)	(1.91)	(0.92)	(1.39)	(9.34)	(1.35)	(0.31)
1995-96	3221	2185	171	5625	95	101	237	742	136	39
	(41.77)	(28.33)	(2.22)	(72.94)	(1.23)	(1.31)	(3.07)	(9.62)	(1.76)	(0.51)
2000-01	3408	2612	164	6222	55	55	86	473	121	64
	(42.95)	(32.92)	(2.07)	(78.41)	(0.69)	(0.69)	(1.08)	(5.96)	(1.52)	(0.81)
2005-06	3464	2647	149	6290	29	47	80	557	85	71
	(44.03)	(33.64)	(1.89)	(79.94)	(0.37)	(0.60)	(1.02)	(7.08)	(1.08)	(0.90)
2006-07	3467	2621	154	6268	29	41	70	607	99	76
	(44.10)	(33.34)	(1.96)	(79.74)	(0.37)	(0.52)	(0.89)	(7.72)	(1.26)	(0.97)
2007-08	3487	2609	154	6271	27	30	60	605	108	90
	(44.31)	(33.15)	(1.96)	(79.68)	(0.34)	(0.38)	(0.76)	(7.69)	(1.37)	(1.14)
2008-09	3526	2735	151	6433	22	29	60	527	81	82
	(44.57)	(34.57)	(1.91)	(81.31)	(0.28)	(0.37)	(0.76)	(6.66)	(1.02)	(1.04)
2009-10	3522	2802	139	6480	19	30	62	511	60	83
	(45.51)	(35.41)	(1.76)	(81.90)	(0.24)	(0.38)	(0.78)	(6.46)	(0.76)	(1.05)

Note: Figures in parentheses indicate percentages to the total cropped area.
Source: *Statistical Abstract of Pubjab*, various issues.

to the price fluctuation. Actually, fluctuation in potato prices is a major factor behind the increase or decrease in the area under potatoes. Generally, its market price is fixed according to the forces of demand and supply. This crop is also not covered effectively under the public procurement programme.

All this reveals that foodgrains, particularly wheat and paddy have come to dominate the cropping pattern in the state in the wake of new farm technology and the axe has fallen mainly on the pulses and oilseeds. As already discussed, this outcome is the consequence of higher profitability of the wheat and paddy cropping system. There the cropping pattern has added another dimension to the agrarian problem. Pulses and oilseeds are legumes and their cultivation was an important natural source of restoring the soil fertility. The decline in their area has resulted in reduced availability of natural sources of fertilisation of soils. Moreover, there is also concern over the long range effects of the cereals dominated cropping pattern particularly the rice cultivation and also overall exploitative agriculture which could have a deleterious effect on the soil health and underground water.

3.5 Over-Exploitation of Ground Water

In the post-Green Revolution period, the even-rising area under paddy cultivation and fast growth in number of electric tube-wells for irrigation purposes has become reality. There were nearly 12,000 tube-wells in the state in 1960-61.This number increased to 1.92 lakhs in 1970-71, 6.00 lakhs in 1980-81, 7.73 lakhs in 1990-91, 10.73 lakhs in 2000-01 and 11.68 lakhs in 2004-05. At present, about 75 per cent of the irrigation is done through these tube-wells and the remaining 25 per cent by the canals. Since paddy is a water-intensive crop, this phenomenon has resulted in over-exploitation of ground water. For instance, just 45 per cent of development blocks in the state (Table 5.4) had fallen in the category of over-exploited blocks in the year 1984. This proportion increased to 76 per cent during 2004. The number of white blocks constituted 31 per cent in 1984 which declined to about 12 per cent in 2004. Similarly, the share of grey blocks declined from 19 per cent in 1984 to six per cent in 2004.

Due to the declining underground water table, already more than one lakh tube-wells have been replaced with submersible pumps and around 3.9 lakh centrifugal pumps will have to be replaced by the submersible pumps in the next few years, costing crores of rupees and increasing energy requirements three-fold to pump-out the same quantity of water (Aulakh, 2004). The PAU experts always advise the farmers not to transplant paddy before June 15 because transplantation of paddy before this date results in fall of water table. For example, paddy transplanted on May 1 results in 70 cms decline in water table, 60 cms in the case of May 10, 50 cms on May 20, 28 cms on May 30 and 10 cms on June 10. For the last two decades, the PAU advice to the farmers did not have a significant impact in this regard. According to the press reports, some farmers of Moonak block (Sangrur district) transplanted paddy as early as on April 20, 2006 (Sharma, 2006). In central Punjab, the water table is declining very fast which would have wide implications in the years to come. From the years 1982-87, the water table in central Punjab declined by 18 cms per year. This figure increased to 25 cms in the years 1992-97, 42 cms in 1997-2002, 69 cms in 2003-04 and 74 cms in 2004-05 (GOP, 2006). Keeping in view these facts, the State Government has put a ban on transplantation of paddy before June 10 every year.

The district-wise categorisation of water table in Punjab during 1984-2004 is given in Table 5.5. It revealed that the 100 per cent blocks of Amritsar, Faridkot, Fatehgarh Sahib, Jalandhar, Kapurthala, Mansa, Moga and Sangrur were over-exploited where the withdrawal of ground water was more than 100 per cent of the recharge. This figure was about 91 per cent for Ludhiana district, 89 per cent for Patiala district, 70 per cent for Ferozepur district, 57 per cent each for Bathinda and Gurdaspur districts, 29 per cent for Ropar district and 20 per cent for Hoshiarpur district. As far as the state as a whole was concerned, about 76 per cent of the water blocks were over-exploited. The share of dark blocks was about seven per cent, grey blocks about six per cent and white blocks about 12 per cent.

Table 5.5: Groundwater Exploitation in Punjab, 1984 to 2004

Water Blocks	*Year*				
	1984	*1989*	*1991*	*1997*	*2004*
Over-Exploited	53	62	62	73	104
	(44.92)	(52.54)	(52.54)	(52.90)	(75.91)
Exploited	7	7	8	11	9
	(5.93)	(5.93)	(6.78)	(7.97)	(6.57)
Grey	22	20	15	16	8
	(18.64)	(16.95)	(12.71)	(11.59)	(5.84)
White	36	29	33	38	16
	(30.51)	(24.58)	(27.97)	(27.54)	(11.68)
Total Number	118	118	118	138	137
of Water Blocks	(100.00)	(100.00)	(100.00)	(100.00)	(100.00)

Note: (i) Figures in parentheses indicate percentages to the total number of water blocks

(ii) Over-exploited blocks are those where withdrawal of groundwater was more than 100 per cent of the recharge of water. Dark blocks are those where the withdrawal of groundwater was between 85 per cent and 100 per cent of recharge of water. In grey blocks, the withdrawal of groundwater was between 60 per cent and 85 per cent of recharge of water. In white blocks, the withdrawal of groundwater was less than 60 per cent of the recharge of water.

Source: Water Resources Directorate, Punjab, Chandigarh.

Table 5.6: District-wise Categorisation of Water Blocks in Punjab, 2004

District	*Over-Exploited (OE)*	*Dark (D)*	*Grey (G)*	*White (W)*	*Total Water Blocks*
Amritsar	16	-	-	-	16
	(100.00)				(100.00)
Bathinda	4	-	1	2	7
	(57.14)		(14.29)	(28.57)	(100.00)
Faridkot	2	-	-	-	2
	(100.00)				(100.00)
Fatehgarh	5	-	-		5
Sahib	(100.00)				(100.00)

Ferozepur	7	1	-	2	10
	(70.00)	(10.00)		(20.00)	(100.00)
Gurdaspur	8	2	2	2	14
	(57.14)	(14.29)	(14.29)	(14.28)	(100.00)
Hoshiarpur	2	2	3	3	10
	(20.00)	(20.00)	(30.00)	(30.00)	(100.00)
Jalandhar	10	-	-	-	10
	(100.00)				(100.00)
Kapurthala	5	-	-	-	5
	(100.00)				(100.00)
Ludhiana	10	1	-	-	11
	(90.91)	(9.09)			(100.00)
Mansa	5	-	-	-	5
	(100.00)				(100.00)
Moga	5	-	-	-	5
	(100.00)				(100.00)
Muktsar	-	-	1	3	4
			(25.00)	(75.00)	(100.00)
Nawan	3	-	-	2	5
Shahr	(60.00)			(40.00)	(100.00)
Patiala	8	-	1	-	9
	(88.89)		(11.11)		(100.00)
Ropar	2	3	-	2	7
	(28.57)	(42.86)		(28.57)	(100.00)
Sangrur	12	-	-	-	12
	(100.00)				(100.00)
Punjab	104	9	8	16	137
	(75.91)	(6.57)	(5.84)	(11.68)	(100.00)

Note: Figures in parentheses indicate percentages to the total.

Source: Water Resources Directorate, Punjab, Chandigarh

Keeping in view the problem of the declining water table and other related issues, the Punjab Government constituted the Committee under the Chairmanship of Dr. S.S. Johl—an eminent agricultural economist—to suggest various measures for diversification of agriculture in Punjab. The Committee suggested that an area of one million hectares each under paddy and wheat may be replaced with other crops, particularly oilseeds and pulses. According to the existing water resources of the state, Punjab can sustain paddy cultivation on 16 lakh hectares only. But owing to various reasons, the recommendations of this Committee have not been implemented as such by the Government of India. Actually, a severe drought in the year 2002-03 resulted in the fall of foodgrain production in India by about 38 million tonnes in a year. The buffer stocks also declined considerably; rather India was forced to import about seven million tonnes of wheat during 2006-2008. Since food security of the country is in the hands of the Punjab farmers, therefore, shifting of 10 lakh hectares of paddy area to other crops in the near future will be a very difficult task. The policy framework and market infrastructure indeed favour the wheat and paddy crops in the state.

3.6 Growth Rates of Area, Production and Yield of Different Crops

The compound growth rates of area, production and yield for important crops of the state are shown in Table 5.6. A perusal of these figures shows that rice production recorded the higher growth, i.e. 18.41 per cent per annum from 1966-67 to 1980-81. The contribution of area and yield was 11.00 per cent and 6.67 per cent respectively. Among the cereals, wheat was the next crop to record a high production growth rate (6.48 per cent per annum) during this period. The contribution of area in this was 3.34 per cent and the yield contributed 3.05 per cent. Potato and American cotton also recorded significant production growth rates of 13.30 per cent and 8.09 per cent respectively in this period. In the case of potatoes, the contribution of area was 9.38 per cent and that of yield 3.66 per cent. In the case of cotton (A), the increase in production mainly occurred as a result of increase in area (7.37 per cent) and contribution of yield was (-) 0.11 per cent. Sugarcane witnessed a negligible growth rate of 0.23 per cent. The other crops like maize, barley, bajra, pulses, oilseeds and cotton (D) had negative growth rates for production during this period. This happened primarily on account of decrease in the area under these crops. Area released from maize crop in the kharif season was largely replaced by the paddy crop and that from pulses and oilseeds to wheat in the rabi season. The area under cotton (D) has mainly been replaced by cotton (A).

The compound growth rates of area, production and yield of important crops in the state for the period 1981-82 to 1990-91 revealed that the rice crop again recorded the highest production growth rate; grew at 5.61 per cent per annum. The contribution of area was 4.85 per cent and that of yield 0.72 per cent. Wheat also records 3.70 per cent per annum production growth rate. The contribution of area was 0.97 per cent and that of yield 2.70 per cent. The cotton (A) recorded 11.16 per cent per annum growth rate in production and the contribution of area and yield was 2.79 per cent and 8.15 per cent respectively. Sugarcane also did not show a high growth rate in this period. The crops like maize, barley, bajra, pulses, oilseeds, potato and cotton (A) showed the negative production growth rates. It happened mainly due to a decrease in area under these crops.

During the period 1991-92 to 2000-01, the production growth rates of rice and wheat were low compared to the earlier periods, i.e. 1966-67 to 1980-81 and 1981-82 to 1990-91. Among the cereals crops, the production growth rate of rice was 2.86 per cent per annum during the years 1991-92 to 2000-01. The increase in production was mainly due to increase in area, i.e. 2.72 per cent per annum. The contribution of yield was non-significant, i.e. 0.12 per cent per annum. The major reason for increase in rice area during this period was replacement of cotton (A) by the farmers with the rice. Owing to the attack of American bollworm on the cotton (A) crop on a large scale during this period, the farmers had no option but shift to paddy crop in the kharif season. In the cotton belt, the ground water is brackish and unfit for water-intensive crops like paddy. But economic hardships faced by the farmers due to failure of the cotton (A) crop forced them to shift to rice cultivation.

Wheat crop recorded the production growth rate of 2.48 per cent per annum during the period 1991-92 to 2000-01. The contribution of area and yield was 0.36 per cent and 2.13 per cent respectively. The potato crop witnessed a significant production growth rate, i.e. 14.56 per cent per annum during this period. The contribution of area and yield was 14.59 per cent and 0.18 per cent respectively. Sugarcane production also witnessed the growth rate of 2.07 per cent per annum but it was not significant. The cotton (D) showed 5.57 per cent production growth rate which was not found to be significant, whereas cotton (A) production declined by 13.29 per cent per annum. The other crops like barley, bajra, pulses and oilseeds showed negative production growth rates. The maize crop witnessed non-significant 1.54 per cent production growth rate.

During the period 2001-02 to 2009-10, the production growth rate of rice was 2.95 per cent per annum. The increase in production was due to increase in area, i.e. 1.16 per cent per annum and yield, i.e. 1.77 per cent per annum. The wheat crop recorded a non-significant production growth rate of 0.64 per cent per annum during the period 2001-02 to 2009-10. The contribution of area and yield was 0.45 per cent and 0.49 per cent respectively. The maize crop witnessed 3.60 per cent production growth rate which was mainly due to increase in yield, i.e. 4.85 per cent per annum. Potato crop witnessed significant production growth rate, i.e. 6.70 per cent per annum during this period. The contribution of area and yield was 4.85 per cent and 2.42 per cent respectively. The cotton (A) showed 10.79 per cent production growth rate, whereas cotton (D) production declined by 16.68 per cent per annum. The other crops like barley, bajra, pulses, oilseeds and sugarcane showed negative production growth rates.

The overall growth rate of area, production and yield of important crops for the period 1966-67 to 2009-10 indicated that the rice crop was at number one having the highest production growth rate, i.e. 7.68 per cent per annum. The contribution of area and yield was 5.42 per cent and 2.13 per cent respectively for increasing rice production. The wheat was the next important crop having 3.53 per cent growth rate in production. The contribution of area was 1.36 per cent and yield 2.14 per cent. The growth rate of production of cotton (A) was 2.98. The contribution of area was 1.77 per cent and that of yield was 1.15 per cent. Potato was another important crop which showed the growth rate of production, i.e. 4.61 per cent per annum. The contribution of area and yield was 3.60 per cent and 0.92 per cent respectively. Sugarcane recorded the production growth rate of 0.52 per cent per annum. This increase was mainly due to increase in productivity. The other crops, like maize, bajra, pulses, oilseeds and cotton (D), recorded negative growth rates in production.

Table 5.6a: Compound Growth Rate of Area, Production and Yield of Important Crops in Punjab
(Figures in per cent per annum)

S. No.	*Crop*	*Area*	*Production*	*Yield*
		1966-67 to 1980-81		
1.	Rice	11.00***	18.41***	6.67***
2.	Wheat	3.34***	6.48***	3.05***
3.	Maize	-1.33*	-0.90NS	0.42NS
4.	Barley	-4.44*	-0.30NS	4.21***
5.	Bajra	-7.92***	-7.27***	0.71NS
6.	Pulses	-3.36***	-4.05***	-0.72NS
7.	Oilseeds	-2.91***	-2.91***	-0.0009NS
8.	Sugarcane	-4.15***	0.23NS	4.55***
9.	Potato	9.38***	13.30***	3.66***
10.	Cotton (A)	7.37***	8.09***	-0.11NS
11.	Cotton (D)	-1.77*	-2.91**	-1.65***
		1981-82 to 1990-91		
1.	Rice	4.85***	5.61***	0.72NS
2.	Wheat	0.97***	3.70***	2.70***
3.	Maize	-5.72***	-7.08***	-1.40NS
4.	Barley	-8.79***	-3.32NS	6.08***
5.	Bajra	-18.46***	-19.66***	-1.63NS
6.	Pulses	-7.15***	-4.39*	2.97*
7.	Oilseeds	-6.01***	-4.16NS	2.21*
8.	Sugarcane	0.95NS	0.77NS	-0.80NS
9.	Potato	-2.77NS	-2.01NS	-0.08NS
10.	Cotton (A)	2.79NS	11.16***	8.15**
11.	Cotton (D)	-9.07***	-3.52NS	6.09*
		1991-92 to 2000-01		
1.	Rice	2.72***	2.86***	0.12NS
2.	Wheat	0.36*	2.48***	2.13***
3.	Maize	8.23 NS	1.54NS	3.42**
4.	Barley	-4.60***	-2.36*	2.48***
5.	Bajra	-7.92**	-5.80NS	-2.80*
6.	Pulses	-5.62***	-7.97***	-2.50**

S. No.	*Crop*	*Area*	*Production*	*Yield*
7.	Oilseeds	-7.41**	-9.64***	-2.40***
8.	Sugarcane	2.29 NS	2.07NS	0.23NS
9.	Potato	14.59***	14.56***	0.18NS
10.	Cotton (A)	-5.21***	-13.29***	-8.53**
11.	Cotton (D)	6.23 NS	5.57NS	-0.62NS
		2001-02 to 2009-10		
1.	Rice	1.16***	2.95***	1.77***
2.	Wheat	0.45***	0.64 NS	0.19 NS
3.	Maize	-0.75*	3.60*	4.85**
4.	Barley	-6.94***	-6.57***	0.35 NS
5.	Bajra	-8.51**	-6.02***	4.38**
6.	Pulses	-10.79***	-8.53***	2.53*
7.	Oilseeds	-5.89***	-2.14NS	3.98 NS
8.	Sugarcane	-8.75***	-6.14**	-0.04 NS
9.	Potato	4.85***	6.70**	2.42 NS
10.	Cotton (A)	3.23 NS	10.79**	7.32**
11.	Cotton (D)	-22.18***	-16.68***	7.21**
		1966-67 to 2009-10		
1.	Rice	5.42***	7.68***	2.13***
2.	Wheat	1.36***	3.53***	2.14***
3.	Maize	-3.35***	-1.86***	1.91***
4.	Barley	-3.98***	-0.45NS	3.67***
5.	Bajra	-9.98***	-10.13***	-0.03 NS
6.	Pulses	-7.42***	-7.42***	0.04 NS
7.	Oilseeds	-3.86***	-2.67***	1.15***
8.	Sugarcane	-0.49*	0.52**	0.97***
9.	Potato	3.60***	4.61***	0.92***
10.	Cotton (A)	1.77***	2.98***	1.15***
11.	Cotton (D)	-4.42***	-3.28***	1.12***

Note: NS, ***, **, * indicate non-significant and significant at 1 per cent, 5 per cent and 10 per cent levels respectively.

The overall comparison of growth rates of different periods show that Punjab agriculture is now facing the problem of stagnation in production, particularly in the last one decade. The slow down in the growth rates of different crops had a negative impact on the income and employment of the farmers as well as the agricultural labourers. The area under different crops has almost reached the maximum possible level. Any increase in area of a particular crop will result in decline of another crop. In this way, the overall picture of Punjab agriculture may not change significantly in the near future.

3.7 Stagnated Production and Productivity Across Major Crops

Undoubtedly, the rice and wheat production have shown remarkable progress in the state during the last 45 years. But during the last few years, wheat production has declined from 159 lakh tonnes in 1999-2000 to nearly 142 lakh tonnes in 2002-03. The production of wheat crop is almost stagnant since 2000-01. It was 155.51 lakh tonnes in 2000-01 and increased marginally to 157.33 lakh tonnes during 2008-09 and declined to about 152 lakh tonnes during 2009-10. Similarly, rice production has declined from about 92 lakh tonnes in 2000-01 to about 89 lakh tonnes in 2002-03 and it increased to about 112 lakh tonnes during 2009-10. It may be mentioned here that weather conditions also played an important role in production of these crops. Sometimes, it is favourable or at other times unfavourable to the crop/s. For instance, flash floods in Punjab during the month of September 1988 damaged the rice crop on a large scale and consequently, the rice production declined to 49 lakh tonnes during 1988-89 compared to 54 lakh tonnes in 1987-88 and 59 lakh tonnes in 1986-87. The severe drought condition in 1987-88 also adversely affected the rice production of the state. Similarly, production of cotton (A) has declined during the 1990s due to the attack of American bollworm. The production of other crops, except sugarcane and potato, has declined through all time.

Productivity measured as the yield per unit of area is an indication of the efficiency in production. The yield figures of important crops show that in the case of wheat, the productivity after showing an increase during the initial years (during 1966-67 to 1971-72) showed no improvement during 1972-73 to 1976-77 and stagnated around 24 quintals per hectare. In the later years, however, there was an improvement in the productivity, although it was marked by the inter-year fluctuations. In the recent years, the maximum yield of wheat was 4696 kgs per hectare in 1999-2000. After that peak yield, it had started declining. As already discussed, the weather also played an important role in this regard.

In the case of rice, the productivity increased from 1185 kgs per hectare in 1966-67 to 3507 kgs per hectare in 1993-94. This meant about three times increase in productivity during the period. After that, the yield witnessed a decline up to the year 1999-2000 but again showed increase in 2000-01. It was 3506 kgs per hectare in this year. It went to the level of 3545 kgs per hectare in 2001-02 but marginally declined to 3510 kgs per hectare in 2002-03 and increased to 4010 kgs in 2009-10. There were also inter-year fluctuations in rice yield. This happened due to the occurrence of floods, drought, and diseases to the crops. There is need for technological breakthrough in the case of rice, particularly in the hybrids.

The productivity of cotton (A) also rose from 335 kgs per hectare in 1966-67 to 636 kgs in 1992-93. During this period also, there were inter-year fluctuations in the productivity because of various factors. After 1992-93, the cotton yield (A) started declining owing to the attack of American bollworm and it reached the lowest level of 179 kgs per hectare in 1998-99. In the subsequent years, it picked up largely due to BT cotton. The yield of cotton (A) was 673 kgs per hectare in 2009-10. Further, productivity analysis of other crops reveals that yield of maize, sugarcane, potato, oilseeds and barley crops has increased overtime although there were inter-year fluctuations for various reasons. The productivity of pulses and cotton (D) did not show any remarkable improvement. To increase the production of various crops, there is need for technological breakthrough in the productivity.

3.8 Slow Down in Agricultural GSDP

The productivity analysis reveals that technological breakthrough has been achieved mainly in a few crops like rice, wheat, sugarcane, potato, maize and barley. However, except the wheat and rice, the area under other crops in the state is not quite large. There are marketing constraints for other crops because public procurement is effective only in the case of wheat and paddy. In the case of pulses, cotton (D) and bajra, the productivity has almost stagnated. Overall, the contribution of the agriculture sector in Punjab's gross state domestic product (GSDP) is slow-down. For instance, the growth rate in agricultural GSDP had been 2.40 per cent per annum in Punjab for the period 2000-01 to 2007-08 against 3.20 per cent per annum for the country (Table 5.7). Gujarat state had the highest agricultural GSDP growth rate of 11.70 per cent, followed by Chhattisgarh (9.40 per cent), Rajasthan (5.80 per cent), Maharashtra (5.60 per cent), and Madhya Pradesh (5.50 per cent). Even Haryana and Himachal Pradesh which were part of Punjab up to October 31, 1966 achieved a high growth rate of 3.60 per cent and 4.00 per cent respectively. The slow-down in the agricultural GSDP growth in Punjab in recent years is a matter of concern. It is a red signal for the policy planners at the state and national level.

Table 5.7: State-wise Agricultural Gross State Domestic Product Growth Rate, 2000-01 to 2007-08

(per cent per annum)

S. No.	*State*	*Agri. GSDP Growth Rate (at 1999-2000 prices)*	*S. No.*	*State*	*Agri. GSDP Growth Rate (at 1999-2000 prices)*
1.	Punjab	2.40	14.	Uttaranchal(Uttarakhand)	2.50
2.	Madhya Pradesh	5.50	15.	Gujarat	11.70
3.	Jammu & Kashmir	3.60	16.	Maharashtra	5.60
4.	Rajasthan	5.80	17.	Puducherry	3.10
5.	Arunachal Pradesh	3.20	18.	Uttar Pradesh	1.70
6.	Orissa	4.60	19.	Bihar	1.50
7.	Andhra Pradesh	5.60	20.	Manipur	2.50
8.	Haryana	3.60	21.	Assam	0.50
9.	Tripura	4.60	22.	Karnataka	1.20
10.	Himachal Pradesh	4.00	23.	Kerala	0.70
11.	Meghalaya	4.20	24.	Tamil Nadu	2.50
12.	Chhattisgarh	9.40	25.	West Bengal	2.10
13.	Sikkim	5.40	26.	**India**	**3.20**

Source: Business Standard, Chandigarh dated April 14, 2011, p. 10

3.9 Extent of Exploitation of Potential Yield and Future Possibilities

Table 5.8 shows the information regarding the extent of exploitation of potential yield of various kharif and rabi crops. A perusal of the data reveals that among the Kharif crops, the extent of exploitation of potential yield was the highest in Bt cotton, i.e. 84.95 per cent followed by paddy (83.21 per cent),

Table 5.8: Extent of Exploitation of Potential Yield

S. No.	*Crop*	*Potential Yield (q)*	*State Average Yield (q)*	*% Potential Exploited*
Kharif Crops				
1.	Paddy	29	24.13	83.21
2.	Bt Cotton	10.5	8.92	84.95
3.	Moong	4.5	3.59	79.77
4.	Basmati	14	10.50	75.00
5.	Desi Cotton	9	6.41	71.22
6.	Sugarcane	325	231	71.08
7.	Maize	20	13.77	68.85
8.	Arhar	6	3.92	65.33
9.	Sesamum	2.1	1.36	64.76
10.	Soyabean	6	3.65	60.83
11.	Mash	4	1.99	49.75
12.	Groundnut	9	3.78	42.00
13.	Bajra	14	4.26	30.42
Rabi Crops				
1.	Wheat	20	18.06	90.30
2.	Sunflower	7.8	7.09	90.90
3.	Barley	15.8	13.94	88.23
4.	Gobhi Sarson	7	4.87	69.57
5.	Gram	7	4.71	67.28
6.	Field Peas	7.5	4.77	63.60
7.	Lentils	4.8	2.62	54.58
8.	Toria	5	-	-
9.	Linseed	4.7	-	-
10.	Winter Maize	28	-	-

Source: Department of Economics & Sociology, PAU, Ludhiana

moong (79.77 per cent), basmati (75.00 per cent), desi cotton (71.22 per cent), sugarcane (71.08 per cent), maize (68.85 per cent), etc. The lowest exploitation of the potential yield was in the case of bajra (30.42 per cent) followed by groundnut (42.00 per cent), mash (49.75 per cent), soyabean (60.83 per cent), etc. In the case of rabi crops, the extent of exploitation of potential yield was the highest in sunflower, i.e. 90.90 per cent followed by wheat (90.30 per cent), barley (88.23 per cent), gobhi sarson (69.57 per cent), etc. The lowest exploitation of potential yield was in the case of lentils (54.58 per cent) followed by field peas (63.60 per cent), gram (67.28 per cent), etc. Hence, there is an ample scope of further exploitation of potential yield of the crops where the exploitation is less which calls for the need of adequate extension services and providing the technical know-how to the farmers. There are sizeable productivity differentials among districts which are otherwise more or less homogeneous with respect to availability of irrigation facilities and soil type. It should be possible to increase the productivity levels in these districts by giving due attention to the limiting factors in these districts.

In the light of these observations, it is often talked that Punjab may not be able to add much to its agricultural production because it is already near the saturation point as far as exploitation of new areas under cultivation is concerned. Besides, water is going to become the most limiting resource in the further intensification of agriculture. One view is that unless the state makes rational use of its irrigation resource, it would be difficult to maintain even the present type of cropping pattern in the long run. Already, the state is facing the problem of the falling water level across the vast areas in central Punjab. This is coupled with the water logging problem in some parts of the south-western districts where the underground water is brackish. This does not, however, mean that there is no scope to increase agricultural production. Even with the known level of technology, it is possible to enhance agricultural production by bridging the adoption gaps between potential yield and actual yield of major crops.

Further, there are sizeable productivity differentials among the districts which are otherwise more or less homogeneous with respect to availability of irrigation facilities and soil type. It should be possible to increase the productivity levels in these districts by giving due attention to the limiting factors in these districts. As far as diversification of crops is concerned, the authors are of the view that alternative crops should provide net returns almost equal to the wheat and paddy crops. Only then, the farmers will shift to those crops. In this regard, production technology and marketing will have to play a crucial role. At present, the farmers face problems related to these issues.

4. Summary and Conclusions

Wheat is the principal crop of Punjab which has about 46 per cent of the cropped area followed by rice which has about 35 per cent area. In this way, these two crops taken together occupy about 81 per cent of the area. Rice is not a traditional crop of Punjab. The area under rice was just 227 thousand hectares in 1960-61 which increased to 390 thousand hectares in 1970-71, 567 thousand hectares in 1980-81, 1183 thousand hectares in 1985-86 and 2015 thousand hectares in 1990-91. It reached the level of 2612 thousand hectares in 2000-01 which further increased to 2802 thousand hectares in 2009-10. In the post-Green Revolution period, the number of tube-wells for irrigation purposes has increased very fast. There were only 1973 tube-wells in the state in 1950-51.This number increased to about 12000 in 1960-61, 1.92 lakhs in 1970-71, 6.00 lakhs in 1980-81, 7.73 lakhs in 1990-91, 10.73 lakhs in 2000-01 and 13.15 lakhs in 2009-10. At present, about 72 per cent of the irrigation is through tube-wells and the rest about 28 per cent by canals. This phenomenon resulted in over-exploitation of ground water in the state.

The overall comparison of growth rates of different crops/ periods show that Punjab agriculture is facing the problem of stagnation in production, particularly in the last one decade or so. The slow down in the growth rates of different crops has a negative impact on the employment and income of the farmers as well as agricultural labourers. The area under different crops has almost reached the maximum possible level. Any increase in area of a particular crop will result in a decline of another crop. In this way, the overall picture of Punjab agriculture may not change significantly. The productivity analysis reveals that technical breakthrough in the productivity has been achieved mainly in a few crops like rice, wheat, sugarcane, potato, maize and barley. Except wheat and rice, the area under other crops is not quite large. There are marketing constraints for other crops because public procurement is effective only in the case of wheat and paddy. In the case of pulses, desi cotton and bajra, the productivity has almost stagnated. Overall, Punjab's agriculture is facing the problem of stagnation in production and productivity. It may be stated that actual yield in the state is already more than 80 per cent of the potential yield in the case of principal crops like wheat, paddy, Bt cotton, sunflower, etc. This means that there is limited scope to increase the yield of these crops at the farm level. For other crops where there is potential to increase the yield, the farmers are not willing to bring more area under those crops for various reasons.

Punjab's agriculture which was growing fast earlier has now reached a sort of plateau in terms of productivity and production. In the wake of a declining land man ratio, it is not able to generate gainful employment and sufficient income for the growing population. Farm profitability has witnessed a decline in the recent years due to cost price squeeze. There is almost stagnation in farm income. Farming alone is not able to generate sufficient income for the small and marginal farmers. Owing to economic distress, a large number of farmers and agricultural labourers committed suicide in the state. At present, the rural indebtedness is to the extent of about Rs 35,000 crores. The Punjab farmers are in a deep economic crisis. For sustainable agricultural development, non-farm employment opportunities for the rural youth may be created. It is the need of the hour. A delay of a few years will not be in the interest of the state and country.

REFERENCES

Aulakh, K.S. (2004), Re-Fixing Priorities Can Save Agro-Economy, *The Tribune*, Chandigarh, Vol. 124 (73), March 15, p. 16.

Ghuman, Ranjit Singh (2008), Socio-Economic Crisis in Rural Punjab, *Economic and Political Weekly*, Vol. 43 (7), pp. 12-15.

GOP (2006), *Agricultural and Rural Development of Punjab : Transforming from Crisis to Growth*, The Punjab State Farmers Commission, SAS Nagar (Mohali), pp. 1-72.

GOP (2009), *Budget Speech of the Finance Minister, Punjab*, Chandigarh.

GOP (2011), *Statistical Abstract of Punjab 2010*, Economic and Statistical Organisation, Punjab, Chandigarh.

HT Correspondent (2006), Debt Trap is Killing Farmers, Say Experts, *The Hindustan Times*, Chandigarh, Vol. 82 (47), February 24, p. 6.

Mander, H. (2004), 'Of Human Bondage', *The Hindustan Times*, Vol. 80 (178), July 27, p.6.

Nibber, G.S. (2004), Over 2000 Farmers' Suicides in Punjab in 15 Years: Report, *The Hindustan Times*, Chandigarh, Vol. 80 (253), October 22, p. 2.

PAU (2009), *Farmers and Agricultural Labourers Suicides Due to Indebtedness in Punjab State: Pilot Survey in Bathinda and Sangrur Districts*, Department of Economics and Sociology, Punjab Agricultural University (PAU), Ludhiana.

Sharma, H.L. (2006), Early Paddy: Good or Bad, Plant We Will, *The Hindustan Times*, Chandigarh, Vol. 82 (94), April 21, p. 6.

Sidhu, M.S., A.S. Joshi and Lavleen Kaur (2006), *Problems and Prospects of Agriculture in Punjab, Research Report*, Department of Economics and Sociology, Punjab Agricultural University (PAU), Ludhiana, pp. 1-41.

PART III

Emerging Alternatives for Sustainable Agriculture in Punjab

6

Growth and Performance of the Dairy Sector in Punjab

Parminder Kaur, A.S. Bhullar, Inderpreet Kaur and Harpreet Kaur

Introduction

The Indian dairy industry has made rapid strides in milk production, processing and marketing during the last three decades. This sub-sector occupies an important place in the agricultural economy of India as milk is the second largest agricultural commodity contributing to the national product, next to rice. Though the contribution of agriculture and allied sectors to the Nation's Gross Domestic Product (GDP) has declined during the last few decades, yet contribution of livestock has increased overtime. Sustained economic/income growth, fast growing urban population and rising integration of the global agri-food markets are fuelling the rapid growth in demand for animal products in India. This implies tremendous potential for future growth of the livestock sector and new opportunities for livestock owners, especially the small holders (Birthal, 2008).

Punjab is the leading agrarian state of the Indian economy. It not only contributes a large chunk in the pool of grain stocks, but its contribution to India's milk production is also very significant. Due to the growing significance of livestock in the agrarian economy of the state, its share in the Net State Domestic

Product (NSDP) accruing from agriculture increased over time and that of crops and allied activities declined. The share of livestock in the NSDP from agriculture and allied activities increased from 33.52 per cent in 1980-81 to 40.41 per cent in 2005-06 at constant prices. In fact, livestock in general and dairy in particular are regarded as the engine of growth of Punjab's agricultural sector in recent years. Dairy enterprises are considered as a treasure of the state's economy particularly for rural systems, where the dairy farming provides nutritious products, draft animal power, organic manure, supplementary employment and generates continuous flow of income and acts as a cushion against income shocks arising due to crop failure. Further dairying provides a support system to milk producers without disturbing their agro-economic systems. Dairying in recent decades has also been considered as a vital component in the diversification of agriculture. It seems that to improve the income, to provide gainful employment and to stabilise income flow, the diversification of agriculture with dairying emerges as a major strategy in the state. Therefore it is absolutely essential to examine the trends in the growth of dairy, which is reflected in the increase in milk output and its sources.

This chapter is an attempt to examine (a) compositional changes in bovine population; and (b) the trends in the growth of milk output and the sources of milk output growth. It is based on both the primary and secondary data. The secondary data was collected from various published sources such as Statistical Abstracts of Punjab and Livestock Censuses of Punjab. Besides tabular analysis, per annum growth rates were computed to indicate an increase or decrease in bovine population during inter-census periods as follows:

$$\frac{Pt}{P_0} = \left(1 + \frac{r}{100}\right)^1$$

Where P_t is bovine population in the tth period; P_o is the bovine population in the base year; r is the compound growth rate; and t is the time in years.

In case of milk production, the compound growth rates have been computed by fitting the exponential function of the form, when the time series data without any gap was available, as follows:

$$\mathbf{Y = A\ B^t}$$

where Y is the variable for which the growth rate is to be worked out; t is the time; B = 1+r, where r is the compound growth rate; and A is the constant.

To analyse the relative contribution of bovine population and increase in milk yield to growth in milk production, The 'Additive Decomposition Model' developed by Minhas and Vaidyanathan (1965) was used. The model is as under:

$$M_t - M_{t-1} = (P_t - P_{t-1})\ Y_{t-1} + (Y_t - Y_{t-1})\ P_{t-1} + (P_t - P_{t-1})\ (Y_t - Y_{t-1})$$

where 'M' refers to total milk production by species; 'P' refers to population of milch animals; 'Y' refers to yield per milch animal; 't' and 't_{-1}' refers to the terminal and base years respectively.

And, to examine the productivity of milch bovines, lactating efficiency was worked out as under:

$$\text{Lactation efficiency} = \frac{\text{Adult female bovine numbers in milk}}{\text{Total adult female bovines}}$$

In order to examine the growth of the dairy sector, Punjab has been divided into three regions, namely sub-mountain region, central region and south-western region. These regions broadly correspond to the three agro-climatic zones of Punjab depending on cropping pattern, soil type, physiography and water availability.The districts falling under these regions are as follows:

I. Sub-Mountain: Nawan-Shehar, Hoshiarpur and Rupnagar (3).
II. Central: Gurdaspur, Amritsar, Kapurthala, Jalandhar, Ludhiana, Moga, Sangrur, Patiala, and Fatehgarh Sahib (9)
III. South-Western: Ferozepur, Faridkot, Bathinda, Muktsar and Mansa (5).

The analysis has been divided into five sections. Section I deals with the introduction and methodology of study. Section II describes the growth and composition of bovines in the state.

Section III presents the growth of milk production in the state. The sources of milk output growth are presented in Section IV. Section V presents the constraints inhibiting the growth of the dairy sector in the state.

II

Bovine Population: Growth and Composition

This section examines the growth and compositional changes in the total bovine population in the state. The total bovine population in Punjab during different inter-census periods is presented in Table 6.1. It makes it clear that the total bovine population in the state increased from 7421.80 thousand in 1977 to 8810.5 thousand in 1997, but then declined to 8033.00 thousand in 2003 and 6796.55 thousand in 2007; showing an annual compound growth rate of 0.86 per cent during 1977-1997, and declining growth rate of 2.56 per cent per annum during 1997-2007. And, during 1977-2007, the total bovine population declined at the rate of 0.29 per cent per annum. Further, the buffalo population in the state recorded 0.68 per cent annual growth rate during 1977-2007, while the stock of cattle declined at the rate of 2.08 per cent during the same period. The sharpest decline was witnessed in the population of indigenous cattle, i.e. at the compound growth rate of 6.09 per cent per annum.

Owing to wide differentials in growth rates, the composition of the bovine population in the state has also changed over the last three decades. The composition based on the breed shows that due to fast growth of buffaloes and negative growth of cattle, their respective shares in 2007 turned out to be 74.09 per cent and 25.91 per cent in the total bovine population. These trends in the size and composition of the bovine population stock in the state show that a shift has taken place in favour of more productive milch animals. It means that population of less productive bovines (indigenous cattle) has declined, and that of productive animals like crossbred cows and buffaloes have increased.

Table 6.1. Total Bovine Population in Punjab by Animal Census Periods

	Bovine Population (000)					*CGR (%)*		
Category	*1977*	*1990*	*1997*	*2003*	*2007*	*1977-1997*	*1997-2007*	*1977-2007*
1. Cattle	3311.80 (44.62)	2832.50 (33.67)	2639.8 (29.96)	2038.5 (25.38)	1760.92 (25.90)	-1.12	-3.96	-2.08
i. Indigenous	3311.80 (44.62)	1253.00 (14.89)	810.50 (9.19)	508.00 (6.33)	502.53 (7.39)	-6.79	-4.16	-6.09
ii. Crossbreed	-	1579.50 (18.78)	1829.30 (20.77)	1530.50 (19.05)	1258.39 (18.51)	2.11	-3.67	-1.32
2. Buffaloes	4110.00 (55.38)	55.77 (66.33)	6170.70 (70.04)	5994.50 (74.62)	5035.63 (74.09)	2.05	-2.01	0.68
Total Bovine Population	7421.80 (100.00)	8410.5 (100.00)	8810.5 (100.00)	8033.00 (100.00)	6796.55 (100.00)	0.86	-2.56	-0.29

Figures in parentheses are the percentages to the total bovine population

Compositional Changes and Growth Rate of Adult Bovine

Bovine population that comprises buffaloes and cattle was further classified on the basis of sex, age and purpose for which these animals are reared. Growth and composition of adult bovine in Punjab during inter-census periods is presented in Table 6.2. Stock of adult male bovine, referred as 'work animals' declined by almost four times between 1977 and 2007; showing a negative annual compound growth rate of 5.05 per cent. The rate of decline was slightly slower for he-buffaloes (3.94 per cent) as compared to he-cattle (5.31 per cent). In 2007, these work animals constituted 77.82 per cent of cattle and 22.18 per cent of buffaloes. The reason for the sharp decline in the stock of adult male bovine was the large-scale mechanisation of agriculture in the state making this section of bovine population redundant.

Stock of adult female, which are mainly reared for milk and to some extent for breeding purposes, increased from 3110.7 thousand in 1977 to 5049.9 thousand in 1997, but declined to

4217 thousand in 2003 and 3870.34 thousand in 2007; witnessing an annual growth rate of 0.73 per cent. The population of in-milk bovine increased at the rate of 1.11 per cent per year during the same period. The total number of cows increased during the intervening period, but declined later on. It is interesting to note that the number of indigenous cows declined very sharply, whereas the number of crossbred cows increased at the annual compound growth rate of 0.06 per cent during 1990-2007; indicating a replacement of indigenous cows by crossbred cows. Further, the stock of other bovines consisting of permanently dry and infertile cows and buffaloes declined from 66.7 thousand to 43.63 thousand with the negative annual growth of 1.40 per cent during 1977-2007. However, the stock of adult bovine which had not calved even after attaining the age of calving increased up to 2003, but declined in 2007.

Classification of adult female bovine based on species indicates that stock of buffaloes increased at the rate of 1.06 per cent per annum, whereas the stock of indigenous cows experienced negative growth exceeding five per cent per annum. The growth rate comes to -0.17 per cent when the crossbred cows are also included. These differences in growth rates raised the share of buffaloes in adult female bovine maintained for milk and breeding purposes from 69.63 per cent in 1977 to 76.82 per cent in 2007. About 18.43 per cent bovine reared for milk purposes during 2007 were crossbred cows. Another silver lining is that the proportion of in-milk cows and buffaloes has increased from 62.26 per cent to 69.83 per cent during this period indicating a qualitative increase in the total bovine stock.

Density of Animals

Region-wise density of animals per hectare of net sown area (NSA), area under fodders and availability of fodders is presented in Table 6.3. It shows significant regional disparities in the stocking rates in the state. On an average, every hectare of NSA in the state sustained 1.94 bovine population. The number of animals per hectare of area under fodders was found to be 14.20 and per day per animal availability of fodders was observed to be 11.17 kgs in the state against the national average of 5 kgs (Government of India, 2006). The density of animals per hectare of NSA was the highest in the central region (2.15 animal) and the south-western region accounted for the least (1.49 animal). The central region had the highest bovine density of 15.13 animals per hectare of area under fodder, followed by the sub-mountain region 13.40 animals and the south-western region accounted for the lowest of 12.52 animals. Per day per animal availability of fodders was the highest in the south-western region (11.61 kgs), followed by central region (11.14 kgs) and sub-mountain region (10.46 kgs) respectively.

Table 6.2: Growth and Composition of Adult Bovine in Punjab

Category			*Population (000)*			*CGR (%)*
	1977	*1990*	*1997*	*2003*	*2007*	*(1977-2007)*
Adult Male	1599.4	876.1	484.4	540.9	336.96	-5.05
i. Buffaloes	249.9	147.7	125.2	99.6	74.75	-3.94
ii. Cattle	1349.5	728.4	359.2	441.3	262.21	-5.31
Adult Female Species	3110.7	4435.7	5049.9	4217.0	3870.34	0.73
i. Buffaloes	2166	3297.6	3752.1	3281.7	2973.19	1.06
ii. Total Cows	944.7	1138.1	1297.8	935.3	897.15	-0.I7
a) Indigenous Cows	944.7	432.8	328.9	142.5	183.84	-5.30
b) Crossbreed Cows	-	705.3	968.9	792.8	713.31	0.06
Type:						
In-milk	1936.7 (62.26)	2786.8 (62.83)	3285.8 (65.70)	3049 (72.30)	2702.5 (69.83)	1.11
Dry	999.6 (32.13)	1166.8 (26.30)	1266.0 (25.07)	922.0 (21.86)	957.9 (24.75)	-0.14
Breedable	2936.3 (94.39)	3953.6 (89.14)	4551.8 (90.14)	3971.0 (94.16)	3660.4 (94.58)	0.73
Not Calved	107.7 (3.47)	444.1 (10.01)	460.7 (9.12)	225.3 (5.35)	166.33 (4.29)	1.45
Others	66.7 (2.14)	38.0 (0.85)	37.4 (0.74)	20.7 (0.49)	43.63 (1.12)	-1.40

Figures in parentheses are the percentage to the total adult female species

Source: Livestock Censuses of Punjab (various years).

Therefore, per day per animal availability of fodders in the sub-mountain region was found to be the lowest in the state.

Table 6.3: Density of Animals Per Hectare of NSA, Area Under Fodder and Fodder Availability in Punjab, 2005-06

Regions	*Area Under Fodder ('000 ha)*	*Average Yield of Fodder (qtl/ha)*	*Total Production of Fodder ('000 qtl)*	*Per Hectare Number of Animal/s of*		*Per Day Per Animal Availability of Fodder (in kgs)*
				Net Sown Area	*Area under Fodder Crop*	
Region I	70.68	511.89	36180.61	2.12	13.40	10.46
Region II	342.50	615.51	210815.94	2.15	15.13	11.14
Region III	156.65	530.95	83174.73	1.49	12.52	11.61
State as a Whole	569.83	579.41	330171.29	1.94	14.20	11.17

Source: *Statistical Abstract of Punjab* (various years).

III

Growth of Milk Production

Milk production and its per capita availability in Punjab is presented in Table 6.4. Over the last three decades, the state has made progress in its milk production in leaps and bounds. The state currently occupies a much higher position in milk production owing to sustained and concerted efforts towards total dairy development in the state. A significant growth in milk production was observed during the last two decades. The total milk production in 1980-81 was 3.22 million tonnes which increased to 9.38 million tonnes during 2009-10. Punjab produces about 8.64 per cent of the country's total milk production. The growth is largely on account of both improvements in productivity and shift in priorities towards buffaloes and crossbred cattle. It is remarkable to note that the per capita per day availability showed a substantial increase in the state from 541 gms to 915 gms during the said period which is much higher compared to the national average of 258 gms per day. Further increases in per capita income and changing consumption pattern would lead to acceleration in demand for milk and milk products in the state, which would give a boost to this sector (Radhakrishna and Ravi, 1994; Gandhi and Mani, 1995; Kumar, 1998 and Dastagiri, 2001).

Table 6.4: Milk Production and Per Capita Availability of Milk in Punjab

	Punjab		*India*	
Year	*Milk Production (million tonnes)*	*Per Capita Availability (gms/day)*	*Milk Production (million tonnes)*	*Per Capita Availability (gms/day)*
1980-81	3.22 (10.18)	541	31.6	128
1985-86	4.03 (9.16)	597	44.0	160
1990-91	5.14 (9.53)	682	53.9	176
1995-96	6.42 (9.69)	798	66.2	197
2000-01	7.77 (9.64)	870	80.6	220
2005-06	8.90 (9.16)	930	97.1	241
2009-10	9.38(8.64)	915	108.5	258

Note: Figures in parentheses are percentages to all India milk production

Source: Statistical Abstract of Punjab, (various issues)

The growth in milk production during different phases of Operation Flood (OF) Programme in the state is presented in Table 6.5. During OF-I (1970-71 to 1980-81), milk production in the state increased significantly at the rate of 4.49 per cent per annum. The rate of growth in milk production during OF-II slowed down, but in the OF-III phase, it jumped at the rate of 4.86 per cent. The overall rate of growth of milk production during the period 1980-81 to 2009-10 was observed to be 3.96 per cent in the state, which was slightly less than the national level growth rate of 4.27 per cent.

The production of milk depends upon the productivity of milch animals and the total breedable population. Productivity of milch animals was considered on the basis of two factors: (a) average milk yield per milch animal; and (b) ratio of adult female in-milk to total adult females known as lactation efficiency. As the average milk yield per indigenous cow, crossbred cow and buffalo was 2.83 kgs, 9.05 kgs and 7.11 kgs respectively during 2005-06 in the state which was found to be more than the national average of 1.94 kgs per indigenous cow, 6.39 kgs per crossbred cow, and 4.28 kgs per buffalo (Government of India, 2007). It can be inferred that the average productivity went up substantially in the case of cows. There is an increase in milk yield of buffaloes also, but it is less sharp than that of crossbred cows. Buffaloes have higher yields than indigenous cows, however, crossbred cows are more productive than either indigenous cows or buffaloes. The lactation efficiency of dairy animals has also improved over time in the state. Among these milch animals, buffaloes and crossbred cows had the highest lactation efficiency compared to indigenous cows. Lactating efficiency in crossbred cows was 62.46 per cent in 1990 which increased to 65.13 per cent and 71.49 per cent in 1997 and 2005 respectively; whereas in the case of buffaloes, it increased from 63.48 per cent to 65.49 and 72.32 per cent respectively during the aforesaid periods; indicating qualitative improvement in the breeds of milch animals.

IV

Sources of Growth in Milk Production

Increase in population and productivity of milch animal are the two sources of growth in milk production. About 40.66 per cent growth in the bovine milk production during 1977-2005 was due to yield effect, 31.55 per cent due to population effect and the remaining 27.79 per cent due to interaction effect (Table 6.6). The contribution of yield effect increased from 42.74 per cent during 1977-90 to 53.73 and 60.24 per cent during 1990-97 and 1997-2005 respectively. The contribution of population effect showed a declining trend, i.e. from 42.46 per cent during 1977-90 to 38.15 per cent during 1990-97 and then to 34.58 per cent during 1997-2005. The same trend was observed in the case of interaction effect. It declined from 14.80 per cent during 1977-90 to 8.12 per cent and 5.18 per cent during 1990-97 and 1997-2005, respectively. The dominance of yield effect was true in the growth of milk production from the cows as well as buffaloes.

Table 6.5: Growth in Production of Milk during Operation Flood Phases in Punjab and India

Operation Flood Period		*Compound Growth Rates (%)*	
		Punjab	*India*
Phase I :	1970-71 to 1980-81	4.49*	4.51*
Phase II :	1980-81 to 1984-85	4.46*	6.91*
Phase III :	1985-86 to 1995-96	4.86*	4.23*
Post Phase-III :	1996-97 to 2005-06	2.80*	3.65*
After Phase I:	1980-81 to 2009-10	3.96*	4.27*

Note: * indicates that compound growth rates are significant at one per cent level

Source: Statistical Abstract of Punjab, (various issues)

Table 6.6: Percentage Contribution of Increase in Milch Animal Population, Productivity Growth and Interaction between Productivity and Population to Growth in Milk Production

Output	*Source of Contribution*	*1977-1990*	*1990-1997*	*1997-2005*	*1977-2005*
Bovine Milk	Population Effect	42.46	38.15	34.58	31.55
	Yield Effect	42.74	53.73	60.24	40.66
	Interaction Effect	14.80	8.12	5.18	27.79
Cow Milk	Population Effect	-	33.37	-47.01	11.38
	Yield Effect	-	57.88	157.44	82.45
	Interaction Effect	-	8.75	–10.43	6.17
Buffalo Milk	Population Effect	-	40.31	46.70	39.67
	Yield Effect	-	51.85	46.85	46.06
	Interaction Effect	-	7.84	6.45	14.27

Source: Kaur, 2008

A comparison of the relative contribution of sources of growth in the milk production of cows and buffaloes revealed that from 1990-97, the contribution of population effect in the case of cow milk was positive (33.37 per cent). However, it declined drastically during 1997-2005. Yield effect emerged as a very strong factor in the growth of cow milk production. The contribution of yield across the cow milk was 57.88 per cent during 1990-97 and it jumped to 157.44 per cent during 1997-2005; showing a very significant increase in yield levels of cow milk. The contribution of yield effect for the total period, i.e. during 1990-2005 was 82.45 per cent. The contribution of the interaction effect was 8.75 per cent in 1990-97 and became negative (-10.43%) during 1997-2005. It can be inferred that in the case of cow milk production, the contribution of yield factor consolidated over time and the effect of population weakened. In case of buffalo milk, both population and yield were major contributing factors during 1990-97, but its contribution declined in subsequent periods. During 1990-97, the contribution of population effect was 40.31 per cent; it then increased to 46.70 per cent during 1997-2005. The contribution of yield effect in percentage terms in the case of buffalo milk during 1990-97 was 51.85 per cent and it declined to 46.85 per cent during 1997-2005. Overall contribution of yield effect was 46.06 per cent during 1990-2005 and that of population effect was 39.67 per cent during the same period. The contribution of interaction effect was observed to be 14.27 per cent for buffalo milk production during 1990-2005. In a nutshell, it can be inferred that a structural shift in the composition of milk production had taken place in the state and distribution of animals have shifted from low to high milk yield animals. The productivity of milch animals, as measured by their yields, indicated a steady increase, reflecting the positive contribution of technological change in breeding and feeding.

V

Constraints and Policy Implications

Although Punjab has achieved a distinction by producing the highest milk production in the country, yet there are some major constraints which hamper the growth of the dairy sector in the state. Some of these basic problems require immediate attention of the planners and administrators for dairy development in the state. It is also desirable to resolve these problems so as to develop the dairy sub-sector on a sound footing. These problems are elaborated below:

Shortage of Fodders

The major constraint in livestock production in the state is the scarcity of fodder. In Punjab, fodder crops are mostly grown under irrigated conditions, which is a major source of green fodder to the animals. The state produced about 33.01 million tonnes of fodder from 0.56 million hectares of land during 2005-2006 (Government of Punjab, 2008). The cultivated area devoted to fodder production was 7.22 per cent of the total cultivated area during 2005-06. Apart from this, a small area under forests (2.83 lakh hactares), permanent pastures (0.05 lakh hactares) and barren and fallow lands (1.0 lakh hactares) was available for grazing the animals (Puri and Tiwana, 2007). Though the fodder availability in Punjab is the highest in the country, it is still not sufficient to meet the minimum requirements of green fodder for animals.

Table 6.7: Region-Wise Estimates for Green Fodder Availability and Requirements in Punjab, 2005-06

Regions	*Adult Bovine Population (000')*	*Fodder Requirement (Million Tonnes)*	*Fodder Availability (Million Tonnes)*	*Deficiency (Million Tonnes)*	*Deficiency as Percentage of Requirement*
I	522.4	7.62	3.61	4.01	52.62
II	2785.1	40.66	21.08	19.58	48.15
III	909.6	13.28	8.32	4.96	37.35
Total	4217.1	61.56	33.01	28.55	46.38

The estimates for green fodder availability as well as requirements in different regions of the state are presented in Table 6.7. These estimates reveal the fact that in Punjab, including the different regions, there was a deficit of stock of green fodder. Among regions, the central region had the highest availability of green fodder, while the sub-mountain region had the lowest. The fodder requirement in region I, II and III for adult bovines is 7.62 million tonnes, 40.66 million tonnes and 13.28 million tonnes respectively. The total deficit of green fodder in the state was 28.55 million tonnes. The deficiency of fodder as percentage to the requirement was the highest in region-I (52.62%) followed by region-II (48.15%) and region-III (37.35%). Overall, there was a deficit of 46.38 per cent of green fodder in the state. It is suggested that to reduce the demand and supply gap of fodders, the total area under fodders in the state has to be increased to 1062.675 thousand hectares which would be about 13.51 per cent of the total cropped area against the existing area of 7.22 per cent in the state (Kaur, 2008). So, fodder production must be increased substantially to provide sufficient feed of good quality.

Low Productivity of Animals

No doubt, the performance of Punjab's dairy sector appears to be impressive in terms of bovine population and total milk production. Unfortunately, yield of milch animals in the state is not in consonance with the levels attained in the developed countries. In spite of remarkably high potentials of milk compared to other states, existence of wide gaps in the yield of different milch animals was corral truth. The study revealed that the realised yield in the case of indigenous cows was 48.05 per cent of the potential yield, while in the case of crossbred cows and buffaloes realised yield was 39.43 and 72.29 per cent respectively of the potential yield in the state. Yield gaps both in absolute as well as relative terms are larger in the crossbred cows as compared to the buffaloes. This is interesting to note that buffalo yield is comparatively closer to the attainable yields. Thus, yield gap statistics suggests that there is a large potential which can be managed by exploiting the existing technologies and/or by replacing them with some appropriate need-based doable dairy technologies.

Animal Health Constraints

Since the introduction of an extensive crossbreeding programme, the susceptibility of these exotic breeds to various diseases has also increased. Though the state has been provisionally free from Foot and Mouth disease (FMD) as no such case was reported in the state during 2005-06 (Government of India, 2007), however, twenty outbreaks of Hamorthagic Septicalmia were reported from the districts Ludhiana, Ropar,

Kapurthala, Ferozepur, Amritsar, Jalandhar and Fatehgarh Sahib. And, about 201 animals were affected and 92 animals died from this disease. Beside these outbreaks, incidence of reproductive disorders in buffaloes and cows is quite common in the state. For instance, incidence of reproductive disorders was 19.11 per cent in buffaloes and 15.05 per cent in cows (Singh, 2004). Further, major reproductive disorders in buffaloes and cows were the anestrus and repeat breeding with a incidence of 31.98 per cent and 35.06 per cent respectively in Punjab. These diseases reduce milk potential of livestock and cause numerous economic losses to farmers. In India, livestock output worth Rs. 50 billion is lost annually due to such diseases (Birthal and Jha, 2005). It was about Rs. 540 crores in the Punjab due to the mastitis disease. Economic losses due to these diseases in Amritsar district were of Rs. 84.66 crores in 2001-02 (Singh et al. 2005). Therefore, to tackle the menace of anestrus, repeat breeding and other related problems in dairy animals, exclusive infertility campaigns and animal welfare days should be organised.

Not Calved Bovines

A large majority of indigenous/crossbred cattle as well as buffaloes fall in the category of 'not calved' adult females across these regions during various censuses thereby posing threats to the state's dairy industry. The high incidence of 'not calved' bovines is a serious matter of concern which may also be due to deterioration in maintenance, upkeep and diet of such animals. Therefore, the animal scientists have to disseminate their technologies to convert these unproductive milch animals to productive ones on one hand, while the planners and policy makers have to re-orient their policies to strengthen field infrastructures on the other.

Unproductive/Useless Animals

The problem of unproductive animals who are just wandering about in streets/fields and not yielding anything, but still managing to eat away some fodder which can be made available to other lactating animals who can give more milk must be taken on priority basis. These stray animals, besides adversely affecting milk production, are damaging the crops of the farmers and are becoming a traffic hazard. Therefore, it is suggested that these unproductive animals should be culled. It seems to be a desirable goal of policy makers to resolve this problem so as to put the dairy sector on a sound footing.

Some Future Policy Approaches

From the ongoing discussion, it is evident that scarcity of feed/fodder, quality of animals, veterinary care, etc. are the major constraints in raising milk production in the state. Therefore, there is need to improve the feed and animal resources both quantitatively and qualitatively. For increasing fodder production, measures should be taken in the sub-mountainous region where per animal availability of fodder is the least. More efforts are to be made for upgrading and replacement of indigenous cattle in the south-western districts of the state. Reproductive disorders, mainly anoestrous and repeat breeding, must be encountered in the state with the help of removing micro-nutrient deficiencies in the animal diet. Moreover, incidence of rising proportion of 'not-calved' bovines should also be solved at the earliest possible time.

REFERENCES

Birthal, P.S. and A.K. Jha (2005), 'Review on Emerging Trends in India's Livestock Economy: Implications for Development', *Indian Journal of Animal Sciences*, Vol. 75 (3), pp. 1227-32.

Birthal, P.S. (2008), 'Linking Small Holder Livestock Producers to Market: Issues and Approaches', *Indian Journal of Agricultural Economics*, Vol. 63 (1), pp. 19-37.

Dastagiri, M.B. (2001), 'Demand for Livestock Products in India: Current Status and Projections to 2020', *Agricultural Economics Research Review (Conference Proceedings)*, Agricultural Economics Research Association, New Delhi, pp. 176-80.

Gandhi, V.P. and G. Mani (1995), 'Are Livestock Products Rising in Importance? A Study of Growth and Behaviour of Their Consumption in India', *Indian Journal of Agricultural Economics*, Vol. 50 (3), pp. 283-93.

Government of India (2007), *Basic Animal Husbandary Statistics 2005-06*, Department of Animal Husbandry and Dairying, Ministry of Agriculture, Government of India, New Delhi.

Government of India (2006), *Indian Livestock Census*, Directorate of Economics and Statistics, Department of Agriculture and Cooperation, Ministry of Agriculture, New Delhi

Government of Punjab (2008), *Statistical Abstract of Punjab 2007*, Economic and Statistical Organisation, Punjab, Chandigarh.

Kaur, Parminder (2008) 'Role of Dairy Farming in the Structural Transformation in Agriculture in Punjab', *Unpublished Ph.D. Dissertation*, Punjab Agricultural University (PAU), Ludhiana.

Kumar, P. (1998), 'Food Demand and Supply Projections in India', *Agricultural Economics Policy Paper 98-01.* Indian Agricultural Research Review, New Delhi.

Minhas, B.S. and A. Vaidyanathan (1965), 'Growth of Crop Output In Indian–1951-52 to 1958-61: An Analysis of Component Elements', *Indian Journal of Agricultural Statistics*, Vol. 17 (2), pp. 32-8.

Puri, K.P. and U.S. Tiwana (2007), 'Forage Production Potential and Quality of Various Rotations Round the Year', Paper Presented in National Symposium on *A New Vista to Forage Crop Research* held at BCKV, Kalyani from September 10-11, 2007

Radhakrishna, R. and C. Ravi (1994), *Food Demand in India*, Centre for Economic and Social Studies, Hyderabad, Mimeu.

Singh, J. (2004), 'Study on Incidence of Reproductive Disorders in Dairy Animals vis-a-vis Various Management Practices', *Unpublished M.Sc. Thesis*, Department of Veterinary and Animal Husbandry Extension, Punjab Agricultural University (PAU), Ludhiana.

Singh, R., M. Kaur and M.K. Sekhon (2005), 'Occurrence of Diseases in Dairy Animals:An Economic Analysis', *Indian Journal of Dairy Science*, Vol. 58 (2), pp. 359-64.

7

Organic Farming for Sustainable Agriculture in Punjab

G.S. Romana

I

Introduction

One of the most important achievements during the last six decades of India's post-independence history is the attainment of self-sufficiency in food grains production. The state of Punjab has led the country in this much acclaimed revolutionary change. With better fertile land, water and human resources, the state has come to symbolise the success story of the Green Revolution. The Green Revolution made the country self-sufficient in food grains and Punjab's role in achieving food security is well recognised. In Punjab, the agricultural production, gross cropped area, irrigated area, cropping intensity and fertiliser use have increased tremendously over the period of time. Having only 1.53 per cent of the total geographical area of the country, the state contributed about 42 per cent of wheat, 29.5 per cent of paddy and 13 per cent of the total cotton production in the country during 2009-10. The cropping intensity in the state increased from 126 per cent in 1960-61 to 190 per cent in 2009-10. The increasing load of crops over per unit area has increased the demand for various inputs particularly the major soil nutrients like nitrogen, phosphorus and potash (NPK) from 762 thousand metric tonnes in 1980-81 to 1866 thousand metric tonnes in 2009-10 (Government of Punjab, 2012).

However, this vertical growth in the agriculture has occurred at the cost of degradation and depletion of natural resources such as soil fertility and water. Increasing cropping intensity along with maintaining productivity levels has led to depletion of both macro and micro nutrients in the soils (Dasgupta, 2000). The paddy, being nutrient responsive and high water requiring crop, has increased the fertiliser use on the one side, whereas it depleted the underground water table on the other side. To meet water requirement of the crop, the underground water table in the state declined at the rate of 29 cms to 43 cms per annum across the three agro-climatic zones in Punjab during 1990-2005. It has been estimated that the underground water table would go down more than 26 metres by the year 2023 compared to 16 metres in 2003 (Aulakh, 2004). And, during the next 15-20 years, a huge investment of about Rs. 3000 crores will be required for deepening the existing tubewells in the state (Government of Punjab, 2002). Interestingly, the average depth of the water table has increased from 3.15 metres in 1994 to 6.69 metres in 2004 in the districts of south-west Punjab where the underground water is brackish in nature and not fit for repeated irrigations (Romana, 2006). The ever-increasing use of farm inputs followed by the rising cost of cultivation and stagnant yield have reduced the profit margins of farmers from this crop.

On the other side, more and more use of inputs in the wheat crop have also increased cultivation cost, however, rise in the wheat yield over time kept this crop always economical in the state. Now, due to the mono-cropping pattern of wheat-paddy over a long period of time, per hectare yield of wheat has started decreasing in the new millennium. Moreover, the share of cotton crop in the gross cropped area of the state did not increase over time. It remained around 15 per cent of gross cropped area till the mid-1990s. After 1995-96, the rising incidence of pests on cotton especially the American bollworm seriously eroded its productivity and caused a reduction in the area under cotton. But after the advent of Bt cotton hybrids since 2004-05, the cotton productivity is stable over time. Further, the increasing level of fertilisers to maintain the same yield level confirmed the decreasing fertility status of soils. Per hectare consumption of fertilisers in Punjab increased from 1.33 kgs in 1960-61 to 447.37 kgs in 2009-10; an increase of 335 times. The all India average of per hectare fertiliser consumption is still less than 100 kgs (Government of India, 2007). The number of tractors, per thousand hectares, increased from 2.4 during 1964-65 to 102 in 2009-10 in Punjab.

This has further led to a high degree of diminishing returns to inputs. The per annum per hectare trend growth of net returns in wheat (on variable cost at 1970-71 prices) was minus 3.51 per cent during the 1970s, which however, improved to 3.93 per cent during the 1980s but declined to minus 0.35 per cent during the 1990s. The corresponding trend growth rate in paddy was 1.90 per cent during the 1980s but declined to minus 2.83 per cent during the 1990s. The trend growth rate in cotton declined from 9.21 per cent during the 1980s to minus 14.24 per cent during the 1990s (Ghuman, 2002). The negative trend growth rate of return during the 1990s resulted in the shrinkage of farmers' income and piling up their debt-burden. Beleaguered in this severe crisis, the farmers in Punjab started committing suicides (Gill and Singh, 2006; Singh, 2008).

For sustainable agricultural development, crop yield must increase along with rising costs of cultivation so as to balance the increasing cost of production over a period of time and to ensure the net positive returns over these costs. The declining trend in productivity over a period of time has, however, made these crops unsustainable. This chapter, keeping in view these facts, examines the unsustainability of the presently dominant cropping pattern in Punjab agriculture as well as builds a case in favour of organic farming for sustainable agriculture in the state. This chapter has been divided into four sections. Section I introduces the problem of Punjab agriculture in brief. Section II examines the various parameters that question the sustainability of its agriculture in the long run. The organic farming as an alternative to chemical agriculture has been examined in Section III. And, Section IV deals with policy issues to make organic farming a viable option.

II

Parameters of Unsustainability of Punjab Agriculture

There are a number of ecological and social factors, interalia, which may be held responsible for this. These are:

2.1 Ground Water Quality

The quality of water used for irrigation plays a significant role in raising agriculture production. Water quality not only affects the crop growth during a particular irrigation cycle, but also influences the soil productivity for subsequent crop production. In Punjab, out of the total cultivable area, about 75 per cent is irrigated by ground water through the tubewells and 25 per cent by surface water through network of canals. Taksi and Chopra (2002) found that in the south-western Punjab, ground water quality deteriorated with the depth of soil. Table 7.1 illustrates that, at the depth of 10 metres, fresh water (quality water) was available in 62.18 per cent of the area, whereas marginal water and poor quality (unfit) water was available in 20.54 per cent and 17.28 per cent of the total area respectively. Interestingly, with the increase in ground depth, the fresh water reservoir reduced, while the area under marginal and poor quality water increased. At the soil depth of 30 metres, the area under fresh water reduced to 28.75 per cent, whereas the area under poor quality water increased to 50.15 per cent.

Table 7.1: Depth-wise Distribution of Ground Water Quality in the Cotton Belt of Punjab, 2002

Quality of Ground Water	*Percentage of Area Distributed at the Soil Depth*				
	10 metres	*15 metres*	*20 metres*	*25 metres*	*30 metres*
Fresh	62.18	53.36	55.14	38.48	28.75
Marginal	20.54	24.24	17.00	27.00	21.10
Unfit	17.28	22.40	27.86	34.52	50.15

Source: Takshi and Chopra (2002).

Romana's study (2006) also observed that that in paddy-wheat growing Bhikhi and Phool blocks of south-western Punjab, the quality of water has deteriorated from Category I to Category II with the increase in the depth of water table (Table 7.2). The situation is quite different in Muktsar block, where the quality of water has improved from Category IV to Category II, because the underground water there was of already poor quality due to the waterlogged conditions. Thus, irrigation with poor quality of underground water has affected productivity of both rice and wheat over a period of time in these blocks. On the other side, in the cotton-wheat growing blocks where the ground water is already saline and unfit for irrigation, the rising water table has further aggravated the problem by increasing the soil salinity and water logging areas, thus, decreasing quality of water from Category II to Category III. The increasing salinity has affected the productivity of both cotton and wheat.

Choudhary, et al. (2001) studied the affects of sodic irrigation waters on the yield and fibre quality of cotton in Punjab. They pointed out that plant height and fibre quality in cotton decreased to some extent with the application of more and more sodic water. Takshi and Chopra (2002) while studying the monitoring and assessment of ground water resources in Punjab state also reported the underground water quality is saline in about 40 per cent area of the state that falls mostly in south-western Punjab. Similarly, Bajwa, et al. (1992) also found that the level of residual sodium carbonate (RSC) in irrigation water had increased through continuous irrigations with brackish water in cotton-wheat rotation areas of Punjab. Thus, all these studies state that the deteriorating quality of ground water has reduced the quantity as well as quality of agricultural production in the state over a period of time.

2.2 Depletion of Soil Fertility

No doubt, cropping intensity has increased from 126 per cent in 1960-61 to 190 per cent in 2009-10 along with improving productivity levels of main crops in the state. In fact, this intensive agriculture has depleted the macro- as well as micro-nutrients in the soils of the state. The increasing trend of important nutrient use in the state to maintain the same yield status of the crops shows the decreasing fertility level of Punjab soils. For instance, in Punjab, fertiliser consumption in the form of NPK has tremendously increased from 762 thousand tonnes in 1980-81 to 1866 thousand tonnes in 2009-10. Paddy-wheat is an exhaustive cropping system in the state. Against an addition of 300 kgs of NPK per hectare in this cropping system every year, nearly 500-800 kgs of NPK per hectare get consumed (Nayyar, 2002). Thus, nutrients in the form of NPK are consumed at a rate faster than their application by this system. A net deficit of 200-500 kgs of NPK per hectare per year leads to decreasing fertility of soils and hence, it will reduce the productivity of both paddy and wheat, if is not supplemented.

Table 7.2: Depth-wise Water Quality in Paddy-Wheat Growing Blocks in South-West Punjab

Year	*Bhikhi*		*Phool*		*Muktsar*	
	Depth (metres)	*Category**	*Depth (metres)*	*Category*	*Depth (metres)*	*Category**
1994	2.7	I	4.8	I	1.95	IV
1999	6.5	II	9.5	II	2.1	III
2004	13	II	17.5	II	3.8	II
Year	Jhunir		Sangat		Lambi	
1994	8.6	II	11	II	8	II
1999	6.5	III	7.5	II	3.8	III
2004	7	III	7	III	5.3	III

Source: Romana, G.S. (2006), * Category I – Quality Water, II – Medium Quality, III and IV – Poor Quality, Unusable.

Romana (2006) found that in paddy-wheat crop rotations, the level of P, Zinc and other micro-nutrients has increased over the period of time to maintain the yield levels of these crops. The quantity of nitrogen and phosphorus has increased in the case of paddy from 72 kgs and 5 kgs per hectare in 1994 to 170 kgs and 48 kgs per hectare in 2004 respectively, whereas in the case of wheat these nutrients increased from 117 kgs and 48 kgs to 174 kgs and 72 kgs per hectare respectively during the same period (Table 7.3). Further, the use of zinc and other micro-nutrients has also increased from 8 kgs and 1 kg per hectare to 27 kgs and 10 kgs per hectare during 1994-2004 in the paddy crop. The overall average annual increase in the use of above

Table 7.3: Fertiliser Uses in Paddy-Wheat and Cotton-Wheat Rotation in South-Western Punjab, 1994-2004

Crop	*Nitrogen (N) (kgs/ha)*			*Phosphorus (P) (kgs/ha)*			*Zinc (Zn) (kgs/ha)*			*Others* (kgs/ha)*			*Annual Av. Increase (%)*			
	1994	*1999*	*2004*	*1994*	*1999*	*2004*	*1994*	*1999*	*2004*	*1994*	*1999*	*2004*	*N*	*P*	*Zn*	*Others*
Paddy	72	127	170	5	18	48	8	23	27	1	1	10	13.6	86	23.8	90
Wheat	117	140	174	48	57	72	0.2	0	0.1	1	0	0.7	4.9	5	5	3
P-W System	189	267	344	53	75	120	8.2	23	27.1	2	1	10.7	8.2	12.6	23	43.5
Cotton	40	69	129	16	8	43	0.3	1	8	0.2	0	0.2	22.2	16.9	256.7	Nil
Wheat	111	136	170	44	55	73	0	1	4	0.2	0.3	9	5.3	6.6	NA	440
C-W System	151	205	299	60	63	116	0.3	2	12	0.4	0.3	9.2	9.8	9.3	390	220

Note: * Includes manganese, iron, sulphur, gypsum and bio fertiliser.

Source: Romana, (2006).

nutrients is comparatively more in the case of paddy crop compared to wheat crop because paddy crop responded better to these nutrients over wheat.

Further, on an average, application of nitrogen and phosphorus in cotton has increased from 40 kgs and 16 kgs per hectare in 1994 to 129 kgs and 43 kgs per hectare in 2004 respectively at the annual growth rate of 22.2 per cent and 16.9 per cent. The use of zinc as a micro-nutrient has also increased from 0.3 kg per hectare to 8 kgs per hectare during the same period. Similarly, in wheat crop, the use of nitrogen and phosphorus has also increased from 111 kgs and 44 kgs to 170 kgs and 73 kgs per hectare respectively during 1994-2004 along with zinc and other micro-nutrients from zero and 0.2 kg per hectare to 4 kgs and 9 kgs per hectare respectively during the same period. Here again, an increase in the nutrient consumption was more in the cotton over the wheat crop.

Brar and Chibba (1994) also reported that the fertility of Punjab soils (Table 7.4) has reduced with the deficiency of nitrogen and phosphorus contents increasing over the years. The fertility of soils was low in the form of nitrogen (N) and phosphorus (P) in 52 per cent and 16 per cent of the blocks in Punjab during 1970-77. These proportions have grown to 67 per cent and 44 per cent, during the 1981-90 period respectively; indicating rising incidence of soil degradation in Punjab. However the concentration of potash (K) has improved over this period of time.

Table 7.4: Percentage of Blocks with Low Fertility Soils in the Form of N, P and K in Punjab

Fertility Status	*Percentage of Blocks during 1970-77 with the Deficiency of*			*Percentage of Blocks during 1981-90 with the Deficiency of*		
	N	*P*	*K*	*N*	*P*	*K*
Low	52	16	13	67	44	-
Medium	48	65	58	33	55	43
zHigh	-	19	29	-	1	57

Source: Brar, 1979; Brar and Chhibba, 1994.

Further, according to the report of the Indian Council of Agriculture Research, most of the soils in Punjab are deficient in organic carbon, which has come down from 0.5 per cent in the 1960s to 0.2 per cent in 2002. Organic carbon is an important and vital constituent of the soil health. It improves the biological activities of the soils. In a nutshell, over a period of time, the cultivation of paddy-wheat and cotton-wheat system has reduced the fertility of soils in the state. Declining soil fertility is one of the important reasons behind stagnant/decreasing productivity of paddy, cotton and wheat in Punjab.

2.3 Growing Incidence of Pests

After the coming of the Green Revolution, the cultivation of high-yielding and fertiliser responsive dwarf varieties of paddy and wheat, increasing cropping intensity, monoculture of paddy-wheat rotation, higher use of agro-chemicals, etc., has increased the problem of different weeds, pests including insects and diseases on the crops in Punjab. Over the period of time, the problem of new weeds like Kanki (*Ischeamum rugosum)* and Gharilla (*Ceasulia axillaris)* in paddy, 'Itsit' in cotton, Jangli palak (*Rumax spinosus*) and Maina (*Medicago denticulate)* in wheat has become serious with *swank* and *gulli-danda* as the predominant weeds in these crops respectively (Table 7.5). In paddy, butachlor (a weedicide) had been extensively used for the control of different weeds. With the continuous use of this herbicide, certain tolerant weed species like kanki (*Ischaemum rugosum),* gharilla (*Caesulia* sp) and other species like *Sphenoclea* species and *Ammania* species have emerged (Kolar and Mehra, 1992).

Table 7.5: Changing Levels of Pest-Incidence on Important Crops in Punjab

Crop	*Earlier, Around the 1970s*	*Now, at Present*
Weeds		
Paddy	*Echinocloa* (swank) was predominant.	*Echinocloa* is predominant. New weeds in some pockets have emerged: *Ischeamum rugosum* (Kanki), *Ceasulia axillaris* (Gharilla),

		Sphenochlea zylancia.
Wheat	Broad leaf weeds and wild oats were predominant.	*Phalaris minor* (Gulli danda) is predominant. New weeds in some areas are *Rumex spinosus* (Jangli palak), *Medicago denticulate*, (Maina). *Phalaris minor* has become resistant to Isoprturon through continuous use.
Cotton	Weed-free crop	*Itsit* is a serious weed of cotton
Insects/Pests		
Paddy	Pest-free crop	Yellow stem borer and leaf folders are the key pests. Other important pests are white-backed plant hopper and rice hispa.
Wheat	Pest-free crop	Aphids, armyworm, shoot fly and pink stem borer are becoming important pests.
Cotton	Cotton whitefly was a minor pest and American bollworm was reported in localised areas.	Cotton whitefly has become a key pest due to excessive use of synthetic pyrethroids. American bollworm has become an epidemic eroding the productivity of the crop completely.
Diseases		
Wheat	Yellow and brown rust	High-yielding resistant varieties have been developed, but some have become susceptible to new races of brown rust.
	Flag smut	Wheat–rice rotation has minimised its incidence.
	Karnal bunt	Karnal bunt became widespread. The other diseases like head scab and leaf blight have become important now.
Paddy	Disease-free crop	Bacterial leaf blight (BLB) is a major disease in PR106 and Pusa44 varieties. Other observed diseases are sheath blight, sheath rot, false smut, kernal smut
Cotton	Disease-free crop	Cotton leaf curl virus (CLCV) is a serious disease of cotton.

Source: Department of Agronomy, Entomology and Pathology, PAU Ludhiana.

Further, it is to be noted that paddy was a pest-free crop in the 1970s, but now the yellow stem borer and leaf folder are the key pests of this crop. The other important pests of paddy are white-backed plant hopper and rice hispa. Similarly, wheat was also a zero pest crop in the 1970s but now with the appearance of aphids and armyworm, the average number of insecticide sprays on wheat has also increased. In cotton, out of more than 160 insects/pests of this crop in India, 16 are of economic importance in different zones of the country. Among these, cotton jassid, whitefly, pink bollworm, spotted bollworm and American bollworm are pests of national concern damaging the crop in all the cotton-growing zones of the country. In Punjab, the pest situation on cotton has changed considerably during the last three decades and attained a dangerous proportion in the cotton-wheat rotation zone. For instance, American bollworm and whitefly, which were minor pests of cotton in the 1970s, have now become key pests on cotton after the mid-1990s. The tobacco caterpillar is another emerging pest of cotton in future (Dhawan, et al. 2000). Earlier, termites was a problem of wheat in the cotton-wheat rotation zone, but now a number of aphids, armyworm and American bollworm have been causing serious damage.

Over the period of time, new diseases, like head scab, leaf blight, ear-cockle, tundu in wheat and sheath blight, sheath rot and kernel smut in paddy, have appeared (Sokhi et al., 1992). Cotton, which was a disease-free crop in the 1970s, has been infested now with cotton leaf curl virus (CLCV). Since mid-1990s, the CLCV has been a silent killer of cotton crop (Singh et al., 1994). Research done by Romana (2006) also confirmed the increasing number of harmful insects in the cotton belt of Punjab. The average number of insects in paddy-wheat growing blocks has increased from 4 to 11, whereas in cotton-wheat growing blocks from 5 to 11 during 1994-2004 (Table 7.6).

Thus, with the introduction of short stature high-yielding varieties of wheat, paddy and cotton, the problem of weeds, insects/pests and diseases have become more serious pushing back the yield/productivity of these crops considerably. Resultantly, the dependence of agriculture on agro-chemicals

Table 7.6: Harmful Insects of Important Crops in the Cotton Belt of Punjab

Year	*Paddy-Wheat Growing Blocks*			*Cotton-Wheat Growing Blocks*			*Average of Blocks Growing*	
	Bhikhi	*Phool*	*Muk-tsar*	*Jhu-rni*	*San-gat*	*Lambi*	*Paddy-Wheat*	*Cotton-Wheat*
1994	3	4	4	5	4	5	4	5
1999	6	6	8	9	6	9	7	8
2004	10	9	13	13	7	14	11	11
Average	6	6	8	9	6	9	7	8

Source: Romana, (2006).

is increasing over a period of time. As such, the cost of cultivation has risen enormously in the state.

2.4 Pesticide Residue

It is true that pesticides/insecticides played a great role in controlling the pests/insects from infecting the crops, animals and human beings. Increasing use of these chemicals have greatly increased the agricultural production and saved millions of lives from insect-borne diseases. However, the mono-cropping pattern over time has made many pests/insects like American bollworm, spotted bollworm, whitefly, etc. more serious. Ultimately, pesticides have been highly exploited in this belt against these pests. Punjab constituted 16 per cent of the total consumption of pesticides in India and, further, more than 90 per cent of these pesticides are used in the cultivation of paddy, cotton and vegetables. The indiscriminate use of pesticides over a period of time has caused pollution in our food chain and the environment. The pesticide residue studies in various food components and the environment have been conducted in the Department of Entomology, Punjab Agricultural University Ludhiana from time to time. These studies have revealed the presence of various pesticide residues in different food and environmental components as:

(a) Soil and Crop Produce: Large proportions of pesticides applied to plants reach the soil and the soil acts as a reservoir for these chemicals. Earlier studies by the Punjab Agricultural University on pesticide residues in soils revealed the presence of mainly DDT (Di-chloro Di-phenyl Tri-chloro ethane) followed by HCH, Lindane, Methyl Parathion 50EC, Phorate, etc. The highest mean level of DDT (0.08 mg kg $^{-1}$) was found in the cotton-growing area which was four times more than the mean level of 0.017 mg kg^{-1} for Punjab soils (Kalra and Chawla, 1983). Similarly, Singh and Dhawan (2001) reported the residues of Colfos 40 EC (Ehtion + Cypermethrin) in soil, cotton seed and cotton lint in the cotton-growing area of the state. These residues remained above the minimum detecting limits for about 7 days after the spray.

Similarly, Kumar (1978), Sharma and Aggarwal (1988), Singh, et al. (1990), Singh, et al. (1991), Battu, et al. (1992) and Singh, et al. (2001) studied the residues of commonly used synthetic as well as non-synthetic insecticides in the soils, cotton seed and cotton lint in cotton-growing blocks of Punjab. All these studies found the residues of different insecticides / pesticides in soils, cottonseed and cotton lint. Although these residues were found in very small quantities and even for a shorter period of time yet these are polluting the environment, soil health as well as crop produces. Singh, et al. (2001) in the study conducted in the Department of Entomology, PAU Ludhiana found the residues of about 11 insecticides in the first picking of cotton crop in south-west Punjab. Thus, excessive use of pesticides in cotton is a great curse for the farmers as well as for the society as a whole.

(b) Milk and Milk Products: Though it is very difficult to produce crops that contain zero chemical residue, yet pesticide residues in food items is a matter of serious concern. All living things are exposed to the pesticide-contaminated feed. Animals feeding on this contaminated feed ultimately produce contaminated milk and meat. The studies conducted in this direction have identified the residues of different organo-chlorine insecticides in various food items and cattle-feed (Table 7.7). During 1976-80, detectable amounts of DDT and HCH residues were found in all the 215 samples of bovine-milk collected from different localities of Punjab (Kalra and Chawla,

1983). Out of these, residue level exceeded the maximum residue limit (MRL) of 1.25 mg per kg (1.25 mg kg^{-1}) in 81 per cent of the samples. Again during 1985-86, all 142 samples of animal-milk were found contaminated with DDT and HCH (Anonymous, 1989). Further, 70 per cent and 49 per cent of these milk samples exceeded the MRL for DDT and HCH respectively. Similarly, about 50 per cent of the milk samples collected during 1989-93 were contaminated with DDT and HCH above their respective MRL (ICMR 1993). Kalra and Chawla (1983) also found that all the samples of popular brands of butter were contaminated with DDT and HCH residues, but below their respective MRL during 1983. Further, during 1989, again all 95 samples of butter were found to be contaminated with these pesticides but within the MRL (Anonymous, 1989).

(c) Cereals: Wheat grown in the cotton-wheat rotation also got contaminated with these pesticides. Joia, et al. (1978) found DDT and HCH residues in almost all 140 samples of wheat flour collected from different cities in Punjab. Sixty-one per cent of the samples contained DDT residues above the MRL of 0.01 mgs per kg. During 1989, however, only one out of the thirty samples was contaminated with DDT residues above the MRL of 0.01 mgs per kg. Although the ban on the use of DDT and HCH in agriculture introduced during 1988 has reduced their residue in the cereals, but over use of other pesticides is posing a great threat to food items and to the society.

(d) Human Milk: Mother's milk is the primary food for an infant. Kalra and Chawla (1983) found that all 130 samples of mother's milk collected from Punjab during 1979-80 were contaminated with residues of DDT and HCH at a far higher level (DDT 0.52 mgs and HCH 0.18 mgs per kg of milk) than reported in other countries of the world and MRL of 0.01 mgs per kg of milk. The problem was more severe in the cotton belt of Punjab where use of pesticides is comparatively more. The contamination level of DDT and HCH in 122 samples of mother's milk analysed during 1988-90 from the cotton belt of Punjab was almost high from the previous samples (DDT 0.55 and HCH 0.26 mgs per kg of milk) (Joia and Battu, 1990). However, the analysis of 22 samples during 1999-2000 revealed the low level of DDT (0.07 mgs) only while no HCH contamination was found (Anonymous, 2000)

Table 7.7: Pesticide Residues in Different Food Items in Punjab, 1976-2000

Year	*Samples Analysed (No.)*	*Contaminated Samples (No.)*	*Nature of Residue*	*Samples Above MRL**	*References*
			Bovine Milk		
1976-80	215	215	DDT	174	Kalra and
		215	HCH	75	Chawla (1983)
1985-86	142	142	DDT	99	Anonymous
		142	HCH	69	(1989)
1989-93	263	257	DDT	133	ICMR (1993)
		236	HCH	145	
1999-2K	24	2	DDT	nil	Anonymous
		23	HCH	23	(2000)
			Butter		
1983	120	120	DDT	nil	Kalra and
		120	HCH	nil	Chawla (1983)
1989	95	95	DDT	nil	Anonymous
		95	HCH	nil	(1989)
			Cereals		
1978	140	140	DDT	85	Joia et al. (1978)
1984-85	30	30	DDT	1	Anonymous
	30	30	HCH	nil	(1989)
			Human Milk		
1979-80	130	130	DDT- 0.52	130	Kalra and
	130	130	HCH - 0.18	130	Chawla (1983)
1989-90	122	122	DDT - 0.55	122	Joia and Battu
	122	122	HCH - 0.26	122	(2000)
1999-2K	22	22	DDT- 0.07	nil	Gill (2000)
			Animal Feed and Fodder		
1990-98	105	85	DDT	nil	Anonymous
	105	105	HCH	nil	(2000)

* MRL = 0. 01 mgs/kg for cereals and human milk, 1.25 mgs/kg for bovine milk, 0.1 mgs/kg for animal feed. Residual limit of DDT had decreased while that of HCH still remained above its MRL in the samples.

(e) Animal Feed: Although use of DDT and HCH were banned in agriculture in 1988, but these are still easily available in the market and farmers are occasionally using them against the cotton pests. Further, these pesticides were openly used in the malaria control programmes of the health department and have recently been banned. The pesticides applied to fodder and cereals directly contaminate the animals' feed. The wheat straw was highly contaminated with DDT and HCH residues. The animals feeding on such contaminated feed, thus, produce contaminated milk, eggs and meat. In the recent years (1990-98), although the residual level of pesticides especially of the DDT and HCH was below their respective MRL of 0.1 mgs per kg in 81 per cent of the contaminated samples (Anonymous, 1989), but a large number of pesticides and fertilisers used in agriculture still posed a serious concern for human health in the state.

Thus, over the period of time, uses of pesticides in different crops have polluted the whole scenario and their residual effect in the daily used food items can be clearly seen from the above reports.

2.5 *Environmental Pollution*

In the cotton-wheat and paddy-wheat crop cultivation, overuse of agro-chemicals, especially pesticides over the period of time has made the environment unhygienic by polluting the soil, water and air. The rural, as well as urban, population is now forced to live under the pesticide umbrella. Thus, exposure to the polluted atmosphere is resulting in many incurable diseases in human beings. Gurunadha Rao, et al. (2004) while studying the assessment of ground water quality in Ludhiana and Muktsar districts of Punjab reported that with the continuous use of nitrogenous and phosphatic fertilisers in the cotton–wheat and paddy-wheat crop rotations, the concentration of Chloride, Sulphate, Nitrate as N and Fluoride content in ground water has increased (>5 mgs/litre) above the standard limit (1.5 mgs/litre) of WHO in about 60 per cent and 75 of the Mukatsar district, respectively. Thus, cultivation of cotton, paddy and wheat over a period of time has polluted the underground water. In another study, Josan, et al. (1996) found that the irrigations with saline and sodic irrigation water, prevailing in south-west Punjab, adversely affecting the soil health. The sodicity as well as salinity increased in the soils of the state.

Recognising that the environment is a complex composition of a large variety of variables such as soil, water, pest resistance, bio-diversity, air pollution, etc., Singh's study (2004) tried to quantify some of these factors and estimate their effects on the paddy yield by using the Cobb-Douglas production function as:

$$Y = 3.1830\ S^{-0.\,0367}\ W^{0.\,.3610\,**}\ P^{0.\,1850\,*} \quad (R^2 = 0.5796^{**})$$

Note: * 5 per cent level of significance and ** 1 per cent level of significance

The major variables that could explain the fall in the paddy yield (Y) were the depletion of soil fertility (S) measured by increase in the use of micro-nutrients, fall in the water table (W) making irrigation costlier and rising use of pesticides, particularly the weedicides (P). These three variables explained the decline in rice productivity by 58 per cent (R^2 =0.5796), whereas the depleting water table (W) alone explained 36 per cent (with regression coefficient value 0.3610) yield in this crop. The increasing use of weedicides (P) had 18.5 per cent (with regression coefficient value 0.1850) and micro-nutrients (S) as 3.7 per cent (with regression coefficient value 0.0367) effect on fall in the average yield of paddy in Punjab during the past 20 years.

Further, the total factor productivity (TFP) growth in paddy and cotton over a period of time showed that in spite of the higher and higher use of inputs, it was difficult to sustain the output growth of these crops and thus, the TFP was declining (Romana, 2006). For the crop to be sustainable, the TFP index must be positive and high. The TFP growth in these crops is declining due to deteriorating soil health, depletion of water resources, resurgence of sucking pests, pest resistance, pesticide residue problem, pollution of soil health, air, water, etc. over the time period.

2.6 Farmers' Perceptions

Farmers, actual sufferers of the ill-effects of the present cropping systems in south-west Punjab, were also assessed (Romana 2006). About 75 per cent of the farmers reported the increasing problem of joint pains, asthma, rusting of teeth, hypertension and diabetes in the cotton-wheat growing blocks in 2004, while 65 per cent of the paddy-wheat growers reported the same problems over the last decade (Table 7.8). Further, among the cotton-growers, 55 per cent reported the problems of cancer and heart attack. Half the population from both paddy-wheat and cotton-wheat growing blocks felt that reddening, irritation and early weak eyesight were some of the health-hazards becoming common among the adults and children in the sampled villages these days. There was hardly any such problem before.

Regarding the animal health, 85 per cent of the farmers from both cotton-wheat and paddy-wheat growing blocks were of the view that over the last decade, on an average, milk yield in buffaloes has decreased from an average 14 -15 litres to 7-8 litres per day per animal respectively. About 55 per cent farmers reported many reasons for lower milk yield like polluted feed, increased incidence of diseases like more tics (sucking insects), choking of milking teats, breeding problems, etc.

Air pollution, an environmental hazard, was reported by more than 80 per cent of sampled farmers. The fresh air in the villages has now been replaced by the foul smell emanating from stagnated water full of stinking pesticides and smoke clouds from burning of paddy and wheat straw. It is very hard to breathe outside in the open sky during the harvesting period of the paddy and wheat crop. Further, it is very difficult to move along the cotton and paddy fields often sprayed with pesticides.

Further, 75 per cent of the paddy growers responded that the concentration of carbon dioxide and pesticide poison is increasing in the air causing many secondary diseases like burning of eyes, asthma, etc. Likewise, 90 per cent of the farmers from both cotton-wheat and paddy-wheat growing blocks confirmed the foul smell of pesticide gases during the crop season. All respondents have also reported the contamination of food items caused by overuse of agro-chemicals. Farmers were of the view that quality of roti and milk has deteriorated over a period of time. They have to consume another meal after 2-3 hours as the nutritive value of roti has come down. Earlier, there was no need to consume the meal for the whole day as the wheat was of better quality, enriched with more food nutrients. Also, the quality of milk has deteriorated over time. The taste and food value of milk is comparatively poor than in the earlier times. This is because cereals and animals are highly exposed to agro-chemicals whose contamination is polluting the food items and animal products. Apart from these, all the paddy growers in south-west Punjab have mentioned the most serious impact of water table falling. They reported the average annual fall of the water table as 0.80 metres. On the other hand, the farmers from the cotton-wheat growing blocks are more worried about the rising water table that is increasing in the waterlogged areas.

Table 7.8: Health Hazards and Ecological Implications of Cotton-Wheat and Paddy-Wheat Rotation in Sampled Villages of the Cotton Belt of Punjab

Implications	*1994*	*1999*	*2004*	*Farmers (%)*
Deteriorating Human Health	Joint pains were only at the old age, very few problems.	Problems were there but comparatively low.	Joint pains, asthma, rusting of teeth, Diabetes increasing.	75 (C-W)* 65 (P-W)**
	Very rare deaths by this cause.	Not very common.	Cancer, heart attacks and deaths are common.	55 (C-W)
	No problem till 40, very rare in children.	Problem persists but not so serious.	Eyesight weakens early, even in children.	50 (Both)
Deteriorating Animal Health	Better yield @ 14 kgs/ day, more productive.	Yield was better @ 10 kgs /day, diseases were less.	Poor milk yield @ 7 kgs per day, more diseases.	85 (Both)
	No tics, hardly any repeat case.	Repeats more, tics were rare.	Repeats more, tics problem increasing.	85 (Both)

Air Pollution	Hardly any problem due to no burning of wheat straw was there.	Problem was not so serious.	Due to straw burning co_2 conc. high, causing asthma.	50 (C-W) 90 (P-W)
	No problem at all, healthly environment.	Problem was there but not so serious.	Foul smell of pesticide, not easy to breathe.	90 (Both)
Drug Addiction in Rural Youth	Hardly 25 per cent take drugs. Liquor, and cigarettes, only.	Ratio was around 70 per cent Liquor, *bhuki*, poppy and cigarettes.	More than 90 per cent youth are drug-addicted. Liquor, *bhuki*, poppy, fancy injections, cigarettes, etc.	90 (Both) 80 (C-W)
Work Culture	Work was done as worship, avoid labour.	Work culture was not so disturbed.	Youths avoid work, can't work, weak and druggy, prefer casual labour.	60 (C-W) 80 (P-W)
Pesticide Contamination	High quality meals, no need to eat for 8-10 hours.	Almost similar taste but slightly better.	Roti not so tasty, have to take meals after 2-3 hours.	100 (Both)
	Tasty and healthy milk, easy to digest.	Almost the same quality.	Bitter and contaminated milk, less nutritive, one could not drink much.	100 (Both)

* C W - Cotton-Wheat growing farmers.
**PW - Paddy-Wheat growing farmers.

Source: Romana, 2006.

Further, more than 90 per cent of the rural youths in this zone have been reported to be trapped in the clutches of the drug mafia. All types of drugs are easily available in these villages. The continuous failure of cotton crops after the mid-1990s and the decreasing size of holdings year after year have made the rural youth frustrated and drug addictive. Another limitation of agriculture is the deteriorating work culture among the youth. Eighty per cent of the farmers in the paddy-wheat area and 60 per cent in the cotton-wheat area have reported that youths in agriculture prefer to do the easy and machine-operated jobs. They avoid heavy work and prefer to get it done through casual labour irrespective of their cost and efficiency of work.

Thus, a chain of problems persists in the villages that have made rural life totally miserable. Both cotton and paddy crops are feeding the society with certain economic, social and ecological problems over time.

III

Organic Farming : An Answer to Chemical Agriculture

Organic farming is a production system which avoids the use of synthetically manufactured fertilisers, pesticides and growth regulators. Organic farming system relies on crop rotations, crop residues, animal manure, legumes, green manure, off-farm wastes and biological pest control to maintain the soil fertility, to supply plant nutrients and to control pests. Farming organically is more than just abandoning chemicals. It requires the elimination of persistent chemicals from soil. Therefore, there is need for the conversion period from chemical to organic farming. Generally, a three-year transition period is required from the chemical to organic farming.

3.1 Consumer Preference

To assess the demand, price to be paid, source of supply and the crops to be grown under organic farming, Singh, et al. (2011) conducted a survey on 100 respondents in south-western districts of Punjab during the year 2010-11. Results showed that about 88 per cent consumers preferred organic products if they were easily available to them. Out of them, 34 per cent are prepared to pay 1.5 times higher price and another 10 per cent can even afford double the normal price. Only 9 per cent consumers reported the availability of wheat as the only organic food in their area. About 7.5 per cent of the respondents did not prefer organic food due to lack of guarantee by the organic producers. As far as the price for organic products is concerned, 50 per cent consumers were willing to pay 1.5 times additional price for the organic products, while 14.5 per cent were willing to pay the double price for organic products. Daily consumable vegetables were the most preferred and most of them demanded organic products as reported by 46.5 per cent of the respondents. Further, 68.5 per cent of the respondents preferred farmers' field as the source for purchase of organic food. Thus, a sufficient market is available for the organic food produced with quality norms and made easily available to the consumer.

3.2 *Area Under Organic Cultivation*

In India, about 4.8 million hectares area are reported to be under the organic cultivation out of which 1 million hectares are cultivated while the rest of the area is wild. Further, in Punjab, about 5200 hectare area is cultivated organically. At national level, the National Commission for Organic Farming (NCOF) is looking after the promotion of organic farming in the country, while its Hisar Chapter is responsible for organic farming in the state. The organic cultivation is also promoted by some NGOs like the *Kheti Virasat Mission, Green Peace, etc.* in the state. Some farmers in the state have now started growing organic crops without the use of chemicals owing to the fear of chemical contamination in the food grain crops. Even, the Punjab Agro Food Grain Corporation (PAFC) had also included the organic cultivation in its contract farming programme of 2005-06.

3.3 *Economic Viability*

Some of the organic crops like cotton, basmati rice, moong and guara in the kharif season and wheat, gram and sarson in the rabi season have been grown in the state. Although yields of organically produced crops decreased during the initial years but it reaches the normal level after 3-4 years. The economic analysis of these crops to assess their costs and returns has been reproduced in Table 7.9 (Romana 2006). In the kharif season, cotton was the highest paying crop with returns over variable costs (ROVC) equal to Rs. 13,008 per hectare followed by the basmati, guara and moong crops with ROVC worth Rs. 6020, Rs. 4520 and Rs. 2988 per hectare respectively. Moong remained the least paying crop in this season. In the rabi season, gram was at the top with returns worth Rs. 13,444 per hectare, while sarson and wheat paid Rs. 11,647 and Rs. 10,775 per hectare respectively. Organic cotton-wheat rotation as a whole paid ROVC worth Rs. 23,784 per hectare.

Table 7.9: Economics of Organic Crops Grown in the Cotton Belt of Punjab, 2003-04 (Rs/ha)

Particulars	*Kharif Organic Crops*				*Rabi Organic Crops*			*Cotton + Wheat*
	Cotton	*Moong*	*Basmati*	*Guara*	*Gram*	*Sarson*	*Wheat*	
Preparatory Tillage	1113	962	1272	888	1050	1130	1362	2475
Sowing / Transplanting	2318	875	1610	806	950	388	1303	3621
Plant Protection	6250	1000	750	250	250	250	313	6563
Fertilisers	250	0	750	0	0	750	4250	4500
Inter – culture	2537	1000	375	200	375	500	350	2887
Irrigation	957	250	3655	426	500	500	1056	2013
Harvesting	2783	800	0	798	850	783	1943	4726
Threshing	830	1125	1568	947	1075	1198	1997	2827
Transport & Marketing	1663	2500	2000	529	4481	610	5802	7465
Total Variable Cost	**18701**	**10512**	**11980**	**4844**	**9531**	**6109**	**18375**	**37076**
Yield-Main P (Qtl./ha)	12.5	3.75	10	8.75	10	12.5	20	NA
Price-Main P (Rs/qtl.)	2418	3500	1800	901	2250	1380	1370	NA
Yield-By P (Qtl./ha)	26.5	10	NA	15.75	9.5	11.5	15	NA
Price-By P (Rs/qtl)	56	50	NA	94	50	44	100	NA
Gross Returns	31709	13500	18000	9364	22975	17756	29150	60859
ROVC	13008	2988	6020	4520	13444	11647	10775	23784

Note: ROVC stands for Returns over Variable Cost and P for Product.

Source: Romana, 2006.

3.4 Comparative Economics

The comparative economics of some organic crops with the respective inorganic crops being grown in the state have been prepared in Table 7.10, which shows that all the crops produced organically paid less returns when these were produced with the use of chemicals. Further, although the variable costs in organic cotton-wheat rotation came down by 10 per cent over that of chemically produced cotton and wheat, but their yield had drastically reduced resulting in the poor returns over the variable costs. While shifting from inorganic cultivation to organic cultivation, the returns from cotton had come down from Rs. 14,287 per hectare to Rs. 13,009 per hectare while in wheat from Rs. 13,537 per hectare to Rs. 10,775 per hectare respectively. In the cotton-wheat rotation, against 10 per cent decrease in variable cost, the returns came down by about 15 per cent in organic cultivation. Further, in wheat, the marketing cost had increased by Rs.4000 per hectare due to grading, packing and special marketing of the organic produce, while no special price was received for the organic cotton. In organic moong, although the gross returns increased due to better prices in the market, but the increasing marketing costs had reduced the returns over variable costs from the organic moong. Guara also failed at this front, as there was no special market for the organic crop, but the yield reduced this way. Basmati rice, being prone to stem borer insects proved uneconomical when produced organically due to significant reduction in its yield.

Similarly, in the rabi season, organic sarson paid almost equal returns to that of inorganic crop, as there was no special price for the organic sarson. However, the decrease in its yield was compensated by the decrease in its variable cost. The returns over variable costs from gram crop reduced due to decrease in its yield in spite of the increased price for the organic crop. Thus, in organic crop cultivation, although the pesticide and fertiliser costs can be reduced significantly, but the yield also declines. In the kharif season, organically produced cotton, moong, basmati and guara were unable to equalise their returns to that of chemically produced crops, while in the rabi season, organic wheat and gram had poor returns, while sarson paid almost equivalent returns over variable costs equal to that from chemically-produced sarson.

Table 7.10: Comparative Economics of Organic and Inorganic Crops Grown Both in Kharif and Rabi Seasons in the Cotton Belt of Punjab, 2003-04

Crop	*Av. Yield (Qtl/ha)*		*Market Price of Organic Crops (Rs/qtl.)*	*Gross*/ Returns from Organic (Rs/ha)*	*Operational Costs of (Rs/ha)*		*ROVC Organic Crops (Rs/ha)*	*Difference in ROVC Over Inorganic Crop (Rs/ha)*
	Inorganic	*Organic*			*Inorganic*	*Organic*		
Wheat	46	20	1370	29150	15123	18375	10775	-6186
Sarson	13	12.5	1380	17756	6614	6109	11647	-207
Gram	14.5.	10	2250	22975	6006	9531	13444	-3050
Cotton	16	12.5	2418	31709	27393	18701	13008	-1279
Moong	7.5	3.75	3500	13500	7212	10512	2988	-1050
Basmati	37.7	10	1800	18000	12510	11980	6020	-15400
Guara	10	8.75	901	9364	4911	4520	4520	-1261

* Gross returns include returns from crop by-product/s also.

Source: Romana, 2006.

3.5 Ecological Sustainability

By opting for organic cultivation of crops, chemical fertilisers and pesticides were totally replaced with the organic bio-pesticides and bio-fertilisers being environment-friendly. Table 7.11 shows that investment on fertilisers and pesticides had reduced significantly by replacing them with organic fertilisers and pesticides in all the crops except wheat. In wheat, the substitute cost of chemical fertilisers was Rs. 4250/ha against the chemical fertiliser worth Rs. 3,148. During the initial years of organic cultivation, yield of crops reduces considerably but revives in the later years. Although, the natural resources like soil health and environment are improved with the organic cultivation of crops but keeping in view the increasing demand for food, the process can be implemented in a phased manner.

Table 7.11: Resource Use Pattern of Organic Crops in the Cotton Belt of Punjab, 2003-04

Crop	*Fertilisers Used (Rs./Ha)*		*Pesticide Used (Rs./Ha)*		*Resources Saved by Organic Cultivation (Rs./Ha)*	
	Inorganic	*Organic*	*Inorganic*	*Organic*	*Fertilisers*	*Pesticides*
Wheat	3148	4250	1930	313	-1102	1617
Sarson	1500	750	370	250	750	120
Gram	600	0	500	250	600	250
Cotton	2293	250	12624	6250	2043	6374
Moong	400	0	2100	2000	400	100
Guara	28	0	485	250	28	235
Basmati	1156	750	2755	750	406	2005

Source: Romana, 2006.

3.6 Viable Options for Organic Farming

As discussed earlier, no chemical fertiliser as well as pesticide is used in organic cultivation. Although, by this way the crop, yield gets decreased, but the costs on account of not using chemicals fertilisers and pesticides are saved, thus, reducing the variable costs as well. Thus, by adding the fertiliser and pesticide savings in their respective returns, the estimated yield and price level at which the organically produced major as well alternative crops in the state can be made equally economical to that of chemically-produced crops (Table 7.12). The estimates of yield and price at which these organic crops can become comparable to inorganic crops have been made in two options.

In option-I, with the present yield level of the organic crops; the estimated prices required for these crops to become comparable are significantly high like Rs. 1,741 per qtl in wheat, Rs. 2,518 per qtl in gram and Rs. 3,747 per qtl in moong crop against their actual market prices of Rs. 1,370, Rs. 2,250 and Rs. 3,500 per qtl respectively. However, in cotton, on account of large savings by not using pesticides has made this crop economical only at the price of Rs. 1,966 per qtl against the present market price of Rs. 2,418 per qtl. Thus, the minimum required prices need to be protected for making these crops economical.

In option-II, the minimum yield level at which these crops can be compared with the inorganic crops has been calculated. The required yield level at the available market prices for these organically produced crops is also high in all the crops except the cotton and sarson. In these two crops, the required yield level is 10.16 qtls per hectare and 12.39 qtls per hectare respectively to replace the inorganic crop yielding level of 12.5 qtls per hectare each. In other crops like wheat, gram and moong, the minimum yield estimated for their adoption is 25.79 qtls, 11.57 qtls and 4.16 qtls per hectare against their actual yield level of 20 qtls, 10 qtls and 3.75 qtls per hectare, respectively. Thus, in organic farming, the yield of the crops decreases at the faster speed in the absence of chemical fertilisers that must be compensated with the sufficient supply of bio-fertilisers so as to overcome the nutrient deficiency. Further, in guar, sarson and cotton, there is no special market for the organic produce.

Table 7.12: Economic Viability of Organic Over Inorganic Crops Grown in Cotton Belt

Crop	*Gross Returns Excluding By-product (Rs/ha)*	*ROVC Including Savings Due to Organic Farming (Rs/ha)*	*Difference in ROVC Over Inorganic Crops (Rs/ha)*	*For Making Organic Crops Comparable with Inorganic*			
				Option–I		*Option–II*	
				At Present Yield (Qtl/ha)	*Minimum Price (Rs/ha)*	*At Present Price (Rs/qtl)*	*Minimum Yield (Qtl/ha)*
Wheat	27400	9540	-7421	20	1741	1370	25.42
Sarson	17250	12011	157	12.5	1367	1380	12.39
Gram	22500	13819	-2675	10	2518	2250	11.19
Cotton	30225	19941	5654	12.5	1966	2418	10.16
Moong	13125	3113	-925	3.75	3747	3500	4.01
Basmati	18000	6283	-15137	10	3314	1800	18.41
Guara	7884	5775	-6	8.75	902	901	8.76

Source: Romana, 2006

IV

Policy Implications

As it is clear from the foregoing discussion that organic farming is the right answer to the depleting natural resource base, pesticide pollution and environmental pollution caused by the present cropping system using chemicals. Thus, a strong support system to this new era should be developed to combat the deteriorating eco-system in the state. Further, the majority of the population is in favour of organic food, provided it is easily available and the guaranteed produce. Till date, there is no state support so far as easy testing of organic food, viable certificates, proper checks, any promotion programme or campaign and any reserve national/international market for the organic produce. Thus, to make the organic crops viable in the state, the government must:

- Assure minimum support price during the initial years of its production to compensate the poor yield of the organically produced crops or assure minimum support price as calculated in option-I for making the organic crops viable over the present cropping system.
- Start promotional programmes to popularise organic farming to minimise the chemical use in agriculture and to protect the natural resource base.
- Develop and reserve the different markets for organic crops both at the national as well as at the international level through Punjab Agro, Markfed, Nafed, etc.
- Support the organic producers in grading, packing and providing the marketing base for the organic produce through some special department for this purpose.
- Authorise the agency at the state level as well as at the national level that can test or can issue the certificate of organic produce or organic farming.
- Earmark a strong vigilant department to check the production, packing, marketing and quality of the organic produce so as to win the consumer's faith as most of the consumers reported doubts about the authenticity of organic food. Thus, internationally accepted quality of the organic produce must be assured.

REFERENCES

Anonymous (1989), 'All India Coordinated Research Project on Pesticide Residue', *Consolidated Report 1984-1989*, Ludhiana.

Anonymous (2000), 'All India Coordinated Research Project on Pesticide Residue', *Annual Report 1999-2000*, Punjab Agricultural University, Ludhiana.

Aulakh, K.S. (2004), 'Meeting the Emerging Challenges in Agriculture', *Progressive Farming*, Vol. 40 (4), pp. 1-4.

Battu, R.S., P.P. Singh and B. Singh (1992), 'Residues of Endosulphon in Cotton', *Journal of Insect Science*, Vol. 5, pp. 101-02.

Brar, J.S. and I.M. Chhibba (1994), 'N, P and K Status of Punjab Soils', *Indian Journal of Ecology*, Vol. 21 (1), pp. 34-8.

Brar, S.P.S. (1979), 'Fertility Status of Punjab Soils', *Journal of Research*, Vol. 16 (3), pp. 272-81.

Bajwa, M.S., O.P. Choudhary and A.S. Josan (1992), 'Effect of Continuous Irrigation with Sodic and Saline-Sodic Waters on Soil Properties and Crop Yields under Cotton-Wheat Rotation in North-Western India', *Agricultural Water Management*, Vol. 22, pp. 345-56.

Choudhary, O.P., A. S. Josan and M.S. Bajwa (2001), 'Yield and Fibre Quality of Cotton Cultivars as Affected By Build-Up of Sodium in the Soils with Sustained Sodic Irrigations Under Semi-Arid Conditions', *Agricultural Water Management*, Vol. 49, pp. 1-9.

Dasgupta, Kumkum (2000), 'Undoing the Green Revolution Damage', *available at www.cropwatchindia.org*

Dhawan, A.K., G.S. Dhaliwal and S. Chelliah (2000), 'Insecticide Induced Resurgence of Insects/Pests in Crop Plants', in G.S. Dhaliwal and B. Singh (eds.) *Pesticides and Environment*, Commonwealth Publishers, New Delhi, pp. 86-127.

Ghuman, Ranjit Singh (2002), 'WTO and India Agriculture: Crisis and Challenges: A Case Study of Punjab', *Man and Development*, Vol. 23 (2), pp. 67-98.

Gill, Anita and Lakhwinder Singh (2005), 'Farmers' Suicides and Response of Public Policy: Evidence Diagnosis and Alternatives from Punjab', *Economic and Political Weekly*, Vol. 41 (26), June 30, pp. 2762-68.

Government of Punjab (2002), *Agricultural Production Pattern Adjustment Programme in Punjab for Productivity and Growth*, Chief Minister's Advisory Committee on Agricultural Policy and Restructuring.

Government of Punjab (2012), *Statistical Abstract of Punjab 2011*, Economic and Statistical Organisation, Punjab, Chandigarh.

Government of India (2007), *Agricultural Statistics at a Glance.*

Gurunadha Rao, V.V.S., S. Sankaran, B.A. Prakash, K. Mahesh, P. Yadaiah and S.V.N. Chandrashekhar (2004), 'Assessment of Groundwater Quality in Ludhiana and Muktsar Districts, Punjab', Paper Presented in the Workshop on *Sustainable Agriculture: Problems and Prospects,* Punjab Agricultural University (PAU), Ludhiana, November 9-11, 2004, Conference Proceedings, pp. 47-55.

Josan, A.S., O.P. Choudhary and M.S. Bajaj (1996), 'Water Quality and Irrigation Management of Cotton Crop', *Progressive Farming,* April, a Monthly Magazine of Punjab Agricultural University (PAU), Ludhiana, pp. 11-3.

Joia, B.S., R.P. Chawla and R.L. Kalra (1978), 'Residues of DDT and HCH in Wheat Flour in Punjab', *Indian Journal of Ecology,* Vol. 5, pp. 120-7.

Joia, B.S. and R.S. Battu (2000), 'Occurrence of DDT and HCH Residues in Breast Milk in Punjab', *Indian Journal of Environmental Toxicology,* Vol. 10 (1), pp. 16-8.

Kalra, R.L. and R.P. Chawla (1983), 'Studies on Pesticide Residue and Monitoring Pesticidal Pollution', *Final Technical Report,* Pl 480 Project, Punjab Agricultural University, Ludhiana.

Kolar, J.S. and S.P. Mehra (1992), ' Changing Scenario of Weed Flora in Agro Eco-systems in Punjab', in G.S. Dhaliwal, B.S. Hansra and N. Jerath (eds.), *Changing Scenario of Our Environment,* Punjab Agricultural University, Ludhiana, pp. 252-60.

Kumar, A. (1978), 'Residues of Different Insecticides on Cotton Lint and Cotton Seed', *Unpublished M.Sc. Thesis,* Punjab Agricultural University, Ludhiana.

Nayyar, V.K. (2002), 'Effect of Rice-Wheat Cropping System on Soil Health.' Paper Presented in the Refresher Course on *Socio-Economic Implications of Rice-Wheat System in Indo-Gangetic Plains of India* Punjab Agricultural University (PAU), Ludhiana, August 21 to September 10, 2002.

PAU, *Annual Reports* (Various Years), Department of Agronomy, Entomology and Pathology, Punjab Agricultural University (PAU), Ludhiana.

Romana, Gurjinder Singh (2006), 'Sustainability of Alternative Cropping System in Cotton Belt of Punjab', *Unpublished Ph.D. Dissertation,* Department of Economics, Punjabi University, Patiala.

Sharma, J.P. and R.A. Aggarwal (1988), 'Residues of Synthetic Pyrethroid in Seed and Lint of Upland Cotton', *Indian Journal of Plant Protection*, Vol. 16 (1), pp. 111-5.

Singh, B., N.S. Butter and K.K. Chahal (1991), 'Residues of Some New Synthetic Pyrethroid in Cotton Seed and Lint', *Pestology*, Vol. 15 (11), pp. 27-9.

Singh, B., P.P. Singh, R.S. Battu and R.L. Kalra (1990), 'Residues of Synthetic Pyrethroid in Seed and Lint of Upland Cotton', *Indian Journal of Agricultural Sciences*, Vol. 60 (11), pp. 775-6.

Singh, J., A.S. Sohi, H.S. Mann and S.P. Kapoor (1994), 'Studies on Whitefly, *Bemisia Tabaci* (Gen.) Transmitted Cotton Leaf Curl Diseases in Punjab', *Journal of Insect Science*, Vol. 7, pp. 194-7.

Singh, B., Gaganjyot Singh and R.S. Buttar (2001), 'Residues of Cypermethrine and Ethion in Cotton Seed and Lint', *Pesticide Research*, 313 (2), pp. 195-8.

Singh, Gurpreet (2008), Farmers' Suicides in Punjab: A Socio-Economic Analysis, *Unpublished M.Phil. Dissertation*, Department of Economics, Punjabi University, Patiala.

Singh, Gaganjyot and A.K. Dhawan (2001), 'Residues of Calfos 40 EC in Soils, Cotton Seed and Lint', paper Presented at *National Conference on Plant Protection: New Horizons in the Millennium*, Maharana Partap University, Udaipur (Rajasthan), February 23-25, 2011.

Singh, Gurdeep and G.S. Romana (2011), 'Consumer Preperences and Quaries regarding Organic Produce', *Unpublished Survey Report*, Krishi Vighan Kendra, Mansa (Punjab).

Singh, J. (2004), Economic Cost of Environment Degradation in Indian Punjab Agriculture, *Unpublished Research Report*, Department of Economics and Sociology, Punjab Agricultural University (PAU), Ludhiana.

Sokhi, S.S., P.P. Singh and R.K. Grewal (1992), 'Disease Scenario of Crops in Modern Agriculture', in G.S. Dhaliwal, B.S. Hansra and N. Jerath (eds.), *Changing Scenario of Our Environment,* Punjab Agricultural University, Ludhiana, pp. 261-70.

Takshi, K.S. and R.P.S. Chopra (2004), 'Monitoring and Assessment of Groundwater Resources in Punjab State', Paper Presented at National Level Workshop on *Ground Water Use in North-West India,* Organised by the Centre for Advancement of Sustainable Agriculture, April 13, 2004 at INSA, New Delhi.

PART IV

Consequences of Agrarian Distress in Punjab

8

Political Economy of Agrarian Distress in Punjab

Kesar Singh Bhangoo

Introduction

During the neo-liberal policy regime, agriculturally advanced regions of the country, have been witnessing a scourge of rural suicides among the farmers and agricultural labourers. Many studies on the subject clearly point out that the rising incidence of suicides is the manifestation of an unprecedented agrarian distress in the countryside. Punjab, known as the granary of India, has also been experiencing the occurrence of farmers' suicides due to the emerging agrarian distress with higher intensity. The unabated suicides among the farmers and agricultural labourers are the most striking and horrible expression of the desperation of the farming community. Actually, the structural transformation of the economy during the neo-liberal regime has also witnessed a decline in the share of agriculture in the gross domestic product of India's economy. Further, the formation of the World Trade Organisation (WTO) in 2005 and its subsequent policies added to the woes of farmers, as this had prematurely pushed the country's farming community to compete with the farmers of developed countries enjoying high subsidies/state support without a level playing field. The strong political position gained by the farmers during the Green Revolution period has been weakened and fragmented during the 1980s and 90s, and now, they are living on the margins owing to a shift in the political affiliations and disjuncture between the interests of farmers and the politicians (Suri, 2006).

Along with the changing agrarian political economy, changes in the interests of politicians, bureaucracy, etc. has clearly been manifesting in the state agrarian policies. Punjab politicians, who once advocated the cause of agricultural development and farmers' interests, have developed their strong interests in the industry and business activities. And, they are no longer interested in agriculture as the agricultural income no more remained the main source of their total income (Bhangoo, 2005). In such a situation, the agriculture sector in Punjab has continuously been marginalised and, consequently, the economy of farmers and agricultural labourers has been hit very hard. It is, therefore, of paramount importance and desirable to explore the causes, problems and related intricacies of agrarian distress in the state.

This chapter makes a modest attempt to analyse the prevailing economic structure of Punjab's economy with a special reference to the agriculture sector to ascertain the causes of agrarian distress, rural indebtedness and rising incidence of suicides among the farmers and agricultural labourers. The analysis has been organised in six different sections. Section I presents the review of existing literature on the subject in Punjab state. Section II discusses the changing structure of the Punjab economy and emerging agrarian distress. Section III analyses the problem and extent of farmers' indebtedness in Punjab. Section IV discusses and elaborates the phenomenon of suicides among the farmers and agricultural labourers in Punjab. Section V traces the plight of some suicide victims of the state and Section VI concludes the discussion and also suggests remedial measures to mitigate the agrarian distress in Punjab or elsewhere in the country.

I

Review of Literature

The surfacing of agrarian distress and suicides among the

farmers has become a subject of debate, analysis and evaluation among the economists, sociologists and policy makers. The state government has already admitted 2116 farmers' suicides in the state due to indebtedness (MASR, 2001). Being a matter of grave concern having severe political, social and economic ramifications, the state government and its agencies have funded some studies (Sidhu, et al. 2011; Shergill, 2010 & 1998; NSSO, 2005; IDC, 1998 & 2006; PSFC, 2006 & 2007) to gauge the gravity of the situation. And, some individual scholars on their own (Bhangoo, 2006 & 2005; Gill and Singh, 2006; Satish, 2006; Chahal, 2005; Gill, 2005; Iyer and Manick, 2000; AFDR, 2000) have also studied the phenomenon empirically and analytically at the micro and macro levels relying on the primary as well as secondary sources. The review of these studies states that three approaches were adopted to analyse the problem; first, representational and journalistic (MASR, 2001; Sridhar, 2005) to draw the attention of the government/policymakers to the distressing plight of the farmers and remains at the level of impressionistic observations. Second, research studies based on the field surveys, primary and secondary information which have analysed and evaluated the issue of suicides (Sidhu, et al. 2011; IDC, 2006 & 1998; AFDR, 2000; Iyer and Manick, 2000; Chahal, 2005; Satish, 2006; Bhangoo, 2006) have been carried out in different parts of the state. Third, analytical studies (Gill, 2005; Johdka, 2006; Gill and Singh, 2006; Satish, 2006; Bhangoo, 2005) analyse the problem on the basis of existing literature and secondary information.

These studies have identified the state's cotton belt comprising Sangrur, Bathinda, Mansa, Ferozpur and old Faridkot districts with high incidence of farmers' suicide proneness area during 1991-2005 (Sidhu, et al., 2011; IDC 1998 & 2006; Chahal 2005; Bhangoo, 2006). Literature also reveals that the central plain and sub-mountainous districts of the state respectively fall under the moderate and low incidence of farmers' suicide-proneness areas. It has also been reported that non-remunerative prices of crops, successive crop failures, uncertainty of good yield, lack of marketing alternatives, non-implementation of the crop diversification programme, increasing costs of cultivation, exorbitant interest rates charged by the moneylenders and banks have landed the farming community of Punjab, especially the small and marginal farmers into the debt trap. In fact, the grave situation of farmers' indebtedness in Punjab (Shergill, 2010 & 1998; NSSO, 2005; PSFC, 2007) and the resultant suicides have been hitting the headlines continuously. Actually, suicides among the farmers due to indebtedness are heartrending and awful especially in a prosperous state like Punjab, which has seen strong peasant movements and notwithstanding the fact that political leadership of the state comes predominantly from farming communities, especially the Jat-Sikhs who committed the maximum suicides (IDC, 2006 & 1998; AFDR, 2000; Iyer and Manick, 2000; Chahal, 2005; Bhangoo, 2006). The literature has also thrown light on the issues of economic distress, causes and magnitude of indebtedness and of suicides. However, because of the divergent estimates and conclusions, a precise and concrete idea and possible solutions to tackle this crisis remains lacking. At the same time, some gaps have remained and some studies have been found to be incoherent.

II

Contours of Agrarian Distress and the Punjab Economy

The Punjab economy has been showing structural changes since 1966. The primary sector of the state witnessed a decline in its share of gross state domestic product (GSDP) as well as the share of workforce and rural workforce (Table 8.1 and Table 8.2). This sector accounted for 55.11 per cent of GSDP in 1970-71 which declined to 24.92 per cent in 2009-10. On the other hand, the share of secondary and tertiary sectors has increased from 18.09 per cent and 26.80 per cent in 1970-71 to 31.58 per cent and 43.53 per cent during the same period respectively. During the period of 1970-71 to 2009-10, the share of agriculture and live-stock alone in the GSDP produced in the primary sector has remained more than 95 per cent. On the other side, the share of agriculture in the total workforce of the state stood at 62.66 per cent in 1971 and declined to 39.36 per cent in 2001 (Table 8.2). The cultivators and agricultural labourers accounted for

78.84 per cent of the rural workforce in 1971 which declined to 53.50 per cent in 2001. And, 46.50 per cent of the rural workforce was engaged in non-agricultural activities in 2001. It is evidently clear from Table 8.1 and Table 8.2 that agriculture and livestock continue to be the backbone of the state's rural economy. The industrial sector has not become an important sector of the Punjab economy as its share in the state's GSDP, total workforce and rural workforce remained quite low during the period of 1970-71 to 2009-10.

Table 8.1: Structural Change in the Distribution of the Gross State Domestic Product in Punjab, 1970-71 to 2009-10

(%age figures)

Years	*Primary Sector*	*Secondary Sector*	*Tertiary Sector*	*Total*
1970-71	55.11 (98.46)	18.09	26.80	100
1980-81	49.45 (99.05)	19.76	30.79	100
1990-91	48.33 (98.55)	22.46	29.21	100
2000-01	36.60 (98.38)	15.10	48.30	100
2004-05	32.53 (95.32)	24.78	42.69	100
2005-06	31.16 (95.16)	25.75	43.09	100
2006-07	29.10 (92.35)	28.33	42.57	100
2007-08	27.67 (95.35)	30.39	41.94	100
2008-09^{P}	26.60 (95.25)	30.37	43.03	100
2009-10^{Q}	24.92 (95.16)	31.55	43.53	100

Source: Statistical Abstracts of Punjab, Relevant Issues, Chandigarh.

Note:

1. Figures for 1970-71, 1980-81 and 1990-91 are at 1980-81 prices and for 2000-01 are at 1999-2000 prices and 2004-05 onwards at 2004-05 prices.
2. Figures in parentheses are percentages of the share of GSDP of agriculture and livestock in GSDP of the Primary Sector
3. P - Provisional Q - Quick estimates.

It is also true that the success of the Green Revolution strategy has resulted in rapid growth in the state income at the rate of 5 per cent per annum during the period of 1966-67 to 1988-89 which led to reduction in rural poverty. As a result of this high growth, Punjab's per capita income ranked number one for so many years in the country. Unfortunately, the gains of the Green Revolution could not be sustained in the long run as the agrarian sector of the state in subsequent years has been passing through an unprecedented crisis. The rate of growth of the state's agriculture sector, which was 3.18 per cent per annum during 1967-80, rose to 4.87 per cent per annum during 1981-91, but declined to a very low level to 0.37 per cent per annum during the period 1992-99 (Government of Punjab, 2004). Further, it was 2.9 per cent in 2000-01 and 0.6 per cent in 2001-02 as a result of which the overall growth rates of the Punjab economy slipped to the third lowest in the country and Punjab state lost its per capita income number one status to Delhi, Haryana and Maharashtra in 2002-03 (IDC, 2006). It is interesting to note that the projected growth rate of Punjab's agriculture for the Eleventh Five Year Plan (2007-12) lies between 2.07 per cent and 2.56 per cent per annum (Mathur, et al., 2007).

Table 8.2: Percentage Distribution of Workforce and Rural Workforce of Punjab, 1971-2001

Years	*Cultivators*	*Agricultural Workers*	*Industrial Workers*	*Services and Others*	*Total*
1971	42.56	20.10	11.30	26.04	100
	(53..64)	(25.24)	(8.19)	(12.93)	(100)
1981	35.86	22.16	13.16	28.82	100
	(46.11)	(32.77)	(8.36)	(12.76)	(100)
1991	31.45	23.81	12.28	32.46	100
	(44.39)	(32.28)	(8.27)	(15.06)	(100)
2001	22.96	16.40	8.41	52.23	100
	(31.50)	(22.00)	(3.10)	(43.4**)	(100)

Source: Census of India

Note: 1. **Construction and other than household industry included in services. 2. Figures in parentheses are percentages of rural workforce.

Factually, the prevailing agrarian distress in the state was diagnosed as early as the mid-1980s when the experts expressed concern about stagnating productivity levels and recommended the diversification of agriculture as a remedy to the problems of sustainability of the agriculture sector of the state. Agrarian distress in the state is the result of policies pursued by the government and many other factors like the stagnation of yield, especially of the wheat and decline in the rice and cotton crops (Government of Punjab, 2000; IDC, 2006) and successive cotton crop failures due to natural and man-made factors (spurious pesticides, seeds, fertilisers, etc.) along with failure and non-implementation of the crop diversification programme due to uncertain yields, prices and marketing of alternative crops.

Agrarian distress in Punjab has also been supplemented by the rising operational as well as fixed costs of cultivation and consequently declining farm incomes. During the liberalisation and globalisation policies era, prices of wheat and rice at home remained stagnant, but continuously declined in the international market, hitting the agriculture sector hard and making it unviable and non-competitive. Moreover, agricultural input prices increased by 25 to 45 per cent, but the increase in agricultural output prices was only 9.0 to 9.5 per cent since 1967 (IDC, 2006). Further, the cost of rice cultivation increased by 5 percentage points from 44 per cent to 49 per cent during the period 2000-01 to the 2005-06 period over the 1995-96 to 2000-01 period, and for wheat it increased by 8 percentage points during the same period. As a consequence, gross income was reduced by 33 per cent for rice and almost by 100 per cent for wheat from 1995-96 to 2000-01 to 2000-01 to 2005-06 respectively (IDC, 2006). The cost of cotton cultivation increased 17 times and the income from cotton rose only by 11 times during 1975-76 and 2001-02 (Narayanamoorthy, 2006) and its continuous failure almost for a decade in Punjab due to the attack of American bollworm and water logging (Rangi and Sidhu, 2000) has negatively affected the incomes of cotton growers. Even in such a situation, the minimum support prices (MSP) for major crops grown in Punjab has been increased nominally, the yield really stagnated and cost of cultivation skyrocketed due to rising prices of farm inputs added to the woes of the farmers. Thus, stagnant/declining yields and incomes from major crops are painful for the farmers facing economic hardships and unable to repay their debts.

In Punjab, around 30 per cent of the operational holdings (Table 8.3) are small and marginal, and their economic viability, existence and continuation is suspected due to the squeezing profitability of major crops and increasing production costs.

Small and marginal farmers are facing hardships and fighting for their survival which is under threat. The marginal, small and semi-medium operational holdings together account for 62.60 per cent in the numbers and operating 30 per cent land area in 2000-01 are under greater distress due to their uneconomic size of land holding (Rangi and Sidhu, 2000). This marginalisation of operational holdings, sub-division and fragmentation of land holdings have also contributed to the agrarian distress. In Punjab, the average size of operation holdings has declined from 4.07 hectares in 1970-71 to 3.16 hectares in 2000-01 (Table 8.3). Further, Punjab agriculture is also facing (i) over capitalisation and mechanisation with underutilisation of farm machinery, (ii) transfer of agricultural land for non-agricultural purposes and (iii) unfavourable terms of trade for agriculture. These factors further deepened the agrarian distress and have contributed hardships especially to the small and marginal farmers of the state.

Further, onslaught by the WTO policies added to the woes of farmers as these policies prematurely pushed them to compete with farmers of developed nations enjoying high subsidies/state support without a level-playing field. The new economic agenda focused on the industry and other sectors and it has resulted in stagnated public investment in agriculture (Mathur, et al., 2007) that has marginalised the agrarian sector and wreaked havoc with farmers. The changing agrarian political economy also contributed to agrarian distress as state politics turned against the interests of the farmers, as the strong political position of farmers emerging during the Green Revolution period weakened and fragmented in the 1980s and now on the margins during the liberalisation period due to the shift in the political affiliations and disjuncture between interests of farmers and the politicians. Punjab politicians who once advocated the cause of agriculture development and farmers' interests developed interests in industry and business and were no longer interested in agriculture as agriculture no more remained the main source of their income. As a result, small and marginal farmers suffered and marginalisation of agriculture further deepened the crisis.

Table 8.3: Percentage Distribution of Operational Holdings by Size and Average Size of Operational Holdings in Punjab

Size Group (Hectare)	*1970-71*	*1980-81*	*1990-91*	*1995-96*	*2000-01*	*2005-06*
Marginal & Small (Below 2)	56.54	38.62	44.73	35.43	29.70	31.64
Semi-Medium (2-4)	20.44	27.99	25.85	29.31	32.90	31.85
Medium (4-10)	18.02	26.20	23.41	27.98	30.20	29.45
Large (Above 10)	5.00	7.19	6.01	7.28	7.20	7.06
Total	100	100	100	100	100	100
Average Size (Hactare)	4.07	3.79	3.61	—	3.19	—

Source: Statistical Abstracts of Punjab, ESO, Punjab (Relevant Issues).

Finally adverse adult and juvenile sex ratio, especially in rural Punjab due to the son preference, prevalence of dowry system, break up of joint family system resulting in individualisation of farm operations, increasing alcohol and drug abuse, rising consumption standards determined by peak income levels, collapse of rural education/health infrastructure, large educated unemployed youth, stressful mounting indebtedness and the increasing suicides among farmers and agricultural labourers are the causes and consequences of the emerging agrarian crisis.

The discussion makes it clear that although agriculture is experiencing a decline, yet it remains an important sector of the Punjab economy. Further, the growth pattern of the Punjab economy has not adhered to the growth theory which suggests a reduction of the economy's dependence on agriculture and shifting of surpluses both of the labour and capital resources to the industrial sector as a natural course of development. In fact, the state's agrarian crisis is the result of stagnated yield in agriculture, successive crop failure/damage and non-implementation of the crop diversification programme. Also, increasing production costs, low farm returns, non-viability of small and marginal holdings, over capitalisation and farm mechanisation with underutilisation of farm machinery, marginalisation of the agriculture sector and weakened political position of the farmers during the new policy regime doomed the farmers' economy especially of small and marginal farmers and this has compelled them to borrow heavily under the expectations of revival of agriculture.

III

Punjab Farmers: Indebtedness

Rural indebtedness is not a new phenomenon in India as well as in Punjab, but the farmers' suicides are. Long ago, Darling, a Britisher, rightly described that Punjab, though one of the most prosperous provinces was probably the most indebted province of British India (Darling, 1925). Today's situation has, however, deteriorated so much as the indebtedness compelled many farmers in the state to commit suicide. Indebtedness depends on the availability of credit, cost of credit, ability to service it and cost of cultivation. Agriculture credit is not a bad thing till it is used for productive purposes and serviced timely through the income generated from farm produce and would not be turned into indebtedness (Satish, 2006). Unproductive use of credit and loans at exorbitant interest rates, mainly from the moneylenders/commission agents, are disturbing dimensions of indebtedness (Shergill, 1998; 2010; and NSSO, 2005). Various research studies highlighted the gravity of indebtedness among the farming community in Punjab as the outstanding loans against farmers of the state increased from Rs. 5,700.91 crores in 1997 (Shergill, 1998) to Rs. 12,506. 37 crores in 2002 (Satish, 2006), to Rs. 24,000 crores (PSFC, 2007) and to Rs. 30,394.91 crores in 2007-08 (Shergill, 2010).

The National Sample Survey Organisation also reported that in 2003 (NSSO, 2005) at the all India level, 48.6 per cent farm households were reported to be indebted, leading by Andhra Pradesh (82 per cent) and followed by Tamil Nadu (74.5 per cent) and Punjab (65.4 per cent). Average outstanding loans per farm household at all India level was Rs. 12,585. And, it was the highest in Punjab (Rs. 41,576), followed by Kerala, Haryana, Andhra Pradesh and Tamil Nadu. Another estimate put per farm household outstanding loan equal to Rs. 45,193 and Rs. 28,082 against the small and marginal farmers of Punjab respectively (Chahal, 2005). All these estimates about the farmers' indebtedness pointed out the grave/crisis like situation prevailing in the state which corroborates the views of Darling (1925). An analysis of farmers' indebtedness in Punjab suggests that the farmers in the state preferred and depended largely on the institutional sources (commercial banks and cooperative agencies) for their long-term productive credit needs (Shergill, 2010). For the short-term productive credit needs, the farmers mainly depend upon informal and non-institutional sources (Shergill, 2010). For non-productive credit, Punjab farmers completely depended on informal sources (Shergill 2010 and 1998, Satish, 2003).

Overall, credit needs of the farmers in Punjab seem to be very high when compared with the farmers of other states because of the highly intensive and mechanised agriculture in the state. However, available formal credit in the state is not enough to fulfil, one-half of the credit demanded by the farmers (Gill and Singh, 2006). Naturally, for their credit needs, they are highly dependent on the informal sources of credit (NSSO, 2005). As a result, business of moneylenders and commission agents continues to flourish in Punjab despite the fact they charge high and exorbitant interest rates. The main merit in their dealings is that they advance loans easily or immediately or on demand for productive/unproductive purposes and sometimes without collateral or mostly by engaging the produce as collateral. For instance, about 40 per cent of total credit amount negotiated by the farmers in the state was for unproductive purposes (NSSO, 2005; Chahal, 2005) such as for the consumption, social ceremonies (death or marriage), house construction, illness, etc. So far as the debt position across the various farm-size categories of farmers are concerned, per acre debt is the highest among the small farmers and the lowest among the large farmers. Other studies on debt also suggest the precarious position of the small farmers in the state (Shergill, 2010). The fact is that the agrarian distress played havoc with small and marginal farmers in the state as this category of farmers with less operational land area were hopelessly involved in the indebtedness.

Living members of suicide victims' families and close relatives also indicated abnormally high farm input prices and crop failures/damages as leading causes of indebtedness. Excessive consumption expenditure due to penetration of consumerism, indulgence in conspicuous consumption, social ceremonies like dowry in marriages, low prices of farm products/failures of non-farm business/excess debt than income, low/stagnant yields, etc. have also been reported as important causes of farmers' indebtedness (Table 8.4).

Table 8.4: Percentage Distribution of Farmers' Perceptions about Causes of Indebtedness in Punjab

Perceptions	*Shergill 1998*	*AFDR 2000*	*Chahal 2005*	*IDC 2006*
1. Abnormally High Farm Input Prices	30.80	—	—	—
2. Crop Failure/Damage	18.50	21.50	24.65	42.44
3. Excessive Expenditure on Consumption, Social Ceremonies, Illness etc.	36.10	24.60	27.28	—
4. Low Prices of Farm Products/ Non-farm Venture Failed/Excess Debt than Income	7.30	9.60	33.12	43.60
5. Low/Stagnant Yields/Poor Quality of Land	4.60	15.10	14.95	—
6. Over Expenditure on Farm Machinery	1.50	—	—	—
7. Lack of Hard Work and Drug Abuse	1.20	1.40-	—	6.40
8. Any Other	—	27.8	—	7.56

The analysis makes it clear that the Punjabi farmers are highly indebted for the wrong reasons and this trend is on the rise. Undoubtedly, they are driven to the debt trap not only because of imprudently heavy borrowings from informal sources and for non-productive purposes, but also because of fall in net farm incomes far below the expectations of the farming community. Further, Punjab farmers are borrowing too heavily for farm machinery, digging/deepening of tube wells, replacing old bore wells with submersible pumps and for cultivating input-intensive high value crops in the expectation of high yield and prices. Non-realisation of these expectations has been identified as the major cause of indebtedness by the experts and farm studies.

IV

Punjab Farmers and Agricultural Labourers: Suicides

Suicides among the farming community of Punjab, especially in the cotton belt of Malwa region, have been hitting the headlines for the last couple of years. This frightening and shocking phenomenon continues without any sign of abatement and reveals the plight of victims and also of the farmers who are alive but whose condition resembles/worse than that of the victims. The Punjab government initially tried to sweep the issue under the carpet till it blew out of proportion and perceived it as one of the repercussions of the neo-liberal policy regime pursued since the 1990s. Though it admits late that the farmers in Punjab are committing suicides due to economic distress and indebtedness, but it does little or nothing to resolve the problems of heavy indebtedness faced by the small and marginal farmers. The print and electronic media, farmers' unions, agricultural scientists and experts, concerned economists, NGOs working for the betterment of the farming community and political parties, mainly the opposition, raised a hue and cry about this phenomenon.

Truly, the suicides occur in modern society for many other counts (social tensions, psychological, cultural, etc.) but the worrisome and disturbing aspect is that the suicides are taking place among the farmers and agricultural labour of a prosperous state like Punjab and largely due to the indebtedness. The farmers' suicides has become a subject of debate, analysis and evaluation among all those concerned. The state government has also admitted 2116 farmers' suicides in the state owing to the indebtedness (MASR, 2001). Being a matter of serious concern with serious political, social and economic implications, the state government and its agencies, to gauge the gravity of situation, have sponsored some studies (Shergill, 1998, NSSO,

2005, IDC, 1998 & 2006), and some scholars did these on their own (Gill and Singh, 2006; Satish, 2006; Chahal, 2005; Gill, 2005; Iyer and Manick, 2000; AFDR, 2000) empirically and analytically at the micro and macro levels relying on the primary as well as secondary sources.

Most of these studies have been conducted in Sangrur, Mansa and Bathinda districts of Punjab where the bulk of farmers' suicides has been reported. These areas are comparatively socially, economically and humanly poor and backward than that of the other parts of the state (Government of Punjab, 2004). Some studies (IDC, 1998 and 2006) have also covered the Doaba and Majha regions of the state which reported fewer cases of farmers' suicides. Important characteristics of the farmers who committed suicides have been presented in Table 8.5. It is evident from these characteristics that (i) a higher proportion of farmers committed suicide than that of agricultural labourers/non-farming persons; (ii) the number of small and marginal farmers committed suicides was the maximum during 1990-2006; (iii) a large majority of deceased persons were married as well as illiterate; (iv) nearly one-half of the grieved farmers (varied from 20.50 per cent to 68.20 per cent) used loans for unproductive purposes. Similarly, regarding sources of debt, one can easily infer from these studies that nearly 50 per cent of deceased farmers took loans exclusively from informal sources, 30 per cent exclusively from formal sources and 20 per cent from both sources (Table 8.5).

Small and marginal farmers of Punjab were forced to sell/mortgaged their land and other assets because of poor economic conditions and economic distress (Government of Punjab, 2004; Chahal, 2005). This led to family disputes/feuds and which supplemented indebtedness and continuous harassment/insults in full public view by the lender for committing suicides to be relieved of the daily agonies of life (Iyer and Manick, 2000, Chahal, 2005; Bhangoo, 2006). Regarding the main causes of suicides, these studies suggest (Table 8.6) that most of the deceased farmers committed suicide due to indebtedness alone, indebtedness-related problems like harassment by moneylenders/commission agents/bank officials, conflict at home, family discord, loss of social status, alcohol and drug abuse, and economic distress were the major causes of suicides reported by the close relatives of suicide victims. Crop failure/ damage, low crop yield and livestock loss were also reported as the causes of suicides.

Table 8.5: Profile of Farmers' Committed Suicides in Punjab Surveyed by Different Studies

Characteristics	*IDC 1998*	*Iyer & Manick 2000*	*AFDR 2000*	*Chahal 2005*	*IDC 2006*	*Bhangoo 2006*
Districts/Areas Covered	*Sangrur Mansa, Gurdaspur, & Ludhiana*	*Sangrur*	*Patiala, Sangrur, Mansa, & Bathinda*	*Gurdaspur Ludhiana Sangrur & Faridkot*	*Faridkot Bathinda, Sangrur Amritsar & Jalandhar*	*Bathinda*
No. of Suicide Households	53	80	79	42	200	50
No. of Villages Covered	14	11	29	12	24	17
Persons Committed Suicide (Percentage)						
a. Farmers	55.00	68.75	84.80	100	62.00	86.00
b. Agriculture Labourers	45.00	31.25	15.20	Nil	38.00	12.00
c. Small/Marginal Farmers	24.50	53.75	65.70	54.76	81.00	40.00
d. Married	81.10	NA	76	NA	62.00	86.00
e. Illiterate	58.50	66.25	74.70	50.00	71.00	64.00
Status of Debt: (Percentage)*						
a. Exclusively from Moneylenders	36.32	67.50	27.40	52.32	65.70	12.00
b. Exclusively from Banks/Cooperatives	46.56	12.50	6.80	47.68	22.17	10.00
c. Multiple Sources	7.12	13.75	65.80	—	11..63	76.00
Unproductive Use of Loan	68.20	51.62	20.50	38.98	45.33	NA

Note: * The percentages may not add up to 100, as the remaining victims were free from debt.

Table 8.6: Reported Main Causes of Suicides in Punjab

Causes	*IDC 1998*	*Iyer & Manick 2000*	*AFDR 2000*	*Chahal 2005*	*IDC 2006*	*Bhangoo 2006*
1. Indebtedness Alone	17.89	—	15.20	28.57	30.00	36.00
2. Crop Failure/ Damage	1.05	26.25	5.10	7.14	—	16.00
3. Low Crop Yield	—	—	—	—	—	—
4. Conflict/ Family Discord at Home	35.79	11.25	—	28.57	16.00	4.00
5. Alcohol and Drug Abuse	17.89	10.00	1.30	7.14	2.50	—
6. Poverty/Poor Position of Family	6.32	20.00	19.00	—	14.00	4.00
7. Harassment by Lender/Loss of Status	16.84	—	—	25.00	—	20.00
8. Multiple with Indebtedness as One Reason	—	32.50	53.1	—	30.50	16.00
9. Others/Don't Know	4.22	—	6.30	3.57	7.00	4.00

Note: Figures in percentages.

Further, the analysis makes it clear that economic distress leads to indebtedness and indebtedness, in turn, leads to humiliation/ harassment (actual or imaginary) which becomes a driving force behind such suicides. But, in reality, emerging agrarian distress leads to economic, social and cultural distress among the farmers, and inadequacies of credit system leads to a situation of indebtedness, indebtedness-linked problems (family feuds, alcohol and drug abuse, conflict with others, court cases and notices, harassment/threats/humiliation before the public, etc.) and ultimately to the suicides. To a larger extent, unproductive use of credit, diversion of productive credit to unproductive purposes, and failure of formal credit to fulfil farmers' credit needs are also responsible for farmers' indebtedness leading to suicides.

Interestingly, the information about the modes used by the farmers/agricultural labourers to commit suicide clearly related to the agrarian operations as most of them consumed insecticides/pesticides which are easily available at the farm or in the households. This has been substantiated in almost all the studies conducted on the subject in the state. The other modes adopted for committing suicides were like jumping before running trains, hanging at homes and self-immolation (Table 8.7).

Table 8.7: Distribution of Suicides by Different Modes Used to Commit Suicide

Mode	*Bhangoo 2006*	*IDC 2006*	*Chahal 2005*	*AFDR 2000*	*Ayer & Manick 2000*	*IDC 1998*
1. Consuming Pesticides	80.0	77.0	83.3	76.2	76.25	58.5
2. Jumping Before Running Train	10.0	2.5	2.4	5.1	2.5	1.9
3. Self-Immolation	2.0	2.0	2.4	2.5	5.0	9.4
4. Hanging	4.0	9.0	11.90	15.2	10.0	9.4
5. Others	4.0	9.5	-	1.0	6.25	20.8
Total	100	100	100	100	100	100

Note: Figures in percentages.

V

Plight of Farmers: Some Sample Cases of Suicide Victims

Most of the studies found very high incidence of farmers' suicides in Bathinda district of Punjab (AFDR, 2000; IDC, 1998 and 2006; Bhangoo, 2006; Sidhu, et al., 2011) and even the Government of Punjab in one of its reports highlighted this fact. To investigate ground realities and gravity of the situation, the author visited some villages of Bathinda district and interviewed the nearest 100 household heads, family members and relatives of suicide victims. A few typical cases of suicide victims' families have been enumerated below:

1. Jagjit Singh s/o Kirpal Singh, village *Chathewala*,

committed suicide on September 21, 2003. His operational holding was five acres; 2 acres of his own land and 3 acres leased-in land. Ranjit Kaur, his wife (widow), said that her husband committed suicide because of indebtedness, economic distress and grabbing of crops by the owner of the leased-in land. He was indebted to the owner on account of land rent and interest on it to the tune of Rs. 1.5 lakhs, and subsequently, he received an auction notice for his property due to the court case. He was also indebted to the commercial banks (Rs. 3.93 lakhs), cooperative society (Rs. 0.45 lakhs) and commission agent (Rs. 0.80 lakhs). On the date of survey, the family was living in miserable conditions and on the brink of selling owned land for survival.

2. Gurjant Singh, village *Myser Khana* committed suicide on July 2, 2003. His wife Jasvir Kaur said that the cause of suicide was heavy debt burden (Rs. 9.29 lakhs) and constant pestering by the pesticide dealer and commission agent. He was indebted to a pesticide dealer (Rs. 0.57 lakhs), commission agents (Rs. 3.82 lakhs), commercial bank (Rs. 4.0 lakhs) and cooperative society (Rs. 0.90 lakhs). Though the family owned 12 acres of land, but of which 6 acres were mortgaged to the commission agents and 4 acres to the commercial bank.
3. Kulwant Singh s/o Nand Singh, village *Chathewala,* committed suicide on February 9, 2005. His wife Kamaljeet Kaur reported that suicide was largely due to the repeated cotton crop failure due to the attack of American bullworm and mounting debt burden. His loan burden consisted of Rs. 1.84 lakhs from the commercial bank, Rs. 1.38 lakhs from commission agents and Rs. 50,000 from relatives. Now the family has 4 acres of land of which 3 acres have been sold to clear off the debt.
4. Mithu Singh, village *Sandoha,* committed suicide on May 29, 2001. His son Bindu Singh blamed the

commission agent who procured loans from banks by forging the signature of his father. This case remained a bone of contention among farmers' unions and associations of commission agents of the area for a long time. He was indebted to banks (Rs. 3.83 lakhs) and commission agent (Rs. 1.25 lakhs). The family had to sell 1 acre and the remaining 5 acres are pledged to the bank and the family's economic condition is very precarious.

5. Sabia Singh, village *Harkrishanpura* committed suicide in March, 1998 and his wife Nasib Kaur in March, 1999. Kunda Singh, brother of Sabia Singh, said that the reason for suicides was indebtedness, failure of cotton crop due to American bollworm and pressure exerted by lenders. The family was indebted to banks (Rs. 2.35 lakhs) and commission agents (Rs. 1.60 lakhs). The family had to sell 9 acres of land to pay the debt. Left with 6 acres of which 2 are mortgaged, the family has undergone the process of pauperisation and immiseration.
6. Malbeet Kaur w/o Gurjant Singh, village *Harkrishanpura* committed suicide in 2001. Her husband reported that mounting indebtedness and pressure exerted by the lenders on the family had become a cause of her suicide. Actually, the family was indebted to the tune of 3.5 lakhs; the Housefed (Rs. 2.00 lakhs), Commercial Bank (Rs. 1.0 lakhs) and relatives (Rs. 0.50 lakhs).The family was forced to sell 2 acres of land and are now left with 3 acres. The family's economic condition was so deplorable at the time of survey that they were thinking of selling the remaining land to clear the debt.
7. Jagraj Singh s/o Teja Singh, village *Harkrishanpura* committed suicide in 2001. The father of the deceased mentioned that the causes of suicide were debt burden, low crop yield and repeated failures of cotton crop. To clear the loan of Rs. 4.5 lakhs of banks and commission agents, the family sold 7 acres of land. Still, the family

owned 8 acres, of which 6 acres are dry land. As a result, the economic condition of family is still not good.

8. Harcharan Singh s/o Sucha Singh, village *Jivansinghwala* committed suicide on May 12, 2003. His father blamed a commission agent for confiscating the whole wheat crop which came into the market for sale purposes on May 7, 2003, at which the family felt humiliation and it become a triggering point for suicide. The family was indebted to the commission agent (Rs. 130,000), bank and cooperative society (Rs. 85,000) and relatives (Rs. 24,000). The family has 2.5 acres of cultivable land, but are now left with no other male earner and the economic condition of the family was pathetic during the survey.
9. Baldev Singh of village *Mour Charat Singh* having three young daughters committed suicide on June 6, 2005. His wife observed that repeated crop failure, low crop yield, lack of irrigation facilities, mounting debt burden and pressure exerted by the lenders were the reasons behind his suicide. This case also remained a bone of contention among farmers' unions and associations of commission agents. The family's outstanding debt was Rs. 1.15 lakhs. After selling one acre of land, the family is now left with 5 acres of barren land and the deceased's widow has to arrange the marriage of her three daughters.
10. Jagrup Singh s/o Ajit Singh, village *Chhatewal* committed suicide on May 5, 2002. His widow, Mrs. Jaspal Kaur stated that her husband committed suicide due to the burden of Rs.2.50 lakhs loan and humiliation meted out by the commission agent. His two brothers—Kulbir Singh and Booti Singh—had also committed suicide for the same reason, his mother died due to shock a few months later and the father under stress got a paralytic attack. The family's accumulated debt rose to Rs. 4.50 lakhs mainly of the banks and commission agents. The family sold some land and is

left with 2 acres. The economic condition of the family went from bad to worse and the widow, in the absence of social support, has to bear the entire economic burden of the family.

VI

Conclusions and Policy Implications

The analysis clearly suggests that agrarian distress, indebtedness and farmers' suicides in the state are interlinked, deep-rooted, complex and multi-dimensional phenomena which can be tackled and resolved through the multi-pronged short-term and long-term policy initiatives. In the first place, the Punjab government must release a relief package immediately in the form of financial support to the affected farmers' families on the basis of the survey conducted by the Punjab Government in two districts and being underway in other districts of the state. Further, more urgent steps should be taken for the rehabilitation of families of suicide victims by providing pensions for the widows/dependent children, employment to one family member, free education and job/skill-oriented education for the dependent children. Scaling down of interest rates and waiving of entire farm loans are some other suggestions.

Secondly, any type of harassment of indebted farmers and labourers must immediately be banned and the guilty should be penalised. Remunerative prices of farm products should be ensured to the farmers after considering the cost of cultivation. Crop insurance must be introduced and, in case of crop failure/damage, compensation at the market rate of farm production should be given. The state government must ensure adequate quality and reasonably low prices of various farm inputs.

Thirdly, cost of credit of both sources—commission agents and banks—should be reduced and monitored by the state. Corruption in sanctioning/advancing loans by the credit agencies and the malpractices of moneylenders/commission agents should be strictly dealt with and offenders must be punished. Budget provisions should be raised sufficiently for rural development and provisions of priority sector lending, of which agriculture as the main constituent, must be enforced upon so that the entire credit needs of the farmers, especially of the small and marginal farmers, be fulfilled. Some concrete steps must be taken to support the small and marginal farmers for their non-productive credit needs like the expenditure on consumption items, education and health from which they cannot escape.

Fourthly, the state government on its own or on cooperative basis should establish machinery/input delivery centres in a cluster of villages for small and marginal farmers. And, all machinery and input requirements of these farmers should be met at subsidised rates through these centres. Special measures should be taken in high suicide-prone cotton belt areas, namely, adequate supply of canal water for irrigation, especially to tail end villages, control over sale of spurious pesticides and seeds and timely purchase of cotton at remunerative prices. On the social front also, rural society must be sensitised on social problems such as dowry, female foeticide, alcoholism and drug abuse, ostentatious expenditure on social functions and to cultivate hard work ethics. The changing agrarian political economy in the state on one hand and disjunction between the interests of farmers and political elite, the farmer/*kisan* unions must be consolidated and led the farming community to fight the onslaught of the new capitalist regime by reorienting and reorganising their efforts and present a united force to press upon the state to initiate policy changes so that agrarian distress be phased out.

Finally, long-term policy measures to raise farm incomes on a sustainable basis should be initiated to develop rural physical and social infrastructure through large investments in the agriculture and related sectors. Extension of formal credit institutions, fulfilment of entire credit needs of small and marginal farmers and agricultural labourers at low rates of interest, modernising and refurbishing the canal irrigation systems along with social infrastructure of health and education require proper attention. Agriculture research should be strengthened to develop new high-yielding variety seeds, low cost cultivation techniques and the confidence of the farmers must be restored in agriculture research institutions and their extension services.

REFERENCES

AFDR (2000), *Suicides in Rural Areas of Punjab: A Report* (in Punjabi), Ludhiana.

Bhangoo, K.S. (2005), 'Agrarian Crisis: Indebtedness and Farmers' Suicides in Punjab', *Journal of Agriculture Development and Policy*, Vol. 17 (2), pp. 43-60.

Bhangoo, K.S. (2006), 'Farmers' Suicides in Punjab: A Study of Bathinda District', *Journal of Agriculture Development and Policy*, Vol. 18 (1&2), pp. 13-32.

Chahal, T.S. (2005), *Forced Fall: A Case of Punjab Farmers*, ID&P, Amritsar.

Darling, M.L. (1925), *Punjab Peasant in Prosperity and Debt*, Oxford University Press, London.

Gill, Anita and Lakhwinder Singh (2006), 'Farmers' Suicides and Response of Public Policy', *Economic and Political Weekly*, Vol. 41 (26), pp. 2762-68.

Gill, S.S. (2005), 'Economic Distress and Suicides in Rural Punjab', *Journal of Punjab Studies*, Vol. 12 (2), pp. 219-37.

Government of Punjab (2000), *Punjab Development Report*, Chandigarh.

Government of Punjab (2004), *Punjab Human Development Report*, Chandigarh.

Iyer, K.G. and M.S. Manick (2000), *Indebtedness, Impoverishment and Suicides in Rural Punjab*, Indian Publishers and Distributors, New Delhi.

Johdka, Surinder S. (2006), 'Beyond Crises: Rethinking Contemporary Punjab Agriculture', *Economic and Political Weekly*, Vol. 41 (16), pp. 1530-7.

IDC (1998), *Suicides in Rural Punjab*, Institute of Development and Communication (IDC), Chandigarh.

IDC (2006), *Suicides in Rural Punjab*, Institute of Development and Communication (IDC), Chandigarh.

Mathur, Archana S., Surajit Das and Subhalakshmi Sircar (2007), 'Status of Agriculture in India: Trends and Prospects', *Economic and Political Weekly*, Vol. 41 (52), pp. 5327-36.

MASR (2001), *Representation to the Union Minister for Agriculture on Suicide Deaths in Punjab*, Movement Against State Repression (MASR), Chandigarh.

Narayanamoorthy, A. (2006), 'Relief Package for Farmers: Can It Stop

Suicides?', *Economic and Political Weekly,* Vol. 41 (31), pp. 3353-55.

NSSO (2005), *Indebtedness of Farmer Households,* 59th Round, Publication No. 498, Government of India, New Delhi.

PSFC (2006), *Agricultural and Rural Development of Punjab: Transforming Crisis to Growth,* Punjab State Farmers' Commission, Government of Punjab, Chandigarh.

PSFC (2007), *Flow of Funds to Farmers and Indebtedness in Punjab,* Punjab State Farmers' Commission, Government of Punjab, Chandigarh.

Rangi, P.S. and M.S. Siddhu (2000), 'A Study of Contract Farming of Tomato in Punjab', *Agricultural Marketing,* Vol. 42 (4), pp. 15-23.

Satish, P. (2006), 'Institutional Credit, Indebtedness and Suicides in Punjab', *Economic and Political Weekly,* Vol. 41 (26), pp. 2754-61.

Shergill, H.S. (1998), *Rural Credit and Indebtedness in Punjab,* Institute of Development and Communication (IDC), Chandigarh.

Shergill, H.S. (2010), *Growth of Farm Debt in Punjab 1997 to 2008,* Institute of Development and Communication (IDC), Chandigarh.

Sidhu, R.S., Sukhpal Singh and A.S. Bhullar (2011), 'Farmer Suicides in Punjab: A Census Survey of the Two Most Affected Districts', *Economic and Political Weekly,* Vol. 46 (26 &27), pp. 131-7.

Sridhar, V. (2004), 'An Agrarian Tragedy', *Frontline,* Vol. 21 (13), June 19-July 2, Chennai.

Suri, K.C. (2006), 'Political Economy of Agrarian Distress', *Economic and Political Weekly,* Vol. 41 (16), pp. 1523-9.

9

Economic Conditions of Agricultural Labourers and Public Policies in Punjab

Sukhpal Singh and Sangeet

Punjab, the most prosperous state of the country till the 1990s, is now amidst an acute agrarian crisis. Its predominantly agrarian economy is at the crossroads as the declining agricultural productivity, nearly stagnant output prices and rising costs of production have hit the agricultural sector as a whole. An abrupt rise in the number of suicide cases in Punjab is clearly an indication of the sorry state of affairs of the agrarian structure of the state. According to the Census Survey of two districts—Bathinda and Sangrur—of Punjab, 2890 farmers and agricultural labourers have committed suicide during the 2000-2008 time period. As per these figures, the suicide rate per lakh per annum among the rural community was very high—63 per lakh for the farmers and 59 for the agricultural labourers (PAU, 2009). This shows that incidence of suicides among farmers and agricultural labour is almost the same in the state. Indebtedness and economic hardships are the major causes behind the rural suicides in Punjab. In an agrarian distress, agricultural labourers are likely to be the worst hit directly in agriculture through stagnated wages, reduced workdays and deep debt traps, and, indirectly in non-agriculture through multiplier effects. The debt trap is so serious that more than 70 per cent of agricultural labourers of Punjab faced indebtedness (Ghuman, et al., 2007). For them, the living crisis is so severe that a large number of agricultural labourers sleep without any roof. According to the Punjab Government Survey in 2010, out of the total 50,183 homeless families in the state, about 89 per cent belong to the Scheduled Castes (SCs) and Backward Classes (BCs) who are working as agricultural labourers (Government of Punjab, 2010).

Although the number of agricultural labourers has been declining, but agricultural labour is still the largest category of rural workers accounting for nearly 16 per cent of the total rural workforce (main and marginal workers together) after the cultivators in Punjab. Further, nearly 4.5 lakh migrant workers are also working in Punjab's agriculture sector in a given year. The use of tractors and harvester combines has displaced farm labour on a large scale, especially the women and unskilled workers. On the basis of per hectare labour use in the crop year, demand for human labour is estimated to have fallen from 479.3 million man-days in 1983-84 to 421.93 million man-days in 2000-01 (Sidhu and Singh, 2004). It has also been noted that the permanent agricultural labourers are turning to casual labourers due to the mechanisation of major farm operations, slow down of agricultural growth, mono-culture of wheat-paddy crops and inflow of migrant labour in the state.

Many recent reports and studies have shown that the Green Revolution technology has squeezed the employment opportunities in the farm sector, which pushed the agricultural labour towards deprivation and pauperisation (Singh, et al., 2007a; Singh, et al., 2007b; PAU, 2009). This chapter is largely based on an empirical analysis of the economic conditions of agricultural labourers by estimating employment status, levels of income and consumption of such labour households. The impact of various government welfare schemes on these households in the state has also been examined. A total number of 300 agricultural labour households were selected, choosing 50 households from each of the six villages (two in each district) in three districts, namely, Fatehgarh Sahib, Bathinda and Ferozepur; representing three different zones of crop productivity areas of state. The data were collected from the respondent agricultural labour households through the structured schedules by the personal interview method during 2008-09.

The chapter has been divided into three sections. Section I examines the various impacts of the agrarian crisis on the agricultural labour households. Section II scrutinises the meagre benefits derived by agricultural labour households from government welfare schemes in the state. A summary of main conclusions and public policy issues has been reproduced in Section III.

I

Dimensions and Magnitude of the Agrarian Crisis

1.1 Impact on Employment and Income

The capitalistic mode of production has squeezed employment opportunities which eroded the income of farmers in an agrarian economy. An analysis of data shows that agricultural labour has nearly five members (4.98 persons) per household. Of them, 1.92 persons are the main earners and 1.18 persons are semi-earners. It means that every agricultural labour household in the state has 3.10 persons as earners. Further, an agricultural labour household consisting of 3.10 workers is actually able to get 400 days of employment only, whereas the household should have got 930 days of employment per annum (Table 9.1). The proportion of the actual number of employment days to the potential days of employment works out to 43.01 per cent. In spite of the liberal norm of 300 days as the full employment situation for a given year, these workers remain unemployed for 530 days, i.e. about five months in a year. All these facts confirm that (i) the rural workforce in agricultural labour households did not get adequate days of employment in a year; and (ii) in a battle of man versus machine, the man is a loser with reduced days of work for his/her livelihood.

While studying the different sources of income of agricultural labour households in Punjab, it has been observed that an average agricultural labour household earns Rs. 30,785 per annum from all the sources (Table 9.2). As expected, the main source of their income is from hiring out casual labour in the agriculture as, on an average, about 45 per cent of the total income is exclusively earned from this source. The next important source of income is hiring out labour in the construction works (20 per cent) in neighbouring cities and towns, especially during the lean period of farming. Permanent agricultural labour which was meant for the whole year had been considered as the key area of employment and income of agricultural labour in rural areas during the decades of the 1980s and 90s. At that time, they earned almost 40-50 per cent of their income from this source which has drastically declined to just 13.80 per cent of their average income in 2008-09. The mono-culture of crops and capital-intensive Green Revolution model have narrowed down the season and reduced the working days which turned the permanent labour into the casual ones. Apart from this, the agricultural labourers also enhance their income from the non-farm activities. For instance, some of them earn income from tiny enterprises like vending and shopkeeping (8 per cent), working as domestic servants (4 per cent) and dairying (2 per cent). Salaries and pensions account for just 1.50 per cent of their average income which indicates that agricultural labour families are under great constraints of the job market. In some cases, they receive old age pensions of Rs. 250 per month, which is also of an irregular

Table 9.1: Employment Pattern of Agricultural Labour Households in Punjab

Description	*Per Household*	*Per Capita*
Family Size	4.98	-
Earners	1.92	0.39
Semi-Earners	1.18	0.24
Earners plus Semi-Earners	3.10	0.62
	(62.25 % of family size)	
Estimated Working Days if Earners and Semi-Earners Get Work for 300 Days Per Year	930	300
Days Actually Worked	400	129
Days of Unemployment	530	171
Days Actually Worked (%)	43.01	-

Source: Primary Survey.

nature, as collaborated by another study (Gill, Singh and Brar, 2012).

Table 9.2: Sources of Income of Agricultural Labour Households in Punjab

Source of income	*Average Income (Rs/annum)*	*%age*
Casual Agricultural Labour	13687	44.46
Labour in Construction/Brick Kiln	6158	20.00
Permanent Agricultural Labour	4247	13.80
Shop and Vendors	2463	8.00
Industrial Labour	1430	4.64
Domestic Servants	1230	4.00
Dairying	615	2.00
Salaries and Pensions	462	1.50
Others (sale of manure, remittances)	493	1.60
Total	**30785**	**100**

Source: Primary Survey.

1.2 Consumption Pattern

On an average, per annum consumption expenditure for an agricultural labour household is Rs. 33,982 (Table 9.3). Amongst different components of the consumption expenditure, as expected, food items take away the major share, i.e. about 66 per cent followed by the services (10.12 per cent), socio-religious ceremonies (9.05 per cent), non-durables (8.22 per cent) and durables (6.34 per cent). Among the food items, cereals and pulses account for the major proportion, followed by edible oils, sugar and tea, milk and milk products, fruits and vegetables, intoxicants, spices and salt. Services include health care treatment, education, travelling, electricity, and phone/mobile bills. Non-durables include clothes, footwear, fuel, washing and toilet articles. Durables include house construction/repair, scooters/cycles, radios, televisions, watches, hand pumps, sewing machines, fans and utensils. In a similar study for rural labour Punjab, it was found that the rural poor households spend more than 62 per cent of their income on food, 24 per cent on clothing and fuel, and the remaining 14 per cent on recreation activities (Singh, 2008).

Table 9.3: Consumption Pattern of Agricultural Labour Households in Punjab

Consumption Items	*Average Consumption Expenditure Rs/Annum*	*Rs/Per Capita Daily*	*% age*
Food	22521	12.39	66.27
Services	3439	1.89	10.12
Socio-Religious Ceremonies	3076	1.69	9.05
Non-Durables	2791	1.54	8.22
Durables	2155	1.19	6.34
Total Consumption Expenditure	33982	18.70	100.00

Source: Primary Survey.

Further, per capita daily consumption expenditure of an agricultural labour household was found to be abysmally low, i.e. Rs. 18.70; of which Rs. 12.39 is allocated to food items only. Other components of average consumption expenditure of an agricultural labour household measured by per capita per day basis are too minimal to count. In fact, one of the larger social dimensions of the agrarian crisis witnessed in Punjab is mirrored through declining income and consumption levels of the agricultural labourers. Extensive diet surveys carried out in India and across states over the last several years have also shown that the diet of a sizeable proportion of our population, who belong to the poor income groups, are inadequate according to the accepted standards (Gopalan, et al., 1982).

1.3 Incidence of Poverty and Indebtedness

The term 'poverty' is defined, in terms of head count ration, as the inability of an individual to meet a certain minimum desirable standard of living. All those agricultural labour households which have per capita consumption below Rs. 2,500 are considered as poor households. Per capita income among the sampled agricultural labour households is equal to Rs. 6,181 against the per capita consumption expenditure of Rs. 6,824. In this way, it is found that about 26 per cent of the agricultural labourers are living below the poverty line. Average propensity to consume is 1.10 (Table 9.4). Further while studying various factors affecting the poverty among the agricultural labourers, it is found that about 79 per cent of variations in the per capita consumption of agricultural labourers are explained by the magnitude of farm employment, family size, number of earners in the non-farm sector, income level and repayment of loan as shown in Table 9.5. All these factors except the family size and repayment of loan are found to contribute positively towards the poverty among households. All this may be due to the low education level amongst the agricultural labour families.

Regarding the debt condition of labour households, the study revealed that the average amount of debt per indebted household is Rs. 23,438 per annum while the same is Rs. 18,750 for an average sampled household in the state (Table 9.6). Further, 68 per cent of agricultural labour households are under debt. It is also noticed that they borrow about 91 per cent of their loans from non-institutional sources, out of which the major part comes from the landlords and village moneylenders who charge exorbitant rates of interest. Further, it is found that about 91 per cent of the loan is used for consumption purposes like food, recreation, social functions, etc. and only about 9 per cent is spent on productive purposes. The extent of outstanding loan is observed to be considerably high in the case of those agricultural labour households, who use the loan for unproductive purposes. Thus, they remain in the clutches of landlords and village moneylenders.

Table 9.4: Poverty Among Agricultural Labour Households in Punjab

Parameters	*Values*
Per Capita Income (Rs.)	6181
Per Capita Consumption (Rs.)	6824
Average Propensity to Consume (APC)	1.10
Persons Below Poverty Line (%)	26.37

Source: Primary Survey.

Table 9.5: Factors Affecting Poverty Among Agricultural Labour Households—Results of Log-Linear Regression Function (Dependent Variable-Per Capita Consumption)

Factors	*Regression Coefficient*	*t-Value*
Constant	0.1137NS	1.487
Farm Employment (Days/Capita)	0.4334***	3.261
Family Size\ Dependency Ratio (No.)	-0.2156NS	1.361
Earners in Non-Farm Sector (No.)	0.4963***	3.959
Income Level (Rs./Annum)	0.4135**	1.985
Repayment of Loan (Rs./Annum)	-0.0814**	2.092
R^2	0.7884***	

*** Significant at 1 % level, ** Significant at 5 % level, NS: Non-Significant.

Source: Primary Survey.

Table 9.6: Debt Position of Agricultural Labour in Punjab

Description	*Agricultural Labour*
Households Under Debt (%)	68.00
Debt Per Household (Rs.)	18750
Debt Per Indebted Household (Rs.)	23438
Source of Finance (%)	
a. Institutional Sources	8.98
b. Non-Institutional Sources	91.02
Purpose of Credit (%)	
a. Productive Purpose	9.10
b. Consumption Purpose	90.90

Source: Primary Survey.

II

Least Benefits Derived from Government Schemes

Although a large number of schemes and programmes have been started for the upliftment of weaker sections in our country, but still a vast proportion of population has been living in poverty and deprivation. There is always a question mark on the access and delivery mechanism of the state welfare schemes. The study, therefore, analyses the access of agricultural labourers to these schemes (Table 9.7) and makes a modest attempt to quantify the financial benefits of these welfare schemes gained by them (Table 9.8). An assessment of the data reveals that only 10 per cent of the sampled families visit public health centres and the major chunk of these people go to private doctors. This shows that public health system has collapsed in the rural areas. Only 2.46 per cent of labour families have access to private public schools. And, about 37 per cent children of agricultural labour families are going to the primary schools for education, nearly 28 per cent in the high schools and 20 per cent in the secondary education. Further, only 34 per cent of them visit the banks merely for withdrawing old age pensions or MGNREGS wages as otherwise the agricultural labourers do not have enough earnings for the savings. About 24 per cent have access to the veterinary hospitals. Only 1.25 per cent of the labour households visit cooperative societies for various purposes as these societies mainly provide agricultural credit and inputs to the members of the society.

As regards benefits received by the labour families from different government schemes, it is found that about 31 per cent of families are getting old age pension of Rs. 920 per year and only about 28 per cent are satisfied with it (Table 9.8). The Shagun scheme for marriage of young girls is noted for about 21 per cent of families with the average amount being Rs. 1,430 per year and about 18 per cent of the labour families are satisfied with it. And, those who are getting free education constitute 35 per cent of total families and just 30 per cent among them are happy with the amount, i.e. Rs. 400 per year. Only 1.67 per cent of the families got residential plots and out of these, only one per cent felt satisfied. Free electricity is available to about 76 per cent families at the charges of Rs. 2,600 per year and only 18 per cent are happy with it because of severe power cuts. Interestingly, about 99 per cent of agricultural labour households are enjoying the facility of having a ration card, however, only 20 per cent are satisfied with the benefits of ration cards as most of them are unable to get any worthwhile financial benefits like getting subsidised items such as sugar, kerosene, etc due to the prevailing malpractices and black marketing in the public distribution system of the state.

Table 9.7: Agricultural Labour Families Having Access to Different Social Amenities

Amenity	*Proportion of Families Having Access (%)*
Health Centre	10.00
Primary School	36.50
High School	28.30
Secondary School	20.00
Public School (Private)	2.46
Banks	34.00
Veterinary Hospital	24.30
Cooperative Society	1.25

Source: Primary Survey.

Table 9.8: Benefits to Agricultural Labour Households from Government Schemes

Government Schemes	*Proportion of Beneficiary Households*	*Amount (Rs./Annum)*	*Level of Satisfaction (%)*
Residential Plots	1.67	184	1.00
Shagun Scheme	20.67	1430	18.33
Old Age Pension	30.66	920	28.33
Free Education	35.00	400	30.00
Free Electricity	75.67	2600	18.33
Ration Cards	98.66	-	20.00

Source: Primary Survey.

III

Main Conclusions and Public Policy Issues

The agriculture sector in Punjab is facing an unprecedented and multi-faceted crisis. In fact, the crisis has been manifested in the decelerated growth in agricultural output, overall profitability and employment elasticity in agriculture. In a period of such agrarian distress, agricultural labourers are likely to be the worst hit, and become the most vulnerable section of the rural labour force to find adequate employment in the agricultural sector itself. The prevalence of high unemployment and under-employment among the agricultural labourers resulted in low income, under consumption and indebtedness. As a result, malnutrition prevails among the agricultural labourers which keep them un-healthy and under constant physical stress. The quantity and quality of civil amenities enjoyed by these poor sections is far from satisfactory. The living conditions of these people are vulnerable as greater numbers of agricultural labour families are either homeless or living in unhygienic conditions. Only 20 to 30 per cent of the agricultural labour families were found to have access to the different social amenities like safe drinking water, toilets, etc. There should be a progressive increase in wage rates of agricultural labourers. Also, steps should be taken for development of the rural non-farm sectors so that gainful employment can be created for them. Moreover, the functional efficiency of government institutions needs to be improved. Agricultural labourers are under heavy debt burden, particularly of farmers and petty-shopkeepers who charge exorbitant rates of interest from them. Therefore, the flow of institutional credit must be increased at low rates of interest with easy repayment facilities to this vulnerable section of rural society. In the given socio-economic and political structure, all these measures may be helpful for solving some of the problems of agricultural labourers in the state.

REFERENCES

Ghuman, R.S., Inderjit Singh and Lakhwinder Singh (2007), *Status of Local Agricultural Labour in Punjab,* Punjab State Farmers Commission, Government of Punjab, Mohali, Punjab.

Gill, S.S., Sukhwinder Singh and Jaswinder Singh Brar (2012), *Social Security in Punjab: A Blend of State and Central Schemes, Working Paper 21,* HiVOS Knowledge Programme, Centre for Development Studies, Trivandrum (Kerala), Amsterdam Institute for Social Science Research (AISSR), University of Amsterdam and Humanist Institute for Cooperation in Developing Countries (HiVOS), The Hague, The Netherlands, pp. 1-32.

Government of Punjab (2010), *Survey Information,* Department of Rural Development and Panchayat, Chandigarh.

Gopalan, C., B.V. Ramasastri and S.C. Balasubramanian (1982), *Nutritive Value of Indian Foods,* National Institute of Nutrition and Indian Council of Medical Research, Hyderabad, (India), pp. 42-7.

PAU (2009), *Farmers' and Agricultural Labourers' Suicides Due to Indebtedness in the Punjab State: A Pilot Survey of Bathinda and Sangrur Districts,* Punjab Agricultural University, Ludhiana.

Sidhu, R.S. and Sukhpal Singh (2004), 'Agricultural Wages and Employment in Punjab', *Economic and Political Weekly,* 39 (37), September 11, pp. 4132-5.

Singh, K., Sukhpal Singh, and H.S. Kingra (2007a), *Status of Farmers Who Left Farming in Punjab,* A Joint Study by the Punjab State Farmers' Commission and Punjab Agricultural University, Ludhiana, pp. 1-51.

Singh, K., Sukhpal Singh, M. Kaur, and H.S. Kingra (2007b), *Flow of Funds to Farmers and Indebtedness in Punjab,* A Joint Study by the Punjab State Farmers' Commission and Punjab Agricultural University, Ludhiana, pp. 1-70.

Singh, Satjit (2008), Human Capital, Household Inequality and Public Policy: A Case Study of Rural Punjab, *Unpublished Ph. D. Thesis,* Department of Economics, Punjabi University, Patiala.

PART V

Gender Employment and Social Security Perspectives in Punjab

10

Gender Dimensions of Employment in Punjab

Kanwaljit Kaur Gill

Introduction

Employment growth rate is an important indicator of economic growth and development of an economy. Employment rate shows the proportion of working people to the total population of a country. The participation of the workforce in the labour market varies from country to country, region to region, and within the region. It also varies between males and females. Females constitute almost half the population of each country. It is generally expected that the benefits of development will trickle down and disperse evenly among the masses, males and females, and in lieu of that, they participate in the labour market, provide their services and contribute to the national GDP.

Article 39 of the Indian Constitution declares that, 'the citizens, men and women equally, have the right to an adequate means of livelihood', and 'there is equal pay for equal work for both men and women'. But, unfortunately these principles/ rights are not fully translated into practice and the benefits of economic development are not equally distributed among the males and females. In fact, women are being discriminated against in almost all facets of life. And, this discrimination starts in a woman's life even before she actually takes birth, even during the embryonic stage and moves along with her from childhood (malnutrition, less food, less and poor quality of education as compared to her male siblings in the family) to adulthood (early marriage, repeated births, etc.) to as mature woman and up to her old age. Truly, this patriarchal society does not have a rational and positive attitude towards females. They are rated as second rate citizens, bound by duties only to carry on the traditional norms and values, sometimes even at the cost of their health.

Although over a period of time, some positive changes have occurred that are favourable to females, but still a lot is to be done to make them equal partners and consumers in the development process and development benefits respectively. For instance, many significant changes are taking place in the labour market at the international level, and these changes are visible in gender dimensions of the Indian labour market as well, specifically after the implementation of the new economic policy backed by the ideology of globalisation, liberalisation and privatisation. These changes and shift in the female workforce participation rates have given rise to certain issues which need immediate attention. As being noticed, a major chunk of the female labour force still remain unemployed; either due to lack of work opportunities or due to mismatch between the acquired skills and the high-tech work available. And, in the present phase of mechanisation, there are certain trends working against the female workers like the feminisation of work but women are being marginalised in the labour market; more and more casual/contract work now available in the unorganised private sectors, hence more casual opportunities for the female workers; and because of more and more female employment in the unorganised private sectors, differentials in wage payments are also becoming a common phenomenon.

Moreover, the overall percentage of persons in India's labour force, as per the different NSSO Rounds, has declined from 66.5 per cent in 1983 to 64.5 per cent in 1993-94 and further to 61.8 per cent in 1999-2000 (GOI, 2002). This decline was as high as 13.28 per cent for females and just 4.13 per cent for males during this period. And, across the states, the decline in labour force participation was observed during this time period almost in all the states; except for the states of Haryana, Andhra Pradesh, Himachal Pradesh and some small north-eastern states, where a marginal increase was observed between 1983 and 1993-94, but thereafter again followed by a decline. Even, in the developed Indian states like Kerala, Punjab, Haryana, Gujarat and Maharashtra, the decline in labour force participation rates was observed.

The (economically) advanced/developed states (Kerala, Punjab, and Haryana), as expected, do not have higher female work participation and neither has the rising female literacy direct/positive impacts on more female employment, rather in some states, higher female literacy is showing a lower female work participation rate as it was witnessed in Kerala. This paradoxical scenario has been investigated in this chapter with special reference to the state of Punjab, where all development indicators show, that Punjab is one amongst the top most developed states, better in literacy, limited population living below the poverty line, but still it does not enjoy a comfortable position with respect to the female work participation rate. The nature and structure of the female work participation rate still reflects the social prejudice against females in the patriarchal society of Punjab.

Punjab undoubtedly is one of the most developed states across the major states of India. With respect to HDI rank, it maintained its second position since 1981. Though Haryana is also emerging as an equal competitor, as in per capita income, but Punjab as per 2001 HDI rank is just next to Kerala. At one point of time, Punjab was known for its rich culture, open and broad minded people, adjustable to the changing environment (social, political, and even economical) and her strong and healthy young males always ready to face any adverse situation. But somehow, this socio-cultural richness is dying and the economy is not moving in the desired directions of development. In spite of the fact that Punjab is better in the literacy rate, agricultural production and per capita income, its youth is migrating to other countries in search of better employment opportunities and living standards. It has many implications on the indigenous employment scenario. In fact, the nature and structure of employment is changing over time, especially in the case of female employment. These trends in female work participation indicate that there is a gradual upward tendency in female employment over the past two decades (since 1983 to 2005-06 as per NSSO rounds) or so. But, it might be noted that most of the additional employment perhaps went to the women as subsidiary workers with very marginal gains as the principal workers (Mazumdar and Sarkar, 2008, in Rustagi, 2010). Although the female work participation rate is increasing all over the world, but it is still lower than that of males, and secondly, women workers are disproportionately represented in the non-standard and lower-paid forms of work, contract work, casual, part-time, home-based work, self-employment and work in small and micro-enterprises (*World Women's Report, 2000*). Hence, it becomes important to investigate if quantitatively female work participation has increased than what is its nature? Further, sectoral shift from the primary sector to the tertiary sector, and from the self-employed to casual worker needs state intervention to devise employment policy in general and for female employment, in particular, to create regular jobs. Skill formation is equally important to make their entry easy in the manufacturing sector as well.

Measuring Gender Gaps in Employment in Punjab

It is true that the overall work participation rate in India as a whole has remained higher for males compared to their counterpart females both in the rural as well as in the urban areas. This also holds true for Punjab. The NSSO data produce additional evidence to this. The agrarian nature of the Punjab economy gave a justification to explain that the overall work participation rate in rural areas is higher than in urban areas. Table 10.1 gives an overall scenario of employment trends. From 1983 to 1999-2000, there is decline in the work participation rate for males both in India and Punjab. After that during 2004-05, an increasing trend has been observed. And, if someone takes the male-female WPR individually, then the scene becomes clearer as it indicates that whether there is decline or rise in the WPR, the gender gap remains there.

Further, the analysis shows that, during 1993-94, the gender gap in the WPR in Punjab increased to 39.3 per cent from 33.5 per cent in 1983. This phase was the phase of turmoil in Punjab. Political disturbances forced the industrial units to either slow down existing production or shift from Punjab to some other peaceful states. The agriculture sector also suffered a lot during that period. All these had negative long-term impacts on the employment both for males and females even during 1999-2000. The FWPR was just 20.2 per cent and MWPR came down from 55.9 per cent in 1983 to 53.9 per cent in 1999-2000, thereby, giving the gender gap of about 34 per cent. FWPR in Punjab has remained less than that of the national average throughout this period of 1983 to 1993-94 which is the pre-reform period and from 1993-94 to 2004-05 the post-reform period. Further, it is noted that the gender gap in WPR is even less at all-India level, and over a period of time, the gender gap has declined from 32.2 per cent in 1983 to 26.0 per cent in 2004-05, whereas in Punjab it has remained almost the same during this period. This reflects Punjab's social reality and social prejudice against females.

Table 10.1: Distribution of Usual Status (PS+SS) of All Workers

Year	*Male*	*Female*	*Total*	*Gender gap*
India				
1983	53.8	21.6	42.0	32.2
1993-94	54.5	28.6	42.0	25.9
1999-00	52.7	25.9	39.7	26.8
2004-05	54.7	28.7	42.0	26.0
Punjab				
1983	55.9	22.4	39.1	33.5
1993-94	55.0	15.7	36.4	39.3
1999-00	53.9	20.2	38.1	33.7
2004-05	56.1	22.8	40.9	33.3

Source: NSSO, 38th, 50th, 55th and 61st Rounds.

In terms of growth rate, the data reveals that the average annum compound growth rate (ACGR) in FWPR of Punjab does not match that of India. For example, ACGR for males in India was

2.53 per cent during the pre-reform period (1983 to 1993-94) and for females, it was as high as 5.26 per cent. But, in Punjab, it was only 1.82 per cent for males, and was negative (-) 1.57 per cent for females during the same period. Most plausibly, it might be due to the disturbed political situation in Punjab which has an adverse impact on the state's economy in the form of discouraging further investments. During the post-reform period (1993-94 to 1999-2000), FWPR experienced a great spurt when from a negative growth rate in employment, ACGR increased to 4.71 per cent per annum. It means that the post-reform period has shown an encouraging effect on the growth rate of female employment as it further increased to 5.52 per cent per annum during the period of 1993-94 to 2004-05, whereas for males, it is even less than half (2.15 per cent) than that of females. This negates the supposition that globalisation has a negative impact on FWPR.

Table 10.2: Average Annual Compound Growth Rate of Usual Status Workers, 1983 to 2004-05

Time Period	*Male*	*Female*	*Total*
India			
1983 to 1993-94	2.53	5.26	2.37
1993-94 to 1999-2000	1.11	0.31	0.84
1999-2000 to 2004-05	1.93	2.81	2.18
1993-94 to 2004-05	2.12	2.12	2.09
1983 to 2004-2005	3.01	4.74	2.89
Punjab			
1983 to 1993-94	1.82	-1.57	1.25
1993-94 to 1999-2000	1.19	4.71	2.03
1999-2000 to 2004-05	1.89	2.95	2.29
1993-94 to 2004-05	2.15	5.52	3.04
1983 to 2004-2005	2.58	2.61	2.80

Note: Calculated from Table 10.1

Source: NSSO, 38th, 50th, 55th and 61st Rounds.

Again, a question arises in one's mind not regarding the rising quantity of female work, but whether females are able to get quality employment in the development process, especially in the unorganised private sector of the state. For this purpose, an exercise involving occupational shift of workforce at regional level is required to grasp the reality. The next discussion has been devoted to this.

Changing Female Employment Scenario in Punjab

The employment scene at rural level and their structural shift from the agriculture sector to the tertiary sector reflects economic growth on one side and rising quality of human capital on the other. The rural-urban divide of WPR in Punjab indicates (Table 10.3) that the proportion of rural males in the total male workforce declined from 58.1 in 1983 to 53.0 in 1999-2000 and then increased to 54.9 per cent in 2004-05. But, the FWPR experienced a sharp decline in the initial phase of 1983 to 1993-94 (from 31.9 per cent to 22.0 per cent), and then again, it increased to 28.0 per cent in 1999-2000 and to 32.2 per cent in 2004-05. A similar trend was observed at the urban level also when in the pre-reform period, the FWPR declined from 12.9 per cent in 1983 to 9.3 per cent in 1993-94, but during the post-reform period, it increased to 12.5 per cent in 1999-2000 and further to 13.3 per cent in 2004-05. Gender gap at rural level is less as compared to the urban level, indicating that more and more females are engaged in work at the rural level, mostly in the primary, the agriculture sector.

Table 10.3: Distribution of Usual Status Workers in Punjab by Sex and Region, 1983 to 2004-05

Year	*Rural*			*Urban*			*Total*			*Gender Gap in WPR*		
	M	*F*	*P*	*M*	*F*	*P*	*M*	*F*	*P*	*R (1-2)*	*U (4-5)*	*T (7-8)*
	(1)	*(2)*	*(3)*	*(4)*	*(5)*	*(6)*	*(7)*	*(8)*	*(9)*	*(10)*	*(11)*	*(12)*
1983	58.1	31.9	45.0	53.7	12.9	33.3	55.9	22.4	39.1	26.2	40.8	33.5
1993-94	54.6	22.0	39.2	55.3	9.3	33.6	55.0	15.7	36.4	32.6	46.0	39.3
1999-00	53.0	28.0	41.0	54.9	12.5	35.3	53.9	20.2	38.1	25.0	42.4	33.7
2004-05	54.9	32.2	45.2	57.2	13.3	36.5	56.1	22.8	40.9	22.7	43.9	33.3

Source: NSSO Reports of 38th, 50th, 55th and 61st Rounds

Further, an assessment of data in Table 10.4 makes it clear that the average annual growth rate in WPR was much higher for females in rural areas (4.12 per cent) during 1993-94 to 1999-2000 compared to males (0.53 per cent) during the same period. The same rising trend in ACGR in WPR continued for females when it reached 4.95 during the next period of 1993-94 to 2004-05. This implies that, as compared to the pre-reform period, more rural females were able to get work during the post-reform era (Gill and Kaur, 2010b). Also, FWPR increased at the higher rate in the urban areas (6.81 per cent) during this period compared to the males (3.86 per cent). This was partially due to an increase in work opportunities in information technology and call centres. Though such types of jobs are contract basesd and low paid, yet these work opportunities have widespread impacts on females' jobs in urban areas.

Table 10.4: Annual Compound Growth Rate of Usual Status Workers in Punjab by Sex and Region, 1983 to 2004-05

Period	*Rural*			*Urban*			*Total*		
	M	*F*	*P*	*M*	*F*	*P*	*M*	*F*	*P*
1983 to 1993-94	0.96	-2.09	0.21	3.21	-0.41	2.99	1.82	-1.57	1.25
1993-94 to 1999-00	0.53	4.12	1.50	2.47	6.37	3.13	1.19	4.77	2.03
1999-00 to 2004-05	1.32	2.82	2.21	3.01	3.11	2.81	1.89	2.95	2.29
1993-94 to 2004-05	1.28	4.95	2.60	3.86	6.81	4.21	2.15	5.52	3.04
1983 to 2004-05	1.46	1.90	1.69	4.61	4.21	4.71	2.58	2.61	2.80

Source: Calculated from Table 10.3 by using population data of Census 1981, 1991 and 2001.

Moreover, the occupational distribution of usual status women workers at rural and urban levels in India also indicates that in the category of professionals, technical and related works, an overall increase was there for the females compared to the males during the period of 1993-94 to 2004-05 both at rural and urban levels (Rustagi, 2010). This is largely due to an increase in female literacy during this time in India as well as in Punjab. For instance, female literacy increased from 50.41 per cent in 1991 to 63.55 in 2001 (rural female literacy was 57.91 compared to urban female literacy 74.63 in 2001). Urban female literacy, to some extent attainment of professional education, has helped them joining the professional, technical and related works, administrative, executive and managerial workers (though only 3 to 5 per cent share) and other service sectors. In rural areas, more and more females are engaged in the activities related to farming, collecting firewood, cooking, making cow-dung cakes, bringing potable water (not very common in Punjab) and other similar work. While in the urban areas, most of the females are engaged in the production and related works and also in the construction activities.

Structural Change in Female Employment and Quality of Work in Punjab

With the process of economic development, the structure and occupational pattern naturally undergoes a qualitative as well as the quantitative changes. Generally, labour shifts from the primary to the secondary and tertiary sectors during the course of development. It is quite expected that Punjab, being one of the most developed states, where the majority of population engaged in agricultural (primary) activities developed on the capitalist lines along with positive developments in small-scale industries and the tertiary sector, has witnessed occupational shifts and structural changes in female employment (Gill and Kaur, 2010b).

Table 10.5 presents sectoral distribution of female workers (usual status) in Punjab. The data indicates that in rural Punjab, 92.4 per cent females were engaged in the primary sector in 1983. After a marginal increase of 0.3 percentage points during 1993-94, it declined to 90.6 in 1999-2000 and to 89.7 per cent in 2004-05. An increase in FWPR was observed from 2.8 per cent in 1983 to 5.7 per cent in 1993-94 in the tertiary sector at the rural level which further increased to 6.8 per cent in 1999-2000 (Gill and Kaur, 2010a).

However, the secondary sector did not gain much from this structural shift as the share of FWPR declined from 4.2 in 1983 to 1.5 per cent in 1993-94. After that, it observed an increase from

2.6 per cent in 1999-2000 to 3.8 per cent in 2004-05, but it was just half of those who were engaged in the tertiary sector (Table 10.5). Most of the females that shifted from the primary sector to the secondary sector were those engaged in self-employment with the tiny or small domestic and manufacturing units. Others shifted to the service providers, community services, or home-based services like petty professionals (tailoring, beauty parlour, crèches, etc.) or sales workers like running shops, etc.

Table 10.5: Sectoral Distribution of Rural Usual Status (Ps+ss) Female Workers, 1983 to 2004-05

Sector/s	*NSSO Rounds by Year*							
	1983		*1993-94*		*1999-00*		*2004-05*	
	India	*Punjab*	*India*	*Punjab*	*India*	*Punjab*	*India*	*Punjab*
1. Primary Sector	87.8	92.4	86.6	92.7	85.7	90.6	83.6	89.7
a. Agriculture, Hunting, Fishing, Forestry,etc.	87.5	92.2	86.2	92.7	85.4	90.6	83.3	89.7
b. Mining & Quarrying	0.3	0.2	0.4	0	0.3	0	0.3	0
2. Secondary Sector	7.1	4.2	8	1.5	8.6	2.6	9.9	3.8
a. Manufacturing	6.4	4.2	6.4	1.3	7.6	2.3	8.4	2.3
b. Public Utilities (electricity, gas, water)	0	0	0.1	0.2	0	0.2	0	0
c. Construction	0.7	0.1	0.9	0	1.1	0.1	1.5	1.5
3. Tertiary Sector	4.8	2.8	5.6	5.7	5.8	6.8	6.6	6.4
a. Trade & Hotels	1.9	0.6	2.1	1	2	1.1	2.5	2.5
b. Transport, Communication, & Storage	0.1	0.1	0	0	0.1	0	0.2	0.2
c. Other Services	0	0	0	0	0.1	0	0.1	0.1
Financial/Community	3	2.1	3.3	4.7	3.6	5.7	3.8	3.8

Source: NSSO Reports, 38th, 50th, 55th and 61st Rounds.
Note: Financial services include financial insurance, real estate and business services. Community services include community, social and personal services.

However, the trends across sectoral distribution of female workers are entirely different in urban Punjab. For instance, the urban FWPR in the primary sector has come to half in 2004-

05 (15.2 per cent) when compared to 31.1 per cent in 1983. In the secondary sector, more females were visible in the small manufacturing units at the urban level. In 1983, FWPR in the secondary sector was 23.9 per cent which declined to half (12.0 per cent) in 1993-94. But, after that, due to increasing privatisation and shrinkage of regular jobs, females engaged themselves in self-employment and others who were reasonably literate; they accepted even low paid jobs on contract and part-time basis. This raised their work participation rate from 15.5 per cent in 1999-2000 to 25.1 per cent in 2004-05, the majority of them were employed in the manufacturing sector (Table 10.6).

Table 10.6: Sectoral Distribution of Urban Usual Status (Ps+ss) Female Workers, 1983 to 2004-05

Sector/s	*NSSO Rounds by Year*							
	1983		*1993-94*		*1999-00*		*2004-05*	
	India	*Punjab*	*India*	*Punjab*	*India*	*Punjab*	*India*	*Punjab*
1. Primary Sector	31.6	31.1	25.3	27.6	18.1	20.1	18.3	15.2
a. Agriculture, Hunting, Fishing, Forestry, etc.	31.0	31.5	2.4.7	27.6	17.7	20.1	18.1	15.2
b. Mining & Quarrying	0.6	0.0	0.6	0.0	0.4	0.0	0.2	0.0
2. Secondary Sector	30.0	23.9	28.5	12	29	15.5	32.2	25.1
a. Manufact-uring	26.7	22.8	24.1	10.2	24	13.4	28.2	23.1
b. Public Utilities (Electricity, gas, water)	-0.2	1.2	0.3	0.8	0.2	0.7	0.2	1.2
c. Construction	3.1	0.0	4.1	1	4.8	1.4	3.8	0.8
3. Tertiary Sector	37.6	42.5	46.3	60.2	52.9	64.3	49.5	59.6
a. Trade & Hotels	9.5	5.3	10.0	8.2	16.9	25.1	12.2	4.6
b. Transport, Communication, & Storage	1.5	0.8	1.3	0.4	1.8	2.1	1.4	0.8
c. Other Services	0.3	0.5	0.9	0.1	0.5	0.3	0.2	0.6
Financial/Community	25.3	33.9	33.1	49.5	31.7	35.8	32.7	51.6

Source: NSSO Reports, 38th, 50th, 55th and 61st Rounds.

Note: Financial services include financial insurance, real estate and business services. Community services include community, social and personal services.

Interestingly, the FWPR for self-employed in the rural areas has remained higher compared to the urban areas. Whereas the FWPR as casual workers was almost the same for the rural and urban females, there was a considerable difference in their participation as regular workers. However, the major chunk of female workers is engaged in the tertiary sector in the urban areas due to their advantage of access to education and other facilities, whereas the rural females lack such facilities. The urban females are also entering the administrative, financial and community services. The growth rates of rural females in work participation lead us to conclude that during the pre-reform period of 1983 to 1993-94, there was negative growth in the rural primary sector (-2.06 per cent) in the state. It is important to note that immediately after the implementation of reforms, the FWPR in the rural primary sector increased from 3.81 per cent during 1993-94 to 1999-2000 and further to 4.62 per cent during 1993-94 to 2004-05. Higher percentage in non-farm activities in the agriculture sector, as self-employed marginal workers was perhaps the main cause of this. Punjab experienced a robust increase in the annual compound growth rate of female work participation (11.81 per cent) in the manufacturing sector during the period of 1993-94 to 1999-2000 which increased in the later period to 14.60 per cent. The service sector could not grow with as much faster rate in the rural area, rather the ACGR declined from 6.53 per cent during 1993-94 to 1999-2000 to 6.10 per cent during 1993-94 to 2004-05 (Table 10.7).

In urban Punjab, this scenario was somewhat bit different (Table 10.8). As expected, ACGR of FWP declined in the primary sector during the post-reform era of 1993-94 to 2004-05, when it was less than one (0.94 per cent) compared to 2.08 per cent during the immediate post-reform era of 1993-94 to 1999-2000, On the other side, a sharp increase was observed in the manufacturing sector alone (15.40 per cent)—the secondary sector (14.53 per cent) during the post-reform era of 1993-94 to 2004-05. A similar trend was registered in public utility services (10.99 per cent). A very high growth rate in FWP was observed immediately after the new phase of reforms—1993-94 to 1999-00— in the services sector, i.e. the trade and hotels (22.98 per cent) and a very high rate in transport, storage and communication (31.89 per cent. But, all these sectors are notorious for low paid sectors where females are either casual or contract workers. More and younger females were able to get jobs with telecommunication companies as receptionists, or on desks to attend complaints, or to perform activities of receiving bills or other payments. This gave a spurt in their numbers to be in the job market in the tertiary sector. In the next phase, however, the rate of growth declined to 14.05 per cent, as the nature of jobs, and the quality of work may not be according to their qualifications and they have to work longer hours.

Table 10.7: Annual Compound Growth Rates of Rural Usual Status (Ps+ss) Female Workers by Industry, 1983 to 2004-05

Sector/s	*1983-1993-94*		*1993-94 to 1999-2000*		*1993-94 to 2004-05*		*1983 to 2004-05*	
	India	*Punjab*	*India*	*Punjab*	*India*	*Punjab*	*India*	*Punjab*
1. Primary Sector	1.53	-2.06	0.04	3.81	1.49	4.62	1.96	1.71
a. Agriculture, Hunting, Fishing, Forestry, etc.	1.52	-2.04	0.05	3.81	1.5	4.62	1.96	1.72
b. Mining & Quarrying	4.64	—	-3.49	—	-0.91	—	2.27	—
2. Secondary Sector	2.89	-11.67	1.27	11.81	3.9	14.6	4.44	1.26
a. Manufacturing	2.58	-12.93	1.25	12.11	3.6	25.22	4.04	6.44
b. Public Utilities (electricity, gas, water)	—	—	—	4.12	—	—	—	—
c. Construction	4.26	—	2.82	—	6.87	—	7.3	20.84
3. Tertiary Sector	3.06	5.12	0.87	6.53	3.6	6.1	4.34	7.34
a. Trade & Hotels	2.69	3.04	-0.46	5.41	3.52	14.46	4.05	11.48
b. Transport, Communication, & Storage	—	—	—	—	—	—	6.83	6.44
c. Other Services	—	—	—	—	—	—	—	—
Financial/Community	2.64	6.12	1.31	6.75	3.2	2.86	3.81	5.77

Source: Calculated from Table 10.5.

Thus, rising FWR in the case of regular workers both in the rural and urban areas is an indication of increase in the education level and changing perceptions regarding employment jobs

Table 10.8: Annual Compound Growth Rates of Urban Usual Status (Ps+ss) Female Workers by Sectors, 1983 to 2004-05

Sector/s	*1983 to 1993-94*		*1993-94 to 1999-2000*		*1993-94 to 2004-05*		*1983 to 2004-05*	
	India	*Punjab*	*India*	*Punjab*	*India*	*Punjab*	*India*	*Punjab*
1. Primary Sector	1.32	-1.59	-3.5	2.08	0.28	0.94	1.01	-0.39
a. Agriculture, Hunting, Fishing, Forestry, etc.	1.27	-1.72	-3.48	2.08	0.4	0.94	1.07	-0.47
b. Mining & Quarrying	3.59	—	-4.38	—	-6.81	—	-2.44	—
2. Secondary Sector	3.06	-7.04	1.01	9.96	4.6	14.53	5.02	4.53
a. Manufacturing	2.54	-8.11	0.73	10.2	4.95	15.4	4.91	4.29
b. Public Utilities (electricity, gas, water)	7.88	-4.37	-4.38	4.54	-0.49	10.99	4.55	4.21
c. Construction	6.53	—	2.87	11.11	2.66	4.57	5.9	—
3. Tertiary Sector	5.77	3.12	2.54	7.28	4.06	6.7	6.38	6.45
a. Trade & hotels	4.13	4.03	7.88	22.98	5.37	1.12	6.21	3.28
b. Transport, Communication, & Storage	2.12	-7.08	5.13	31.89	4.13	14.05	4.1	4.21
c. Other Services	7.6	-2.13	4.44	-0.05	8.63	8.99	10.65	4.46
Financial/Community	6.42	3.43	0.22	1.99	3.28	7.23	6.25	7

Source: Calculated from Table 10.6.

among the educated females. Further, instead of doing low paid jobs with long working hours in the factories, they now prefer self-employment and long for a dignified decent life. A cursory look at the recent NSSO data of the 62nd Round gives a clear picture of gender disparity in the status of employment existing in Punjab, in spite of the fact that females' education levels have increased and the educated females are becoming more and more aware of their rights and other matters of life. As per NSSO data (62nd Round), the proportion of self-employed to total employed persons both at the rural and the urban levels indicate that at the rural level, 82.3 per cent females are self-employed as compared to 51.4 per cent males in Punjab. At the urban level, this percentage is equal to 43.7 for females and 48.8 for males.

More females are engaged as the self-employed in the rural and urban levels taken together (76.1 per cent) compared to the males (50.7 per cent). It indicates that the males are more engaged in regular work, or they shift to the urban areas to do some work leaving their female partners to look after domestic and other chores along with doing some work which fetches them income.

Table 10.9: Category-wise Persons Employed (Percentage) to the Total Employed in Punjab, 2005-06

Area Sex	*Self-Employed*	*Regular*	*Casual*
Rural			
Male	51.40	18.20	30.36
Female	82.30	7.99	3.00
Persons	61.4	14.90	30.49
Urban			
Male	48.8	41.1	10.00
Female	43.7	49.6	7.06
Persons	48.0	42.3	9.67
(Rural + Urban)			
Males	50.7	25.9	23.48
Females	76.1	15.0	20.59
Persons	57.6	22.8	23.25

Source: Unit Level Data NSSO 62nd Round Employment and Unemployment Situation in India, Report No. 522, 2005-06.

Summing Up

The employment scenario in the country has undergone important changes, but all these are on expected lines. The accelerated economic growth of the Indian economy as a whole has many significant impacts on the employment situation, especially in the agriculture sector, more so on the female employment and their participation rates. In fact, the process of economic liberalisation initiated in the 1990s accompanied by encouraging exports/imports, promoting foreign direct investment and increasing incentives for investments and innovations has accelerated growth of the economy from 5.29 per cent per annum during the 1980s to 6.06 per cent during 1991-92 to 2005-06 (Bhalla, 2009) Accordingly, the share of agriculture declined from 30.01 per cent in 1993-94 to 25 per cent in 1990-2000 and to 20.22 per cent during 2004-05. However, a corresponding decline in share of agriculture in the employment (as per NSSO's usual status workers) was not of that speed. Contribution of agriculture in the employment was 60.24 per cent in 1999-2000 which declined to 56.47 per cent in 2004-05. Surprisingly, the Punjab economy, where the agriculture sector still dominates, had experienced a negative growth rate across workers employed in agriculture (-0.32 per cent) during 1983 to 1993-94. But, growth rate in agriculture employment picked up to 1.04 per cent per annum in the post-reform period (1993-94 to 2004-05). In the secondary sector, growth rate of employment was much higher (7.11 per cent) in the post-reform period compared to the earlier period, e.g. 2.44 per cent per annum during 1983 to 1993-94.

Further, the employment scenario in Punjab shows a gender gap to the tune of more than 33 per cent since 1983 to 2004-05. The gender gap was around 40 per cent in 1993-94, when the FWPR registered a decline from 22.4 per cent in 1983 to 15.7 per cent in 1993-94 and the MWPR was 55.0 per cent in 1993-94. By marking 1983 to 1993-94 as the pre-reform period, and 1993-94 to 1999-2000 and to 2004-05 as the post-reform period, the NSSO data, in a nutshell, concludes that:

- FWPR registered a decline in Punjab during the pre-reform period (-1.57 per cent), and after that, it has picked up to 5.52 per cent per annum during 1993-94 to 2004-05 (Table 10.2).
- Rural-urban distribution of usual status workers showed a gender gap of 26.2 percentage points in 1983 and 32.6 percentage points in 1993-94 (Table 10.3). However, in the post-reform period, this gender gap in the state declined, leading us to conclude that more females are joining the labour market not only in the urban areas, but in rural areas also. Though the CGR of female employment in urban Punjab was much higher (6.81 per cent per annum) in the post-reform period compared to rural Punjab (4.95 per cent per annum) during the same period, whereas the CGR for rural

females was negative (-2.09 per cent) compared to the urban females (-0.41 per cent) in the pre-reform period (Table 10.4).

- Regarding nature of employment, the study observes that nearly 89 per cent rural female workers are self-employed and their proportion has marginally declined over time. Rural females as casual labourers have also declined, undoubtedly a healthy sign. But, when compared with their male counterparts, the females as casual and marginal workers were more than twice such male workers as per population Census–2001. Similarly, as the main workers, females' percentage share was just 14.7 per cent compared to the males' 45.3 in 2001.
- However, structural shift in the employment in Punjab has favoured the males, shifting from the primary to the manufacturing sector. In urban areas, more females are entering into service/tertiary sectors compared to the rural females. But more and more females are now feeling good in self-employment activities, especially the rural females.

All these trends clearly show that the economic growth in Punjab has definitely brought out growth, though a moderate rate, in the female employment, and the females are now entering the professions which earlier were altogether denied to them, but still the social prejudices against females came in their way to upward mobility, especially when they aspire for the higher administrative and managerial positions. A general reluctance on the part of the officials towards females, however qualified and efficient, is visible and this is prevalent in the so-called developed nations of US, Canada, UK, etc. also. This attitudinal gender bias demands immediate concern on the part of the policy makers.

Moreover, the spread of education among females is an important determinant to increase their participation in the labour market to match the changing quality of labour demanded. To improve the quality of employment, more efforts should be made to create regular jobs. Contract appointments, whether in the companies or educational institutions, have a dampening effect on efficiency and performance. And, in the urban areas, increased female work participation which is mostly of a casual nature or contract jobs even in the organised sector, should be seriously addressed.

'To achieve decent work for all, as suggested by the ILO (1999), promote more employment opportunities for women and men to obtain decent and productive work, in conditions of freedom, equity and security and human dignity'. Female self-employment workers in the unorganised sector, specifically in agriculture, face discrimination with respect to wage differentials also. In Punjab, they get two-third wages in agriculture compared to the males, and surprisingly, their real wage-rates have declined over the time period. There seems to be no solid explanation why they are paid less when they perform equally well and are equally efficient.

A rising proportion of self-employed women suggest that training of these professions should be included in the traditional education programme. Further, community centres set up by the state, self-help groups and NGOs can play an important role to impart such training to rural poor women who do not have any formal education but are willing to work. MG-NREGS is doing well in rural areas and this is one scheme where workers are paid equally, irrespective of their gender. Payment by cheque is another check on any bungling in payment and accounts. More and more such schemes should be implemented to have such equality. Thus, in order to bridge the gender gap in employment, not only more and more women-centric investments should be made, but also focus on 'what investment is good for women' for their real upliftment and empowerment. It will help having 'gender equality' and reduce gender disparity in the state.

NOTE

1. Klenke (1997) used the term leadership and information labyrinth in discussing the challenges that women leaders face, especially in the field of information technology, quoted in, Eagly and Linda, 2007.

REFERENCES

Bhalla, G.S. (2009), 'Globalisation and Employment Trends in India', in J. Krishnamurthy and R.P. Mamgain (eds.) *Growth, Employment and Labour Markets: Perspectives in the Era of Globalisation in India*, Indian Society of Labour Economics and Institute of Human Development, New Delhi, pp. 403-39.

Eagly, A.H. and L.C. Linda (2007), *Through the Labyrinth: The Truth About How Women Become Leaders*, Harvard Business School Press, Boston, Massachusetts, USA.

Gill, Kanwaljit Kaur and Navjeet Kaur (2010a), Economic Reforms and Gender Differentials in Employment in India: A Case Study of Kerala and Punjab, *Man and Development*, Vol. 32 (2), June, pp. 1-12.

Gill, Kanwaljit Kaur and Navjeet Kaur (2010b), 'Changing Dimensions of Female Employment in Rural Punjab', *Journal of Agricultural Development and Policy*, Vol. 20, January-June, pp.19-26.

GOI (2002), *National Human Development Report 2001*, Planning Commission, New Delhi.

ILO (1999), *Report of the Director-General: Decent Work*, International Labour Conference, 87th Session, International Labour Office, Geneva.

Majumdar, Dipak and Sandip Sarkar (2008), *Globalisation, Labour Markets and Inequality in India*, Routledge Studies in the Growth Economics of South Asia, International Development Research Centre, London and New York.

NSSO (1987), *Employment and Unemployment in India 1983*, 38th Round (January–December 1983), Report No. 341.

NSSO (1997), *Employment and Unemployment in India 1993-94*, 50th Round (July 1993–June 2004), Report No. 409.

NSSO (2001), *Employment and Unemployment Situation in India 1999-2000*, (Part I & II), 55th Round (July 1999-June 2000), Report No. 458.

NSSO (2006), *Employment and Unemployment Situation in India 2004-05*, (Part I & II), 61st Round (July 2004–June 2005), Report No. 515.

NSSO (2008), *Employment and Unemployment Situation in India 2005-06*, 62nd Round (July 2005–June 2006), Report No. 522.

Rustagi, Preet (2010), Continuing Gender Stereotypes or Signs of Change: Occupational Pattern of Women Workers, *Indian Journal of Labour Economics*, Vol. 53 (3), July-September, pp. 481-500.

World Women's Report 2000—*Progress of World's Women 2000:* UNIFEM Biennial Report, United Nations Development Fund for Women.

11

Affluence, Vulnerability and Social Security Evidence from Punjab

Varinder Jain

I. Introduction

In a discourse on extension of social security to the poor, Kannan et al. (2006) point out that 'a measure of social security helps to develop a healthy and contented workforce capable of enhancing their contribution to national income and thus enhance the capacity of the economy to grow. A workforce with higher capability and security could contribute to higher growth, which in turn, would enhance the aggregate demand in the economy through higher purchasing power of this vast mass of the workforce'. Further, on the question of what form of social security is desired for a developing economy, scholars like Guhan favour three broad forms of social security, viz. 'promotional, preventive and protective', for developing countries (Guhan, 1994). It is said that the promotional measures are needed for improving endowments, exchange entitlements, real incomes and social consumption; preventive measures are desired for averting deprivation in specific situations; and protective measures are needed to protect an individual/ household from a downfall in living standards at the onslaught of a sudden contingency.

For providing social security through these measures, an active role of the state is also desired. As far as the rationale for the state role is concerned, Barr (1989) provides an economic argument rooted in the equity and efficiency principles for the state to come forward in the provision of social security. It is argued that the state, in contrast to the market, is the best agency as the latter provides an efficient outcome only when a number of conditions concerning perfect information, perfect competition and the absence of market failures are met—which is a rare phenomenon as the failure of one or more of these conditions generally makes the resulting market equilibrium inefficient. And, in India, under the neo-liberal approach to development, the state's role in the economic spheres is largely curtailed. In such a situation, any urge for the state to extend social security brings into account the fiscal implications as the state in the developing nations is becoming largely a resource-constrained state. Such a concern for resource constraint is recognised and the financing models based on either the full or the partial contributions are advocated in literature (see, e.g. Kannan, 2002).

However, some Indian states like Kerala, Tamil Nadu, etc. could make relatively better provision of social security at moderate levels of per capita income. Given this, it may be hypothesised that the provision of social security need not be conditioned merely by economic affordability as even the economically better-off states need not have better provision of social security. One may test this hypothesis in the Indian context as there are both the affluent and the deprived states owing to prevalence of regional inequality. For the purpose, this chapter focuses on an affluent state, viz. Punjab that has consistently maintained its highest position in terms of per capita income till 2001-02 (Table A1). Its economic prosperity is also reflected in the higher levels of monthly per capita consumer expenditure vis-à-vis other Indian states (Table A2). A very low level of absolute poverty also corroborates the affluence attained by this state in the overall Indian context.

This chapter has five sections including the introductory section. The next Section II depicts the state of affluence of Punjab's economy. Other sides of growth are illustrated through the diagnosis of vulnerability among the working masses in Section III. Following this contrast of economic affluence on the one hand and pervasive vulnerability on the other, Section IV evaluates the social welfare efforts made by the state both in terms of policy initiatives and actual expenditures. The final section provides concluding remarks.

II. State of Affluence in Punjab

2.1 Economic Situation Before the State's Reorganisation

The evolution of the Indus Valley Civilisation in Greater Punjab had made it a place of historical significance and the passage of five perennial rivers (Jhelum, Chenab, Ravi, Sutlej and Beas) along with the availability of vast fertile plains had made this region economically attractive to the invaders from the far West. Being the last state annexed by the British in 1849 it remained relatively less vulnerable to plunder and exploitation. The area had seen development of canals and railway networks during the British rule (Paustian, 1930; Calvert, 1936) and owing to these interventions made by the British, commercialisation of agriculture on a significant scale had taken place here.[1]

However, the agricultural surpluses were largely squeezed by the British. Besides frequent hikes, the inelasticity of land revenue to market fluctuations and bad harvests resulted in the mortgage of agricultural land on a significant scale—a phenomenon that forced the British to enact the Punjab Alienation of Land Act, 1901 for preventing the non-agricultural classes from owning the agricultural land.[2] However, the dependency on loans continued but with a substitution of village moneylenders by rich landlords. Thus, there took place accumulation of (whatever limited) agrarian surplus within the agricultural sector, and thereby the enhanced prosperity of the countryside—a fact quite contrary to the experience of other states like Bengal (Mukherjee, 1985). There also took place growth in commerce and industry. It is said that on the eve of independence, Greater Punjab was a well-balanced economic region possessing economic resources in such a way that every sub-region was vital for the prosperity of the other (Vakil, 1950).

The shock of partition (in 1947) led to the bifurcation of Greater Punjab into 'East Punjab' (on the Indian side) and 'West Punjab' (on the Pakistan side). In this bifurcation, East Punjab remained at a disadvantage as a large part of the irrigated area under canal colonies went to West Punjab. East Punjab got only three million canal irrigated acres out of a total of over fourteen million acres. The soil quality of land in East Punjab was not at par with that in the West Punjab. The refugee farmers had to bear a net loss of about two million acres of land and the Hindu merchant class and industrialists had to lose their generations-long sunk capital in industrial plants and machinery. By one estimate, the non-Muslims had lost 400 industrial units (valued at Rs. 40 crores) in the industrial centres of Rawalpindi, Sialkot, Lahore, Wazirabad and Gujranwala (Rai, 1965). There were very few who could bring some wealth, otherwise a majority had to run bare-handed for saving their lives amidst bloodshed.

The partition left East Punjab as an economically backward region with an additional burden of rehabilitating 2.46 million refugees (GoP, 1950). The damage caused was so wide and rampant that a strenuous effort by the state was needed to rehabilitate the dislodged economy. Consequently, effective strategies were charted out by both the state and central governments. As a result, the economy of East Punjab started gaining recovery. Its industrial segment regained and became a home for a large number of small-scale industries in no time. At such times, another setback arose due to the state's reorganisation on a linguistic basis in 1966 and as a result, the state once again lost its developing industrial complex around Delhi to Haryana besides losing (whatever limited) mineral and forest resources to Himachal Pradesh.

2.2 Economic Attainment Since the State's Reorganisation

The timing of the state's reorganisation coincided partly with the advent of the 'Green Revolution'—a phenomenon by which a voluminous rise in wheat and rice output had been witnessed. A variety of factors like the adoption of high-yielding variety (HYV) seeds on a large scale coupled with an extensive programme of land consolidation and land reforms, vast expansion of rural roads and rural electrification, provision of short-term credit, etc. shaped the success of the 'Green Revolution' in the state. As a result, the agriculture sector grew by 2.87 per cent per annum during the 1970-71 to 1979-80 periods. This growth had been the highest during the 1980-81 to 1989-90 period (Table 11.1). Other primary sub-sectors such as forestry and logging, fishing, mining and quarrying recorded relatively fast growth for most of the time period under consideration but they could not emerge as the major sectors due to the dominance of the agricultural sector in the state's Net State Domestic Product (NSDP).

Owing to multiplier effects, the agricultural growth facilitated the expansion of sectors like manufacturing, services, etc. Bhalla (1995) points out that the increasing use of new agricultural technology stimulated the demand for intermediate inputs like fertilisers, pesticides, power, diesel, capital goods (like electric motors, diesel engines, tractors, threshers, etc.) and other consumption goods. In response to this newly emerging demand, engineering and hand-tool industries became more vibrant. There also appeared industries for processing agricultural products. Rising per capita income levels of rural population provided a push to all sorts of consumption good industries. The food processing industries like dairying, grain mills, edible oil manufacturing and beverages recorded rapid expansion. Similarly, a big spurt had taken place in the production of textiles and durable consumer goods like sewing machines, radios, bicycles, televisions, etc.

The manufacturing sector recorded the highest exponential growth rate of 9.94 per cent in the period just immediate to the advent of the Green Revolution, i.e. 1970-71 to 1979-80. Despite the ruinous impact of militancy and religious fundamentalism in the state during 1980-94, the manufacturing sector made significant growth, but in the subsequent periods, it did not reveal an encouraging performance. Similarly, various sectors related to services also recorded significant growth over the time period. As a result, there took place a decline in the contribution of the primary sector from 58.36 per cent in 1970-71 to 35.73 per cent in 2009-10. The share of the secondary and tertiary sector increased with the latter recording a relatively high increase over a period of time (Figure 1).

The overall growth rate of the Punjab economy remained positive since the state's reorganisation. During the decade of the 1990s, a decline in growth rate led the scholars to hint at deceleration of economic growth in Punjab (Ahluwalia, 2000; Singh and Singh, 2002). Though the performance of the Punjab economy in the subsequent decade improved marginally, it remained lower than that recorded by other major Indian states. In fact, during the post-1990 period, most of the states recorded faster growth than Punjab—as a result, Punjab's rank of NSDP growth declined to thirteenth for 1990-91 to 1999-2000 and

Table 11.1: Exponential Growth Rate (%) of Punjab's Economy Since 1970-71, Base=1999-2000 Prices

	1970-71 to 2009-10	*1970-71 to 1979-80*	*1980-81 to 1989-90*	*1990-91 to 1999-00*	*2000-01 to 2009-10*
A. Agriculture	3.35	2.87	4.49	2.87	4.34
B. Forestry and Logging	5.77	5.16	-3.51	3.58	17.27
C. Fishing	11.45	5.33	16.12	12.79	1.64
D. Mining and Quarrying	5.60	-5.99	4.59	0.01	8.31
Primary Sector (A+B+C+D)	**3.39**	**2.88**	**4.37**	**2.92**	**4.47**
E. Manufacturing	5.33	9.94	8.29	3.89	4.40
F. Construction	4.86	3.20	3.75	4.56	11.74
G. Electricity, Gas and Water Supply	6.15	17.34	7.03	10.15	5.51
Secondary Sector (E+F+G)	**5.26**	**8.11**	**6.89**	**4.55**	**5.93**
H. Transport, Storage and Communication	6.06	6.49	8.50	9.13	6.16
I. Trade, Hotels and Restaurants	5.07	9.33	6.03	1.26	7.34
J. Banking and Insurance	7.77	9.21	7.62	8.62	5.25
K. Real Estate Ownership of Dwellings & Business Services	6.75	2.93	-1.39	12.30	0.10
L. Public Administration	7.17	3.51	7.22	8.49	4.39
M. Other Services	6.19	7.12	5.38	8.75	4.58
Tertiary Sector (H+I+J+K+L+M)	5.93	7.83	5.65	5.96	5.61
Net State Domestic Product	**4.64**	**5.24**	**5.29**	**4.34**	**5.26**

Source: Based on EPWRF (2003) and http://mospi.nic.in/

subsequently to seventeenth for 2000-01 to 2007-08 (Table 11.2). Nonetheless, it is noteworthy that the state maintained its highest rank in terms of per capita income till 2001-02. During the 2002-05 period, it remained at the second rank but in recent years, it is at the fifth rank and is overtaken by states like Haryana, Maharashtra, Kerala and Gujarat (Table A1). Similar to per capita income, evidence on monthly per capita expenditure also hints at the relative affluence of the Punjab economy (Table A2).

2.3 Magnitude of Revenue Mobilisation by the State

It is noteworthy that the state in spite of the non-taxation of agricultural income that constitutes a large proportion of NSDP, could mobilise its tax revenue and non-tax revenue from various sources such as the taxes on property and capital transactions, taxes on commodities and services, share in central taxes, own non-tax revenue and the grants from the centre. However, during the 1980-90 decade, Punjab state's revenue as per cent of its Gross Domestic Product (GDP) remained at the lowest level than that of other states. A somewhat similar pattern had been revealed by the growth rate of its total revenue when it remained lower than that recorded by the states of Haryana, Maharashtra and Gujarat. In terms of revenue buoyancy, Punjab's performance remained worse than all the states during this decade except Tamil Nadu (Table 11.3).

During the 1990-2000 decade, the ratio of total revenue to state GDP improved from its average level recorded in the earlier decade. Its total revenue had risen at the growth rate of about four per cent with the buoyancy of 0.77. Such revenue performance seems to be somewhat satisfactory in comparative inter-state analysis. Though one does not observe such robust performance of the Punjab state in terms of the ratio of total revenue to state GDP and the growth rate of total revenue, it is noteworthy that in terms of revenue buoyancy, Punjab emerged as one of the better performing states. Though all the states witnessed a decline in revenue buoyancy during the 1990s, Punjab did not record a sharp decline which reveals its better revenue mobilisation during this decade.

Figure 1: **Sectoral Composition (%) of Punjab's NSDP Since 1970-71**

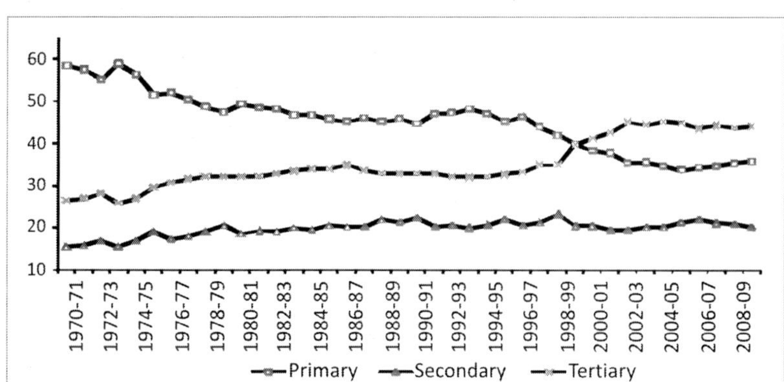

Note: Primary sector includes agriculture, fishing, forestry, logging, mining and quarrying; Secondary sector includes manufacturing, construction, electricity, gas and water supply; Tertiary sector includes transport, storage and communication, trade, hotels and restaurants, banking and insurance, real estate and ownership of dwellings, public administration and other services.

Source: Same as Table 1.

Punjab's revenue-generating capacity improved further in the post-2000-01 period when the ratio of total revenue to state GDP improved to a considerable extent. It placed Punjab at the top among the high-income states. In terms of growth rate of total revenue, the state recorded a somewhat similar pattern by being at the second position. Its revenue buoyancy of 1.48 placed it at the top position. Clearly, such high revenue buoyancy along with a high ratio of total revenue to the state GDP during the current period along with the earlier decade of the 1990s negates the argument of resource scarcity with the Punjab state; rather it depicts a sound and sustainable revenue profile of the Punjab state.

3. Other Sides of Growth: Pervasive Livelihood Vulnerability

It is a noteworthy fact that the economic growth process in Punjab had been largely inequitable and exclusive. In the case of the agricultural sector, the process of the Green Revolution induced certain changes in the rural society that in one way or

Table 11.2: Exponential Growth Rate (%) of Real NSDP Across States

States	*1970-71 to 2007-08*		*1970-71 to 1979-80*		*1980-81 to 1989-90*		*1990-91 to1999-00*		*2000-01 to 2007-08*	
	GR (%)	*R*	*GR (%)*	*R*	*GR (%)*	*R*	*GR (%)*	*R*	*GR (%)*	*R*
Andhra Pradesh	5.35	4	3.17	8	5.15	5	5.13	9	7.77	6
Assam	3.31	17	2.61	13	3.26	15	2.17	17	4.71	16
Bihar*	3.45	15	2.94	12	4.63	11	2.58	16	6.87	10
Gujarat	5.63	3	4.58	4	4.72	8	7.68	1	10.46	1
Haryana	5.73	1	4.71	3	6.07	1	4.60	11	8.88	3
Himachal Pradesh	4.92	7	3.05	9	4.44	13	6.02	7	6.63	11
Jammu & Kashmir	3.69	14	4.27	5	1.93	17	4.54	12	5.12	15
Karnataka	5.24	5	4.16	6	5.13	6	6.84	2	7.39	7
Kerala	4.25	11	1.71	16	2.54	16	5.69	8	8.45	4
Madhya Pradesh*	4.08	12	1.12	17	3.51	14	4.91	10	5.86	13
Maharashtra	5.70	2	5.60	1	5.42	3	6.66	3	7.82	5
Orissa	3.45	15	2.37	15	4.68	9	3.94	14	8.94	2
Punjab	4.64	10	5.24	2	5.29	4	4.34	13	4.68	17
Rajasthan	5.14	6	2.99	10	5.77	2	6.32	5	7.33	8
Tamil Nadu	4.70	9	3.38	7	4.87	7	6.21	6	7.13	9
Uttar Pradesh*	4.07	13	2.58	14	4.67	10	3.43	15	5.24	14
West Bengal	4.90	8	2.97	11	4.48	12	6.63	4	6.19	12

Note 1: The exponential growth rates are estimated with regression function, $\ln Y = a + bt$.

Note 2: * implies that from 1993-94 onwards, real NSDP of Bihar, Madhya Pradesh and Uttar Pradesh is inclusive of the real NSDP for Jharkhand, Chhattisgarh and Uttarakhand respectively.

Source: Same as Table 11.1.

the other contributed to the vulnerability of the masses dependent on agriculture. In its initial stages, almost all sections of the peasantry benefited from the Green Revolution due to increased viability of even the small farms (Saini, 1976). But, over a period of time, the cultivation process became more capital-intensive due to rising input cost. The small and marginal farmers found it very difficult because of their limited access to credit. The increasing non-viability of small farms due to declining productivity of agriculture added further to their woes (Bhalla and Chadha 1982).

There is also a significant inequality in asset ownership. As per the 59th Round of the National Sample Survey Organisation (NSSO), only nine per cent rural cultivating households own forty-five per cent of assets, whereas seventy-six per cent households own only twenty-four per cent of total assets.[3] Such inequality in asset ownership also led to inequalities in the earnings from crop production (Chopra, 1984). Land is the major asset and the distribution of operational land holdings assumes significance per se. By Visualising the distribution pattern in

Table 11.3: Revenue Generating Capacity of Punjab in a Comparative Perspective

Time	*Punjab*	*Haryana*	*Gujarat*	*Maharashtra*	*Tamil Nadu*
	Total Revenue as % of State GDP				
1980-90	11.54	14.81	14.07	14.02	15.85
1990-2000	12.44	15.09	12.56	11.01	13.66
2000-08	13.58	12.49	11.76	11.53	14.11
	Trend Growth Rate of Total Revenue (%)				
1980-90	4.97	7.44	6.67	6.77	4.67
1990-2000	4.01	4.74	6.29	4.20	4.01
2000-08	7.23	11.29	7.68	10.01	10.27
	Revenue Buoyancy				
1980-90	0.93	1.17	1.12	1.15	0.90
1990-2000	0.77	0.80	0.74	0.56	0.48
2000-08	1.48	1.26	0.74	1.25	1.44

Notes: 1. Growth rates are 'trend' growth rates and are computed after deflating total revenue by state GDP deflators (base 1999-2000) for the respective years.

2. Revenue buoyancy is the ratio of the growth rate of real total revenue and real state GDP (base 1999-2000).

Source: EPWRF (2004) and Reports on State Finances, published by the Reserve Bank of India.

Figure 2, it becomes clear that there are large inequalities in the ownership pattern of land. For instance, the share of farmers with operational land holdings below one hectare which has been about thirty-eight per cent in 1970-71 has reduced to about twelve per cent in 2000-01, whereas the share of farmers having more than two hectares has increased.

***Figure 2:* Distribution of Operational Land Holdings in Punjab**

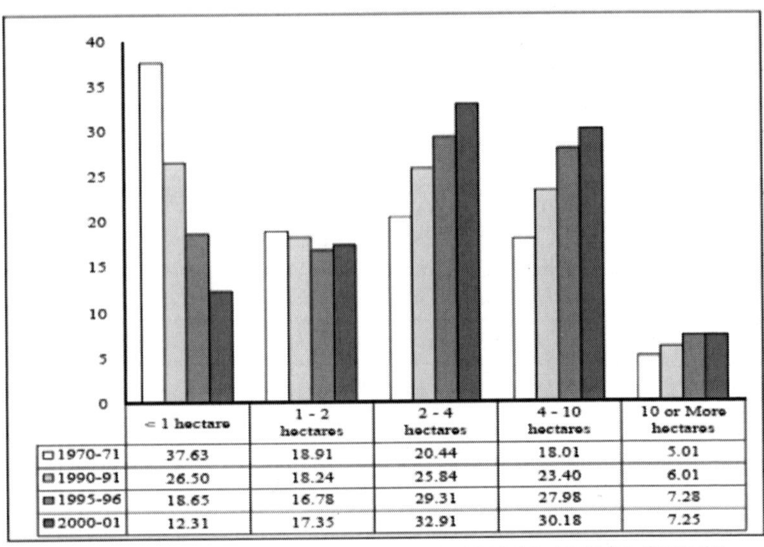

	< 1 hectare	1 - 2 hectares	2 - 4 hectares	4 - 10 hectares	10 or More hectares
1970-71	37.63	18.91	20.44	18.01	5.01
1990-91	26.50	18.24	25.84	23.40	6.01
1995-96	18.65	16.78	29.31	27.98	7.28
2000-01	12.31	17.35	32.91	30.18	7.25

Source: Agricultural Census, Punjab: 1970-71, 1990-91, 1995-96, 2000-01

Besides asset and land ownership, the declining share of cultivators in the agricultural workforce provides another indication for the prevalence of vulnerability in the agricultural segment. This share has declined from about sixty-eight per cent in 1971 to about fifty-eight per cent in 2001 (GOP, 2006). Though one may attribute such a decline in the share of cultivators to the increase in the share of labour due to the inflow of migrants, it is difficult to deny in light of the above evidence on land inequality that a new class has emerged who has lost land and is working as agricultural labour. Besides the cultivating class, evidence on the plight of agricultural labour is also available. Studies like Rangi et al. (2004) point out an increasing incidence of casualisation in Punjab's agriculture. Nonetheless, most of this literature has remained focused on migrant workers.[4] It is revealed that the migrant labour has to face exploitation not only in terms of working conditions but also in terms of remuneration. There are instances where it suffered as bonded labour as well (Singh, 1997).

For portraying the vulnerability situation in other non-agricultural segments like construction, transport, trade, hotels, etc., some evidence from NSSO data (61st Round), as there is dearth of literature on non-agricultural segments in Punjab's context, reveals that in 2004-05, the share of casual and own account workers was twenty-two per cent and thirty-three per cent respectively. An exploration of vulnerability-related aspects such as the nature of contract, duration of wage receipts, access to paid sick leave and social security benefits provides interesting insights about the prevalence of vulnerability in these segments. It is learned that about seventy-two per cent workers work without any (written) contract with their employers and about twenty-five per cent receive their wage payments on a daily basis. About sixty-two per cent do not have any access to paid sick leave and about sixty-nine per cent do not receive any kind of social security benefit (Jain, 2010c).

An examination across sectors reveals that most of the casual employment is generated in the construction sector. The situation is relatively worse in rural areas as here about seventy-one per cent of the employment generated by the construction sector is casual. The share of casual employment is also high in the transport, storage and communication. With respect to the nature of job contract, the overall situation is not very attractive as a majority of the employment is provided without any (written) job contract.[5] A large set of workers in the construction sector do not have any (written) job contract. Similarly, about ninety per cent of employment generated by trade and hotels do not have any job contract and the situation is relatively the same in both the rural and urban areas. The segment of transport, storage and communication also provides a large part of its employment without any job contract. Though the situation in other sectors is also not very encouraging, they may be termed as relatively better due to the fact that a majority of employment generated by them is based on some sort of written contract.

In terms of the duration of wage receipts, one finds that a majority of construction sector workers receive wage payments on a daily basis. A small proportion of the workers in the transport/storage/communication sector also receive their wage payments on a daily basis. The situation remains somewhat better in other sectors where a majority receive wage payments on a monthly basis. In terms of access to paid sick leave, there is not an encouraging picture as a majority of the workers do not have access to paid sick leave except the sectors like electricity, gas and water supply and financial, real estate and other services. It is noteworthy that a large part of both these sectors belongs to the organised segment of the Punjab economy. On the other hand, the remaining segments of construction, transport and trade/hotels—a large part of which belong to the unorganised segment, clearly reveal that a majority of the workers in these sectors do not have access to paid sick leave. The situation is with respect to workers' access to any sort of social security benefits across these sectors.

Thus, the construction sector followed by the transport, storage and communication, and trade and hotels are the major sectors which contribute to the vulnerable employment. Much of this vulnerability may be attributed to the recruitment processes, which are highly informal. Moreover, the working conditions are too degraded that they often face implications for the occupational health and safety of the workers. Besides wage earnings being very low, there are limited chances of skill formation and occupational mobility in these segments. The lax implementation of labour laws aggravates the situation. Added to these, one can find incidence of vulnerability among wageworkers and self-employed workers in Punjab's urban unorganised manufacturing sector, where such workers experience a range of insecurities (Jain, 2010d). Not only this, their households also remain victims of the work-related vulnerability of these informal workers.

Such pervasiveness of vulnerability along with a remarkable

economic attainment of the Punjab state during the post-reorganisation period raises the expectation that the state might have developed a sound social welfare system to alleviate the plight of its masses.[6] But, has it been so? The answer follows in the next section.

4. State Provision of Social Security in Punjab

4.1 Existing Policy Framework for Containing Vulnerability

In any policy framework for mitigating vulnerability, legislations and policies/schemes are two major constituents. Legislations emerge out of procedures specified in the Constitution and thereby are the commitments binding on the state to perform its role. They are generally enforceable and permanent in nature. The policies/schemes on the other hand are enacted by the respective governments in response to various considerations such as election commitments, party ideology, favouring priority sector/s, etc. These may have a transitional character. As far as the former constituent is concerned, it is noteworthy that Punjab has not enacted any major legislation to protect unorganised poor workers as done by many other states like Kerala, Maharashtra, Madhya Pradesh, etc. Generally, the nature and scope of the enforced legislations in Punjab has remained confined to only those enacted by the central government.[7] Nonetheless, the state is supposed to facilitate the implementation of these legislations effectively in its territory. But, it seems that the state has failed in this respect as well.

The Minimum Wage Act, 1948, for example, urges the payment of minimum wages to the workers across all the organised and unorganised segments. But, as pointed out by Jain (2010a) that the wages received by 71 per cent of the unorganised manufacturing sector workers falls below the stipulated minimum wage rates in the state. The severity of the reward differential (gap between minimum and the actual wage as the ratio of the minimum wage) is high[8] for about forty-three per cent of the wageworkers. Similarly, the incidence of bonded labour in agriculture is well documented by studies like Singh (1997)—a finding indicating the violation of the Bonded Labour

System (Abolition) Act, 1976. The studies on wage discrimination like Kapoor (1987) and Jain (2010b) indicate the violation of the Inter-State Migrant Workmen (Regulation of Employment and Conditions of Service) Act, 1979.

Similarly, there has been a lack of concern with the state to implement the Building and Other Construction Workers (Regulation of Employment and Conditions of Service) Act, 1996. Though passed by the central government in 1996, it has taken about thirteen years for Punjab to initiate its implementation in the state. At present, the state is collecting one per cent cess on all public, private and commercial construction works in the state and by one estimate, it has hitherto collected Rs. 36 crores in the welfare fund. But, the labour welfare board has registered only 5,000 construction workers out of about three to four lakh workers in the state (Singh, 2010).

In conclusion, one can say that merely having the legislation on paper does not serve the purpose; what matters is its effective implementation as the ultimate outcomes depend on this. It is not so that there is an absence of much-needed institutional structure. The labour welfare board was constituted in the state in 1974 under the Punjab Labour Welfare Fund Act, 1965. This board is responsible for the implementation of various labour laws and to design schemes for the welfare of working masses. However, the welfare schemes implemented so far have remained limited to the benefit of the organised workforce. It has not introduced any major scheme for promoting the welfare of unorganised workers.

In terms of policy as well, Punjab does not find any specific policy/scheme to alleviate the plight of vulnerable masses in Punjab's agricultural and non-agricultural segments, except having some general pensionary schemes for the elderly, widows, disabled, SCs, etc. Some of the main features of these schemes are highlighted in Table 11.4. However, the assistance provided by these schemes is very limited as well as meagre. For example, the amount of monthly pension under the State Old Age Pension Scheme is merely Rs. 250, which is lower than the neighbouring state of Haryana. The Haryana government provides a monthly pension of Rs. 500 to all and Rs. 750 to widows and destitute women and Rs. 600 to the handicapped (GOH, 2010). Similarly, another neighbouring state of Himachal Pradesh provides a monthly pension of Rs. 330 to the elderly, Rs. 330 to widows and destitute women and Rs. 300 to the disabled (GOHP, 2010).

Table 11.4: State-Funded Social Security Schemes in Punjab

Scheme's Name	*Introduced in*	*Eligibility Conditions*	*Benefits*
Old Age Pension Scheme	1964	Age: 60 years for women & 65 years for men if they belong to BPL family	Rs. 250 per person
Financial Assistance to Widow & Destitute Women	1968	Widows/unmarried women < 60 years of age; Also available to unmarried destitute > 30 years	Rs. 250 per month
Financial Assistance to Dependent Children	1968	Orphans & destitute children (< 21 years) if they belong to BPL family	Rs. 250 per month per child
Financial Assistance to Disabled Persons	1982	Disabled with > 50 % disability and monthly income < Rs. 1,000	Rs. 250 per month
Shagun/ Ashirwad Scheme	1997	> 18-years-old girls of BPL, SC/Christian/ Widow families with Punjab domicile; also included are the BCs and economically backward families[9]	Rs. 15,000, limited to two girls per family[10]
Atta-Dal Scheme	2008	BPL families	-

Source: Various Websites of the Punjab Government

4.2 State Social Welfare Effort: Some Empirical Evidence

In light of the fact that Punjab has been one of the prosperous states of India, such lack of sound social security policy framework indicates the state's apathetic attitude towards the vulnerable masses. But, before concluding so, one needs to delve into the social welfare efforts made by the state.[11] For this purpose, actual expenditure statistics provided by the Reserve Bank of India's publications on State Finances has been studied. The time period considered is from 1980-81 onwards till the latest available (2007-08). The social sector expenditure, in these reports, is reported under twelve heads, viz. (1) education, sports, art and culture, (2) medical and public health, (3) family welfare, (4) water supply and sanitation, (5) housing, (6) urban development, (7) welfare of scheduled castes, scheduled tribes and other backward classes, (8) labour and labour welfare, (9) social security and welfare, (10) nutrition, (11) relief on account of natural calamities, and (12) others. But, there are primarily three heads, viz. (7), (8) and (9) together that form exclusively the state's social welfare expenditure.

To get a real picture of the state's social welfare efforts, social welfare expenditure figures in real terms[12] (base=1999-2000) in Punjab as proportion of the state's gross domestic product (GDP) has been estimated as:

$$\text{Social Welfare Effort}_{ij} = \frac{\text{RSWE}_{ij}}{\text{RGDP}_{ij}} \times 100$$

where RSWE and RGDP stand for real social welfare expenditure and real gross domestic product respectively and the subscripts i and j stand for year and state respectively.

Figure 3 provides the relative performance of Punjab state in terms of social welfare effort vis-à-vis other high-income states of Haryana, Gujarat, Maharashtra and Tamil Nadu. It can be observed that Punjab has made the lowest social welfare effort for most of the time period under consideration. In a few years (1989-90 to 1991-92), its performance has improved but it has remained lower than that made by its counterpart states.

Figure 3: **Social Welfare Effort Across High-Income States Since 1980-81**

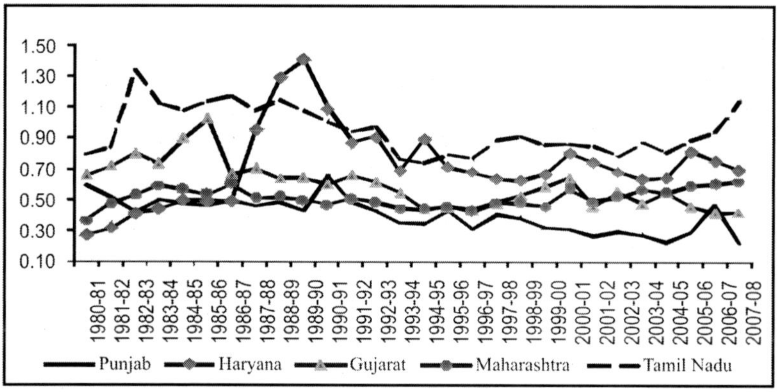

Source: Same as Table 3

5. Concluding Remarks

Thus, Punjab despite being an affluent state did not do much to protect the interests of vulnerable masses. Its efforts, in terms of policy and expenditure, for curbing vulnerability have remained minimal. In spite of their existence, the legislative measures protecting the working poor have remained largely ineffective. Similarly, institutions like labour welfare board, etc. has not been of much help to the working poor. Even the implementation of social security schemes like the pensions to old, widows/destitute women, dependent children and disabled persons are not only low, but also are irregular for most of the time. Moreover, the social welfare efforts made by the state have remained negligible not only in absolute terms, but also in terms of its magnitude vis-à-vis other high income states. Such findings leave much room for disappointment in an affluent state that could have emerged as the 'model' welfare state due to its 'relatively better' endowments. Thus, there is urgent need to provide social security benefits to the vulnerable masses in the state.

Table A1: Rank Distribution of Per Capita Income* Across Major Indian States

Year	Andhra Pradesh	Assam	Bihar#	Gujarat	Haryana	Himachal Pradesh	Jammu & Kashmir	Karnataka	Kerala	Madhya Pradesh#	Maharashtra	Orissa	Punjab	Rajasthan	Tamil Nadu	Uttar Pradesh#	West Bengal
1970-71	15	7	16	9	2	5	3	13	4	14	6	11	1	10	8	17	12
1971-72	14	6	16	9	2	5	4	12	3	11	7	15	1	13	8	17	10
1972-73	15	6	16	14	2	4	3	12	5	11	8	10	1	13	7	17	9
1973-74	14	7	16	9	5	4	2	11	3	13	6	10	1	15	8	17	12
1974-75	11	7	16	13	4	5	2	10	3	12	6	14	1	15	9	17	8
1975-76	15	7	16	9	2	3	4	11	5	12	6	13	1	14	8	17	10
1976-77	15	8	16	9	2	4	3	12	6	14	5	13	1	11	7	17	10
1977-78	15	9	16	8	2	4	3	11	6	14	5	12	1	13	7	17	10
1978-79	14	9	16	8	2	5	3	11	6	15	4	10	1	13	7	17	12
1979-80	12	10	16	8	2	6	3	9	5	15	4	13	1	14	7	17	11
1980-81	14	7	17	8	2	4	3	11	6	12	5	13	1	16	9	15	10
1981-82	10	6	17	8	2	4	3	11	7	13	5	14	1	15	9	16	12
1982-83	10	5	17	8	2	6	3	11	7	13	4	16	1	15	9	14	12
1983-84	12	5	17	6	2	7	3	11	8	14	4	15	1	13	10	16	9
1984-85	12	5	17	6	2	8	3	10	7	13	4	14	1	15	9	16	11
1985-86	12	5	17	8	2	6	3	11	7	14	4	13	1	16	9	15	10
1986-87	13	6	17	7	2	4	3	11	8	16	5	12	1	14	9	15	10

1987-88	12	5	17	11	2	4	6	9	8	13	3	14	1	16	7	15	10
1988-89	10	9	17	5	2	4	6	11	7	15	3	14	1	12	8	16	13
1989-90	10	9	17	5	2	4	8	11	6	15	3	13	1	14	7	16	12
1990-91	10	9	17	7	2	4	8	12	5	14	3	16	1	11	6	15	13
1991-92	10	8	17	11	2	4	7	9	6	15	3	16	1	13	5	14	12
1992-93	11	10	17	4	2	5	8	9	6	14	3	16	1	12	7	15	13
1993-94	10	11	17	7	2	5	9	8	4	13	3	15	1	14	6	16	12
1994-95	9	11	17	4	2	6	10	8	5	14	3	15	1	13	7	16	12
1995-96	9	12	17	6	2	5	11	8	4	14	3	15	1	13	7	16	10
1996-97	9	13	17	4	2	5	11	8	6	14	3	16	1	12	7	15	10
1997-98	11	13	17	4	2	5	12	8	7	14	3	15	1	10	6	16	9
1998-99	10	13	17	4	2	5	12	8	7	14	3	15	1	11	6	16	9
1999-00	10	13	17	7	2	4	11	8	5	14	3	15	1	12	6	16	9
2000-01	9	13	17	8	2	4	11	7	6	14	3	15	1	12	5	16	10
2001-02	10	13	17	7	2	3	12	8	5	14	4	15	1	11	6	16	9
2002-03	10	12	17	7	1	4	11	8	5	14	3	15	2	13	6	16	9
2003-04	8	13	17	6	1	4	12	10	5	14	3	15	2	11	7	16	9
2004-05	8	13	17	6	1	4	11	9	5	15	3	14	2	12	7	16	10
2005-06	9	13	17	6	1	5	11	8	4	15	2	14	3	12	7	16	10
2006-07	8	14	17	6	1	5	12	9	3	15	2	13	4	11	7	16	10
2007-08	9	14	17	4	1	6	12	8	2	15	3	13	5	11	7	16	10

*Notes:** indicates that the per capita income is per capita net state domestic product (at 1999-2000 prices).
implies that from 1993-94 onwards, the per capita income Bihar, Madhya Pradesh and Uttar Pradesh is inclusive of the values for Jharkhand, Chhattisgarh and Uttarakhand respectively.

Source: Same as Table 11.1.

Table A2: Pattern of Monthly Per Capita Total Expenditure (in Rs.), 1972-73 to 2004

State	*27th Round (1972-73)*				*32nd Round (1977-78)*				*38th Round (1983)*				*43rd Round (1987-88)*				*50th Round (1993-94)*				*55th Round (1999-2000)*				*60th Round* (2004)*			
	Ru	*R*	*Ur*	*R*	*Ru*	*R*	*Ur*	*R*	*Ru*	*R*	*Ur*	*R*	*Ru*	*R*	*Ur*	*R*	*Ru*	*R*	*Ur*	*R*	*Ru*	*R*	*Ur*	*R*	*Ru*	*R*	*Ur*	*R*
Andhra Pradesh	39.8	13	56.3	14	69.7	7	93.2	9	115.4	7	153.5	12	160.1	7	230.3	12	288.7	7	408.6	12	453.6	12	773.5	12	557.1	10	1101.7	5
Assam	41.7	9	60.8	9	59.0	14	94.4	8	113.0	8	154.0	11	153.6	10	269.9	3	258.1	13	458.6	6	426.1	13	814.1	10	531.7	12	1019.5	10
Bihar	41.2	11	59.9	10	57.5	15	83.1	14	93.8	16	138.5	15	136.6	15	186.5	16	218.3	16	353.0	16	384.7	15	601.9	16	442.5	14	784.0	16
Gujarat	51.7	4	57.6	13	70.3	6	100.9	3	122.7	5	163.6	9	161.2	5	240.7	9	303.3	5	454.2	8	551.3	4	891.7	7	613.2	4	1092.0	6
Haryana	70.1	2	69.9	3	92.4	3	100.4	4	151.8	2	186.9	1	214.7	2	251.8	5	385.0	3	473.9	5	714.4	3	912.1	4	878.7	3	1050.3	9
Karnataka	44.5	5	57.9	12	64.9	10	87.6	11	116.8	6	166.3	6	149.1	12	222.8	14	269.4	12	423.1	11	499.8	7	911.0	5	501.6	13	937.1	12
Kerala	42.2	7	58.3	11	74.2	5	82.7	15	145.2	3	176.4	4	211.5	3	266.2	4	390.4	2	493.8	3	765.7	1	932.6	3	990.2	1	1371.5	1
Madhya Pradesh	40.7	12	61.9	8	59.9	12	90.2	10	100.5	14	144.9	14	142.0	14	236.0	11	252.0	14	408.6	12	401.5	14	693.6	13	437.3	15	793.4	15
Mahara-shtra	41.6	10	74.8	2	76.9	4	110.3	2	110.4	11	184.4	3	160.8	6	279.5	1	272.7	11	529.8	1	496.8	8	973.3	1	568.9	8	1258.9	2
Orissa	35.0	16	62.4	7	52.5	16	87.0	12	98.8	15	151.4	13	127.5	16	225.2	13	219.8	15	402.5	14	373.2	16	618.5	15	414.1	16	872.1	13
Punjab	74.6	1	77.9	1	114.4	1	121.7	1	170.5	1	185.2	2	244.2	1	270.0	2	433.0	1	510.7	2	742.4	2	898.8	6	946.9	2	1058.8	8
Rajasthan	52.0	3	63.9	5	108.7	2	95.7	7	127.0	4	159.9	10	177.8	4	237.9	10	322.4	4	424.7	10	548.9	5	795.8	11	580.5	6	994.8	11
T. Nadu	37.7	15	54.0	15	63.3	11	86.1	13	112.2	10	163.7	8	154.3	9	248.8	8	293.6	6	438.3	9	514.0	6	971.6	2	603.4	5	1130.5	4
Uttar Pradesh	42.1	8	53.6	16	67.3	9	82.5	16	104.5	13	135.5	16	148.7	13	216.7	15	273.8	10	389.0	15	466.7	10	690.7	14	538.2	11	827.0	14
West Bengal	38.5	14	68.2	4	59.3	13	97.1	5	104.6	12	170.0	5	149.9	11	249.5	7	278.8	9	474.2	4	454.5	11	866.6	8	580.2	7	1133.4	3
All-India	44.2	6	63.3	6	68.9	8	96.2	6	112.5	9	164.0	7	158.1	8	249.9	6	281.4	8	458.0	7	486.1	9	855.0	9	564.7	9	1060.2	7

Ru = Rural, R = Rank and Ur = Urban

Note: *As per Schedule I; R implies Rank in Descending Order.

Source: NSSO's Various Surveys on Household Consumer Expenditure.

NOTES

1. Banerjee (1982) describes the growth of commercial agriculture in Punjab during the British rule.
2. Thorburn (1886) provides a background to this Act.
3. Based on Table 8R (pp. A - 166) of NSSO (2005).
4. A few important studies on migrant labour are Oberai and Singh (1980), Singh (1997) and Sidhu and Rangi (1998).
5. Job contract assumes significance as it ensures job security to a certain extent whereas the absence of such contracts makes the workers vulnerable to the implicit threat of job loss.
6. Such an expectation is deeply rooted in the democratic set-up of the Indian political system by which the state must come forward to protect and promote the well-being of its vulnerable masses as the notion of democracy per se implies 'the rule of the people, by the people and for the people'. This argument goes in line with the 'Rights-based Argument' as put forward by studies like Kannan and Pillai (2007).
7. The details of various labour legislations in Punjab are available at http://punjabgovt.gov.in/punjabrti/Labour.html
8. i.e. more than 0.40.
9. As reported in *The Tribune*, June 1, 2011.
10. Initially, the *Shagun* was limited to Rs. 5,100 but over a period of time, the amount got raised to Rs. 15,000.
11. There is the possibility that besides state, other (semi-government) organisations like welfare boards, etc. may also be contributing significantly to the promotion of social welfare. We do not consider such organisations as our prime focus to evaluate the social welfare effort made by the state.
12. Real values are derived by deflating the nominal values with state gross domestic product deflators.

REFERENCES

Ahluwalia, M.S. (2000), 'Economic Performance of States in Post-Reforms Period', *Economic and Political Weekly*, Vol. 35 (19), pp. 1637-48.

Banerjee, D. (1982), 'Industrial Stagnation in Eastern India: A Statistical Investigation', *Economic and Political Weekly*, Vol. 17 (8), pp. 286-98.

Barr, N. (1989), 'Social Insurance as an Efficiency Device', *Journal of Public Policy*, Vol. 9 (1), pp. 59-82.

Bhalla, G.S. (1995), 'Agricultural Growth and Industrial Development in Punjab', in J.W. Mellor (ed.) *Agriculture on the Road to Industrialisation*, Johns Hopkins University Press, pp. 67-112.

Bhalla, G.S. and G.K. Chadha (1982), 'Green Revolution and the Small Peasant: A Study of Income Distribution in Punjab Agriculture: I and II', *Economic and Political Weekly*, Vol. 17 (20 and 21), pp. 826-33 and 870-77.

Calvert, H. (1936), *The Wealth and Welfare of the Punjab*, The Civil and Military Gazette Ltd, Lahore.

Chopra, K. (1984), 'Distribution of Agricultural Assets in Punjab: Some Aspects of Inequality', *Economic and Political Weekly*, Vol. 19 (13), pp. A29-A38.

EPWRF (2003), *Domestic Product of States of India: 1960-61 to 2000-01*, Economic and Political Weekly Research Foundation (EPWRF), Mumbai.

EPWRF (2004), *Finances of State Governments in India: A Time Series Analysis of State-Wise Budgetary Performances during the 1980s and 1990s*, Economic and Political Weekly Research Foundation (EPWRF), Mumbai.

GOH (2010), *Economic Survey of Haryana 2009-10*, Publication No. 946, Department of Economic and Statistical Analysis, Government of Haryana, Chandigarh.

GOHP (2010), *Economic Survey of Himachal Pradesh 2009-10*, Finance Department, Government of Himachal Pradesh, Shimla.

GOP (1950), *Statistical Abstract of Punjab 1947-50*, Public Relations Department, Government of Punjab.

GOP (2006), *Statistical Abstract of Punjab 2005*, Economic Advisor to Government, Punjab, Chandigarh.

Guhan, S. (1994), 'Social Security Option for Developing Countries', *International Labour Review*, Vol. 133 (1), pp. 35-53.

Jain, V. (2010a), *Unfair Remuneration in Punjab's Unorganised Establishments: An Exploration across the Wage Ladder*, Mimeo, Centre for Development Studies, Thiruvananthapuram, (Kerala).

Jain, V. (2010b), 'Wage Workers' Exposure to Discrimination and Work-Related Insecurity in Punjab's Urban Unorganised Establishments: A Social Class Analysis', in S.S. Gill, Lakhwinder Singh and Reena Marwah (eds.) *Economic and Environmental Sustainability of the Asian Region*, Routledge (Taylor & Francis), New Delhi, pp. 339-66.

Jain, V. (2010c), 'Affluence, Vulnerability and the Provision of Social Security: Assessing State's Concern for the Vulnerable Masses in Indian Punjab', *CDS-ASSR Project on Social Security Working Paper No. 3*, HiVOS, The Netherlands.

Jain, V. (2010d), 'Dynamics of Insecurity in India's Informal Sector: A Study of Manufacturing in Punjab', *Unpublished Ph.D. Dissertation*, Jawaharlal Nehru University, New Delhi.

Kannan, K.P. (2002), 'The Welfare Fund of Social Security for Informal Sector Workers: The Kerala Experience', *The Indian Journal of Labour Economics*, Vol. 45 (2), pp. 243-72.

Kannan, K.P., R. Srivastava and A. Sengupta (2006), 'Social Security for Unorganised Sector: A Major National Initiative', *Economic and Political Weekly*, Vol. 41 (32), pp. 3477-80.

Kannan, K.P. and N.V. Pillai (2007), 'Conceptualising Social Security in a Human Development and Rights Perspective', *Indian Journal of Human Development*, Vol. 1 (1), pp. 33-54.

Kapoor, B. (1987), 'Labour Market Discrimination Against Migrant Workers in an Indian State: The Case of Punjab', *Journal of Development Studies*, Vol. 23 (3), pp. 402-17.

Mukherjee, M. (1985), 'Commercialisation and Agrarian Change in Pre-Independence Punjab', in K.N. Raj, N. Bhattacharya, S. Guha and S. Padhi (eds.) *Essays on the Commercialisation of Indian Agriculture*, Oxford University Press, Delhi, pp. 51-104.

NSSO (2005), *Household Assets and Liabilities in India (as on June 30, 2002), NSS 59th Round (January-December 2003), Report No. 500 (59/18.2/1)*, Ministry of Statistics and Programme Implementation, Government of India, New Delhi.

Oberai, A.S. and H.K.M. Singh (1980), 'Migration Flows in Punjab's Green Revolution Belt', *Economic and Political Weekly*, Vol. 15 (13), pp. A2-A12.

Paustian, P.W. (1930), *Canal Irrigation in the Punjab: An Economic Inquiry Relating to Certain Aspects of the Development of Canal Irrigation by the British in the Punjab*, Columbia University Press, New York.

Rai, S.M. (1965), *Partition of the Punjab*, Asia, New Delhi.

Rangi, P.S., M.S. Sidhu and Harjit Singh (2001), 'Casualisation of Agricultural Labour in Punjab', *The Indian Journal of Labour Economics*, Vol. 44 (4), pp. 957-70.

Saini, G.R. (1976), 'Green Revolution and the Distribution of Farm Incomes', *Economic and Political Weekly*, Vol. 11 (13), pp. A17-A22.

Sidhu, M.S. and P.S. Rangi (1998), 'A Study on Migrant Agricultural Labour in Punjab', *The Indian Journal of Labour Economics*, Vol. 41 (4), pp. 717-27.

Singh, L. and S. Singh (2002), 'Deceleration of Economic Growth in Punjab: Evidence, Explanation and a Way-Out', *Economic and Political Weekly*, Vol. 37 (6), pp. 579-86.

Singh, M. (1997), 'Bonded Migrant Labour in Punjab Agriculture', *Economic and Political Weekly*, Vol. 32 (11), pp. 518-19.

Singh, V. (2010), 'In Punjab, Work 90 Days to Avail Interest-Free Loan', *The Tribune*, Chandigarh.

Thorburn, S.S. (1886), *Musalmans and Money-Lenders in the Punjab*, Reprinted in 1983, Mittal Publications, New Delhi.

Vakil, C.N. (1950), *Economic Consequences of Divided India: A Study of the Economy of India and Pakistan*, Vora & Co., Bombay.

PART VI

Critical Issues in Punjab's Education Sector

12

Public Expenditure on the Education Sector in Punjab: A Comparison with Some Adjoining States

Amarjit Singh Sethi and Baljit Kaur

I

Introduction

Education is considered as an important instrument of social change, which is not merely a mechanism for generating manpower, but it also provides socially responsible citizenry in our democratic society. It improves the quality of human resources, which are simultaneously termed as the means and ends of economic development. Thus, when the Education Commission (1964-66) opined that the 'Destiny of India is being shaped in her classrooms', (Government of India, 1966) it was not a mere slogan; rather it was a directive towards the aspiration of the young nation, although now it appears to be reflecting some sort of wishful thinking. The national development policy has been in favour of a major role for education in the building of the nation. This is amply reflected in the impressive quantitative expansion of education since independence. For instance, during the period 1949-1978, Uttar Pradesh state had experienced a nine-fold increase, in real terms, in public expenditure on education (Muzzamil, 1980). Prasuna and Kumar (1999) empherised that the poor states should make concerted efforts to improve their level of NSDP so as they can be able to step-up the development expenditure.

In India, education is an important constituent of social sector expenditure. This particular activity falls in the Concurrent List, meaning thereby that the central as well as state governments are responsible for effective provision of education facilities to the general masses. Keeping this in view, the present paper envisages studying some dynamic aspects relating to government expenditure on the education and allied activities in Punjab compared to some of the adjoining states. The paper has been divided into three sections including the present one. Section II deals with the data and analytical techniques; and, the discussion and main results are briefly presented in Section III, duly supplementing the meaningful policy implications.

II

Data and Analytical Techniques

Being an empirical investigation, it is based on secondary information, compiled in the form of regular time series for 21 years since the mid-80s (1985-86) to 2005-06 on government expenditure on the education sector (including Sports, Art and Culture) in Punjab (PNB) and its adjoining states, viz., Haryana (HAR), Himachal Pradesh (HMP) and Jammu & Kashmir (JNK). Making use of suitable splicing techniques, such time series data were also compiled on their Gross State Domestic Product (GSDP), both at the current and at 1999-2000 constant prices. Through the GSDP deflators, time series data on public expenditure on the education sector in each state was then generated at constant prices (1999-2000). The required data were compiled through the publications of various official agencies (like RBI, CSO, CMIE, Planning Commission of India, etc.), including their websites.

In order to examine differentials, if any, among the growth rates of in education during the pre- and post-liberalisation policy regime in each of the four states, we have made the estimation of the growth rates (through OLS technique) from an exponential equation involving *dummy variables* technique (as indicated in Sethi, 2006), given by

$$y_t = b_0 b_1^t c_2^{Dt} e^{u_t} \qquad \text{(i)}$$

Then following the methodology as outlined in Sethi (2008), an examination of alternative hypotheses (regarding growth pattern of expenditure on education) was made through graphical portraits of *relative growth rates* (RGR_t) estimated from the behavioural growth paths of the best-fit[1]. Nature of structural changes was examined through temporal shifts in relative shares of government expenditure towards the education sector. An assessment of differentials, if any, in expenditure on education/ allied activities (expressed as a percentage of income) among the four states under study was made through *two-way analysis of variance* approach.

III

Results and Discussion

Results have been discussed, in brief, under the following sub-heads:

3.1. Growth Rates Analysis

Rates of growth were computed over three time spans, *viz.* pre-liberalisation period (*i.e.* from 1985-86 to 1991-92), post-liberalisation period (from 1991-92 to 2005-06) and for the whole time period (*i.e.* from 1985-86 to 2005-06). Such growth rates have been presented in Table 12.1. A perusal of the data clearly depicts that overall rates of growth in public expenditure on the education sector have been meagre ones, and varied within a fairly narrow range. The growth rate was observed to be 3.96 per cent in Punjab in relation to the highest growth rate of 4.64 per cent registered by Haryana. The data further evinces that the policy of liberalisation has induced suppression on state governments' public expenditure on education in each of the selected states. For instance, the state of Punjab experienced growth at a rate of 6.6 per cent during the pre-liberalisation period, whereas it was growing at a rate of 4.3 per cent only during the post-liberalisation period. A further look at Table

12.1 reveals that the growth rate of state governments' expenditure on the education was the maximum (=7.4 per cent) in Himachal Pradesh during the pre-liberalisation period, whereas in the post-liberalisation period, the growth rate declined to 4.4 per cent. Thus, on the whole, it appears that the LPG policy regime has adversely affected the growth process of public expenditure on the education sector in each of the selected states. Devi's study (2005) also observed that the economic reforms, despite resulting in relatively higher levels of literacy and a reduction in poverty before and after their implementation, were not thoroughly successful in bringing out the expected improvement in public expenditure on education in the post-1990s period.

Table 12.1: Exponential Compound Rates of Growth in Public Expenditure on Education in Punjab and Adjoining States during Different Periods

State	*Period*		
	Pre-lib.	*Post-lib.*	*Overall*
PNB	6.59	4.31	3.96
HAR	6.78	4.92	4.64
HMP	7.35	4.36	3.91
JNK	6.28	3.71	3.31

3.2. Evaluation of Alternative Hypotheses Regarding Growth Paths

The above analysis based on sub-periodisation is associated with an inherent limitation of meagreness of degrees of freedom available for the sub-periods and, therefore, may not provide us with a very concrete picture regarding the growth pattern in these states. And, this part of analysis, which aimed at examining validity of alternative hypotheses, has shown a certain improvement in this direction. For this purpose, we have first tried to identify long-term behavioural growth paths of the best-fit (out of a totality of 14 alternatives) traced by the time series data on real public expenditure on the education sector in each of the states through *confluence analysis*. Then, through the so-identified functional forms, *relative growth rates* (RGRs) were worked out (Sethi, 2008) across these selected states and portrayed graphically in Figure 1). A glance at the figure reveals that the state governments of Punjab and Himachal Pradesh have been giving virtually unchanged importance to the education sector, as relative growth rates (at less than 4 per cent) have followed a constancy path. Presence of U-shaped pattern in respect of Jammu & Kashmir implies a deceleration in the public expenditure on education up till 2000, but thereafter acceleration. In Haryana, however, the RGRs have pointed towards the validity of accelerating growth path. On the whole, the picture in respect of Punjab state has not been very conducive.

***Figure 1:* Temporal Pattern of Relative Growth Rates in the Education Sector**

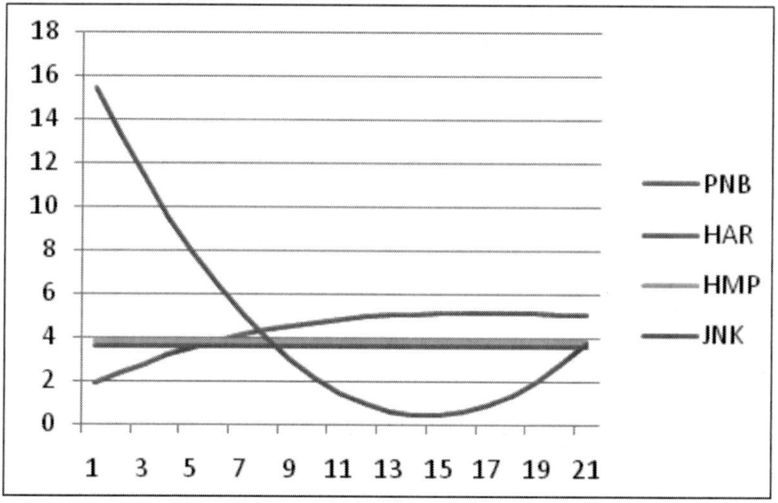

3.3 Structural Changes in Public Expenditure on Education

This section is devoted to an examination of the nature of structural changes with respect to public expenditure on education (as gauged through temporal shifts in relative shares of expenditure on the education sector as a percentage of the aggregated public expenditure) that have been experienced in each of the four states. Table 12.2 presents such computations at three points of time [*viz.* P_1 (1985-86), P_2 (1995-96), and P_3 (2005-06)]. Relative shares of Non-developmental Expenditure (NDE) have also been presented in this table, so as to have a comparative picture on the importance assigned by the state governments to the activities of developmental vis-à-vis non-developmental nature. The data clearly reveal that in all the four states, the relative share of public expenditure on education was fairly high in the period P_1 which, however, has decreased over the span of time. In Punjab, for example, the relative share of the public expenditure on education was 20.3 per cent in the period P_1, which declined to 15.9 per cent in P_2 and further to 13.2 per cent in P_3. Thus, over the study span, the relative share of public expenditure on education in Punjab state has come down through a hefty 35.2 per cent. In the rest of the states as well, the share of this sector has dipped, although through varying extents; the dip being the maximum in the case of Punjab. The findings are in broad agreements with earlier studies done by Sethi and Kaur (2004) and; Kaur and Sethi (2007) in respect of social sector expenditure in India. Decline in the relative share of state government expenditure on this particular activity is, of course, an unhealthy sign from the point of view of social welfare and human capital formation.

Table 12.2: Distributive Shares of Public Expenditure on Education and Non-Development Expenditure (NDE) at Different Points of Time Across Four States

State	*Activity*	*Point of Time*		
		1985-86	*1995-96*	*2005-06*
PNB	Education	20.32	15.89	13.17
	NDE	32.01	53.55	55.12
HAR	Education	17.76	12.15	16.02
	NDE	27.86	47.85	35.87
HMP	Education	18.96	18.57	18.18
	NDE	26.64	32.74	45.92
JNK	Education	14.94	17.22	11.41
	NDE	32.14	37.78	38.58

On the other hand, the relative share of NDE has increased

perceptibly in all the four states (Table 12.2). In the year P_1 (*i.e.* 1985-86), the relative share of NDE was to the tune of 32 per cent in both Jammu & Kashmir and Punjab. In the year P_3 (*i.e.* 2005-06), the share increased to 38.6 per cent in Jammu & Kashmir, but to as high as 55.1 per cent in Punjab. As to what it implies is that, the state of Punjab, which is already facing a severe deterioration in its fiscal health, has been allocating more than half of its aggregated expenditure towards the activities which are non-developmental in nature. This undoubtedly could be a seen as reflector of poor governance in the state.

3.4 Ratio of Public Expenditure on the Education Sector as a Percentage of GSDP

States' expenditure expressed as a percentage of their income is widely accepted to be an important indicator on the part of the concerned governments as to whether a particular activity is given due recognition or not. Prasuna and Kumar (1999) observed a significant empirical relationship between the GSDP of 14 major Indian states and the level of their government expenditure. Long ago, the Kothari Commission (1964-66) also recommended 6 per cent of India's GDP to be spent on the education sector alone (Government of India, 1966). In order to make an assessment of the departures, if any, from the recommendation, an attempt has been made in this section to analyse the states' public expenditure on education expressed as a percentage of the corresponding GSDP (Table 12.3). Such ratios were determined for each of the four states and at each of the 21 years. Regarding years as replicates, the ratios were then subjected to *two-way analysis of variance technique* (Table 12.4), so as to squeeze out a more concise picture regarding comparative performance among the states.

A perusal of Table 12.3, once again, reveals that the education sector has failed to attract the desired attention across all state governments in the sense that this sector has been able to get a very small piece of cake of the total pie. Overall value (for the entire study period) of the ratio was found to be the minimum (=2.4 per cent) in Haryana, followed closely by that (=2.5 per cent) in Punjab. However, the states of Himachal

Pradesh (5.7 per cent) and Jammu & Kashmir (5.2 per cent) were associated with high ratios which were fairly closer to the magic figure of 6 per cent as recommended by India's famous Kothari Commission in the mid-1960s (Government of India, 1966).

Table 12.3: States' Public Expenditure on Education Expressed as a Percentage of their GSDP

State	*Points of Time*					
	1985-86	*1990-91*	*1995-96*	*2000-01*	*2005-06*	*Average (over 21 years)*
PNB	2.49	2.71	2.32	2.49	2.48	2.54
HAR	2.32	2.38	2.19	2.34	2.11	2.35
HMP	5.68	6.59	5.28	5.62	4.59	5.74
JNK	4.08	6.36	5.35	5.00	4.09	5.19

An analysis of data in Table 12.4 finds a highly significant value of 'F' (=2.891) for years indicates that the ratio of public expenditure on education to GSDP has not remained unchanged over the years. Besides, a very large value (= 218.53) of 'F', associated with an exceedingly small value of 'p' for the states provides a very strong evidence that the ratios were grossly different among the states. Furthermore, the paired comparisons among the states (Table 12.5), as made through *critical difference*, indicated that although the ratio for Punjab was comparable to that of Haryana, yet the same was highly significantly lower than that for each of Himachal Pradesh and Jammu & Kashmir. The state of Himachal has, of course, been the clear leader on this front. A similar finding was made earlier by Sethi and Kaur (2008) in the context of social sector expenditure.

Thus, in conclusion, Punjab state in particular needs to learn a lesson from the experiences of its sister state of Himachal Pradesh. No doubt, Punjab state (which used to be a top-ranking state in terms of per capita income in India for a pretty long time) has undergone the turmoil of terrorism, and has remained heavily burdened to spend large sums of state expenditure towards public administration and defence, leading to a rapid slippage in its comparative positioning. Nevertheless, such a retrogressive phenomenon cannot be allowed to continue in

Table 12.4: Two-Way Analysis of Variance of Ratios of Public Expenditure on Education to GSDP

Source of Variation	*Degrees of Freedom*	*Sum of Squares*	*Mean Square*	*F-Value*	*P-Value for F*
Years	20	17.195	0.860	2.891***	0.00079
States	3	194.985	64.995	218.529***	≅ 0
Exptl. Error	60	17.845	0.297		
Total	83	230.025			

*** Significant at 0.001 probability level

Table 12.5: Paired Comparisons Among Four States on Basis of Ratios of Public Expenditure on Education to GSDP

Pair of States	*Means*
PNB-HAR	0.192NS
PNB-HMP	-3.195**
PNB-JNK	-2.652**
HAR-HMP	-3.387**
HAR-JNK	-2.845**
HMP-JNK	0.542**

** Significant at 0.01 probability level

future years; there is urgent need to create a political will (on the part of our polity and bureaucracy) to provide good governance, change their priorities and do something serious to promote educational activities rather than spending enormously on vote-catching and other unproductive measures. In line with the study done by Parekh (2002), a combination of policies promoting higher growth and reduction in population pressure would lead to higher public expenditure on development activities. Concerted efforts must be made to improve the level of the state's income in order to be able to step-up public expenditures and become autonomous in future.

NOTES

1. A totality of fourteen functional forms was estimated from the time series information on education in respect of each of the

four states. The forms were: (1) Simple Linear (SLR); (2) Parabolic (PRB); (3) Cubic (CUB); (4) Exponential (EXP); (5) Exponential Parabolic (EPB); (6) Exponential Cubic (ECB); (7) Geometric (GEO); (8) Hyperbolic (HYP); (9) Modified Exponential (MEX); (10) Gompertz (GOM); (11) Logistic (LGS); (12) Log-Linear (LLR); (13) Log-Parabolic (LPB); and (14) Log-Cubic (LCB). Then, path of the best-fit was identified on the basis of the indicator I (Sethi, 2008), given by an equation:

$I = 1.2\,\varphi - 0.2\,[\,|\,DW - 2\,|\,];$

where j being the coefficient of predictability and DW, the Durbin-Watson statistic. The equation associated with the highest value of I was accepted to be the best-fit functional form. Computations in entirety were made through software developed by the senior author of the present paper.

REFERENCES

Devi, T.N. (2005). 'Role of the State in Social Sector: Some Reflections', *Anvesak,* Vol. 35 (2), pp. 71-84.

Government of India (1966), *Report of the Education Commission 1964-66: Education and National Development* (headed by D.S. Kothari), Manager of Publications, Delhi.

Kaur, B. and A.S. Sethi (2007), 'Liberalisation and Social Sector Expenditure: An Inter-State Analysis in India', *The Journal of Income and Wealth,* Vol. 29 (1), pp. 79-92.

Muzzamil, M. (1980), 'An Enquiry into the Growth of Public Expenditure on Education in Uttar Pradesh: 1949-50 to 1977-78', *The Indian Journal of Economics,* Vol. 61 (240), pp. 75-88.

Parekh, K.M. (2002), 'Some Aspects of State Government Expenditure: A Study of Gujarat (1980-81 to 1997-98)', *Anvesak,* Vol. 32 (1), pp. 1-13.

Prasuna, C.A. and S.N.V. Kumar (1999). 'Pooling Cross-Section and Time-series Data: The Expenditure and Net Domestic Product Relationship for Major Indian States', *The Indian Economic Journal,* Vol. 47 (4), pp. 119-23.

Sethi, A.S. (2006), 'Estimation of Rates of Growth–Some Conceptual Issues', Paper Presented in the *42nd Annual Conference of the Indian Econometric Society* (TIES) at Guru Nanak Dev University, Amritsar, January 5-7.

Sethi, A.S. (2008), 'Some Methodological Aspects of Rates of Growth Computations: Limitations and Alternatives', *South Asia Economic Journal,* Vol. 9 (1), pp. 195-209.

Sethi, A.S. and B. Kaur (2004), 'Public Expenditure and National Income in India: An Investigation of Structural Changes and Causality', *The Journal of Income and Wealth*, Vol. 26 (1 & 2), pp. 45-57.

Sethi, A.S. and B. Kaur (2008), 'Social Sector Expenditure in India: An Examination of Inter-State Divergences', *91st Conference Volume of Indian Economic Association*, pp. 229-41.

Websites Accessed

www.cmie.org.in
www.indiabudget.nic.in
www.mospi.nic.in
www.plannningcommission.gov.in
www.rbi.org.in

13

Market Dispensation, State Contraction and Emerging Practices in Delivery of Higher Education in Punjab

Jaswinder Singh Brar

I. Introduction

The higher education sector in the state of Punjab, during the last decade and a half, has recorded not only the spectacular growth and multiple expansions but also many noticeable changes in all dimensions and components. The process of change, which actually started in a gradual manner with the adoption of the new education policy during the mid-1980s (GOI, 1986) and its revised version during the 1990s (GOI, 1991) at the national level, got a boost with the adoption of a comprehensive package of economic reforms of 1991 and thereafter. The new economic environment constructed upon the edifice of privatisation, liberalisation and globalisation and more so with the decisive and liberal role to the market forces that radically transformed the organisation of economic activities in the country. Along with commodity-producing sectors, the service sector too was opened up for the participation of all forms of private capital comprising both the national and global variety. The service sector reforms paved the way for the supply of all types of services including the educational one in the overall framework which in essence involves the diminished role of the state, opening up of the existing public concerns to the private sector capital, and promotes the further capacity expansion either exclusively through the private sector or joint ventures involving different types of public and private mixing.

This business environment which resulted from market-oriented policy framework drastically altered the whole gamut of supply of education services. The higher education sector expanded in numerous directions by absorbing and acting upon the market signals which emanated from mutual interaction of new education and economic policies. Consequently, the delivery of higher education started in a market mode with the determination of consumer prices on the basis of the cost plus principle. Thus, the planning, execution and relevance of all the activities and courses offered at the level of the higher education system have continuously been viewed and are undertaken within the overall ambit of business dynamics. As a result, the higher education sector in the state of Punjab, as also elsewhere in the country, has witnessed the entry of a large number of private service suppliers with varying profiles and divergent interests. It led to the emergence of the strong private sub-sector in the domain of higher education which precisely fits in the category of for-profit suppliers.

Another note worthy development in the sphere of higher education of this period has been in the form of the curtailment of the supply of public resources to the already existing government-owned as well as government-aided private institutions. The public resource crunch has seriously disturbed the academic and financial equilibrium in the majority of institutions, particularly with small size of operations, situated in unfavourable locations, or those serving purely academic disciplines and known for supplying quality education services at low cost or at fairer terms and conditions. These institutions have been allowed and encouraged to raise their own resources which practically resulted in the enhancement of tuition fees and other charges. The overriding objective of attaining self-sufficiency of finance on the part of institutions amidst resource paucity narrowed down the academic and administrative choices towards professional courses.

Overall, the higher education sector has witnessed too many changes in all spheres from purely academic to administrative, to financial, to staff deployment, to student intake, etc. The higher education system has essentially been transformed and operated in such a manner that the real and ultimate stakeholders (students and parents), other than those of owners and operators, have suffered serious setbacks in numerous ways with far-reaching multilayered implications and outcomes. The loose and ineffective regulations allowed the private interests to override the non-negotiable social (equity) and academic (quality) interests. This chapter against such a background examines and highlights in a holistic way the emerging issues, problems and concerns by focusing on the experiences and evidences of Punjab's higher education sector.

The chapter, overall, runs into six Sections. Section II examines the main policy changes and dynamics. Section III provides the overview of size, composition and patterns of the growth. Section IV and Section V deal with the issues related to fees, funds, and public and private financing. Section VI sums up the major concerns and policy issues.

II. Policy Configurations and Dynamics

The space for opening up and expansion of the higher education sector has practically been created by the overall understanding at the national level among the policy circles that the higher education base of the country must be strengthened in order to bring a large section of the population under the purview of higher level of education and training. Moreover, it has been contemplated that the earlier it happens the better it would be in order to support and carry out the huge programme of modernisation of the national economy. And, it was further decided that the country could reap the benefits of 'demographic dividend' only by expanding its higher education base in a time-bound manner and thereby bring the larger proportion of the relevant age group in the domain of higher education. It was further realised that for the higher education to expand, involvement of private capital is a must because the state alone cannot undertake such a huge task for a variety of reasons such as other developmental commitments and priorities. And, moreover, it was also postulated that there is no solid justification to stop the entry of private players in the areas where they are more than willing to participate and supplement the government efforts. Such type of policy configurations provided a big boost to the emergence of the higher education system with different contours and dimensions.

The whole process of reformatory measures placed the education sector largely in the domain of the market. Consequently, all the types and stages of the education sector responded to the market forces to a larger extent though with differential intensity and depth. In this milieu, the higher education sector has shown a much higher level of flexibility and demonstrated a great degree of change and ultimately over the course of time acquired absolutely a new format and face. These changes have facilitated unlimited possibilities and led to diversification of educational programmes and courses in higher education. The higher education sector, in fact, added more and more new programmes and study courses in order to make it relevant to the needs of the various sectors of the economy. Consequently, the success of the higher education sector has been assessed by the degree of its diversification from the liberal academic courses of the pre-reform period to the professional and job-oriented courses. The skill generation task has assumed unprecedented coverage over the other critical roles/contributions which were normally associated with the acquiring of higher level degrees. Thus, even the existing institutions started adding up the market-friendly courses and the newer ones came up exclusively in the professional and job-oriented courses.

To facilitate the opening up of new programmes/courses, the existing norms and practices related to the affiliation and recognition were considerably restructured at all the levels and for all the categories of education such as the professional, technical and general education. The prevalent entry barriers for the non-state suppliers, comprising all types and varieties of the existing and upcoming higher education services, have either been relaxed or removed under the various pretexts. The regulatory framework changed with the establishment of separate universities exclusively to deal with the provisioning of professional and technical courses. All such initiatives led to the proliferation of higher educational institutions in a relatively shorter span of time of about a decade. The private players entered in a big way to supply higher education and occupied the decisive space. On the other side, curtailing budgetary support has created the situation of resource crunch for all the three categories of institutions, viz. government-owned institutions, aided private institutions, and publicly funded state universities. Fees and funds increased exorbitantly as the students emerged as the only effective way for resources mobilisation. Thus, the higher education sector of the state has changed drastically in every respect: type of courses serviced, curriculum designs, financing practices, ownership modes, cost formation, locational dynamics, staff deployment practices, etc.

Further, expansion of the higher education sector in the state was affected in the situation of the extremely favourable environment generated by the specific demand and supply side factors and tendencies. The capacity addition quickly made its way into the situation of high-intensity of demand for higher education which partly sprouts from the more than normal level of expectations about the social and economic returns of acquiring of higher level of degrees and training on the one side and lack of readily available employment opportunities on the other. The private sector in higher education responded quickly to the situation and succeeded in filling the vacuum by attracting the students by designing the courses with more acceptability in the market by the full use of its publicity and advocacy programmes. The high paying capacity of the middle and rich strata of society of the state came in very handy for the upcoming service suppliers to fully cash in on such type of opportunities and activities. The market acquired almost full control of the higher education sector as the profitability of investment in the education sector has been compared with other sectors by the investors. The existence of such a situation has made the delivery of education as a business preposition subject to cost and benefit considerations in a typical monetary framework.

III. Size, Composition and Ownership

The higher education sector in Punjab experienced a remarkable growth and diversification during the reforms. Overall, it consists of 457 institutions up to 2008 (Table 13.1). Between 2001 and 2008, as many as 150 new educational institutions were added, i.e. nearly 19 institutions per annum. This expansion was essentially driven by the professional education courses as 125 professional institutions were added compared to 25 general education institutions. And, this rapid expansion in professional education has brought out a strong structural change within the higher education sector. For instance, the proportion of professional education institutions in the overall higher education sector has increased from 34.52 per cent in 2001 to 50.55 per cent in 2008. Interestingly, the number of professional institutions surpassed that of the general education institutions in 2008. Within the professional education, the maximum expansion occurred in the case of management, computer and engineering education.

The state's higher education sector also witnessed drastic changes in terms of patterns of ownership. The proportion of private sector institutions increased considerably (Table 13.2). In the case of professional education, the proportion of government institutions declined for the seven categories of education, i.e. Medical, Dental, Ayurvedic and Homeopathic, Nursing, Engineering, Architecture and Pharmacy. In the case of Physiotherapy, MBA, MCA and Law, all new institutions fall in the category of the private sector. In the case of general education (Table 13.3), the overall share of two categories of institutions, namely, 'government-owned institutions' and 'government-aided but privately managed' had declined. And, the share of 'pure privately owned and operated' rose from 14.43 per cent in 2001 to 22.29 per cent in 2008.

Table 13.1: Number of Higher Education Institutions in Punjab (as on December 31)

Institutions	*2001*	*Percentages*	*2008*	*Percentages*
1. Medical	06	5.66	07	3.03
2. Dental	09	8.49	14	6.06
3. Ayurvedic, Homeopathic	13	13.21	16	7.02
4. Physiotherapy	03	2.83	11	4.76
5. Nursing	08	7.55	17	7.36
6. Engineering	25	23.58	54	23.38
7. Architecture	02	1.89	08	3.46
8. MBA/MCA	26	24.53	70	30.30
9. B.Pharmacy	11	10.38	21	9.09
10. Law	02	1.89	13	5.63
(a) Professional (1 to 10)	106	100.00	231	100.00
(b) General Education	201	34.53	226	50.55
Overall (a+b)	307	65.47	457	49.45
		100.00		100.00

Source: (1) AIU, *Universities Handbook* (various years); (2) *www.aicte.ernet.in*

Table 13.2: Proportion of Government Institutions (Other than Universities) in Professional Education in Punjab (as on December 31)

Course/Trade	*2001*	*2008*
1. Medical	50.00	40.00
2. Dental	22.29	19.10
3. Ayuvedic and Homeopathic	11.25	10.05
4. Physiotherapy/MBA/MCA/Law	0.00	0.00
5. Nursing	24.00	13.15
6. Engineering	48.25	29.11
7. Architecture	100.00	29.58
8. B. Pharmacy	36.35	22.20

Source: (1) AIU, *Universities Handbook* (various years); (2) www. aicte.ernet.in

Another structural shift has been noticed in the intake pattern of students in higher education in the state (Table 13.4). During 2001-02, there were 2.34 lakh students enrolled in the higher education. Their number reached 3.04 lakh students

Table 13.3: Ownership–wise Distribution of General Education Institutions in Punjab

(Up to December 31)

Ownership	*2001*	*2008*
1. Government Colleges	23.88	22.35
2. Aided Private Colleges	61.69	55.36
3. Unaided Private Colleges	14.43	22.29
Total	100.00	100.00

Note: The general education is supplied by three categories of institutions: government, government-aided, and private-unaided.

Source: (1) AIU, *Universities Handbook* (various years); (2) www. aicte.ernet.in

Table 13.4: Number and Percentage Distribution of Students in Higher Education in Punjab

	Courses	*2001-02*	*Percentage*	*2007-08*	*Percentage*
1.	Ph.D./D.Sc./ M.Phil.	249	0.11	1,075	0.35
2.	M.A.	9,995	4.28	12,738	4.19
3.	M.Sc.	2,174	0.93	7,768	2.55
4.	M.Com.	928	0.40	1,237	0.41
5.	B.A./B.A.(Hons.)	1,32,731	56.78	127,985	42.09
6.	B.Sc./B.Sc. (Hons.)	16,745	7.16	25,980	8.54
7.	B.Com./B.Com (Hons.)	20,444	8.75	22,143	7.28
8.	B.E./B. Tech. (Engg./B. Arch.)	13,750	5.88	29,623	9.74
9.	Medicine, Dentistry, Nursing, Pharmacy, Ayurvedic & Unani, etc.	6,112	2.61	11,495	3.78
10.	B.Ed.	3,803	1.63	5,987	1.97
11.	Others	26814	11.47	58,042	19.09
	Total	2,33,745	100.00	304,073	100.00

Source: MHRD, *State Profile*, Department of Higher Education, New Delhi, URL: http://education.nic.in/stats/state profile0506.pdf (July 29, 2009).

during 2007-08. The maximum addition took place in the case of engineering courses as the proportion of engineering students in the total students jumped from 5.88 per cent to 9.74 per cent.

The rising proportion of technical education students and of other courses was accompanied by the decline in the proportionate share of students in the B.A. course.

IV. Public Resources in Higher Education

The financing pattern of higher education in the state also changed drastically during the reforms. Truly, the proportion of private resources increased and that of public resources declined. Although the education budget of the state seems to have increased too much when it is viewed in absolute terms and at current prices (Table 13.5), yet its perusal in relative terms presents a different picture. For example, the higher education budget of the state increased from Rs. 211.90 crores in 2000-01 to Rs. 267.85 crores in 2007-08. However, as a proportion of state income, it declined from 0.36 per cent in 2000-01 to 0.21 per cent in 2007-08. Similarly, as the proportion of state budget, it declined from 1.81 per cent to 1.16 per cent during corresponding periods and as proportion of the overall education budget, it too declined from 10.31 per cent to 9.31 per cent. The overall squeeze of higher education budget resulted in declining educational spending on per student basis at current prices from Rs. 11736 to Rs. 8809 during the two reference periods.

Table 13.5: Punjab's Higher Education Budget in Relation to Punjab State Income and Budget

Name of Variables	*2000-01*	*2007-08 (RE)*
1. Higher Education Budget (Rs. Crore)	211.90	267.85
2. Ratio of Higher Education Budget to State Budget	1.81	1.16
3. Ratio of Higher Education Budget to State Income	0.36	0.21
4. Ratio of Higher Education Budget to Education Budget	10.31	9.31
5. Per Student Expenditure on Higher Education, (Rs. at Current Prices)	11736.43	8808.67

Sources: 1. *Budgetary Resources for Education*, MHRD (various issues).
2. *Statistical Abstract of Punjab, Chandigarh*, ESO (various issues).

Moreover, there are certain other disturbing features of the higher education budget of the state. It starts with the lower level of spending on the plan side. For example, the total spending on the plan account was just Rs. 1.42 crores (0.67 per cent) in 2000-01 which increased to Rs. 13.11 crores (4.89 per cent) in 2007.08. It means out of the total budget of the higher education sector, an overwhelming proportion (more than 95 per cent) went to the non-plan account (Table 13.6). It is to be noted that the spending on plan account results in the new capacity creation undertaken for new and fresh activities. The non-plan expenditure goes to the maintenance and running of the already created capacities.

Table 13.6: Plan and Non-Plan Distribution of the Higher Education Budget in Punjab

(Rs. Crores)

Type of Expenditure	*2000-01*	*2007-08 (RE)*
1. Plan	1.42 (0.67)	13.11 (4.89)
2. Non-Plan	210.48 (99.33)	254.73 (95.11)
Total(1+2)	211.90 (100.00)	267.84 (100.00)

Sources: Budgetary Resources for Education, MHRD (various issues).

The other feature pertains to allocation of extremely negligible funds to the significant component, i.e. direction and administration (0.01 per cent in 2007-08) which is necessary for successful functioning of any educational activity. The proportionate share of universities, government colleges and aided colleges increased from 69.30 per cent during 2003-04 to 94.42 per cent during 2007-08 (Table 13.7). It implies that over the short time period, the budget of higher education has taken the form of spending more on the committed accounts only with limited funds available for other crucial activities.

V. Private Resources in Higher Education

The process of opening up higher education witnessed a divergent set of financing practices by the various institutions. All types of institutions, irrespective of their ownership and management base, have tried numerous alternatives of finance.

The government as well as aided institutions coped with the resource scarcity by opening up various self-financing courses. The pure private players flourished by charging the students fees and funds. It becomes abundantly clear from the perusal of data related to financing by the various colleges during 2006-07 (Table 13.8). In the case of professional education, except for the physiotherapy, in all other courses, namely, engineering, law, ayurvedic, MBA, MCA, medical, dental, nursing and architecture, the private institutions were found to be dependent exclusively on the students for financing of their various educational programmes and operations.

In the case of general education, during 2003-04, the share of various sources of finance (Table 13.9) was as follows: students (50.42 per cent), government (45.26 per cent), voluntary (2.02 per cent), and miscellaneous (2.30 per cent). The voluntary sources include the income from donations, contributions by eminent personalities, rich individuals, philanthropy, etc. The miscellaneous sources include the income from rent, consultancy, professional bodies, etc. Further, within the general education, the financing pattern varied according to the nature of ownership and management of the institutions. For example, government colleges were dependent on two sources for their finance, viz. government and students. The share of government

Table 13.7: Distribution of Public Expenditure on Higher Education in Punjab

(Figures in Rs. Crores)

Head	*2003-04*	*Percentage*	*2007-08 (RE)*	*Percentage*
1. Direction & Administration	0.00	0.00	00.04	0.01
2. Assistance to Universities	50.62	20.77	71.77	26.80
3. Government Colleges	55.54	22.78	74.62	27.86
4. Non-Government Colleges	62.78	25.75	106.49	39.76
5. Others	106.40	30.70	14.92	5.57
Total	243.77	100.00	267.84	100.00

Source: *Budgetary Resources for Education*, MHRD (various issues).

was 67.21 per cent and that of students 32.79 per cent. The private-aided colleges had financed their operations by realising 52.08 per cent from students, 43.77 per cent from government and 4.15 per cent from miscellaneous sources. The pure private colleges financed 82.12 per cent from students, 0.45 per cent from voluntary sources, and 17.43 per cent from miscellaneous sources.

Table 13.8: Percentage Share of Students in Overall Financing of Professional Education in Punjab, 2006-07

BFUHS Affiliated Institutions/Courses		*PTU Affiliated Institutions/Courses*	
1. Medical	98.94	1.Engineering	99.53
2. Dental	98.76	2. Architecture	99.78
3. Ayurvedic	98.76	3. MBA	99.31
4. Physiotherapy	51.79	4. Law	99.20
5. Nursing	92.23	5. MCA	99.63

Note: PTU stands for Punjab Technical University; BFUHS stands for Baba Farid University of Health Sciences

Source: Kalia, 2010.

Table 13.9: Financing Pattern of General Education Colleges in Punjab, 2003-04

Type of Management	*Students*	*Govt.*	*Voluntary*	*Miscell-aneous*	*Total*
1. Government Colleges	32.79	67.21	0.00	0.00	100
2. Aided Private Colleges	52.08	43.77	0.00	4.15	100
3. Unaided Private Colleges	82.12	0.00	0.45	17.43	100
Overall	50.42	45.26	2.02	2.30	100

Source: Ghuman, Singh and Brar, 2005.

The funding pattern has also been altered completely in the public universities of the state. It becomes quite clear by examining the funding pattern of a state university, namely,

Punjabi University, Patiala (Table 13.10). This is, in fact, true about all the typical publicly-managed, well-established and affiliated universities of the state. For the triennium ending in 1993, the University had got Rs.15.12 crores (86.40 per cent) from the government sources out of the total income of Rs. 17.50 crores of the University. However, the proportionate share of government sources declined to 26.85 per cent during the triennium ending in 2010. The government sources constituted the grants from three bodies, viz. state government, central government and UGC. Within the government sources, the bulk was contributed by the state government. But its share declined from 96.69 per cent to 78.08 per cent during the two reference points of time. The share of the UGC increased from 2.91 per cent to 21.81 per cent. And, that of the central government declined from 0.40 per cent to 0.11 per cent. Thus, the pattern of university financing in the state has changed drastically since the process of reforms was started in 1991 as shown by the declining proportion of government grants and rising proportion of fees and funds.

Though the grants from the Punjab government to the University has increased from Rs. 14.61 crores for the triennium ending in 1993 to Rs. 27.53 crores for the triennium ending in 2010, yet the University has to raise its own sources like fees and funds from students to finance various expansionary programmes and policies. For instance, the University had realised as high as Rs. 95.94 crores from its own sources for the triennium ending in 2010. Therefore, the share of its own sources in the total income of the University increased from 13.60 per cent for the triennium ending in 1993 to 73.15 per cent for the triennium ending in 2010. The own sources basically include six components, along with respective shares in own sources, as follows: fees and funds (80.56 per cent); receiving of interest (0.42 per cent); donations, recovery of loans, and scholarships (19.02 per cent). It means that the changing pattern of financing university education in the state has by and large shifted the whole burden of funding from government to the students.

In fact, this transformation of the higher education system in the state resulted in exceptionally higher level of fees and funds for all service suppliers (Table 13.11). There are huge variations in the level of fees and funds charged from students across various types of service suppliers. For B.A./B.Sc./ B.Com., the average level of fees and funds in the case of private institutions was Rs. 9,395; 2.43 times more that of government institutions (Rs. 3,859). For M.A./M.Sc./M.Com., average level of fees and funds was 2.19 times higher in the private colleges (Rs. 10,245) than in the government institutions (Rs. 4,678). For B. Tech., fees and funds are by and large the same between the government and private institutions. For the B.Ed., a student pays Rs. 37,402 per annum in private institutions compared to just Rs. 5,925 per annum in government institutions. Similarly, in the M.B.A./M.C.A., and B.Phar./BPT, the overall level of fees and funds is very high. In the BCA, fees and funds in the private institutions (Rs. 28,745) were higher than the government ones (Rs. 18,925).

VI. Emerging Issues and Concerns

The higher education sector in the state at present has acquired the distinction of a full-fledged market-based activity operating under the hardcore considerations of business costs and profits. The educational institutions have been transformed as business concerns standing for profit alone devoid of other larger social and academic concerns. The institutions that were originally established in the public sector have gone very close to the pure private suppliers in terms of imposition of fees and funds. In fact, larger numbers of institutions with even public managements have become privately financed entities in all respects and dynamics. The market in the education sector developed over a shorter span with determination of fees and funds on cost plus profit basis for all types of courses and programmes. The space created by opening up new courses has, in practice, been occupied exclusively by the for-profit suppliers. The presence of not-for-profit private providers, particularly the community-cum-philanthropic ones, has remained very low. Actually, the higher education sector in the state has been striving for the enhancement of commercialisation of degrees with larger frequency of market gimmicks.

Table 13.10: Financing Pattern in a Typical Public University in Punjab: A Case of Punjabi University

Source	*Triennium Ending Average (1993)*		*Triennium Ending Average (2010)*	
	Rs. Crores	*Percentages*	*Rs. Crores*	*Percentages*
(a) Govt. Grants:	15.12	86.40	35.21	26.85
1. Pb. Govt.	14.61	[96.69]	27.53	[78.08]
2. UGC	0.44	[2.91]	7.68	[21.81]
3. Central Govt.	0.06	[0.40]	0.04	[0.11]
(b) Own Sources:	2.38	13.60	95.94	73.15
1. Fees & Funds	2.24	[94.12]	77.29	[80.56]
2. Interest Received	0.02	[0.84]	0.4	[0.42]
3. Donations, Loan Recovery, Scholarships, etc	0.12	[5.04]	18.25	[19.02]
Total Income (a+b)	**17.50**	**100.00**	**131.25**	**100.00**

Notes: 1. Figures presented here refer to the average of three consecutive financial years.
2. Figures in square brackets refer to the percentage share in respective category.

Source: Punjabi University, Patiala, *Annual Budget* (various issues).

Table 13.11: Per Annum Average Level of Fees and Funds in Various Institutions 2010-11

Course	*Type of Institution*	
	Government (Rs.)	*Private Unaided (Rs.)*
1. B.A./B.Sc./B.Com.	3,859	9,395
2. M.A./M.Sc./M.Com.	4,678	10,245
3. B. Tech.	74,595	74,625
4. M.B.A./M.C.A.	n.a.	75,000
5. B. Phar./BPT	63,425	63425
6. B.C.A.	18,925	28,742
7. B.Ed.	5,925	37,402

Note: Total fees and funds mentioned here do not include refundable securities, hostel charges, Parent-Teacher Association charges, etc.

Source: Admission Prospectus, Various Colleges and Universities of Punjab (Session 2009-10).

Further, the higher education sector, particularly its professional segment, has become the domain of private players with profit maximisation as the over-riding goal. Many courses are exclusively being run by the for-profit players. In very few professional courses, even public providers share the market up to a worthwhile degree with the private providers. The private players act as price makers with the strong market power and free hand provided by loose regulations. Actually, there has been emergence of some sort of collusion among the service providers, politicians, administrative decision-makers and regulatory bodies. The ongoing environment in general and the state system in particular has reduced the chances of competitive price-determination to the lowest possible level. There is enough space for manipulations related to the practices adopted in the domain of input use, academic activities, cost reporting, and performance standards.

The state's role as promoter of higher education indeed has diminished in the material sense when viewed in the context of supply of public resources as a proportion of budget, state income and on per student basis which has seriously undermined the capacity of the state sector to deliver quality education at affordable terms and conditions. The diminishing of the proactive role of the state in higher education resulted in weak physical and social infrastructure which has been reflected in lack of undertaking of newer initiatives by public institution operators. The public sector has lost its sheen and glory considerably not only in the existing, but also in the emerging disciplines. The fact of the matter is that the professional segment of higher education has not been attracting the best category of the pass-outs of the competitive tests in the case of those students for whom monetary affordability is not the constraint.

In fact, the working of the education system under the market dispensation resulted in extremely higher level of user charges consisting of larger variety of fees and funds. The charges from students have taken in the form of package as the various components of the charges are not shown separately. The user charges have been de-linked from the socio-economic reality and requirements of the state. The higher level of user charges led to the exclusion of some section of deserving students from the higher education benefits. It has been made abundantly clear from the two recent studies. The proportion of students who had cleared their matriculation or plus two examination from the rurally located schools was 4.07 per cent in the on-campus departments of the universities of the state and their regional centres during the academic session 2005-06 (Ghuman, Singh and Brar, 2006). Similarly, in the higher level professional education, the proportion of rural students was 3.71 per cent during 2007-08 (Ghuman, Singh and Brar, 2009). The user charges are found to be on the higher side of the state income. As per the U.R. Rao Committee Report, the fees and funds charged from students should not be more than 30 per cent of state's per capita income (Ramachandran, 2004). But, in the state, the user charges crossed this threshold in many education courses.

The chances of exclusion increase when the income inequalities and populations which face economic vulnerability are taken into consideration. According to Census 2001, the proportion of the Scheduled Caste population out of the total population was 28.85 per cent. During 2004-05, exactly 5.20 per cent population of the state was below the officially defined national poverty line (Government of Punjab, 2008-09b). As per the *Atta-Dal* scheme (i.e. provision of subsidised wheat and pluses) of the state government, initiated on August 15, 2007, the number of poor families in Punjab was 13.47 lakhs (Government of Punjab, 2008-09a). It means 30.98 per cent of the total families/households (43.48 lakhs) fall in the category of poor families. Those families were included under this scheme whose income was less than Rs. 30,000 per annum (Government of Punjab, 2008-09 b). In the state, in six districts, the proportion of population below the poverty line in rural areas during 2004-05 was reported to be very high as follows: Moga (25.2 per cent), Firozepur (17.9 per cent), Mukatsar (28.3 per cent), Faridkot (23.9 per cent), Bathinda (23.1 per cent), and Mansa (16.6 per cent). These six districts constituted 26.40 per cent of the total rural population of the state (Chaudhuri and Gupta, 2009). Similarly, marginal, small and semi-medium size class of farmers constitutes 62.60 per cent of the total farmers of the state which too has been priced-out in the delivery of education under the market-based mechanism. It is important to mention here that the chances of exclusion increase when user charges for education were raised as corroborated by the experiences of advanced countries too (Pennell and West, 2005).

In a nutshell, the higher education system in the state has drifted away from the pious principles of equity and easy accessibility inherent in the constitutional mandate. The education system caters more to the vested interests of pressure groups and lobbies. Consequently, the credibility of the state sector has reached the lowest ebb and this state erosion has been reflected in the powers related to affiliation, recognition, inspection, monitoring, academic processes, examination, evaluation, practical training, etc., which have a strong bearing on the employability of the pass-outs. The faculty in the higher education sector is grossly under paid without any security of service, associated benefits and faculty improvement programmes. The emerging players are more interested in the graduation level courses, where returns are very high and quick as compared to the postgraduate courses and other research programmes. Such preferences in the selection of courses have made the professional institutions as the exclusive graduate-degree providing bodies and not as the partners in the generation of knowledge. The institutions frequently change the courses in response to the market instead of acquiring the higher level of specialisation in the ongoing programmes. The profit induced under undue haste resulted in over-experimentation in the academic sector which, in turn, disturbs the academic equilibrium. These concerns along with wider access, inclusiveness, and quality of higher education in the country have already caught the imagination of scholars (Thorat, 2006). Thus, the higher education sector in the state demands its complete overhauling based on the credible governance structure which ensures inclusion, transparency, and quality aspects in order to generate high rated human resources with wider participation of meritorious students which could come from adequate availability of public resources in diverse forms, provisions and programmes.

REFERENCES

Chaudhuri, S. and N. Gupta (2009), 'Levels of Living and Poverty Patterns: A District-Wise Analysis for India', *Economic and Political Weekly*, 44 (9), pp. 94-110.

Ghuman, R.S., Sukhwinder Singh and Jaswinder Singh Brar (2005), *Unit Cost of Higher Education in Punjab: A Study of Universities and Their Affiliated Colleges*, Association of Indian Universities (AIU), New Delhi.

Ghuman, R.S., Sukhwinder Singh and Jaswinder Singh Brar (2006), *Rural Students in Universities of Punjab*, Publication Bureau, Punjabi University, Patiala.

Ghuman, R.S., Sukhwinder Singh and Jaswinder Singh Brar (2009), *Professional Education in Punjab: Exclusion of Rural Students*, Publication Bureau, Punjabi University, Patiala.

Government of India (1986), *National Policy on Education-1986*, Ministry of Human Resource Development, New Delhi.

Government of India (1991), *Report of the Committee for Review of National Policy on Education-1986* (Ramamoorthy Committee), Ministry of Human Resource Development, New Delhi.

Government of Punjab (2008-09 a), *Annual Plan*, Vol. 1, Department of Planning, Chandigarh.

Government of Punjab (2008-09 b), *Economic Survey of Punjab*, Economic Adviser to Punjab Government, Chandigarh.

Kalia, S. (2010), 'Cost of Higher Education and Financing Practices among Students in Punjab: A Study of Professional Education', *Unpublished Ph.D. Thesis*, Department of Economics, Punjabi University, Patiala.

Pennell, H. and Anne West (2005), 'The Impact of Increased Fees on Participation in Higher Education in England', *Higher Education Quarterly*, Vol. 59 (2), pp. 127-37.

Ramachandran, R. (2004), 'Education—the Warning Bells: An Article on U.R. Rao Report', *Frontline*, 21 (6), March, pp. 13-26.

Thorat, S. (2006), *Higher Education in India: Emerging Issues Related to Access, Inclusiveness and Quality*, Nehru Memorial Lecture, University of Mumbai, Mumbai, November 24.

PART VII

Emerging Health Scenario in Punjab

14

Exploring Women's Health Issues in Punjab: Current Status, Problems and Emerging Policy Issues

Sukhwinder Singh and Rupinder Kaur

I

Introduction

Women's health is the neglected area of research in developing countries like India. Their health-related issues came into prominence with the holding of the International Conference on Population and Development at Cairo in 1994 and Fourth World Conference of Women at Beijing in 1995 (GOI, 1995). Both these conferences placed immense importance on women's empowerment, health care and reproductive rights as significant means to raise their quality of life. Available empirical evidences also pointed out that, in India, women did not enjoy good health status despite adding many years to their life expectancy at birth (IIPS, 2007). In fact, certain health problems that affect the women more than men are gigantic in nature, although the cost-effective technologies/treatments to tackle these problems are available. Further, high fertility, maternal mortality and morbidity rates in India on the one hand, low socio-economic status, educational and nutritional levels of women on the other, affect their health adversely (Misra, et al. 2003). For instance, in 2007, there were 254 maternal deaths per lakh live births in India compared to 8 and 11 maternal deaths in UK and USA respectively (WHO, 2009).

Women's health is indeed interwoven with their nutrition status and health experiences in their early years of life (GOI, 2002). India's National Population Policy 2000 recognises that her malnutrition starts at the early stage that impairs her physical well-being in adulthood largely due to the societal discrimination against the girl child. It also states that girls' good nutrition in early adolescence is crucial to their well-being as a woman and through her to the children. The policy also recognizes inadequate access of women to existing public health facilities in India. These handicaps show the inherent nature of Indian society which stands in the way of women getting empowerment; seeking adequate health care; availing of public health facilities; and give secondary importance to women's health compared to male members including children of the family (GOI, 2000). Thus, poor health and nutritional status of women in India are linked to their poor social, cultural and economic status in society.

Further, women's contribution in making and sustaining families is often overlooked; their health problems are largely ignored and viewed as an economic burden in India. Moreover, there is a strong son preference in our society as the son/s is/are expected to care for their parents as age advances. This son preference, along with high dowry demands associated with daughter/s marriage, sometimes, results in the maltreatment of daughter/s. Besides low level of education, Indian women have low level in labour force participation, particularly in the formal sector employment. They have typically a little autonomy—living under the control first of their fathers, then their husbands, and finally their sons (IIPS, 2007). All these factors exert a negative impact on their health status. Hence, there is an urgent need to review and reorient policy priorities of the state focusing on women's health care needs and services. These policies must be sensitive to the socio-economic constraints that women face in acquiring the services.

Both in theory and practice, human health has several dimensions and determinants (Larson, 1991). According to the

WHO definition, health is not just the absence of disease or infirmity, but is a state of complete physical, mental and social well-being. Viewing on these lines, an improvement in women's health status is difficult to define in the absence of desirable data in the state. Moreover, there is no single 'standard measure' to judge an improving health status for any population. The available National Family Health Survey-3 (NFHS-3) data, which is mostly related to physical health, have been used to show improvement/s in women's health status in India. It also provides fairly good information on the current physical health status of women across states. And, in Punjab, the NFHS-3 survey generated data by covering 3681 women in the age group of 15-49 years during 2005-06 (IIPS, 2007). On some other key women's issues, various narrative/anecdotal evidences have been used to highlight women's health problems. For instance, demographic data generated by the Population Census 2011 and the Vital Statistics (crude birth/death rates, etc.) were also used to show general health conditions of women in the state.

This chapter made a modest attempt to explore women's health problems in one of the economically advanced states of India, i.e. Punjab. It took into account the past achievements, current status and future problems of women's health in the state. The chapter has been divided into four sections. Section I, besides introducing the problem, outlays the data sources and significance of the study. The demographic and socio-economic conditions prevailing in the state have been highlighted in Section II. Section III deals with the basic problems and determinants of women's health like early marriage, nutritional status, mortality rates, reproductive health and child care, contraceptive use, domestic violence, etc. Section IV presents the summary of main conclusions and public policy issues of study. It also identifies workable strategies for improving health and nutritional status of women in the state.

II

Demographic and Socio-Economic Profile of Punjab

Before identifying women's health problems, it is appropriate to elucidate the demographic profile of the state. As per 2011 population figures, the total population of Punjab was 27.70 million persons (24.3 million in 2001) with a sex ratio of 893 females (876 in 2001) per 1000 males much lower than the all India sex ratio of 940 (933 in 2001). During the decade of 2001-2011, Punjab's population grew by 13.73 per cent against the all India level of 17.64 per cent compared to the previous decade's increase (1991-2001) of 19.76 per cent and 21.34 per cent in Punjab and India as a whole respectively. In Punjab, the population density was 550 persons per square kilometre in 2011 (482 in 2001), much higher than the all India average of 382 people (324 in 2001). Further, the urban population of Punjab in 2011 constituted 37.49 per cent—up from 33.92 per cent in 2001; whereas for India this proportion was 31.16 per cent in 2011—up from 27.81 per cent in 2001. Child sex ratio (0-6 age group) in Punjab was 846 females per 1000 males in 2011—up from 798 in 2001 compared to the all India average of 914 females per 1000 males in 2011 and 927 females in 2001 (Table 14.1).

According to vital statistics prepared by the Government of India, the crude birth rate (CBR) and crude death rate (CDR) for Punjab was 16.6 and 7.0 per 1000 people respectively in 2010. These levels are generally lower than the all India averages of CBR = 22.1 and CDR = 7.2 in 2010. Similarly, the infant mortality rate (IMR) in the state is much lower (34 per 1000 live births) than the all India average of 47 per 1000 live births in 2010 (GOI, 2011a). Life expectancy at birth in the state which was 68.4 years for males and 70.4 years for females during 2002-06 was likely to be 68.7 years for males and 71.6 years for females during 2006-2010. Further, life expectancy at birth in India was slightly lower than that of Punjab for both sexes (65.8 years for males and 68.1 years females) during 2006-10 (GOI, 2011a). Rising life expectancy has become a main cause for the rising number of elderly people in the population and their age-specific health problems (Kumar and Devi, 2010).

Table 14.1: Demographic and Socio-Economic Profile of Punjab vs. India

Characteristic/Variable	*Year/Time*	*Punjab*	*India*
Population (in millions)	2011	27.70	1210.19
	2001	24.36	1028.74
Decadal Change (%)	2001-2011	13.73	17.64
	1991-2001	19.74	21.34
Sex Ratio (overall)	2011	893	940
	2001	876	933
Child Sex Ratio (0-6 years)	2011	846	914
	2001	798	927
Density (persons per sq km)	2011	550	382
	2001	482	324
Urbanisation (%)	2011	37.49	31.16
	2001	33.92	27.81
Crude Birth Rate (per 1000 people)		16.6	22.1
Crude Death Rate (per 1000 people)	2010	7.0	7.2
IMR (per 1000 live births)		34	47
Life Expectancy at Birth (years)	2002-06	68.4 (males)	62.6 (males)
		70.4 (females)	64.2 (females)
	2006-10	68.7 (males)	65.8 (males)
		71.6 (females)	68.1 (females)
Literacy Rate (%)	2011	81.5 (males)	82.1 (males)
		71.3 (females)	65.5 (females)
	2001	75.2 (males)	75.3 (males)
		63.4 (females)	53.7 (females)
Female Work Participation Rate (%)	2001	19.1	25.6
	2010* (R)	24.3	26.1
	2010* (U)	12.4	13.8
Per Capita Income (Rs.)	2000-01	27,865	16,648
(Current Prices)	2005-06	36,142	27,123
	2009-10	60,748	46,492

*Related to NSS 66th Round, 2009-10.

Source: GOI, 2011a &b; GOI, 2012; GOI, 2013.

Further, the literacy rate in the state has improved both for males and females. For instance, the literacy rate, as noted in 2011, was 81.5 per cent for males and 71.3 per cent for females; showing an improvement on literacy figures of 75.3 per cent (males) and 63.3 per cent (females) in 2001. Compared to these, 82.1 per cent males and 65.5 per cent females in India were literate in 2011; up from the literacy rate of 75.3 per cent for males and 53.7 per cent for females in 2001. In Punjab, female work participation rate was just 19.1 per cent in 2001, whereas it was 25.6 per cent for India as a whole. Similarly, work participation rates for rural and urban females were 24.3 per cent and 12.4 per cent respectively in 2009-10 compared to all-India rates of 26.1 per cent and 13.8 per cent for rural and urban areas respectively. It means females' work participation rate in the state is less than that of the females in India.

Undoubtedly, Punjab state has performed very well on the economic front, especially during the mid-1960s to mid-1990s. In fact, the state achieved top rank in terms of per capita income in the early 1960s across all major Indian states and continued to maintain this rank up to the year 1993-94. After that, Punjab economy's growth rate decelerated and even lagged behind compared to a few fast growing states like Maharashtra, Gujarat, Haryana, etc. Owing to the sluggish growth of Punjab's economy during the Tenth Five Year Plan (2002-07) and Eleventh Five Year Plan (2007-12), the state's per capita income slides down further. At present, Punjab ranked 7th in terms of per capita income (GOI, 2013) and 5th in terms of the human development index (IAMR, 2011). Although the state still occupied a much better position on the basis of per capita consumption expenditure (Jain, 2010), yet it could not be a least poverty state as claimed earlier in policy documents (Gill, Singh and Brar, 2013). In 2004-05, 20.9 per cent of its population (22.1 per cent in rural areas and 18.7 per cent in urban areas) was living below the official poverty line (GOI, 2012).

Actually, this dismal performance of Punjab's economy during the economic reforms era (1991-2012), when other Indian states picked up growth momentum, has many worse consequences for the state's economy. First, this slow growth adversely affected livelihood and employment strategies adopted by the people in the state, which, in turn, heavily impinges on the well-being of women in the state. Second, the state government, instead of raising resources for development expenditure, induced many populist measures like free electricity to agricultural pump-sets, no octroi, tax rebate to industries, etc. that increased the fiscal deficit and public debt of the state (Gill, Singh and Brar, 2010). And, this continuous disarray in the fiscal policy has adversely affected state expenditure on the social sectors, particularly the education and health sectors, which in turn led to deterioration in public health services in the state (Kumar, 2011). This impinges women's health more as the reproductive health services are solely in the public domain and provided free in the state (Singh and Jain, 2010).

In India, more so in Punjab, the demographic and socio-economic conditions, particularly the gender ratio, work participation and literacy rates are biased against the females. This is, in fact, a contrast to the most developing countries, where with the rising incomes and economic growth, poverty and mortality rates witnessed a decline which in turn raised the survival chances of females more. However, this has not happened in Punjab state where high female mortality and morbidity rates are still a rule. Malnutrition and anaemia across women continue to be a public health problem in the state. The other factors which are responsible for low health status of women in Punjab are high mortality rates arising out of complications of pregnancy and childbirth, inadequate access to medical care, nutritional deficiency, and early marriage, illiteracy, practice of female infanticide/foeticide, and economic deprivation of females.

III

Problems and Factors Affecting Women's Health in Punjab

A perusal of available literature on women's health pointed out that (i) the women in general faced many serious health problems compared to the men; and (ii) their health problems are affected by several demographic, socio-economic and cultural traits prevalent in the society and economy. For instance, age at marriage, reproductive and child health practices, access to income opportunities and health care, mortality rates, home environment/empowerment, etc. affecting women's health to a large extent (see, IIPS, 2007). This section analysed some of these factors, in detail.

3.1 Early Marriage of Girls/Women

Age at which marriage of girls/women took place has become one of the vital indicators of women's health. In demographic theory also, age at marriage occupies a predominant place because it determines the fertility behaviour of women. Any respectable discussion on fertility trends and its determinants refers to the age at which a woman is married (Mc Donald, 1981). It is also said that late or postponement of marriage makes both the girls and boys mature enough physically, mentally and emotionally. Marriage heralds the beginning of a new family unit with all complicated roles and statuses which the member/s of this unit is/are expected to play. In India, having a child (preferably a son) as early as possible, after marriage, is the rule rather than the exception even today. Hence, the age at which a girl marries, takes thereby home responsibilities and reproduction duties assumes importance to explore women's health. Visualising this, even the National Population Policy (GOI, 2000) states that the percentage of girls marrying below 18 years (legally prescribed minimum age for marriage of girls) in India should be brought to nil by 2010 and that the marriage should take place 'preferably only after attaining 20 years of age' (GOI, 2002).

On this count, the NFHS-3 data revealed that the practice of very early marriage (by age 13/14) has virtually disappeared both in urban and rural Punjab. The median age at which first marriage took place is 19.8 years among the women aged 20-49 at the time of the survey in the state (Table 14.2). There are clear-cut evidences of rising age of marriage in the state over the past three decades (Singh and Jain, 2010). Despite this fact, the data suggests that 9.5 per cent of the women aged 20-49 in Punjab were married before reaching the legal minimum marriageable age of 18 years for girls, as set by the Child Marriage Restraint Act of 1978. It is also evident from the data that even among the younger women aged 20-24 years, 5.4 per cent women still marry before reaching the minimum age at marriage. The analysis of data on age at marriage suggests that illegal child marriages are still a reality in the state, though it is not widely practised. Social compulsion of early and universality of marriage across all women is still very strong among the parents in the state like other Indian states (IIPS, 2007). Early marriages, in the absence of contraceptive use, means early and more pregnancies, abortion of unwanted pregnancies, etc. which in turn affects the health of women adversely.

Table 14.2: Percentage of Women First Married by Exact Age (Age at Marriage) in Punjab

Current Age (Years)	*Percentage of Women First Married by Exact Age*					*Median Age at First Marriage*
	15	*18*	*20*	*21*	*25*	
15-19	1.7	na	na	na	na	na
20-24	5.4	19.7	37.4	na	na	na
25-29	8.0	30.2	49.7	60.6	86.6	20.0
30-34	11.5	34.3	56.7	66.5	91.0	19.4
35-39	12.3	37.5	59.2	70.7	93.4	19.2
40-44	10.8	39.8	61.1	71.2	93.5	19.1
45-49	12.3	38.1	58.3	71.1	92.4	19.3
20-49	**9.5**	**31.6**	**51.9**	na	na	**19.8**
25-49	10.7	35.4	56.4	67.3	91.0	19.4

na = Not available due to censoring.

Source: IIPS, 2007

3.2 Poor Nutritional Status of Women

Nutritional deprivation of women leads to their poor physical and mental growth, and is the main cause of high risk pregnancy, childbirth complications, premature births, low weight babies, etc. Poor nutritional intake is often correlated with the poor economic status of women. Available data from Punjab also shows that there is evidence of gender bias in the food distribution against the girl child at the household level. Further, the nutritional requirements of poor women are not fully met in the state. NFHS-3 collected data on height and weight of women aged 15-49 years, excluding pregnant women at the time of survey or women who gave birth in the preceding two months of the survey. A body mass index (BMI) was constructed: dividing the weight in kilograms by height in metres squared (kg/m^2). For women, a cut-off point of BMI as 18.5 was used to define thinness/acute under-nutrition, and a BMI of 25.0 or above to indicate overweight/obesity.

An analysis of data revealed many interesting results (Table 14.3). First, nearly 51 per cent of women (51.2 per cent) were found to have a healthy weight for their height as 18.9 per cent of surveyed women fell in the category of too thin (BMI <18.5) and another 29.9 per cent were victims of overweight/obesity (BMI >25.0). Second, there were rural-urban differences in the BMI of women. For instance, 17.2 per cent of women in urban areas are too thin compared to 19.9 per cent in rural areas of the state. Similarly, 36.3 per cent of women in urban Punjab were overweight/obese compared to 26.2 per cent in rural Punjab. Third, under-nutrition across Punjabi women is a very serious problem, particularly in the youngest age group (15-19), where 39.2 per cent were too thin; among the never-married, 24.0 per cent were too thin; those in the lowest two wealth quintiles, where 30.5 per cent and 35.8 per cent respectively were too thin; and amongst Hindu and Muslim women, 21.4 per cent and 22.4 per cent respectively were too thin. Fourth, overweight and obesity are most common in the older/adult women, among those living in urban areas, and belonging to the highest wealth quintiles and to the Sikh religion. Fifth, women belonging to the SCs and the lowest income groups have a high prevalence of nutritional deficiency in the state. And, nutritional deficiency decreases substantially with the increase in the households' standard of living, educational level and ageing of women.

Table 14.3: Nutritional Status of Women in Punjab by Socio-Demographic Characteristics, 2005-06

	Percentage of Women Aged 15-49 Years by Body Mass Index in Kg/m² (BMI)*			
	Underweight/Thin		*Overweight/Obese*	
Socio-Demographic Characteristics	*<18.5 (totally thin)*	*<17.0 (moderately/ severely thin*	*>25.0 (overweight or obese*	*>30.0 (obese)*
Age (Years)				
15-19	39.2	17.0	5.3	0.3
29-29	22.1	8.3	18.0	2.9
30-39	11.2	4.2	43.3	13.5
40-49	6.6	2.4	52.7	21.0
Marital Status				
Never Married	34.0	13.9	8.4	0.8
Currently Married	13.5	5.3	37.3	12.0
Widowed/Divorced/ Separated/Deserted	13.6	4.3	43.9	4.3
Residence				
Urban	17.2	7.1	36.3	12.2
Rural	19.9	7.7	26.2	7.3
Education				
No Education	21.0	7.7	27.8	7.5
<5 Years Completed	19.4	11.2	22.9	11.0
5-9 Years Completed	20.7	9.2	30.4	9.9
10 or More Years Completed	16.0	5.8	31.7	9.7
Religion				
Hindu	21.4	9.1	27.4	7.7
Muslim	22.4	6.2	26.0	8.6
Sikh	17.3	6.5	31.9	10.2
Other	7.8	3.8	29.5	9.9
Caste/Tribe				
Scheduled Caste	26.8	11.1	22.6	6.1
Other Backward Class	19.8	7.9	31.7	10.9
Other**	14.3	5.4	33.6	10.6
Wealth Index				
Lowest	30.5	11.0	13.8	0.0
Second	35.8	11.5	11.5	2.1

Middle	29.0	12.9	17.6	2.2
Fourth	21.7	8.9	23.3	7.0
Highest	12.7	4.8	39.2	13.1
Total	18.9	7.5	29.9	9.1

*Excluding Pregnant Women and Women Having Birth in Preceding Two Months.

** Not Belonging to Scheduled Castes/Tribes or Other Backward Classes.

Source: IIPS, 2007.

3.3 Widespread Anaemia Among Women

Iron-deficiency is another form of malnutrition across the women. It is measured by haemoglobin level (counting number of red blood cells - RBCs) in the blood against the 'normal level' for the age and sex of an individual. In fact, iron deficiency is the root cause of anaemia among the children, teenage girls and adult women. The women after conceiving a child usually suffer from iron deficiency which will eventually, if untreated, leads to severe anaemia. Besides posing risks during the pregnancy, anaemia increases women's susceptibility to many diseases such as tuberculosis, frequent infections, etc. and reduces women's energy level to do their daily activities such as household chores, childcare and manual labour. A severe anaemic woman is taxed by most physical activities including walking at an ordinary pace (Kumar, 1990). Anaemia in young girls can lead to retarded growth, impaired cognitive performance as well as increased morbidity from the infectious diseases (IIPS, 2007).

Surprisingly, 38 per cent of women in Punjab have anemia, including 26 per cent with mild anaemia, 10 per cent with moderate anaemia, and 1 per cent with severe anaemia (Table 14.4). Further, a scrutiny of data highlights that anaemia is particularly high among the younger women, SC women and women from the lower wealth quintiles. Women who live in urban areas or who are currently married/never married are also more likely to be anaemic than women living in rural areas or who are currently widowed/ separated/ divorced/ deserted. Interestingly, prevalence of anaemia in Punjab has not changed much since the NFHS-2. For instance, prevalence of anaemia among ever-married women has declined slightly from 41 per cent in the NFHS-2 to 38 per cent in the NFHS-3. However, the prevalence of anaemia among children aged 6-35 months had remained unchanged to 80 per cent in the state (IIPS, 2007).

Anaemia Among Women, Punjab

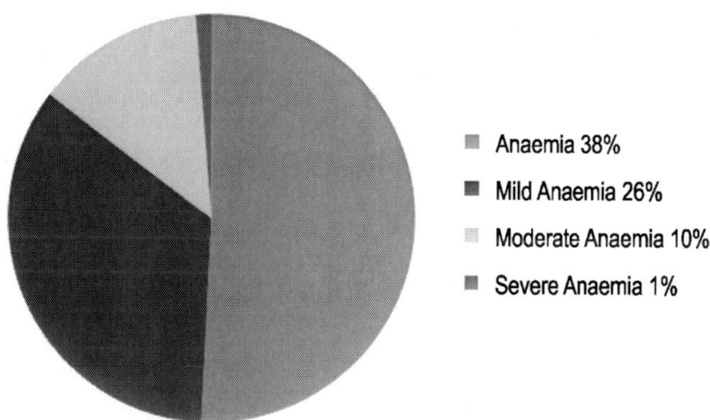

Table 14.4: Prevalence of Anaemia Among Women in Punjab by Socio-Demographic Characteristics

	Percentage of Women Aged 15-49 Years with Anaemic Status by Haemoglobin Level			
Socio-Demographic Characteristics	*Mild (10.0-11.9) g/dl)*	*Moderate (7.0-9.9 g/dl)*	*Severe (<7.0 g/dl)*	*Any Anaemia (<12.0g/dl)#*
Age (Years)				
15-19	27.5	12.3	1.6	41.4
29-29	26.8	10.8	1.3	38.8
30-39	25.5	9.6	1.1	36.2
40-49	25.2	9.1	1.7	36.0
Marital Status				
Never Married	26.1	10.0	1.1	37.2
Currently Married	26.2	10.7	1.5	38.4
Widowed/Divorced/ Separated/Deserted	27.1	7.6	0.0	34.7
Residence				
Urban	28.2	9.7	1.3	39.1
Rural	25.1	10.9	1.4	37.4

Education				
No Education	27.4	11.1	1.6	40.2
<5 Years Completed	26.5	10.6	1.8	38.9
5-9 Years Completed	25.9	11.9	1.8	39.7
10 or More Years Completed	25.6	8.7	0.8	35.0
Religion				
Hindu	26.6	11.4	1.6	39.7
Muslim	30.5	10.7	1.2	42.2
Sikh	25.8	9.4	1.2	36.5
Other	24.9	18.9	0.0	43.8
Caste/Tribe				
Scheduled Caste	29.2	11.7	1.7	42.6
Other Backward Class	20.2	12.3	0.3	32.8
Other*	25.3	9.6	1.4	36.3
Wealth Index				
Lowest	27.3	8.0	2.7	38.0
Second	26.3	12.9	2.0	41.2
Middle	28.6	12.0	1.4	42.0
Fourth	26.4	12.4	2.0	40.9
Highest	25.4	8.6	0.9	34.9
Total	26.2	10.4	1.4	38.0

For Pregnant Women. * Not Belonging to Scheduled Castes/Tribes or Other Backward Classes.

Source: IIPS, 2007

3.4 High Neonatal, Infant and Child Mortality Rates

High neonatal, infant and child mortility rates cannot be studied in isolation from the women's low health status, malnutrition and less empowerment. Most of the causes of infant and child mortality are related to the exogenous factors, mother's health as well as the utilisation of MCH services. Neonatal mortality is termed as the probabilty of dying of infant in the first month of life. Postnatal mortality is the probability of dying after the first month of life but before the first birthday of the infant. Infant mortality is a measure of probability of dying of the infant before the the first birthday. And, child mortality measures the probability of the dying of the child before the fifth birthday. All these rates are measured as per 1000 livebirths for specific age groups. Of these, IMR and CMR are the best indicators of the child's as well as mother's health (IIPS, 2007).

The NFHS-3 data revealed that these rates are very high in the case of Punjab; though improved over the time period. For instance, IMR was estimated at 42 deaths per 1,000 livebirths during the NFHS-3—down from 57 deaths during the NFHS-2. Similarly, the under-five morality rate for Punjab state is 52 deaths per 1000 livebirths—down from the 72 deaths reported in the NFHS-2. The NFHS-3 rates imply that despite decling mortality, more than 1 child in 24 children in Punjab still die within the first year of life and 1 in 19 children die before reaching age five (Table 14.5).

The data also shows that IMRs do not vary greatly between the urban and rural areas of Punjab. Infants whose mothers having no education are likely to die more than one and a half times higher before their first birthday compared to the infants whose mothers have completed at least 10 years of schooling. Infant and child mortality rates are much higher among the Hindu women than the Sikh women. Infants/children of women belonging to the SCs have higher mortality rates than the infants/children whose mothers belong to other castes. Moreover, despite the government's efforts to improve the overall status of SC women, this women's group still remains a socially disadvantaged group and can not secure better access to any type of public services including the health services (Kumar, 2011).

Gender-wise, after the first month of life and before they are five years old, the girls in the state face a much higher mortality risk than the boys. The child mortality rate by sex shows that the gender differentials in mortalilty are particularly higher for children above the age of one year. The child mortality rate for girls is 16 deaths per 1000 children aged 12-59 months compared with 6 deaths for the boys. Further, infant and child mortality rates decline substantially with the increase in household standards of living. This is because the standard of living is closely associated with the better quality and quantity of food the mother and child take, the physical surroundings of the family and other such factors (Singh and Jain, 2011).

Table 14.5: High Infant and Child Mortality Rates in Punajb by Socio-Demographic Characteristics, 2005-06

Socio-Demographic Characteristics	*Different Mortality Rates Per 1000 Livebirths*			
	Neonatal (within 1st month)	*Post-neonatal (after 1st month to 1st birthday)*	*Infant (up to 1st birthday)*	*Child (up to 5th birthday)*
Residence				
Urban	26.2	16.4	42.6	9.2
Rural	32.0	14.2	46.2	10.5
Mother's Education				
No Education	30.9	23.0	53.8	15.9
<10 Years Completed	32.6	12.6	45.2	7.3
10 or More Years Completed	26.3	7.2	33.6	5.0
Religion				
Hindu	29.3	15.9	45.2	11.7
Sikh	31.9	14.7	46.6	8.9
Caste/Tribe				
Scheduled Caste	29.5	16.7	46.2	16.0
Other*	30.6	13.5	44.1	6.8
Wealth Index				
Lowest	na	na	na	na
Second	na	na	na	na
Middle	20.7	18.6	39.3	14.7
Fourth	33.6	18.9	52.5	17.0
Highest	24.7	8.7	33.4	1.3
Child's Sex				
Male	32.9	12.7	45.6	6.0
Female	26.0	18.0	44.0	15.5

* Not Belonged to Scheduled Castes/Tribes or Other Backward Classes.

Source: IIPS, 2007.

3.5 Inadequate Utilisation of Maternal Health Care

Seeking maternal health care is the most important indicator of improving health of women and their infants. NFHS-3 data also provides information about the utilisation pattern of maternal health care like antenatal care, postnatal care, place of delivery and birth attended by health professionals in the state. The data pointed out that nearly 75 per cent of pregnant women having childbirth in the last five years preceding the survey received at least three or more ANC visits of a health professional (Table 14.6). By category of health personnel, 56.1 per cent of women got it from a qualified doctor, 26.5 per cent from skilled health personnel and 7.6 per cent from untrained persons (Dai/TBA). Intriguingly, nearly one-tenth women (9.7 per cent) did not receive any antenatal care visit. As expected, urban women (80.9 per cent) were somehow better placed in the case of receiving three or more ANC visits compared to rural women (71.2 per cent) in the state. Further, more than 92 per cent of women with 10 or more years of education and the same proportion of women who belonged to the highest wealth quintile received such ANC visits. However, just 34.6 per cent of women belonging to the second wealth quintile, 52.4 per cent of women with no education, 54.0 per cent women belonging to the middle wealth quintile, and 51.9 per cent of women having a fourth or higher order birth did not receive three or more ANC visits. Further, nearly three-fourths of women belonging to the Hindu as well as Sikh religion had received three or more ANC visits; whereas only two-third of Muslim women had such visits.

More interesting results were related to the place of child delivery. Almost one-half of the births (49.7 per cent) in Punjab took place at home and the rest (51.3 per cent) used a health facility. By the birth order, in 64.8 per cent of cases of childbirths, the first birth was institutional, compared with only 26.7 per cent of childbirths that were in the order of four or more. The proportion of institutional childbirths increased steadily as one moved upward in terms of education, social status, and wealth index of mothers. Contrary to this, home births were indeed more common among the women who received no ANC check-ups, belonged to the rural areas, women with no education, women belonged to lowest two/three wealth quartiles, SC women, aged women, and women with more than three previous childbirths. Further, 68.2 per cent of childbirths took place with assistance from a health professional (including 44.9 per cent by doctors) and 31.6 per cent were attended by unskilled personnel (dai/TBA, etc). Thus, only 23.3 per cent of childbirths were assisted by a skilled health professional.

Table 14.6: Utilisation of Antenatal, Postnatal and Institutional Care in Punjab by Socio-Demographic Characteristics

	Percentage of			
Socio-Demographic Characteristics	*Women had Three or More ANC Visits*	*Childbirths Delivered in a Health Facility*	*Childbirths Assisted by Health Personnel*	*Women with a Postnatal Check-up within Two Days of Childbirth*
Health Personnel				
Doctor	56.1	51.3 #	44.9	35.3
Skilled Health	26.5	#	23.3	18.9
Personnel	7.6	48.6 $	30.3	9.7
Unskilled	0.1	$	1.3	1.4
(Dia/TBA)				
Others#	9.7	0.1	0.1	34.9
No One				
Mother's Age at Birth (Years)				
<20	72.7	43.3	59.9	56.9
20-34	75.6	53.3	70.4	62.5
35-49	*	21.0	31.4	*
Birth Order				
1	83.6	64.8	78.9	74.1
2-3	74.7	46.5	65.1	58.9
4+	51.9	26.7	46.0	42.7
Residence				
Urban	80.9	57.9	70.3	69.3
Rural	71.2	47.6	67.1	57.7
Education				
No Education	52.4	28.3	46.9	45.3
<5 Years Completed	64.0	47.6	63.4	44.3
5-9 Years Completed	76.2	46.9	67.8	57.3
10 or More Years Completed	92.4	77.3	89.5	79.7
Religion				
Hindu	73.9	48.0	61.9	61.0
Muslim	67.4	34.4	50.6	46.0
Sikh	76.4	56.0	75.4	64.6

Other	*	*	*	*
Caste/Tribe				
Scheduled Caste	63.1	34.0	56.4	46.6
Other Backward Class	72.3	52.8	68.8	54.8
Other**	82.1	62.5	76.6	71.7
Wealth Index				
Lowest	*	14.3	31.3	*
Second	34.6	21.2	39.5	32.9
Middle	54.0	29.9	50.1	50.4
Fourth	70.6	40.8	65.0	54.2
Highest	92.2	74.9	84.9	76.8
Total	**74.8**	**51.3**	**68.2**	**62.0**

and $ meant for inclusion. * Percentage not given; based on fewer than 25 weighted cases.

** Not Belonged to Scheduled Castes/Tribes or Other Backward Classes.

Source: IIPS, 2007.

In medical parlance, each postnatal care visit to a mother helps her to safeguard health and can reduce maternal mortality, however, only 62 per cent of mothers (35.3 per cent by doctors, 18.9 per cent by skilled health personnel and 9.7 per cent by unskilled personnel) had a postnatal check-up within two days of childbirth as per the minimum norm recommended by the medical sciences. Compared to this, more than one-third of mothers (34.9 per cent) did not receive any postnatal care for their last birth. An assessment of data further states that mothers with 10 or more years of education, belonged to the highest wealth quartile, having first childbirth, falling in the 20-34 year age group, living in urban areas and enjoying high caste status (other) received better postnatal check-up compared to their right opposite counterparts. In a nutshell, the birth order, urban location, education level, mothers' age, caste/social and wealth status of women/mothers are the important parameters that explain the better utilisation of ANC, postnatal care as well as place of delivery by mothers in the state.

3.6 Better Knowledge But Poor Use of Family Planning (FP) Methods

Reproductive health of women is largely influenced by their

knowledge about various methods of FP and their actual utilisation. In Punjab, as in India, knowledge of contraceptive methods is nearly universal (Singh and Jain, 2011) because 99 per cent of currently married women were found to know at least one modern contraceptive method (Table 14.7). Of these, female sterilisation is the most widely known method as 96.3 per cent currently married women reported this. Male sterilisation as a FP method was known to 81.3 per cent of currently married women. Across three spacing/temporary methods (pills, IUDs, and condoms) promoted by the state government, 92 per cent of currently married women knew about the pills, 88.5 per cent about the IUDs and 89.7 per cent about the condoms. Further, 82.1 per cent of such women knew about these three spacing methods together. A majority of currently married women (57.6 per cent) also knew about at least one traditional method of FP; 46.0 per cent reported the rhythm methods, 38.1 per cent withdrawal method and 0.8 per cent folk method. However, these traditional methods were not fully safe against pregnancy compared to the modern methods. As expected, urban women were slightly ahead of rural women so far as the knowledge of any contraceptive method was concerned.

Regarding the actual use of FP methods, the information pointed out that 36.7 per cent of currently married women did not use any method and the remaining women (63.3 per cent) were found to be using a method to limit their families (Table 14.8). Of these women, 56.1 per cent used any modern method and 7.2 per cent any traditional method. Across the modern methods, 30.8 per cent of currently married women actually adopted female sterilisation, 15.5 per cent reported the use of condoms/nirodh by their husbands, 5.5 per cent favoured IUD insertions, 2.9 per cent used pills, 1.2 per cent for male sterilisation, and 0.2 per cent injectables. Across the traditional methods, 3.8 per cent of married women favoured the rhythm method and another 3.4 per cent used the withdrawal method.

Table 14.7: Percentage of Currently Married Women Knowing Contraceptive Methods in Punjab, 2005-06

Method	*Currently Married Women*		
	Rural	*Urban*	*Total*
Any Method (Modern and Traditional)	99.0	98.7	98.9
Any Modern Method	98.9	98.7	98.8
i. Female Sterilisation	96.7	95.6	96.3
ii. Male Sterilisation	80.0	83.6	81.3
iii. Condom/Nirodh	87.8	93.0	89.7
iv. Pill	89.9	95.6	92.0
v. IUD	86.8	91.3	88.5
vi. Injectables	41.7	45.6	43.1
vii. Female Condom	10.9	15.9	12.8
viii. Emergency Contraception	11.3	17.6	13.6
ix. Other Modern Methods	0.1	0.1	0.1
x. Pill, IUD and Condom together	79.0	87.5	82.1
Any Traditional Method	53.7	64.2	57.6
i. Rhythm	43.7	49.8	46.0
ii. Withdrawal	33.3	46.3	38.1
iii. Folk Method	0.8	0.9	0.8

Source: IIPS, 2007.

As expected, the current use of modern FP methods, particularly the female sterilisation and condoms/nirodh has been affected by many factors like age, education, caste, location, wealth index, etc. For instance, the data showed that as the education level of the currently married women increases, actual use of female sterilisation decreases, and that of spacing methods (pills, IUDs and condoms) rises in the state. Similarly, wealth status of such women also determines the use of female sterilisation and spacing methods; higher income status of households led to lower utilisation of female sterilisation and higher utilisation of spacing methods and vice versa. Not using any contraceptives was slightly higher in the urban areas (38.3 per cent) than in the rural areas (35.8 per cent). More urban women were found favouring spacing methods (29.1 per cent) compared to the rural women (21.0 per cent). Across the religions, Muslim women as a separate group were the only ones where non-use of

Table 14.8: Percentage of Currently Married Women Using Any Contraceptive Method in Punjab by Socio-Demographic Characteristics

Socio-Demographic Characteristics	*Percentage of Currently Married Women Using Any Contraceptive Method*												*Currently Not Using*	*Total*
	Any Method	*Any Modern Method*	*Female Sterilisation*	*Male Sterilisation*	*Pill*	*14D*	*Injectables*	*Condom/ Nirodh*	*Other Modern Method*	*Any Traditional Method*	*Rhythm*	*Withdrawal*		
Age (Years)														
15-19	6.7	5.4	0.0	0.0	0.0	0.0	0.0	5.4	0.0	1.3	1.3	0.0	93.3	100
20-24	38.5	31.7	4.1	0.2	3.7	6.2	0.2	17.1	0.0	6.8	3.5	3.3	61.5	100
25-29	63.7	54.5	20.1	0.7	4.0	9.9	0.2	19.6	0.0	9.1	5.3	3.8	36.3	100
30-39	74.6	67.7	39.7	0.7	3.7	5.4	0.2	17.9	0.1	6.9	3.5	3.4	25.4	100
40-49	69.0	62.1	47.3	3.1	0.6	2.3	0.1	8.7	0.0	6.9	3.4	3.5	31.0	100
Residence														
Urban	61.7	51.8	21.2	1.4	2.8	4.1	0.1	22.1	0.1	9.9	4.9	na	38.3	100
Rural	64.2	58.6	36.4	1.1	2.9	6.4	0.2	11.5	0.1	5.6	3.1	na	35.8	100
Education														
No Education	66.4	60.4	48.1	1.6	1.8	2.0	0.4	6.3	0.1	6.0	3.8	na	33.6	100
<5 Yrs Completed	56.4	50.9	38.6	1.1	3.3	2.2	0.0	5.7	0.0	5.7	2.3	na	43.5	100
5-9 Yrs Completed	63.4	57.1	30.7	1.0	3.9	6.8	0.0	14.7	0.0	6.4	3.8	na	36.6	100
10 or More Yrs Completed	60.4	51.0	11.2	0.9	3.1	8.5	0.1	27.1	0.0	9.4	3.9	na	39.6	100

Religion														
Hindu	62.2	55.4	30.2	1.7	2.9	3.0	0.3	16.6	0.1	6.8	2.9	3.9	37.8	100
Muslim	49.3	40.5	12.9	0.0	4.3	1.4	1.5	20.4	0.0	8.8	4.4	4.3	50.7	100
Sikh	64.7	57.2	31.2	1.0	2.9	7.7	0.1	14.4	0.0	7.5	4.5	3.0	35.3	100
Other	64.4	61.7	45.5	0.0	0.0	2.6	0.0	13.6	0.0	2.6	0.0	2.6	35.6	100
Caste/Tribe														
Scheduled Caste	62.9	56.8	40.7	1.1	2.6	1.4	0.2	10.6	0.1	6.1	3.5	2.6	37.1	100
Backward Class	60.9	53.9	28.3	2.1	2.9	3.7	0.0	17.0	0.0	7.0	3.3	3.7	39.1	100
Other*	64.2	56.6	25.9	1.1	3.1	8.3	0.2	18.1	0.0	7.5	3.7	3.9	35.8	100
Wealth Index														
Lowest	60.1	53.3	46.5	3.5	0.0	0.0	3.3	0.0	0.0	6.8	3.5	3.3	39.9	100
Second	66.7	59.6	52.5	0.6	3.2	0.0	0.6	2.6	0.0	7.1	5.2	1.9	33.3	100
Middle	63.0	56.8	45.5	1.4	1.1	2.7	0.0	5.9	0.3	6.2	4.1	2.1	37.0	100
Fourth	63.1	57.4	33.3	1.3	3.3	4.9	0.3	14.3	0.0	5.7	2.9	2.8	36.9	100
Highest	63.1	54.8	22.5	1.1	3.2	7.4	0.1	20.5	0.0	8.3	4.0	4.3	36.9	100
Total	**63.3**	**56.1**	**30.8**	**1.2**	**2.9**	**5.5**	**0.2**	**15.5**	**0.0**	**7.2**	**3.8**	**3.4**	**36.7**	**100**

* Not Belonging to Scheduled Castes/Tribes or Other Backward Classes.

Source: IIPS, 2007.

contraceptives were particularly low (50.7 per cent) compared to the women who belonged to other religious groups (35.3 per cent and 37.8 per cent across Sikh and Hindu women respectively). Age of the currently married women is another important factor that determines the use/non-use of any contraceptive. For instance, as one picks up the age ladder, non-use of any contraceptive decreases and vice versa. Similarly, use of female sterilisation also increases as the age of married women advances (Table 14.8).

3.7 Domestic Violence and Health Consequences

Domestic violence has been acknowledged worldwide as a violation of basic human rights of women (IIPS, 2007). Domestic violence against women is widespread in Indian society, so also in Punjab. It has now become a major public health problem because such violence has so many visible as well as invisible impacts on women's physical, mental and reproductive health. In fact, it is a complex social problem with far-reaching health consequences for the girls/women. Though the men can also be victims, domestic violence is nearly a gender-specific crime perpetrated by men against women (Jaisingh, 2002). Females of all ages are victims of this violence, but more so at the adolescent and adult ages. According to Heise, violence against women is detrimental to the economic development because it deprives a woman of her ability to participate fully in the economic activities by reducing her emotional and physical strength. Domestic violence against women can also have negative consequences for the children of the victims (Heise, 1994). It leads to more medical costs, loss of labour hours, disability (if it occurs), and psychological pains amongst the women victims (IIPS, 2007).

Table 14.9: Percentage of Women Aged 15-49 Years Ever Experienced Physical or Sexual Violence in Punjab, 2005-06

Violence Characteristics	*Marital Status of Women*		
	Ever Married	*Never Married*	*Total*
Type of Violence Experienced			
Physical Violence Ever	31.7	24.2	29.9
Sexual Violence Ever	7.4	1.3	5.9
Physical or Sexual Violence Ever	32.7	25.2	30.9
Health Injury Due to Physical or Sexual Violence Ever	49.3	na	na
Person Committing Physical Violence			
Current Husband	44.9	0.0	35.4
Former Husband	3.7	0.0	2.9
Father/Stepfather	10.1	18.4	11.9
Mother/Stepmother	21.1	33.4	23.7
Sister/Brother	11.0	14.6	11.8
Daughter/Son	0.1	0.0	0.0
In-Laws	1.3	0.0	1.0
Teacher	7.8	33.6	13.2

Source: IIPS, 2007.

As per NFHS-3 data, in overall, 30.9 per cent of women aged 15-49 years in Punjab have experienced either physical or sexual violence, which includes 32.7 per cent of ever-married women and 25.2 per cent of never-married women (Table 14.9). Further, 29.9 per cent of women have experienced physical violence ever and another 5.9 per cent sexual violence ever. Close to one-half of ever-married women (49.3 per cent), who experienced either physical or sexual violence, suffered a health injury on their bodies. Further, across 48.6 per cent of physical violence cases across ever married women, violence was committed by either the current/former husband. Father/stepmother and mother/stepmother together were accused by 31.2 ever-married women for physical violence. Amongst never-married women, physical violence was committed by the teachers (33.6 per cent cases), followed by mothers/stepmothers (33.4 per cent cases) and fathers/stepmothers (18.4 per cent cases). In 11.0 per cent and

14.6 per cent cases of ever-married women and never-married women respectively, physical violence was committed by their brothers/sisters. It means physical violence is largely committed by the woman's near and dear ones.

IV

Main Conclusions and Policy Suggestions

The analysis clearly suggests that the health status of women in an economically advanced state is inextricably interwoven to the socio-economic, demographic and cultural factors prevalent in the state. Illiteracy, low education level, rural residence, low work participation and other cultural factors are found to be affecting women's living conditions adversely, which in turn led to low utilisation of health services by women. Even, if the women's work participation, level of earnings and access to health services increased, there are still two prerequisites to be created: First, the women need equality (social, economic and political) for effective participation in decision-making processes at all levels; and second, the women folk need health education and skills for receiving care.

In the absence of these, girls/women are married at early age, exposed to early and repeated pregnancies, became victims of malnutrition and anaemia, and subject to high mortality rates in the state. Further, women's low education and work participation rates affect their individual earnings (measured through wealth status), which in turn led to inadequate utilisation of maternal health care—antenatal, childbirth and postnatal cares. Surprisingly, women aged 15-49 years in the state had nearly universal knowledge about the contraceptives. Across them, however, more than one-third of married women (36.7 per cent) did not currently use any contraceptive method; and those who were using a contraceptive to limit family size, 30.8 per cent favoured women-centric terminal method, 24.1 per cent spacing methods and 7.2 per cent a traditional method. Domestic violence also affected women's health directly as nearly one-half of ever-married women (49.3 per cent), who experienced either physical or sexual violence, suffered a health injury on their bodies. Indeed, such violence is largely committed by the woman's near and dear ones.

Undoubtedly, improved women's health status is one of the most fundamental contours for the development of society as a whole. In fact, there is need to reorganise state policies for better health care of women and their equal participation in all spheres of development. It can safely be said that if the state continues to ignore women's health, one cannot hope ever to attain 'Health for All' in the state. The women not only have special health care needs, but they also do most of the caring for their families. Good health, in fact, is founded in the family itself. So, if women's health is ignored, malnourished and overworked and if they have a large number of children starting at an early age, then their own health as well as of their families will continue to suffer. The study showed that women's purchasing power (income level), education level, social status and locational advantage, to a large extent, determine the health status of future generations of both sexes.

In the light of these observations, the following steps may be suggested which will go a long way in improving women's health in Punjab: (i) efforts must be intensified to postpone the marriages across the adolescent girls. For this, there is need to raise awareness among the girls, their parents, schools and communities about the health consequences of early pregnancy. Legislation prohibiting marriage for girls less than 18 years must be strictly implemented; (ii) efforts must be made to educate the girls since women's education and their health status is closely and positively linked. Education up to, at least, 12 years of schooling for girls be made compulsory and free; (iii) an alternative approach to popularise small family and its benefits be adopted through the parents' counselling and education using the communication strategies, including the mass media; (iv) quality of FP services and proper follow up must be ensured. The role of FP workers needs to be increased to minimise the socio-cultural constraints that women face in acquiring these services; and (v) women's income-generating activities should be enhanced to augment their income and women's empowerment in the state.

REFERENCES

Gill, S.S., Sukhwinder Singh and J.S. Brar (2010), *Globalisation and Indian State: Education, Health and Agricultural Extension Services in Punjab*, Aakar Books, Delhi.

Gill, S.S., Sukhwinder Singh and J.S. Brar (2013), 'Social Security in Punjab: A Blend of State and Central Schemes', in K.P. Kannan and Jan Breman (eds.) *The Long Road to Social Security: Assessing the Implementation of National Social Security Initiatives for the Working Poor in India*, Oxford University Press, New Delhi. pp. 504-38.

GOI (1995), *Fourth World Conference on Women, Beijing 1995, Country Report*, Department of Women and Child Development, Ministry of Human Resource Development, Government of India, New Delhi.

GOI (2000), *National Population Policy 2000*, Ministry of Health and Family Welfare, Government of India, New Delhi.

GOI (2002), *National Health Policy 2002*, Ministry of Health and Family Welfare, Government of India, New Delhi.

GOI (2011a), *SRS Bulletin, Sample Registration System*, Vol. 46 (1), Ministry of Home Affairs, Government of India, New Delhi, December.

GOI (2011b), *Employment and Unemployment Situation in India 2009-10 (66th round)*, NSSO Report No. 537(66/10/1), Ministry of Statistics & Programme Implementation, Government of India, New Delhi.

GOI (2012), *Economic Survey 2011-12*, Ministry of Finance, Government of India, Oxford University Press, New Delhi.

GOI (2013), *Economic Survey 2012-13*, Ministry of Finance, Government of India, Oxford University Press, New Delhi.

Heise, Lori L. (1994), *Violence against Women: The Hidden Health Burden*, Discussion Paper 255, World Bank, Washington DC, pp. 1-72.

IAMR (2011), *India Human Development Report 2011: Towards Social Inclusion*, Institute of Applied Manpower Research and Planning Commission, Government of India, Oxford University Press, New Delhi.

IIPS (2007), *National Family Health Survey (NFHS-3) 2005-06 India*, International Institute for Population Sciences (IIPS), Mumbai (India) and Maryland (USA).

Jain, Varinder (2010), 'Affluence, Vulnerability and the Provision of Social Security: Assessing State's Concern for the Working

Masses in India', *HiVOS Knowledge Programme, Paper 3,* University of Amsterdam, Amsterdam and Centre for Development Studies, Trivandrum, pp. 1-31.

Jaisingh, Indira (2002), *Reconsidered: Dangerous Bill,* India Together, New Delhi.

Kumar, A.K. and D.R. Devi (2010), *Health of Women in Kerala: Current Status and Emerging Issues,* Working Paper No. 23, Centre for Socio-Economic & Environment Studies, Kochi (Kerala), pp. 1-51.

Kumar, Kush (2011), 'State, Market and Utilisation Pattern of Health Services: A Study of Punjab', *Unpublished Ph.D. Thesis,* Department of Economics, Punjabi University, Patiala.

Kumar, Ram (1990), *Women's Health, Development and Administration: Principles and Practices,* Vol. II, Deep and Deep Publications, New Delhi.

Larson, J.S. (1991), *The Measurement of Health: Concepts and Indicators,* Greenwood Publishing Group Inc., Westport.

McDonald, P.F. (1981), *Social Change and Age at Marriage,* Proceedings of the International Conference, Manila.

Misra, R., R. Chatterjee and S. Rao (2003), *India Health Report,* Oxford University Press, New Delhi.

Singh, Sukhwinder and S. Jain (2011), 'Utilisation of Maternal and Child Health Care Services in North-West India: Observations from National Family Health Survey-3', in H.S. Shergill, Sucha Singh Gill and Gurmail Singh (eds.) *Understanding North-West Indian Economy,* Serials Publications, New Delhi, pp. 356-88.

WHO (2009), *World Health Report 2009,* WHO Press, Switzerland.

15

Cancer Suffering Households in Punjab: Economic and Financial Consequences

Inderjeet Singh, Lakhwinder Singh and Parmod Kumar

Introduction

International evidence is indicative of the fact that the agricultural revolution has generated the much needed food security to the nation(s), and at the same time, it has raised alarming signs for the ecology as well. Worldwide, the ground water quantity and quality has been the first victim of this agricultural revolution; the next are the human health and the existence of species (ORG, 2011). The indiscriminate use of agro-chemicals (fertilisers, insecticides/pesticides, etc.) in agriculture has created serious health and environmental problems in so many developing countries. From the ecological perspective, heavy and indiscriminate use of agro-chemicals has contaminated the surface and ground water, damaged fisheries, destroyed freshwater eco-systems, and entered our food chain in a subtle way that the very existence of mankind is facing an extreme danger. Punjab, being the granary of India, has been the leader of the Green Revolution in India. High growth of agricultural output in Punjab has led to the falling water table and ground water overdraft has become a serious problem in the state. Punjab is the leading state in terms of consumption of chemical fertilisers and insecticides/pesticides per hectare. The health ailments, alarmingly on the rise, are being closely identified with indiscriminate use of agro-chemicals in agriculture.

Further, emerging cancer cases across the cotton belt of Malwa region of Punjab have been well-documented by newspaper reports and research studies. Heavy presence of Persistent Organic Pollutant (POP), Nitrate, Phosphate and Uranium in the region has been debated to be the cause of it. Indeed, it is true that a single cancer case in the family derails the economy for several generations in that family. It leads to sharp cut in the essential expenditures, distress sale of assets, and indebtedness. In addition to economic consequences, it has many social consequences for the family too. In this context, the main objective of the present study is to analyse the economic and financial consequences of cancer from the patient's family perspective. Findings of the study will also help to quantify the state support or insurance coverage that can bring the cancer victim's family out of perpetual distress. Further, the outcome of the study will be used to formulate bigger policy support to cover the entire Malwa cotton belt.

Review of Theory and Empirics

Most of the existing studies on cancer have been conducted by medical professionals; a very few social scientists, especially the economists have been involved in this field of research. Most of the international research in developed countries is related to incidence of cancer, morbidity and mortality, prevalence rates and cost comparisons (Parkin, et al. 2001; Shibuya, et al., 2002; Polsky, et al., 2003; Chang, et al., 2004; Brown, et al., 2006; Ferlay, et al., 2010).

Cancer is not a single disease; it is a generic term that refers to more than one hundred distinct type of cancers, and each one is defined by its anatomic site and microscopic features (Barnum and Greenberg, 1993). It is defined as an uncontrollable growth of abnormal cells within the human body. A spate of environmental factors contributes towards the development of cancer, apart from the genetic and dietary factors (Singh, 2008). Many studies have examined the relationship between cancer and environmental factors, particularly in the local context. Carcinogens vary between geographical locations, since their prevalence often depends on local practices. Still this understanding, the interplay of local environmental factors and fatal diseases like the cancer is far from any consensus. The countries like India are expected to see an increase in deaths due to cancer. The World Health Organisation (WHO) estimates that the proportion of deaths from cancer in India will rise from 8 per cent in 2005 to 11.9 per cent in 2030 (WHO, 2002).

In India, a few studies have been conducted on the economic aspects of cancer from the patients' perspective. Our country lacks nation-wide cancer registry of such a high incidence disease. The study by Dikshit et al. (2012) added that tobacco and cervix-related cancers are on the rise and such cancers need early detection to reduce the treatment burden, particularly in the rural areas. Thakur, et al. (2008) estimated higher incidence of cancer cases in the cotton belt of Punjab - a Green Revolution state. This study also identifies multiple factors like indiscriminate use of pesticides, tobacco and alcohol that caused cancer. Even, rising urbanisation, industrial pollution, undesirable lifestyles, poverty—abundance syndrome, social stress and strains; which in turn has contributed to rising incidence of non-communicable diseases (NCDs) like cancer, heart diseases, diabetes, hypertension, arthritis, mental disorders, respiratory disease and accidents (Mohan, et al., 2011). According to one estimate, cancer accounts for one out of eight deaths annually in the world (Mathers and Loncar, 2006). Among all these, cancer is not a consequence of an affluent lifestyle; it occurs most often in the poorer countries (Boyle and Levin, 2008; Parkin et al., 2001). Further, the rising cancer incidence has also been due to the ageing population (Bumgarner, 1992). Some studies show that it is associated with substance abuse (Hamilton, 1986).

A study done by Dikshit et al. (2012) revealed that, in India, the most common cancer among men are of oral cavity, stomach, esophagus, and lungs compared to the most common cancers of cervix, breast and ovaries across women. Cancer causes premature loss of life and thereby the national economic loss.

In India, next to cardio-vascular diseases, that count 52 per cent of NCDs associated mortality and 29 per cent of mortality statistics, the cancer comes to the next; as 25 lakh people are suffering from it. About 8 lakh cases are added every year in India and the cancer deaths are likely to rise from 7.30 lakhs currently to 15 lakhs by the year 2030 (Mohan, et al., 2011). It means the incidence of cancer is on the rise in India.

An ideal health care system of a region should have three characteristics: easy access; low cost treatment; and quality aspect of service. Under the new policy regime, Indian's health system, where out-of-pocket expenses dominate, is highly regressive in nature and iniquitous in practice (Duggal, 2007). It is charcterised by 'imperfect information' and 'imperfect competition'. Incorrect information with the patient about this disease, treatment cost and outcomes become a major cause of drain on financial resources of patients and their families. Cancer patient's families have to indulge in a costly borrowing or selling of their capital assets and cut down their important family or social expenses. Owing to the unmanageable treatment cost, the patients are forced to postpone treatment, or to get substandard treatment or leave the treatment in between.

There is also a dearth of studies relating to the public/ private cost and financing of cancer treatment. These sets of problems are further compounded by the low penetration of health insurance in India. In rural areas, cancer is taken as a stigma. Therefore, a socio-economic analysis of the cancer-affected individuals and their families are the need of time. The present study is targeted to analyse the economic and financial consequences of cancer from the patient's family perspective in Punjab, a province of northern India.

Methodology and Coverage

The reference period of the study is 2012. Keeping in view the main objectives of the study, Muktsar district of Punjab state has been selected for primary survey. Against the World Health Organisation's point of reference, 80 cancer-affected persons amongst one lakh population, the incidence of cancer is the highest in Muktsar district (136.3 per lakh). Further, four villages, namely, Kotbhai, Bhalaina, Doda and Channu have been selected. These villages are well spread across the length and breadth of Muktsar district. Kotbhai has been reported to be a high cancer deaths village (Singh, 2008). Bhaliana and Doda have very high nitrate content in water (Green Peace, India, 2009). Channu has a poor water quality with presence of chemical constituents (like EC, F, As, Fe) more than the permissible limit. The sample of the study fairly represents all types of ecologically affected villages. Since, we have been interested in identifying the cost and financial aspect of cancer from the patient's perspective, the starting point has been the identification of cancer-afflicted families for collection of the data. Our fieldwork covers the living cancer patients and those cancer victims who died in the last eleven years. First house listing of each village and interaction with chemists, political and social activists helped us in identifying the cancer patients' families. A structured interview-cum-schedule has been used for data collection that covers demographic, social and economic aspects relating to the disease. Descriptive statistics and Likart scaling technique for analysis of data have been used. Secondary sources of data are also used to supplement and strengthen the present analysis.

Intensive Agriculture and Empirical Evidence on Cancer

While the success of the Green Revolution in Punjab has been well documented and accepted; but its consequences have recently come under considerable global scrutiny. Issues like the environmental degradation (Conway and Pretty, 1991), separatist violence in Punjab (Corsi, 2006), increasing class disparities, agrarian tensions arising out of wealthier farmers being favoured by the markets, rural-urban migration, loss of biodiversity (Shiva 1991), petering out of productivity (Byerlee, 2006), water issues like water logging, water overuse, and changes in soil salinity (Gupta and Abrol, 2000) have been raised. The Punjab state is now suffering from the adverse consequences of the Green Revolution as well. Fears are being expressed that 'what happens in Punjab today could happen to the rest of the country tomorrow' (Philipose, 1998).

In Punjab, wheat-paddy crop rotation has become a dominant cropping pattern along with wheat-cotton cycle in south-western Punjab. The rising crop intensity from 140 per cent in 1970-71 to 190 per cent in 2010-11 indicates the adoption of intensive agricultural practices that led to the rising trend of consuming chemical fertilisers, pesticides/weedicides and other chemicals. In fact, the state has a chemical centred agriculture system. Further, Punjab's agriculture sector has undergone significant structural changes since the advent of the Green Revolution in the mid-1960s. The traditional agriculture has progressively given way to modern and commercial agriculture. The production of wheat and rice has increased many-fold since the mid-1960s. Apart from high-yielding varieties of wheat and rice, many other factors like consolidations of land holdings, expansion of irrigation facilities, higher use of agro-chemicals (fertilisers, insecticides/pesticides, etc.), farm mechanisation, power and road infrastructure, easy access to inputs and market support mechanism for output have facilitated this process. To meet the ever-growing demand for food of other Indian states, food grains production has been increased by intensive use of farm inputs like water, fertiliser, insecticides/pesticides, etc. However, adoption of this strategy has raised many development-related problems on economic, social and environmental fronts. The adverse effects of intensive chemical-based agriculture on human health are now clearly visible like the emergence of many fatal diseases like cancer and other NCDs in the specific clusters.

In Punjab, the news about cancer deaths first emerged in the late 1990s when the media had reported high cancer mortality in a few villages. Village Gyana and Jajjal in Bathinda district hogged the limelight for being 'cancer-stricken' villages (Pandher, 1999). The state government was initially in a denial mode and even stated that 'there have been no cancer deaths in Punjab' in response to a parliamentary question (Singh, 2008). The denial mode did not last long, and a spate of research reports and publications increased the focus on cancer mortality in Punjab. The state's own agency, the Punjab Pollution Control Board commissioned the Post Graduate Institute of Medical

Education and Research (PGI), Chandigarh to study the cancer issue. The study report (PPCB, 2005) revealed that the prevalence of confirmed cancer cases was 103 per lakh people in Talwandi Sabo block and 71 per lakh at Chamkaur Sahib block of Punjab. An epidemiological study (Thakur, et al. 2008) on cancer cases reported that cancer deaths in Talwandi Sabo block were greater than those in Chamkaur Sahib 'probably due to more use of pesticides, tobacco and alcohol'. A few other studies showed that in the drinking water, presence of heavy metals such as As, Cd, Cr, Se, and Hg was generally higher, and residue of pesticides such as heptachlor, ethion and chloropyrifos were also higher in the samples of drinking water, vegetables and human blood in the villages of Talwandi Sabo as compared to the villages of Chamkaur Sahib.

Another report by the Centre for Science and Environment (CSE, 2005) entitled, 'Analysis of Pesticide Residues in Blood Samples from Villages in Punjab', concluded that out of 28 pesticides analysed, 15 were detected in blood samples as well. The Atlas of Cancer in India (ICMR, 2006) has also reported a spurt in cancer deaths in Punjab, with incidence in the Muktsar district growing from 30 cases in 2001 to 191 in 2002, while it rose from 19 cases to 144 in the Faridkot district during the same time period. These reports, coupled with media scrutiny and increasing public awareness have now forced the state government to announce a series of steps to augment health facilities to tackle the scourge of cancer. The Punjab Government had also estimated 7738 cancer cases in 2009 in the whole of Punjab; of which 32.29 per cent cancer cases were in five districts: Muktsar, Bhatinda, Barnala, Mansa and Faridkot (Government of Punjab, 2013).

Present Status of Cancer in Punjab

The government survey report (released by Health Minister Madan Mohan Mittal on January 28, 2013) of a statewide cancer awareness and symptom-based early detection campaign showed that 33,318 cancer deaths have occurred during the last five years, out of which 14,682 were in the Malwa region alone. The survey data reveal that there are 84,453 persons who have cancer-like symptoms in the state. The survey covered almost 98 per cent of the state's population and it has found that the incidence of cancer is higher than the national and international average. When compared to WHO's point of reference—80 affected persons among a population of one lakh—Punjab's survey discovered that 90 persons in a population of one lakh were suffering from cancer. While 215 people per lakh have died of cancer, another 318 per lakh are suspected of suffering from the disease. Region-wise, Malwa tops the list (107.1 per lakh), followed by Doaba (88.1 per lakh) and Majha (64.7 per lakh). In Malwa, district-wise incidence of cancer was the highest in Muktsar (136.3 per lakh). Among Doaba districts, the incidence of cancer was highest in Kapurthala (99.1 per lakh) (Government of Punjab, 2013).

Description of Study Area

Our primary survey covered four villages of district Muktsar. Muktsar district lies in the south-western part of Punjab and lies between North Latitude 29° 54′ 20″ & 30° 40′ 20″ and East Longitude 74° 15′, 74° 19′ and falls in the Survey of India Toposheet No.44J & 44K and covers an area of 2,630 sq kms which constitutes 5.19 per cent area of Punjab. The district is divided into three sub-divisions, two sub-tehsils and four development blocks, namely Kotbhai, Lambi, Malout and Muktsar for the purpose of administrative control. The district shares its boundary with Faridkot district in the north and north-east, in north-west and eastern side with Ferozpur district. On the east, it is bounded by Bathinda district of Punjab, on the south by Hanumangarh district of Rajasthan and Sirsa district of Haryana state. Physiographically, the area has no river and is covered extensively by the canal network of Sirhind feeder canal to meet the irrigation and drinking water needs of the people. The area is flat and plain and slopes from NE to SW. The climate of the district is dry with sub-humid having grass land type of vegetation. The district receives an annual rainfall of 380 mm in 22 rainy days. About 79 per cent of the annual rainfall occurs during the monsoon period and 21 per cent occurs during the non-monsoon period. The district forms part of the

the Satlej sub-basin and main Indus basin. The district has mostly sierozem type of soil and partly desert soil in its south-western parts. The synoptic view of the district is presented in Box 1. The box highlights that the district falls in the cotton belt characterised by deteriorating water quality.

Box 1: District Muktsar (Fact Sheet)

Geographical Area	2630 Sq. Km.
No. of Panchayats/Villages	235
Population (as per 2011 Census)	7, 77,493
Land Use (sq. km.)	
(a) Forest Area	20
(b) Net Area Sown	2260
(c) Cultivable Area	2210
Area under Principal Crops (sq. km.)	Cotton (1170); Rice (770); and Wheat (2000)
Irrigation by Different Sources (Area)	
(a) Tube Wells	160
(b) Canals	2080
(c) Other Sources	-
Net Irrigated Area	2240
Gross Irrigated Area	4416

Ground Water Quality

(a) Presence of chemical constituents more than permissible limit (e.g. EC, F, As, Fe) Lambi (3510 us/cm); Giddarbaha (3149 us/cm); and Kabarwala (5.36)
(b) Type of Water: Ca-Mg-HCo3 & Na mixed anions
(c) Major Ground Water Problem: Salinity and Water Logging

The broad parameterisation of the sampled households is as follows. Out of 136 cancer cases covered by the study, 103 were dead and 33 are live patients. Caste-wise distribution of the cancer-affected households is characterised by almost equal percentage of Jat and non-Jat families. Occupation-wise distribution shows that 45.59 per cent of the cancer victims have been engaged in agriculture-related operations; 39 per cent of them in household work and the rest in other occupations. Out of the total sampled cancer victims, 55.88 per cent had a direct exposure to pesticides during their lifetime. Only 2.21 per cent of cancer cases have insurance cover; and that too only life insurance and not health insurance. Average length of the cancer ailment has been 1.9 years in the study region. Average expenditure per patient has been Rs. 2.75 lakhs, of which about 60 per cent has been on hospital admission and the rest on day care treatment. To meet this expenditure, 11.76 per cent of the cancer cases depended on their own savings; more than 60 per cent of cancer victims depended on the loans from commission agents or landlords at highly unfavourable terms and conditions.

Out of 136 cancer cases, 65 (47.79 per cent) were males and 71 (52.21 per cent) are females. In two villages, namely, Bhalliana and Kot Bhai, the proportion of females suffering from cancer was 59.38 per cent and 56.67 per cent respectively. In villages Doda and Channo, the proportion of males was slightly higher; it was 53.49 per cent and 51.61 per cent respectively.

To measure the incidence of cancer at the micro level, the number of cases per thousand of population is the best approximation. In the present study area, overall cancer cases per thousand populations come to be 3.88 (Table 15.2); it is 5.96 per thousand in the case of village Channu and 4.78 per thousand in village Bhaliana. In villages of high cancer incidence, the female cancer incidence is also high; it is 6.02 per thousand in village Channu and 5.93 per thousand in village Bhaliana. Gender-wise distribution of cancer cases per thousand of population is indicative of the fact that it is 4.26 per thousand for females as against 3.53 per thousand in case of males. This implies, females are more prone to cancer in the region as compared to the male population.

Table 15.1: Sex-wise Distribution of Cancer Cases in Muktsar District

Name of Villages	*Male*		*Female*		*Both*	
	Number	*Per cent*	*Number*	*Per cent*	*Number*	*Per cent*
Doda	23	53.49	20	46.51	43	100
Channu	16	51.61	15	48.39	31	100
Bhaliana	13	40.63	19	59.38	32	100
Kot Bhai	13	43.33	17	56.67	30	100
Total	65	47.79	71	52.21	136	100

Source: Primary Survey.

Box 2: Broad Parameterisation of Sampled Cancer Cases

Number of Cases	
(a) Dead	103 (75.74 per cent)
b) Alive	33 (24.26 per cent)
(c) Total	136
Caste-wise Distribution	
(a) Jat	66 (48.53 per cent)
(b) Non-Jat	70 (51.47 per cent)
Occupation	
(a) Agriculture Related	62 (45.59 per cent)
(b) Household Work	54 (39.71 per cent)
(c) Other	20 (14.70 per cent)
Exposure to Pesticides	
(a) Direct	73 (55.88 per cent)
(b) Indirect	63 (46.32 per cent)
Insurance Cover Status	
(a) Insured	3 (2.21 per cent)
(b) Not Insured	133 (97.79 per cent)
Average Ailment Length	1.9 Years
Average Per Patient Cost (Rs.)	2.75 Lakh
Source of Finance:	
(a) Commission Agent	45 (33.09 per cent)
(b) Relatives	26 (19.12 per cent)
(c) Landlord	38 (27.94 per cent)
(d) Own Savings	16 (11.76 per cent)
(e) Other	11 (8.09 per cent)

Table 15.2: Number of Cancer Cases Per Thousand of Population in the Study Area

Villages	*Male*	*Female*	*Both*
Doda	3.80	3.65	3.73
Channu	5.91	6.02	5.96
Bhaliana	3.72	5.93	4.78
Kot Bhai	2.12	3.10	2.58
Total	3.53	4.26	3.88

Source: Primary Survey.

Cancer, as reported by many studies, has grown very fast in Punjab in the recent years. To assess the time profile of cancer growth in the region, temporal distribution of the cancer cases and cancer deaths is the best way out. Temporal distribution of cancer cases and deaths in the study region is presented in Table 15.3. Year-wise distribution of cancer detection is not evenly distributed in the last decade. Fifty per cent of the cancer cases were detected during 2002-06 and the remaining fifty per cent cancer cases afterwards. For the last few years, the proportion of cancer cases detected has declined slightly. On the other hand, out of 103 deceased number of cases studied, about fifty per cent of the deaths have occurred in the last four years. The remaining fifty per cent is spread over seven years; and in the first three years of study frame, there have been just 10.67 per cent of the total deaths. Hence, the temporal analysis of cancer cases is indicative of the fact that more than 50 per cent of the cancer ailment cases detected in the first half of the last decade have been crucial in taking the death toll of the last few years to such an alarming level.

It is a commonly held view that exposure to pesticides has a direct bearing on occurrence of cancer. Quite often, in the pesticide belt, the people can be classified on the basis of exposure into: directly and indirectly exposed. Direct exposure is where an individual has been actively associated with the handling, storage and use of the pesticides. On the other hand, indirect exposure-related victims are passive victims of pesticide use. Out of the total cancer cases in the study area (Table 15.4), 53.68 per cent belonged to the direct exposure category and the rest (46.32 per cent) fell in the indirect exposure category. High proportion of brain (100 per cent), blood (63.16 per cent), liver (60.38), throat (64.71 per cent) and other (60.00 per cent) types of cancer cases are prevalent in the 'direct exposure to pesticides' category. It shows that all brain-related cancer cases belonged to the individuals directly exposed to pesticides. On the other hand, most of the female patients with the breast, uterus and food-pipe related cancers belonged to the 'indirect exposure' category. This shows that direct exposure to pesticide handling, storage and use leads to a specific type of cancer such as brain, blood, liver and throat.

Table 15.3: Time Profile of Cancer Cases and Deaths in Study Region

Year of Detection/ Death	*No. of Cancer Cases*		*No. of Cancer Deaths*	
	Number	*Per cent*	*Number*	*Per cent*
2002	15	11.03	3	2.91
2003	17	12.50	4	3.88
2004	12	8.82	4	3.88
2005	15	11.03	11	10.68
2006	12	8.82	10	9.71
2007	8	5.88	8	7.77
2008	15	11.03	11	10.68
2009	15	11.03	7	6.80
2010	10	7.35	15	14.56
2011	9	6.62	16	15.53
2012	8	5.88	14	13.59
Total	136	100.00	103	100.00

Source: Primary Survey.

Figure 1: **Time Graph of Number of Cancer Deaths in Study Region**

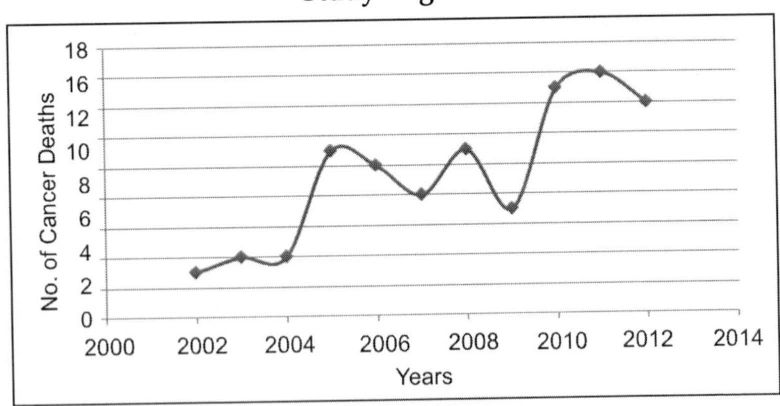

Table 15.4: Cancer Site-wise and Type of Exposure-wise Analysis of Cancer Cases

Cancer Site	*Direct Exposure to Pesticides*		*Indirect Exposure to Pesticides*		*Total Number of Cases*
	Number	*Per cent*	*Number*	*Per cent*	
Blood	12	63.16	7	36.84	19
Breast	7	28.00	18	72.00	25
Liver	32	60.38	21	39.62	53
Throat	11	64.71	6	35.29	17
Uterus	2	28.57	5	71.43	7
Food Pipe	2	33.33	4	66.67	6
Brain	4	100.00	0	0.00	4
Other	3	60.00	2	40.00	5
Total	73	53.68	63	46.32	136

Source: Primary Survey.

Village-wise and cancer site-wise distribution of cases in the study region is presented in Table 15.5 and Figure 2. In the study area, the cancer of liver is the most dominant component; it constitutes 38.97 per cent of cases. It is followed by breast cancer (18.38 per cent) and blood cancer (13.97 per cent). Spatial distribution of cancer cases at disaggregation of four studied villages shows some glaring results. In village Doda (44.19 per cent) and Channu (51.61 per cent), liver cancer cases have the larger proportion. Village-wise analysis of cancer cases shows that in villages Doda Bhaliana and Channu, the top most cancer is the liver, followed by breast and blood cancer. In village Kot Bhai, it is liver cancer, followed by breast and throat cancer. In village Channu, the liver cancer alone constitutes 51.61 per cent of the total cases. Some of the cancers are region-specific, for example, food pipe cancer is prevalent in Bhaliana and Doda; brain cancer is prevalent in village Doda only. Half of the throat cancer cases are in village Kot Bhai only. Different types of cancer occurrence have a spatial specificity.

Table 15.5: Village-wise and Cancer Site-wise Distribution of Cancer Cases

Cancer Site	*Village*				*Total*
	Doda	*Bhaliana*	*Kot Bhai*	*Channu*	
Blood	6 (13.95)	6 (18.75)	2 (6.67)	5 (16.13)	19 (13.97)
Breast	6 (13.95)	6 (18.75)	9 (30.00)	4 (12.90)	25 (18.38)
Liver	19 (44.19)	8 (25.00)	10 (33.33)	16 (51.61)	53 (38.97)
Throat	4 (9.30)	2 (6.25)	8 (26.67)	3 (9.68)	17 (12.50)
Uterus	1 (2.33)	3 (9.38)	0 (0.00)	3 (9.68)	7 (5.15)
Food Pipe	1 (2.33)	5 (15.63)	0 (0.00)	0 (0.00)	6 (4.41)
Brain	4 (9.30)	0 (0.00)	0 (0.00)	0 (0.00)	4 (2.94)
Other	2 (4.65)	2 (6.25)	1 (3.33)	0 (0.00)	5 (3.68)
Total	43 (100.00)	32 (100.00)	30 (100.00)	31 (100.00)	136 (100.00)

Source: Primary Survey.

Besides bearing pain and social costs, financial burden of cancer diseases is measured by the economic costs which include all resources required/used to provide/get a service and the value of foregone opportunities. Theoretically, the economic cost of cancer care and control includes a wide range of costs: expenditures on seeking cancer care services; costs associated with time and effort spent by the patients and their families; and cost of lost productivity due to cancer-related disability or earlier death. Cancer cost is a function of income level, social status, and cultural factors. A typical cancer cost cycle consisting of screening, diagnosis, staging, therapy and follow up costs approximately Rs. 2.5 lakhs to 3.5 lakhs in India. In our study area, the average cost per patient (Table 15.6) on the diagnosis, admission, treatment and follow up comes to Rs 2.75 lakhs. There are spatial variations in this average cost. It is Rs. 3.33

lakhs in village Doda; Rs. 2.42 lakhs in Bhaliana; Rs. 2.77 lakhs in Kot Bhai and Rs. 2.26 lakhs in village Channu.

Figure 2: **Cancer Site-wise Distribution of Cancer Cases in Study Villages**

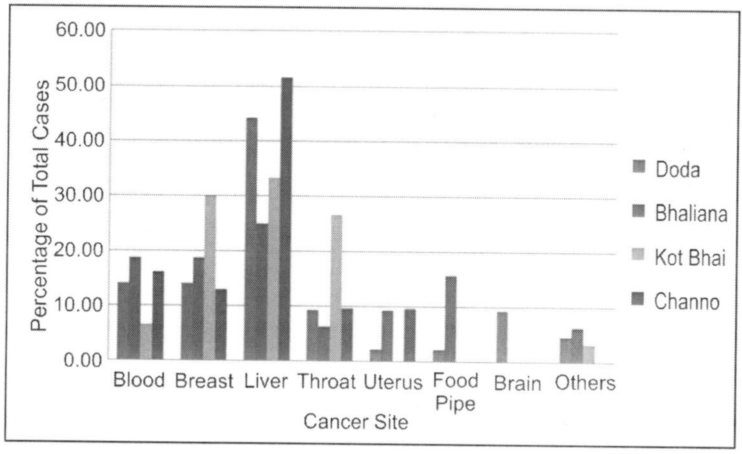

Table 15.6: Average Cost of Cancer Treatment in Different Study Villages

Villages/Area	*Doda*	*Bhaliana*	*Kot Bhai*	*Channu*	*Total Sample*
Expenditure Per Person (Rs. Lakhs)	3.33	2.42	2.77	2.26	2.75

Source: Primary Survey.

These spatial variations in average cost are a function of type of cancer, length of ailment and paying capacity or income status of the patient. Cancer site-wise and average ailment length-wise distribution of average cost is presented in Table 15.7. For total sample, the average cost of cancer treatment is Rs. 2.75 lakhs and average ailment length is 1.9 years. Average cost of cancer treatment is more than Rs. 3.93 lakhs for brain cancer; it is Rs. 3.25 lakhs for food pipe cancer. It is nearly Rs. 3 lakhs for blood and breast cancer. It is as low as Rs. 1.79 lakhs for cancer of uterus and Rs. 2.00 lakhs for other types of cancer. Average ailment length is also different for different types of cancers. It is just 1.1 years for brain, and 3.5 years for food pipe cancer. Karl Pearson's correlation coefficient between average ailment length and average cost of cancer treatment is positive and statistically significant at 1 per cent level of significance. It shows that the average cost of cancer treatment is a function of length of ailment.

Table 15.7: Cancer Site-wise Analysis of Average Ailment Length and Average Cost of Cancer Treatment

Cancer Site	*Average Ailment Length (Years)*	*Average Cost of Cancer Treatment (Rs. Lakh)*
Blood	2.1	3.03
Breast	2.5	3.11
Liver	1.5	2.67
Throat	1.9	2.31
Uterus	1.7	1.79
Food Pipe	3.5	3.25
Brain	1.1	3.93
Other	2.9	2.00
Total	1.9	2.75

Correlation between length of ailment and cost of treatment:
r = 0.230 (d.f.=134), Significant at p=0.01

Source: Primary Survey.

Per patient cost of Rs 2.75 lakhs during mean ailment period of 1.9 years is not a small amount, keeping in view the average level of income and living standards of the study region. Due to meagre in-hand savings, to meet this unplanned eventuality, the cancer victim families have to depend on outside sources of finance (Table 15.8). For meeting the treatment cost, on an average, each cancer suffering family has to arrange finance of Rs. 2.48 lakhs. There is no major difference between the finance arranged for male and female patients. At aggregate level, commission agents and own savings are a source of finance to the tune of more than Rs. 3.00 lakhs. Further, quantum of finance (Rs. 3.00 lakhs) from the commission agents is the same irrespective of the gender. Average amount of finance from relatives is Rs 2.32 lakhs for male and 1.69 lakhs for females.

On the other hand, the average amount of finance from landlords is Rs 1.48 lakhs for males and 2.08 lakhs for females. Different sources of finance are not evenly available with respect to the gender. For cancer suffering families, support of commission agent finance is available irrespective of gender. On the other hand average financial support from relatives is higher for male than female patients; the landlord's financial support is more for the female patient than the male.

Table 15.8: Source of Finance Per Patient (Rs. lakh)

Source of Finance	*Amount of Finance per Cancer Patient (Rs. Lakh)*		
	Male	*Female*	*Persons*
Commission Agents	3.03	2.98	3.01
Relatives	2.32	1.69	2.03
Landlords	1.48	2.08	1.73
Own Savings	2.90	3.34	3.26
Others	3.20	3.33	2.88
Total	2.37	2.59	2.48

Source: Primary Survey.

Further, disaggregate analysis of the sources of finance (Table 15.9) is indicative of the fact that commission agents meet the needs of 33.09 per cent and landlords meet the needs of 27.94 per cent of the cancer-affected families. Thus, about 61 per cent of the families depend on the commission agents and landlords for their financial requirement for the cancer treatment. Income-based disaggregation of source of finance depicts that the landlords are the significant source of finance for the low income group, and the commission agents are the significant source of finance for the middle and high income groups. Relatives, as a source of finance for cancer treatment, are found more in the lower and middle income groups respectively; it is insignificant in the case of the high income group. So, the sources of finance are not evenly available to all the families suffering from cancer.

Table 15.9: Source of Finance by Income Group

Income Group	*Comm. Agents*		*Relatives*		*Landlords*		*Own Savings*		*Others*	
	N	%	N	%	N	%	N	%	N	%
Low	1	2.86	12	34.29	20	57.14	-	-	2	5.71
Medium	26	40.00	13	20.00	16	24.62	7	10.77	3	4.62
High	18	50.00	1	2.78	2	5.56	9	25.00	6	16.67
Total	45	33.09	26	19.12	38	27.94	16	11.76	11	8.09

Source: Primary Survey

It is a proven fact in health economics that the average cost of an ailment is a function of the income level of a family. Table 15.10 presents the average annual family income in relation to average cost of cancer treatment in the study area. As already mentioned, for the total sample, the average cost of cancer treatment is Rs. 2.75 lakhs. The average annual family income of sampled households is Rs. 2.30 lakhs. For low income group, average income is Rs. 0.36 lakhs compared to average cost of treatment Rs. 1.61 lakhs. For middle income group, average income is Rs. 1.29 lakhs against average treatment cost of Rs. 2.71 lakhs; and for high income group, average income is equal to Rs. 6.01 lakhs and average cost is Rs. 2.75 lakhs. The correlation between family income and average cost of treatment is positive and statistically significant at 1 per cent level. Thus the cost of treatment is a function of the paying capacity of the family. For the low income group, the cost of cancer treatment is equivalent to four and a half years income; for the middle income group, it is two years' income and for the high income group, it is just a two-third of one year's income. So, the worst hit by cancer is the low and middle income group patients respectively.

To meet the financial cost and repay the financial debt, the households suffering from cancer have to cut down their essential expenditures; that in turn affect their quality of life and capacity to earn income. Quality of life is affected, if one has to sacrifice one/more of the essential components of quality of life: food, clothing, housing, education, health and social

Table 15.10: Relationship Between Average Income and Average Cost Across Cancer Families

Income Level	*Income (Rs. Lakh)*	*Average Annual Family Income (Rs. Lakh)*	*Average Cost of Cancer Treatment (Rs. Lakh)*	*Gap of Treatment Cost and Family Members (Rs. Lakh)*
Low	Up to 0.4	0.36	1.61	-1.15
Medium	0.4 to 3.0	1.29	2.71	-1.42
High	Above 3.0	6.01	3.92	+2.09
Total	-	2.30	2.75	-0.45

Correlation Between Income and Expenditure: r = 0.330 (d.f. =134), Significant at p=0.01

Source: Primary Survey.

ceremonies. For each aspect of quality of life, a five-point Likert scale method has been used to arrive at the weighted average score (WAS) using -2, -1, 0, 1 and 2 as the weights. The rank based on WAS giving the directly useful magnitude of the effect. An important finding which emerges from the analysis based upon quality of life shows that the cancer suffering households cut expenditure on the basic needs. On the total sample level, due to cancer, in terms of expenditure cut, the food is affected at the first, followed by the health, and clothing, respectively (Table 15.11). For the low income group, the order of effect is in terms of reduced expenditure is the food, education and clothing. For the middle income group, it is in the order of food, clothing and health. For the high income group, it is the health, education and social ceremonies in order of importance. For meeting the cost of cancer treatment, lower income group and middle income group cut down their expenditure on even the food; not to mention health and education. Even, in the case of the higher income group, the health becomes the first victim. In general, the basic ingredients of human capital, the food, education and health have been seriously hit in the cancer victim families. To save these families and their functionalities, an economic package not only for treatment, but also for the food, education and family health is suggested.

Table 15.11: Effect on Quality of Life by Expenditure Cut Due to Cancer Treatment

Expenditure Cut on	*Income-wise Weighted Average Score (WAS) and Ranks*							
	Low		*Medium*		*High*		*Total*	
	WAS	*Rank*	*WAS*	*Rank*	*WAS*	*Rank*	*WAS*	*Rank*
Food	1.31	1	1.11	1	0.19	6	0.92	1
Clothing	1.23	3	1.06	2	0.26	4	0.89	3
Housing	1.03	5	0.82	5	0.25	5	0.73	5
Education	1.26	2	0.89	4	0.47	2	0.88	4
Health	1.11	4	0.91	3	0.69	1	0.90	2
Social Ceremonies	0.69	6	0.55	6	0.42	3	0.55	6

Source: Primary Survey.

Table 15.12: Effect on Quality of Life Due to Cancer

Ailment Lead to	*Income Bracket Weighted Average Score (WAS) and Ranks*							
	Low	*R*	*Medium*	*R*	*High*	*R*	*All*	*R*
Depression/ Anxiety	1.20	4	1.18	3	1.00	3	1.14	3
Decreased HR Utility	1.17	5	1.26	2	0.93	4	1.15	2
Counselling	0.34	8	0.41	7	0.22	7	0.34	8
Social Alienation	0.40	7	0.58	6	0.39	6	0.49	6
Decreased Child Care	1.37	2	1.03	5	0.92	5	1.09	4
Decreased Elderly Care	1.26	3	1.04	4	1.01	2	1.08	5
Relatives Distanced	0.49	6	0.40	8	0.19	8	0.37	7
Financial Stress	1.60	1	1.60	1	1.28	1	1.51	1
Shift to Cheap Treatment	-1.11	9	-0.78	9	-0.92	9	-0.90	9
Left Treatment in Between	-1.14	10	-0.82	10	-0.97	10	-0.94	10

Source: Primary Survey.

In addition to the expenditure-cut, various other parameters of quality of life are also affected at large due to the heavy cost of cancer treatment (Table 15.12). At aggregate level, high cancer cost has led to financial stress, followed by low human resource utility and high anxiety. In the lower income group, the heavy ailment cost has led to decline in child and elderly care. In the middle income group, it leads to low human resource utility, followed by decline in child and elderly care. In the high income group, it leads to low human resource utility and depression. Thus, in addition to financial stress, the first victim of heavy cancer cost is earning capability of the family followed by decreased care of children and elderly.

Further, at the disaggregate level; the analysis revealed that 47 per cent of the families, after starting costly treatment of the cancer patients, shifted to a cheaper treatment. Similarly, 45 per cent of cancer families left the treatment in between and took the patients to their homes in a state of hopelessness. Most such cases belonged to the low and middle income groups. This is precisely because of the reason that except the high income group, the gap between the cost of treatment and the averaging annual income of the household is very high. In the case of low income groups, fund raising capacity as compared to the cancer treatment cost is low. Thus, the cancer suffering households are unable to receive quality treatment.

Table 15.13: District-wise Cases of Cancer Assistance Under Mukh Mantri Punjab Cancer Raahat Kosh (as on December 31, 2012)

S. No.	*District Applications*	*Number of Cases*	*Number of Amount Sanctioned*	*Total per case (Rs.)*	*Amount*
1.	Amritsar	593	593	72602137	122,432
2.	Barnala	194	194	18597349	95,863
3.	Bathinda	509	509	53102176	104,326
4.	Fatehgarh Sahib	90	90	10175650	113,063
5.	Faridkot	266	266	27436654	103,145
6.	Ferozepur	443	443	42006828	94,824

7. Gurdaspur	509	509	66589706	130,825
8. Hoshiarpur	237	237	22946942	96,823
9. Jalandhar	395	395	52301590	132,409
10. Kapurthala	145	145	17107604	117,983
11. Ludhiana	622	622	61504134	98,881
12. Mansa	232	232	22107940	95,293
13. Moga	288	288	28971501	100,595
14. Muktsar	265	265	27211448	102,685
15. Patiala	290	290	32203301	111,046
16. Pathankot	6	6	772600	128,767
17. Roopnagar	56	56	4047860	72,283
18. SBS Nagar	89	89	8638092	97,057
19. SAS Nagar (Mohali)	54	54	6136800	113,644
20. Sangrur	412	412	41364042	100,398
21. Tarn Taran	332	332	33560809	101,087
Total	6027	6027	649385163	107,746

Source: Punjab Government Website.

State Policy Initiatives

There have been various state initiatives for the prevention, diagnosis and treatment of cancer disease in Punjab (Box 3). But still, most of the initiatives are still at design level and their implementation needs a big push in terms of resources and awareness of the masses. The status report of cancer assistance under Mukh Mantri Punjab Cancer Raahat Kosh (Table 15.13) is indicative of the fact that during the reference period, only 6027 cancer patients have availed of this assistance which is a too low figure, if one compares it with the actual number of live cancer patients in the state. The average amount that was sanctioned for a cancer patient comes to Rs. 1.07 lakhs only; in Roopnagar district, it is merely Rs. 0.72 lakhs.

The process for taking state assistance, termed as tedious and time-consuming, is as follows: (a) submission of application with residence proof, cancer test report and estimates of treatment cost from the hospital; (b) approval from the Government Medical College and Hospital Level Committee

(Amritsar, Faridkot, GMCH Chandigarh, PGIMER Chandigrah); and (c) a final sanction from the Office of Chief Minister of Punjab. Existing rules regarding delivering grants to afflicting cancer patients are quite loose and create hurdles in reaching grants to the patients. Therefore, most of the applicants seeking grants face rejection. In some cases, delay in sanction of assistance is more than six months. As per the respondents, government relief of 1.5 lakhs comes after a long chain of formalities, while the treatment cannot wait for a long time. According to the state government's guidelines, a patient will be given money for the treatment after the date of sanction and not during the time period of treatment during which the case was sent for approval. Instead of sanctioning money for treatment, it should provide free hospital admission and medicines to the cancer patients. Further, free education should be given to the living children where the bread winner becomes victim of cancer (ill or dead).

Box 3: State Initiative for Prevention, Diagnosis and Treatment in Punjab

Cancer Prevention

1. Testing of heavy metals in drinking water has been started in the State Public Health Lab.
2. State Government has started installing Reverse Osmosis Systems (RO) in various villages of districts.
3. Health education activities are undertaken to make people aware of the causes, signs/symptoms and prevention of cancer.
4. Steps have been undertaken to control excessive use of pesticides/insecticides.

Diagnosis of Cancer

1. Mammography units have been established at Civil Hospital, Bathinda, Patiala, Jalandhar and Hoshiarpur.
2. Punjab Government had signed a MoU with the NGO 'Roko Cancer Trust' to spread cancer awareness.
3. Cancer Registry has been started:
   (a) Population Based Cancer Registry (PBCR) has been started and it is collecting data of cancer patients and located at Government Medical College, Patiala.
   (b) Hospital Based Cancer Registry (HBCR): It has been

started at the PGI, Chandigarh and is collecting the cancer data.

Free/Cheap Treatment of Cancer

1. Financial assistance under the State Illness Fund through the Punjab Nirogi Society is provided to cancer patients along with other life-threatening diseases belonging to BPL families.
2. Mukh Mantri Punjab Cancer Raahat Kosh Society – Under this scheme, 50.00 crores has been made available by the Government of Punjab for treatment of all cancer patients except government employees and those having health insurance cover. An amount of up to 1.50 lakhs is made available for treatment of every cancer patient.
3. School children suffering from cancer are provided free treatment by the Health Department.
4. Brachytherapy is a type of radiation therapy in which radiation source is used in a focused manner/beam to treat localised cancer. Brachytherapy machine has been installed at Government Medical College & Hospital, Patiala.
5. Radiotherapy Machine & Cobalt Unit has been started at Sri Guru Gobind Singh Medical College, Faridkot also.
6. Cobalt source for the treatment of cancer patients has been installed at Sri Guru Ram Das Institute of Medical Sciences & Research Centre, Amritsar.
7. Regional Cancer Centre at the PGI has been connected to all district hospitals of Punjab via the Tele-Medicine facility.
8. Free travel facility in Punjab Roadways & PRTC Buses is provided to the cancer patients for availing treatment.
9. The state government has executed an agreement with Max Health Care to set up Super Specialty Hospital for Cancer & Trauma Care on the premises of Civil Hospital SAS Nagar (Mohali) and setting up of Super Specialty Cancer & Cardiac Hospital on the premises of Civil Hospital, Bathinda. These hospitals are now fully functional.
10. The National Programme for Prevention and Control of Cancer, Diabetes, Cardiovascular Diseases & Stroke (NPCDCS) has also taken care of cancers.
11. The Cancer Hospital at Bhatinda is being set up with an investment of Rs. 60 Crores by BFUHS. Tenders floated for construction.

Summary and Conclusions

The major findings that emerged from the analysis are as follows:

Punjab, the leader of the Green Revolution since the mid-1960s, is now suffering from the adverse consequences of it as well. The health ailments, alarmingly on the rise, are being closely identified with indiscriminate use of agro-chemicals in agriculture; and cancer is one of them. A recent government survey report on cancer in Punjab, covering 98 per cent of population, showed that 33,318 cancer deaths have occurred during the last five years, out of which 14,682 were in the Malwa region alone. The survey data also reveals that there are 84,453 persons in the state who have cancer-like symptoms—an alarming situation. Against WHO's estimates—80 cancer-affected persons per one lakh population—Punjab's survey reported 90 persons per one lakh population were suffering from cancer. On the basis of cancer incidence region-wise, Malwa (107.1 per lakh) tops the list, followed by Doaba (88.1 per lakh) and Majha (64.7 per lakh). In Malwa, district-wise incidence of cancer was the highest in Muktsar (136.3 per lakh).

This study covers four villages of Muktsar district: Doda, Bhalaina, Kotbhai, and Channu and collected data from 136 cancer cases, of which 103 were dead and 33 are live patients. Occupation-wise distribution shows that 45.59 per cent cancer victims were engaged in agriculture-related operations; 39.71 per cent in household work and the rest in other occupations. Further, 55.88 per cent of sampled cancer victims had a direct exposure to pesticides during their lifetime. Only 2.21 per cent of the total cancer cases had only life insurance cover and not health insurance. Average length of the cancer ailment has been 1.9 years in the study region. And, average cost per patient on diagnosis, admission, treatment and follow up comes to Rs 2.75 lakhs. There are spatial variations in this average cost. Average cost of cancer treatment is a function of length of ailment. Gender-wise distribution of cancer cases indicates that the females (4.26 per thousand) are more prone to cancer in the region as compared to males (3.53 per thousand). Temporal analysis of cancer cases is indicative of the fact that more than

50 per cent of the cancer ailment cases were detected in the first half of the last decade. Direct exposure to pesticide handling, storage and use leads to a specific type of cancer such as brain, blood, liver and throat across sampled villages.

Income-based disaggregation of source of finance depicts that commission agents emerge as the most significant source of finance for the low income group and landlords for the middle and high income groups. Relatives, as a source of finance for cancer treatment, are found in the lower in order of importance; it is insignificant in the case of the high income group. For cancer victim families, support of commission agents to finance treatment cost is available irrespective of gender. On the other hand, average financial support from relatives was higher for male than female patients; the landlord's financial support was more for the female patients than the males.

Cost of treatment is a function of the paying capacity of the family. For the low income group, cost of cancer treatment is equivalent to four and a half years income; for the middle income group, it is two years income and for the high income group, it is just a two-third of one year's income. So, the worst hit by cancer is the low and the middle income group in order. In general, basic ingredients of human capital—food, education and health—have seriously been hit across the cancer victim families. This calls for an economic package not only for treatment, but also for the food and family health. Finally, at disaggregate level, the database revealed that 47 per cent of the families, after taking costly treatment shifted to a cheaper treatment. Similarly, 45 per cent of the families left the treatment in between and took their patient home in a state of hopelessness. Most of such cases belonged to the low and middle income group.

Policy Implications

The size and scale of cancer problems analysed above calls for developing a viable state-supported system. It is high time to develop a system that combines public and private efforts, not only to finance cancer treatment but also to bring the families out of perpetual distress in the long run. In this regard, the following are broad policy implications that emerge from the study:

- For prevention of cancer, the first and foremost step that needs to be taken is to regulate the intensive and uncontrolled use of deadly agro-chemicals (fertilisers, insecticides/pesticides, etc.). If need be, some such agro-chemicals may be banned.
- Masses need to be educated regarding the storage, handling and use of fertilisers and chemicals. This should include first aid in the case of accidents caused due to mishandling of such chemicals.
- Early detection is essential to reduce the burden of treatment costs. Create awareness among people to identify causes and signs for early detection of cancer.
- Ensure safe drinking water to the masses in the region in order to ensure the prevention of cancer to some extent.
- Diagnostic facilities at affordable cost should be provided, at least, one government hospital in each district and that too at block level.
- Cancer treatment facilities need to be strengthened in the public hospitals.
- Procedure to avail cancer-related economic assistance from the state needs to be simplified. It is thus suggested that direct payment may be made to the patient through banks.
- Expenditure incurred by cancer-suffering households varies by the type of cancer and length of the treatment. It is, therefore, suggested that the state government's financial assistance should be variable or flexible as per the level of income, type of cancer and expected length of the treatment.
- Cancer-related state assistance needs to be extended to cover even dead cases, so that the family can support the food, education and health care needs of living family members.

To sum up, different types of cancer in the region are being identified in particular geographical clusters. Against the average cost of cancer treatment of Rs. 2.75 lakhs, average family income at aggregate level is just Rs. 2.30 lakhs. And, average length of cancer ailment is 1.9 years. In the absence of health insurance system and meagre own savings, cancer victim families have to depend on outside sources of finance. Huge treatment costs borne by the cancer victims' families reduces their expenditure on food items, care of children and elderly. State government support to cancer victims is insufficient, untimely and involves procedures that are cumbersome. It is high time to design a financial support system for the cancer victim families that covers not only cancer treatment but also their basic needs, capabilities and functionalities by providing additional financial assistance for looking after the food, health and educational needs of distressed families.

REFERENCES

Barnum, H. and E.R. Greenberg (1993), 'Cancers', in D.T. Jamison, W.H. Mosley, A.R. Measham, and J.L. Bobadilla (eds.) *Disease Control Priorities in Developing Countries,* Oxford University Press, New York, pp. 529-59.

Boyle, P. and B. Levin (2008), *World Cancer Report 2008*, International Agency for Research on Cancer, World Health Organisation, Geneva.

Brown, Martin L., Sue J. Goldie, Gerrit Draisma, Joe Harford, and Joseph Lipscomb (2006), 'Health Service Interventions for Cancer Control in Developing Countries', in D.T. Jamison, W.H. Mosley, A.R. Measham and J.L. Babadilla (eds.) *Disease Control Priorities in Developing Countries,* Oxford University Press, New York, pp. 569-90.

Bumgarner, J. Richard (1992), *China: Long-term Issues and Options in the Health Transition,* The World Bank, Washington D.C.

Byerlee, Derek (2006), 'Technical Change, Productivity and Sustainability in Irrigated Cropping Systems of South Asia: Emerging Issues in the Post Green Revolution Era', *Journal of International Development*, Vol. 4 (5), pp. 477-96.

Chang, S., S.R. Long, L. Kutikova, L. Bowman, D. Finley, W.H. Crown and C.L. Bennett (2004), 'Estimating the Cost of Cancer: Results on the Basis of Claims Data Analyses for Cancer Patients

Diagnosed with Seven Types of Cancer During 1999 to 2000', *Journal of Clinical Oncology*, Vol. 22 (17) pp. 3524-30.

Corsi, Marco (2006) 'Communalism and the Green Revolution in Punjab', *Journal of Developing Societies*, Vol. 22 (2), pp. 85-109.

Conway, G.R. and Pretty J. N. (1991), *Unwelcome Harvest: Agriculture and Pollution*, Earthscan Publisher, London.

CSE (2005), *Analysis of Pesticide Residues in Blood Samples from Villages of Punjab*, Centre for Science and Environment, New Delhi.

Dikshit, R., P.C. Gupta, C. Ramasundarahettige, V. Gajalakshmi, L. Aleksandrowicz, R. Badwe, R. Kumar, S. Roy, W. Suraweera, F. Bray, M. Mallath, P.K. Singh, D.N. Sinha, A.S. Shet, H. Gelband, and P. Jha (2012), 'Cancer Mortality in India: A Nationally Representative Survey in India', *Lancet*, Vol. 379 (9828), pp. 1807-16.

Duggal, R. (2007), 'Health Care in India: Changing Finance Strategy', *Social Policy and Administration*, Vol. 41 (4), pp. 386-94.

Ferlay, J., H.R. Shin, F. Bray, D. Forman, C. Mathers and D.M. Parkin (2010), 'Estimates of Worldwide Burden of Cancer in 2008', *International Journal of Cancer*, Vol. 127 (12), pp. 2893-917.

Government of Punjab (2013), *State Programme for Prevention and Control of Cancer: State-wide Awareness and Symptom-based Early Detection Door to Door Campaign*, Department of Health and Family Welfare, Government of Punjab, Chandigarh.

Greet Peace India (2009), Chemical Fertilisers in Our Water: An Analysis of Nitrates in the Ground water in Punjab, Green Peace India Society, Bangolore, Website: www.greerpeace.org

Gupta, R.K. and I.P. Abrol (2000), 'Salinity Build-Up and Changes in the Rice-Wheat System of the Indo-Gangetic Plains', *Experimental Agriculture*, Vol. 36, pp. 273-84.

Hamilton, S.R. (1986), 'Pathologic Diagnosis of Colorectal and Anal Malignancies: Classification and Prognostic Features of Pathologic Findings', in O.H. Beahrs, G.A. Higgens and J.J. Weinstein (eds.), *Colorectal Tumors*, J.B. Lippincott, Pennsylvania (USA), pp. 107-12.

ICMR (2006), *Atlas of Cancer in India*, Indian Council of Medical Research (ICMR), Bangalore.

Mathers, C.D. and D. Loncar (2006), 'Projections of Global Mortality and Burden of Disease from 2002 to 2030', *PloS Medicine*, Vol. 3 (11), p. 442.

Mohan, S., K.S. Reddy and Prabhakaran, (2011), *Chronic Non-Communicable Diseases in India; Reversing the Tide*, Public Health Foundation of India, New Delhi.

Pandher, Sarbjit, (1999), 'Cancer Cases on the Rise in Punjab Village', *The Hindu*, December 13, 1999.

Philipose, Pamela (1998), 'As Debts Swell and Plots Shrink, Despair Grows in Punjab's Farms', *Indian Express*, November 9, p. 1.

Parkin, D.M., F. Bray, J. Ferlay and P. Pisani (2001), 'Estimating the World Cancer Burden: GLOBOCON 2000', *International Journal of Cancer*, Vol. 94 (2), pp. 153-6.

Polsky, D., J.S. Mandelblatt, J.C. Weeks, L. Venditti, Y. Hwang, J.D. Glick and K.A. Schulman (2003), 'Economic Evaluation of Breast Cancer Treatment: Considering the Value of Patient Choice', *Journal of Clinical Oncology*, Vol. 21 (26), pp. 1139-46.

PPCB (2005), *An Epidemiological Study of Cancer Cases Reported from Villages of Talwandi Sabo Block, District Bathinda*, Punjab Pollution Control Board (PPCB), Patiala.

Shiva, Vandana (1991), *The Violence of the Green Revolution: Third World Agriculture*, Ecology and Zed Books, London.

Singh, Bajinder Pal (2008), *Cancer Deaths in Agricultural Heartland, A Study in Malwa Region of Indian Punjab, March*, Unpublished M.Sc. Thesis, University of Southampton (UK).

ORG (2011), *Re-Imagining the Indus*, Report of Indo-Pakistan Project, Observer Research Foundation, New Delhi, pp. 119-38.

Shibuya, K., C.D. Mathers, B.P. Cynthia, A.D. Lopez, C.J.L. Murray (2002), 'Global and Regional Estimates of Cancer Mortality and Incidence by Site: II (Results for the Global Burden of Disease 2000)', *BMC Cancer*, Vol. 2, pp. 1-33.

Thakur, J.S., B.T. Rao, A. Rajwanshi, H.K. Parwana and Rajesh Kumar (2008), 'Epidemiological Study of High Cancer Among Rural Agricultural Community of Punjab in Northern India', *International Journal of Environmental Research and Public Health*, Vol. 5(5), pp. 399-407.

WHO (2002), *National Cancer Control Programme: Policies and Managerial Guidelines*, World Health Organisation (WHO), Geneva.

About R.S. Ghuman

(DOB: April 6, 1951)

CURRICULUM VITAE IN BRIEF

Positions Being Held Presently

1. Professor and Head, Nehru SAIL Chair, Centre for Research in Rural & Industrial Development (CRRID), Sector 19/A, Chandigarh.
2. Member, Peer Team of National Assessment and Accreditation Council (NAAC), Bangalore.
3. Member, Executive Council, Central University of Gujarat, Ahmedabad.
4. Assessor, Human Resources Division, University of Johannesburg, South Africa.
5. Member, State Advisory Committee of Punjab State Electricity Regulatory Commission, Punjab, Chandigarh.
6. Member, Punjab Government Fee Committee of Private Industrial Training Institutes (ITIs) of Punjab, Chandigarh.
7. External Expert, Faculty of Social Sciences, Punjabi University, Patiala.

Positions/Honours Held Earlier

1. Professor and Head, Department of Economics, Punjabi University, Patiala.
2. Coordinator, UGC's Centre for Advanced Study in Economics, Punjabi University, Patiala.
3. Programme Coordinator, South-West Asia Study Centre, Punjabi University, Patiala.

4. Research Awardee, University Grants Commission (2006-09), New Delhi.
5. Dean, College Development Council, Punjabi University, Patiala.
6. Member, Academic Council, Central University of Gujarat, Ahmedabad.
7. Vice-President, Indian Society of Labour Economics, New Delhi.
8. Member, High Level FICCI led Indian Trade Delegation to Pakistan, April 27–May 2, 1997.
9. Member, Advisory Committee of Indian Council of Social Science Research (North-Western Regional Centre, Chandigarh), Government of India, New Delhi.
10. Visiting Fellow at the Institute of Indology and Department of Political Science, Johannes Gutenberg-Mainz University Johann-Friedrich-Von-Pfeiffer, Mainz, Germany, June 24-27, 2008.
11. Visiting Professor in the Department of Economics (UGC-DRS Department), Madurai Kamraj University, Madurai, Tamil Nadu, January 2004.
12. Chairman, Punjab Government Committee for Minimum Support Price, Chandigarh.
13. Member, Syndicate, and Academic Council, Punjabi University, Patiala.
14. Member, Advisory Committee on 'Go Rural Mission' of Punjab Technical University, Jalandhar.
15. Secretary, Punjabi University Teachers Association (PUTA), Patiala.

Academic Qualifications

Ph.D. (Economics) from Punjabi University, Patiala, 1985.
Ph.D. Thesis: Indo-Pakistan Trade Since 1947.
M.Phil. (Economics) from Punjabi University, Patiala, 1979.
A-Grade, First Position in the University.
M.A. (Economics) from Punjabi University, Patiala, 1973.
First Division with Second Position in the University.

Teaching/Research Experience and Research Supervision

- 40 years of teaching/research experience in higher education institutions.

- Supervised research at Doctoral Level – Completed 8; Ongoing 3.
- Supervised research at M.Phil. Level – Completed 19.

Membership of Professional Bodies

1. International Institute of Asian Studies, Leiden, The Netherlands.
2. Life member, Indian Economic Association.
3. Life member, Indian Society of Labour Economics.
4. Life member, Indian Science Congress.

Areas of Specialisation/Interest

1. Nehruvian Economic Thought and Contemporary India.
2. Corporate Social Responsibility.
3. Growth, Human Development, Poverty and Inequality in South Asia.
4. Indo-Pakistan Economic Relations.
5. Economics of Development and Planning.
6. International Economics and Trade.
7. Advanced Economic Theory – Microeconomics.

Books Authored/Co-Authored

1. *Professional Education in Punjab: Exclusion of Rural Students* (2009), jointly with Sukhwinder Singh and Jaswinder Singh Brar, Publication Bureau, Punjabi University, Patiala.
2. *Status of Local Agricultural Labour in Punjab* (2007), jointly with Inderjeet Singh and Lakhwinder Singh, The Punjab State Farmers Commission, Government of Punjab, S.A.S. Nagar, Mohali.
3. *Rural Students in Universities of Punjab* (2006), jointly with Sukhwinder Singh and Jaswinder Singh Brar, Publication Bureau, Punjabi University, Patiala.
4. *International Economics* (1996), Publication Bureau, Punjabi University, Patiala.
5. *Indo-Pakistan Trade Relations* (1986), Deep and Deep Publications, New Delhi.

Books Edited

1. *Nehruvian Economic Philosophy and Its Contemporary Relevance (2014),* jointly with Indervir Singh, Centre for

Research in Rural & Industrial Development (CRRID), Chandigarh.

2. *Rural Local Self Government in India: Some Developmental Experiences* (2013), with Sukhvinder Singh, Centre for Research in Rural & Industrial Development (CRRID), Chandigarh.
3. *Globalization and Change* (2010), jointly with Surjit Singh and Jaswinder Singh Brar, Rawat Publications, New Delhi.
4. *Globalization, Liberalization and Punjab* (2000), jointly with P.S. Jammu, Publication Bureau, Punjabi University, Patiala.
5. *Post-Independence Punjabi Society* (1999), jointly with P.S.Jammu, Publication Bureau, Punjabi University, Patiala.

Research Projects Completed

1. *Evaluation Report of Corporate Social Responsibility of SAIL for Year 2012-13* (2013).
2. *Evaluation Report of Corporate Social Responsibility Projects by CPSEs in Gonda District of Uttar Pradesh for 2012-13* (2013).
3. *Free Education for Under-Privileged Students: A Case Study of SAIL's CSR* (2013).
4. *Evaluation Report of Sustainable Development Projects of SAIL for 2012-13* (2013).
5. *Free Health Services Under CSR: A Case Study of SAIL* (2013).
6. *Demand Pattern of Steel in Chandigarh and Mohali: A Case Study of Construction Sector* (2012).
7. *Demand Pattern of Various Steel Brands in Rural India: A Case Study of South-West Punjab* (2012).
8. *Brand Awareness and Demand Pattern of Steel in Rural Punjab: A Case Study of Household Sector* (2012).
9. *Urbanisation and Sale of Steel: A Case Study of Dealers in Chandigarh, Mohali and Panchkula* (2012).
10. *Children's Encyclopaedia in Economics* (2011), Commissioned and Funded by Punjabi University, Patiala.
11. *Growth, Human Development, Poverty and Inequality in South Asia: A Study of Development Experience of India, Pakistan and Bangladesh* (2009), Commissioned and Funded by the University Grants Commission, New Delhi.
12. *Losses Suffered by Farmers of Punjab Since 1967-68 Due to Non-*

Linking of Procurement Price of Wheat and Paddy with the Price Index (2009), jointly with P.S. Rangi and M.S. Sidhu, Commissioned and Funded by Government of Punjab..

13. *Professional Education in Punjab: Number, Proportion and Socio-Economic Analysis of Rural Students* (2008), jointly with Sukhwinder Singh and Jaswinder Singh Brar, Commissioned and Funded by Punjabi University, Patiala.
14. *Status of Local Agricultural Labour in Punjab* (2007), jointly with Inderjeet Singh and Lakhwinder Singh, Commissioned and Funded by the Punjab State Farmers Commission, SAS Nagar (Mohali).
15. *Rural Students in the Universities of Punjab: An Exploratory Study* (2006), jointly with Sukhwinder Singh and Jaswinder Singh Brar, Commissioned and Funded by Punjabi University, Patiala.
16. *Unit Cost of Higher Education in Punjab: A Study of Universities and Their Affiliated Colleges* (2005), jointly with Sukhwinder Singh and Jaswinder Singh Brar, Commissioned and Funded by Association of Indian Universities (AIU), New Delhi.
17. *Report on University Finances* (May 2004), jointly with Sucha Singh Gill and Inderjeet Singh, Commissioned by Punjabi University, Patiala.
18. *Indo-Pakistan Trade Relations: A Revisit* (2001), Funded by University Grants Commission, New Delhi.
19. *Suicides in Rural Punjab: A Report* (2000), Commissioned by the Association for Democratic Rights (AFDR), Punjab (completed along with other members of the Task Force).
20. *A Draft Plan of Andana Block, District Sangrur* (1998), jointly with Baldev Singh, G.K. Bhatia and Sukhwinder Singh, Commissioned and Funded by Government of Punjab, Chandigarh.

Research Papers (Published in National/ International Journals and Edited Books)

1. 'Water Supply and Sewerage Services in Ludhiana City: A Study of Financial Constraints' (2013), jointly with Jasdeep Kaur Bedi, *Man and Development*, Vol. 35 (4), pp. 23-32.
2. 'Indo-SAARC Trade Relations since 1985' (2013), jointly with

D.K. Madaan, in Rashpal Malhotra, Sucha Singh Gill and Neetu Gaur (eds.) *Perspectives on Bilateral and Regional Cooperation: South and Central Asia*, Centre for Research in Rural & Industrial Development (CRRID), Chandigarh, pp. 129-44.

3. 'Punjab Economy: Derailed Growth Agenda-High Time to Put It Back on the Track' (2013), in Gurdeep Sharma, Sapna Sharma and Rajiv Kumar (eds.) *Economic Development in North-West Region of India: Challenges & Possibilities*, Aashna Publications, Hoshiarpur (Punjab), pp. 22-31.
4. 'Development Paradigm, Nature of Employment and Need for Social Protection for Workers: Global and Indian Scenario' (2012), Keynote Paper, *Indian Journal of Labour Economics*, Vol. 55 (1), January-March, pp. 77-110.
5. 'Bridging the Rural-Urban Gap: Experiments in Engineering Education in Punjab' (2013), jointly with D.K. Madaan, in Satish Deshpande and Usha Zacharia (eds.), *Beyond Inclusion: The Practice of Equal Access in Indian Higher Education*, Routledge, New Delhi, pp. 145-73.
6. 'Employment Guarantee Scheme in the Agriculturally Developed State of Punjab: A Case Study of Hoshiarpur District' (2012), jointly with Parvinder Kaur, in Ashok Pankaj (ed.), *Right to Work in Rural India: Working of the Mahatma Gandhi National Rural Employment Guarantee Scheme (MGNREGS)*, Sage Publications, New Delhi, pp. 169-93.
7. 'The Sikh Community in Indian Punjab: Some Socio-Economic Challenges' (2012), *Journal of Punjab Studies*, Vol. 19 (1), pp. 87-110.
8. 'Socio-economic Profile of Rural Farm and Non-Farm Workers in Punjab: A Case Study of 24 Villages' (2012), jointly with Dipinder Singh, *The Horizon: A Journal of Social Sciences*, Vol. 3 (1), pp. 41-62.
9. 'A Critical Appraisal of Higher Education And Economic Development in India' (2012), jointly with Saurab Sethi and Wilfred Isioma Ukpere, *African Journal of Business Management*, Vol. 6 (23), pp. 6795-801.
10. 'Education and Rural Transformation: A Case Study of Rural Students in Higher Education in Indian Punjab' (2011),

in Vinayagum (ed.) *Education for Rural Transformation (ERT): National, International and Comparative Perspectives, Institution of International Education*, Stockholm University, Sweden, pp. 213-31.

11. 'Trade and Investment Relations between India and Bangladesh: Status and Possibilities' (2011), jointly with D.K. Madaan, *Man & Development*, Vol. 33 (3), pp. 59-82.
12. 'Agricultural Price Policy, MSP of Wheat and Concerns of Punjab Farmers' (2011), jointly with P.S. Rangi and M.S. Sidhu, *Social Science Research Journal*, Vol. 19 (2), pp. 1-28.
13. 'Employment Scenario in Punjab: A Macro Evidence' (2011), jointly with Dipinder Singh, *Journal of Agricultural Development and Policy*, Vol. 21 (2), pp. 9-22.
14. 'Index Linked vis-à-vis Cost of Production Linked Minimum Support Price: A Case Study of Paddy in Punjab' (2011), jointly with P.S. Rangi and M.S. Sidhu, *Man and Development*, Vol. 33 (1), pp. 47-68.
15. 'Performance of National Rural Employment Guarantee Scheme in Punjab: A Case Study of Hoshiarpur District' (2011), jointly with Parvinder Kaur, in H.S. Shergill, Sucha Singh Gill and Gurmail Singh (eds.), *Understanding North-West Indian Economy*, Serials Publications, New Delhi, pp. 400-29.
16. 'Quality and Quantity in Indian Higher Education: A Critical Analysis' (2011), with Saurab Sethi, *Research Journal of Education*, Vol. 2 (2), pp. 112-9.
17. 'Higher Education and Economic Development within A Globalist Era in India' (2011), jointly with Saurab Sethi and Wilfred Isioma Ukpere, *Journal of Academic Research in Economics*, Vol. 3 (2), pp. 232-41.
18. 'National Food Security: The Strategic Role of Punjab' (2010), jointly with P.S. Rangi and M.S. Sidhu, *Journal of Agricultural Development and Policy*, Vol. 20 (2), pp. 1-16.
19. 'South Asia in Transition: Agrarian and Rural Transformation' (2010), *Man and Development*, Vol. 32 (4), pp. 123-42
20. 'Economic Growth and Human Development in South Asia: Experience of Selected Countries' (2010), jointly with A.S.

Bhullar, *Himalayan Journal of Development and Democracy*, Vol. 5 (1), pp. 72-8.

21. 'Sustainability of the Existing and Alternative Cropping Systems in the South West Punjab' (2010), jointly with G.S. Romana, in Sucha Singh Gill, Lakhwinder Singh and Reena Marwah (eds.), *Economic and Environmental Sustainability of the Asian Region*, Routledge India, New Delhi, pp. 317-36.
22. 'Factors Affecting the Sustainability of Existing Cropping System in Cotton Belt of Punjab' (2010), jointly with G.S. Romana, *PSE Economic Analyst*, Vol. 27, pp. 87-112.
23. 'Agricultural Development and Disparities in India: A Study of Pre and Post-Reform Period' (2010), with Gagandeep Kaur, *Journal of Agricultural Development and Policy*, Vol. 20 (1), pp. 55-76.
24. 'Economic Analysis of the Migrant Labourers in Patiala City' (2010), with Saurab Sethi, *Labour and Development*, Vol. 16-17, June, pp. 160-80.
25. 'Socio-Economic Analysis of the Migrant Labourers in Punjab: An Empirical Analysis' (2010), jointly with Saurab Sethi and Wilfred Isioma Ukpere, *African Journal of Business Management*, Vol. 4 (10), pp. 2042-50.
26. 'Social Analysis of Migrant Labourers in Patiala City' (2009), with Saurabh Sethi, *Indian Journal of Human Rights and Social Justice*, Vol. 4 (1-2), January–December, pp. 195-209.
27. 'Infrastructural Development in India: Pre and Post-Reform Inter-state Disparities' (2009), with Gagandeep Kaur, *Annals of the University of Petrosani Economics*, Vol. 9 (4), pp. 15-26.
28. 'Higher Professional Education in Punjab: Exclusion of Rural Students' (2009), with Sukhwinder Singh and Jaswinder Singh Brar, *Research Journal Social Sciences*, Vol. 17, (1), pp. 1-32.
29. 'Rural Students in Universities of Punjab: A Classic Case of Marginalisation' (2009), jointly with Sukhwinder Singh and Jaswinder Singh Brar, *Journal of Human Development*, Vol. 3 (2), pp. 405-14.
30. 'Capital and Labour in Historical and Emerging Global Perspective: A Brief Comment' (2009), *The Indian Economy*

Review, Vol. 6, pp. 84-8.

31. 'India-ASEAN Trade Relations during Post-WTO Period' (2009), jointly with D.K. Madaan, in Raj Kumar Sen and John Felix Raj (eds.): *WTO and ASEAN Union*, Deep and Deep Publications, New Delhi, pp. 395-406.
32. 'Education, Punjabi Language and Employment' (2009) in Sarbjit Singh (ed.), *Punjabi Language, Present and Future*, Lokgeet Parkashan, Chandigarh, pp. 106-13.
33. 'Changing Character of Rural Economy and Migrant Labour in Punjab' (2009), Jointly with Inderjeet Singh and Lakhwinder Singh, *Journal of Punjab Studies*, Vol. 16 (1), pp. 57-70.
34. 'Trade and Investment in SAARC Countries: SAFTA and Beyond' (2009), jointly with D.K. Madaan, in Neetu Gaur and Vijay Laxmi (eds.), *Cooperative Development, Peace and Security in South Asia*, CRRID, Chandigarh, pp. 29-60.
35. 'NREGA and Rural Employment in Punjab: An Evaluative Study of Hoshiarpur District' (2008), *Comparative Economic Research*, Vol. 11, pp. 55-80.
36. 'Trade Relations among SAARC Countries' (2008), jointly with D.K. Madaan, *Man & Development*, Vol. 30 (1), pp. 77-88.
37. 'Costs of Higher Education in Punjab: Levels, Patterns and Efficiency Issues' (2008), jointly with Jaswinder Singh Brar and Sukhwinder Singh, *Journal of Educational Planning and Administration*, Vol. 22 (2), pp. 153-77.
38. 'Socio-Economic Crisis in Rural Punjab' (2008), *Economic and Political Weekly*, Vol. 43 (7), pp. 12-5.
39. 'Development and Structural Changes in Punjab Since 1960s' jointly with Kanwaljeet Kaur Gill, *Samajak Vigyan Pattar*, Vol. 56, December, pp. 132-54.
40. 'Economic Cooperation between the Two Punjabs' (2007), *South Asian Journal*, April-June, Vol. 7 (2), pp. 88-104.
41. 'Economic Cooperation between India and Pakistan with Special Reference to Two Punjabs' (2007), in Bawa, R.S., P.S. Raikhy and Paramjeet Kaur Dhindsa (eds.), *Globalisation and Punjab Economy: Issues in Agriculture and Small State Industry*, Guru Nanak Dev University, Amritsar, pp. 408-32.

42. 'GATS and Tertiary Education: Global and Indian Scenario' (2007), *Punjab Journal of Business Studies*, Vol. 2 (2), October-March, pp. 10-29.
43. 'Indo-Pak Trade Cooperation and SAARC' (2006), jointly with D.K. Madaan, *Peace and Democracy in South Asia (PDSA)*, Vol. 2 (1 & 2), pp. 71-87.
44. 'Political Economy of Indo-Pakistan Relations and SAARC' (2006), in Kulwant Kaur and Baljit Singh Mann (eds.), *South Asia: Dynamics of Politics, Economy and Security*, Knowledge World, New Delhi, pp. 293-307.
45. 'Comparative Analysis of SAD and Congress Governments Since 1996 (2006), *Business Empire*, Vol. 1, October 2006, pp. 34-8.
46. 'GATS and Higher Education in India' (2005), in Gurdeep Sharma (ed.), *WTO, GATS and Higher Education*, Swami Parmanand Mahavidyalaya, Mukerian, Punjab, pp. 17-27.
47. 'Rural Non-Farm Employment Scenario: Reflections from Recent Data in Punjab' (2005), *Economic and Political Weekly*, Vol. 40 (41), pp. 4473-80.
48. 'Uneven Economic Development and Discontent in South Asia: A Regional Analysis' (2005), in Gopal Singh (ed.), *South Asia Today*, Anamika Publishers, New Delhi, pp. 52-68.
49. 'Softening of Borders between India and Pakistan: An Overview' (2005), *Man and Development*, Vol. 27 (4), December, pp. 29-38.
50. Trade Potentialities and Trade-off between India and Pakistan' (2005), with D.K. Madaan, *The Indian Economic Journal*, Vol. 53 (3), pp. 57-73.
51. 'Economic Cooperation between Two Punjabs (Indian Punjab and Pakistan Punjab) and Punjabi Diaspora' (2004), Theme Paper Published in the Souvenir Released at *World Punjabi Conference* organised by Punjabi University, Patiala on December 1-3, pp. 53-8.
52. 'Rural Employment Scenario in Punjab with Special Reference to Non-farm Employment: A District Level Analysis' (2004), in P. Purushotham (ed.) *Rural Non-Farm Employment*, National Institute of Rural Development (NIRD), Hyderabad, pp. 93-143.

53. 'Punjab Agriculture: Achievements, Problems and Challenges' (2003), *Social Science Research Journal*, Vol. 11 (3), pp. 119-34.
54. 'Rapporteur's Report on Rural Non-Farm Employment in India' (2003), *The Indian Journal of Labour Economics*, Vol. 46 (1), pp. 145-50.
55. 'Non-farm Employment in Rural Punjab' (2002), jointly with Sukhpal Singh and Balwinder Singh, *The Indian Journal of Labour Economics*, Vol. 45 (4), pp. 853-70.
56. 'Socio-Economic Change and Development under the Constitution: A Retrospection' (2002), jointly with Inderjeet Singh, in R.N. Pal (ed.), *Indian Constitution: A Review*, CRRID, Chandigarh, pp. 91-111.
57. 'Changing Agrarian Relations in India: Some Reflections from Recent Data' (2001), jointly with Sucha Singh Gill, *The Indian Journal of Labour Economics*, Vol. 44 (4), pp. 809-826.
58. 'Rural Health–Emerging Punjab Scenario' (2001), jointly with Sucha Singh Gill, in Parkash Singh Jammu (ed.), *Globalisation and Punjab*, Punjab Academy of Social Sciences Literature and Culture, Jalandhar, pp. 221-36.
59. 'Land Reforms in Punjab and Haryana : Trends and Issues' (2001), jointly with Sucha Singh Gill, in Sucha Singh Gill (ed.) *Land Reforms in India: Intervention for Capitalist Transformation in Punjab and Haryana*, Sage Publications, New Delhi, pp. 29-46.
60. 'Crisis of Punjab Economy' (2001), jointly with Sucha Singh Gill, in Parkash Singh Jammu (ed.), *Globalization and Punjab*, Punjab Academy of Social Sciences, Literature and Culture, Jalandhar, pp. 84-105.
61. 'Impact of World Trade Organization on Punjab Agriculture' (2001), in Parkash Singh Jammu (ed.), *Globalization and Punjab, Punjab Academy of Social Sciences, Literature and Culture*, Jalandhar, pp. 106-48.
62. 'WTO and Indian Agriculture: Crisis and Challenges' (2001), *Man and Development*, Vol. 23 (2), pp. 67-98. Also reproduced in S.S. Johl and S.K. Ray (eds.), *Future of Agriculture in Punjab* (2002), CRRID, Chandigarh, pp. 125-59
63. 'Globalization and Developing Economies with Special

Reference to India: A Macro Analysis' (2001), *Indian Management Studies Journal*, Vol. 5 (1), pp. 11-32. Reproduced in P.P. Arya and B.B. Tandon (eds.) *Economic Reforms in India* (2003), Deep and Deep Publications, New Delhi, pp. 31-51.

64. 'World Economic Order, LPG and India: To Whom Would It Serve?' (2001), *Indian Economy and Banks*, Punjab Bank Employees Federation, pp. 21-37.
65. 'WTO Regime: Some Challenges to Indian Agriculture' (2001), jointly with D.K. Madaan, in G.K Chadha (ed.) *WTO and the Indian Economy*, Deep and Deep Publications, New Delhi, pp. 180-90.
66. 'Crisis of Punjab Economy: The Alternative Options and the Role of the Government' (2000), jointly with Sucha Singh Gill, in R.S. Bawa and P.S. Raikhy (eds.), *Punjab Economy: Emerging Issues*, Guru Nanak Dev University, Amritsar, pp. 437-58.
67. 'Punjab Rural Health: Proactive Role of the State' (2000), jointly with Sucha Singh Gill, *Economic and Political Weekly*, Vol. 35 (51), pp. 4474-78.
68. 'World Trade Organization: Challenges to and Prospects for Punjab's Agricultural Economy and Peasantry' (2000), *Association for Democratic Rights*, Punjab, pp. 10-29.
69. 'Indo-SAARC Trade Scenario: Emerging Trends and Trade-off'' (2000), jointly with D.K. Madaan, *The Indian Economic Journal*, Vol. 47 (3), pp. 97-104.
70. 'Handloom Industry in India: A Case Study of Chanderi Saree Industry' (2000), jointly with D.K. Madaan, *The Indian Journal of Economics*, Vol. 80 (319), pp. 431-50.
71. 'Primary Health Services in Punjab and Punjab Government' (2000), jointly with Sukhwinder Singh, in Parkash Singh Jammu and Ranjit Singh Ghuman (eds.), *Globalisation, Liberalisation and Punjab*, Punjabi University, Patiala, pp. 195-203.
72. 'Globalisation and Punjab Agriculture' (2000), in Parkash Singh Jammu and Ranjit Singh Ghuman (eds.), *Globalisation, Liberalisation and Punjab*, Special Issue of *Samajak Vigyan Pattar*, Vol. 47-49, pp. 95-101.
73. 'SAARC and Intra-SAARC Trade Potentials: A Politico-

Economic Approach' (1999), *Politics India*, Vol. 4 (2-3), pp. 47-9.

74. 'Health Care Services in Punjab: Role of Government and Voluntary Organisations (1999), jointly with D.K. Madaan, *Indian Economic Journal*, Conference Volume, pp. 623-32.
75. 'Post-Independence Development of Energy Sector in Punjab' (1999), jointly with Amarjit Singh, in Parkash Singh Jammu and Ranjit Singh Ghuman (eds.), *Punjabi Samaj Azadi Toan Baad*, Punjabi University, Patiala, pp. 89-99.
76. 'Post-Independence Agricultural Development in Punjab and Changing Land Relations' (1999), jointly with S.S. Riar, in Parkash Singh Jammu and Ranjit Singh Ghuman (eds.), *Punjabi Samaj Azadi taon Baad*, Punjabi University, Patiala, pp. 148-73.
77. 'Functions and Finances of PRI's: Implications for Micro Level Planning' (1998), jointly with Baldev Singh, G.K. Bhatia and Sukhwinder Singh, *PSE Economic Analyst*, Vol. 19 (1), pp. 87-103.
78. 'Political Economy of Indo-Pakistan Economic Cooperation: 1947-1996' (1998), in Gopal Singh (ed.), *South Asia: Democracy, Discontent and Societal Conflicts*, Anamika Publishers, New Delhi, pp. 234-46.
79. 'Employment, Wages and Productivity in Public Sector Enterprises in India' (1998), jointly with Lakhwinder Singh, *The Indian Journal of Labour Economics*, Vol. 41 (4), pp. 923-33.
80. 'Need and Progress of Indo-Pakistan Trade' (1997), *Samajak Vigyan Pattar*, No. 43, Punjabi University, Patiala, pp. 53-63.
81. 'New Economic Policy and Indian Economy' (1996), *Samajak Vighan Pattar*, No. 41, Punjabi University, Patiala, pp. 160-68.
82. 'New Economic Policy and Government Budget: Mounting Unemployment and Abject Poverty' (1996), *Politics India*, Vol. 1 (4), pp. 4-46.
83. 'GATT Agreements 1994: Some Implications for South Asian Countries' (1995), in H.S. Deol (ed.), *South Asian Spectrum:*

Problems and Perspectives, Punjabi University, Patiala, pp. 203-32.

84. 'Municipal Finances in Punjab during 1971-91' (1995), in Pardeep Sachdeva (ed.), *Revamping Urban Government in India*, Kitab Mahal, New Delhi, pp. 142-53.
85. 'Wage-Productivity Relationship in Theory and Practice: A Study of Indian Public Enterprises' (1994), jointly with Lakhwinder Singh, *PSE Economic Analyst*, Vol. 15 (1 and 2), pp. 1-13.
86. 'Scope of Raising Agricultural Productivity in Punjab: A Case Study' (1993), jointly with S.S. Riar, *Journal of Agricultural Development and Policy*, Vol. 4 (1 and 2), pp. 45-59.
87. 'Comparative Study of Private Costs in Distance and Conventional Education: A Case Study' (1991), *Pakistan Journal of Distance Education*, Vol. 5-8 (2 and 4), pp. 1-13.
88. 'Role of Municipal Finances in Urban Amenities: A Case Study of Mandi Gidderbaha' (1991), *Nagarlok*, Vol. 13 (3), pp. 90-102.
89. 'Indo-Pakistan Trade Relations in the Historical Perspective' (1991), *The Punjab Past and Present*, Conference Volume, 24th Session of Punjab History Conference, pp. 400-08.
90. 'Private Costs in Distance and Conventional Education in India' (1990), *Journal of Indian Education*, Vol. 15 (5), pp. 40-47.
91. 'Foreign Trade of India: A Macro View' (1989), jointly with Lakhwinder Singh, *Indian Management Studies Journal*, Vol. 1 (1), pp. 95-108.
92. 'Indo-Pak Trade Prospects and Constraints' (1984), jointly with Sucha Singh Gill, in V.D. Chopra (ed.), *Studies in Indo-Pak Relations*, Patriot Publishers, New Delhi, pp. 187-205.
93. 'Green Revolution and Socio-Economic Change' (1983), in Nirmal S. Azad (ed.), *Economy of Punjab*, Publication Bureau, Punjabi University, Patiala, pp. 213-38.
94. 'India's Agricultural Exports: Performance and Some Policy Issues' (1982), jointly with Sucha Singh Gill, *Indian Journal of Agricultural Economics*, Vol. 37 (3), pp. 294-300.

Notes on Editors

Inderjeet Singh is a Professor of Economics and Professor-in-Charge, Planning Commission Chair, at Punjabi University, Patiala (Punjab). His field of specialisation is Economic Development and Planning. His doctoral research work relates to 'Input-Output Analysis of Energy Consumption in India'. His post-doctoral work includes a large number of research papers, books and project reports. He has been associated with following two prestigious research projects: 'Re-Imagining the Indus', a joint project of ORF, India and LUMs, Pakistan and 'Blue Revolution: Charting South Asia's Water Future', a joint project of ORF and PHD Chamber of Commerce and Industry. He is a member of the International Research Group on 'Re-Imagining the Indus'. Most of his recent works relate to structure and dynamics of tertiary sector and economic development. At organisational level, he is associated with many national and international professional associations.

Sukhwinder Singh is currently working as Professor of Economics, Punjabi University, Patiala. His areas of research are the Economics of Health, Regional Economics and Applied Economics. His doctoral research work relates to 'Development and Use of Health Care Services in Rural Punjab'. He has already co-authored six important books on signicant themes like education, health, and regional economy and published more than 30 research papers in national/international journals. He has completed eleven research projects sponsored by the Planning Commission of India; Association of Indian Universities (AIU), New Delhi; National University of Educational Planning and Administration (NUEPA), New Delhi; National Foundation for India (NFI), New Delhi; Centre for Policy Research (CPR), New Delhi; Centre for Development Studies (CDS), Thiruvananthapuram; and the Punjab Government, Chandigarh. He has attended three international conferences held at: Iqra University, Islamabad (Pakistan) in April 2008, University of Kelaniya, Colombo (Sri Lanka) in July 2008 and Seoul National University, Seoul (South Korea) in September 2013. At organisational level, he is associated with a number of national professional associations in the field of economics.

Lakhwinder Singh is Professor of Economics at Punjabi University, Patiala. Prior to this, he has been faculty member of the University of Delhi and National Institute of Public Finance and Policy, New Delhi. He has been Ford Foundation Post-Doctoral Fellow in Economics at Yale University, USA and Visiting Research Fellow, Seoul National University, South Korea. He has been awarded the Asia Fellowship by the Institute of International Education, New York, 2001. He has served as a member, task group, Punjab Governance Reforms Commission, Government of Punjab. His current research interest focuses on the national innovation system, international knowledge spillovers, pattern of development, globalisation and agrarian distress in developing economies. Apart from publishing a number of research papers in journals of national and international repute, he is the founder editor of the journal *Millennial Asia: An International Journal of Asian Studies*, published by the Association of Asia Scholars, since 2010. He has co-edited the book *Economic and Environmental Sustainability of the Asian Region*, Routledge, 2010 and co-authored the book *Economic Cooperation and Infrastructural Linkages Between Two Punjabs: Way Ahead*, CRRID, 2010.

Notes on Contributors

Sucha Singh Gill, Director General, Centre for Research in Rural and Industrial Development (CRRID), Chandigarh. *gsuchasingh@gmail.com*

Lakhwinder Singh, Professor of Economics, Punjabi University, Patiala. *lakhwindergill@pbi.ac.in*

Surjit Singh, Director, Institute of Development Studies, Jaipur. *Surjit07@gmail.com*

M.S. Sidhu, Professor, Department of Economics & Sociology, Punjab Agricultural University, Ludhiana. *mssidhu@pau.edu*

Varinder Pal Singh, Research Associate, College of Dairy Science and Technology, Guru Angad Dev Veterinary and Animal Sciences University, Ludhiana. *dhindsavp@yahoo.com*

Parminder Kaur, Associate Professor, Department of Economics & Sociology, Punjab Agricultural University, Ludhiana. *parminderkaur@pau.edu*

A.S. Bhullar, Professor, Department of Economics & Sociology, Punjab Agricultural University, Ludhiana. *asbhullar1@rediffmail.com*

Inderpreet Kaur, Assistant Professor, Guru Angad Dev Veterinary and Animal Sciences University, Ludhiana. *inderpreetkaur@gadvasu.in*

Harpreet Kaur, Assistant Statistical Scientist, Department of Agriculture, Government of Punjab, Chandigarh. *reetchahal@rediffmail.com*

G.S. Romana, Farm Economist, Punjab Agricultural University Regional Station, Bathinda. *romanabti@gmail.com*

Kesar Singh Bhangoo, Professor of Economics, Punjabi University, Patiala. *kesarbhangoo@gmail.com*

Sukhpal Singh, Professor and Head, Department of Economics and Sociology, Punjab Agricultural University, Ludhiana. *sukhpalpau@yahoo.com*

Sangeet, Research Fellow, Department of Economics and Sociology, Punjab Agricultural University, Ludhiana. *ranguwal@gmail.com*

Kanwaljit Kaur Gill, Professor of Economics, Department of Distance Education, Punjabi University, Patiala. *k_k_gill@yahoo.com*

Varinder Jain, Assistant Professor of Economics, Institute of Development Studies, Jaipur. *vjain2007@gmail.com*

Amarjit Singh Sethi, Professor, Punjab School of Economics, Guru Nanak Dev University, Amritsar. *ajss_gndu@yahoo.com*

Baljit Kaur, Punjab School of Economics, Guru Nanak Dev University, Amritsar. *baljit17_kaur@yahoo.co.in*

Jaswinder Singh Brar, Professor of Economics, Punjabi University, Patiala. *brar_jas@yahoo.ac.in*

Sukhwinder Singh, Professor of Economics, Punjabi University, Patiala. *sohi42pbi@yahoo.com*

Rupinder Kaur, Assistant Professor of Economics, Khalsa College, Patiala. *kkaur2083@yahoo.com*

Inderjeet Singh, Professor and Head, Department of Economics, Punjabi University, Patiala. *inderjeetsidhu@rediffmail.com*

Parmod Kumar, Assistant Professor, Department of Economics, Punjabi University, Patiala. *parmod.agarwal@rediffmail.com*